Cincinnati's 150-Year
OPENING DAY HISTORY

The Hoopla Started with a Parade

RANDY FREKING

Testimonials

· ·

"For a Reds fan, Opening Day is the essential day of the year. And this book is an essential addition to the library of every Reds fan."

Jack Greiner, noted First Amendment attorney, writer, and baseball fan

"For someone who is an avid Reds fans, but not a Cincinnati native, this is a remarkable book. I enjoyed reading about the development of the great Cincinnati tradition I have come to celebrate!"

Les Gunzenhaeuser, Cincinnati anesthesiologist and baseball fan

"For being a 'legal beagle,' Randy Freking shows great bite as a chronicler of his other passion, Cincinnati Reds baseball and more specifically, Opening Day. His engaging love letter embracing Cincinnati's preeminent place in the national pastime is a perfect sidebar on the team's return to prominence."

Dennis Janson, retired WCPO (Channel 9 Cincinnati) sports anchor and member of the University of Cincinnati Journalism Hall of Fame

"This is a 'must have' book for any Reds fan. I have known Randy Freking since our kids were young, and have been his friend for many years. It came as no surprise that Randy authored this sweeping chronicle intertwining the history of Reds Opening Day with the enormous changes in the world since 1869."

Stuart Kunkler, marketing professional and prolific photographer

"As a 52-year veteran of Cincinnati Reds opening days, I can testify that Randy Freking has captured the spirit of this Cincinnati tradition in his enjoyable history."

Mark Painter, retired judge and author

"It's why you take your kids to Opening Day and why they take their kids. Randy Freking captures the hope, joy, and history that make Cincinnati's Opening Day so special. He reminds us of why we love our team and our town. It's about pride, it's about family, it's about belonging to something bigger than yourself."

Carol Williams, retired WCPO (Channel 9 Cincinnati) 30-year news anchor

CINCINNATI'S 150-YEAR OPENING DAY HISTORY
The Hoopla Started With A Parade

Copyright © Randy Freking

Published by Cincinnati Book Publishing Cincinnati, Ohio

Anthony W. Brunsman, president
Sue Ann Painter, executive editor
Greg Eckel, design
Molly Vogele, assistant editor
Kara Thompson, assistant editor
Susan Bradley, freelance editor

www.cincybooks.com

Perfect Bound Edition ISBN: 978-1-7327493-2-0
Hardbound Edition ISBN: 978-1-7327493-1-3
Library of Congress Control Number: 2018911342

Printed in the United States of America

First Edition, 2018

Dedication

To the Cincinnati Reds, who have provided our family
and fellow Cincinnatians with years of enjoyment;

to the Findlay Market Association,
a volunteer organization whose annual parade
has been one of the highlights of Opening Day traditions
enjoyed by our family and the entire region;

to my parents, Bob and Esther Freking,
who inspired my love of baseball and
our Opening Day traditions;

to my aunt and uncle, Jeanne and Harold Freking,
who taught me the value of learning history and
paying attention to current events; and

to the rest of my immediate family,
in-laws, nephews and nieces, and friends
who have celebrated Opening Day with me.

Acknowledgments

··

This book was a labor of love, and I needed love to complete it successfully. This book could not have been researched and written without the incredible support and understanding of my companion on Opening Day for the last 36 years, my wife, Sue. I became a hermit for days and weeks for much of the first half of 2018. I assume she missed me. Each of our children, Becky, Bob, Laura, and Jen also supported me with insight into the text as I was drafting, as well as moral support and encouragement. The whole family has always celebrated Opening Day, but they realize that Opening Day is especially important to me.

I must have an affinity for women named Sue. This book would never have been completed without the incredible work of Susan Bradley, my editor, now a resident of North Carolina. Sue had helped with a previous book many years ago and I called her again to assist me with this Opening Day project. I am particularly impressed with her breadth of knowledge, and her patience with a writer not well versed in document layout, design, and formatting. Sue also displayed a great sense of humor even as my deadline kept creeping forward. During this project, she moved from Minnesota to her new home and never missed a beat. As I have expressed to her, I cannot thank her enough for her diligence and care in assisting me.

I thank coworkers who were understanding during this project, particularly Andrea Dautel, who provided valuable perspective as I began. Karen Pavy was especially helpful with formatting and layout, organization of graphics, and compilation of many of the quotes used in the book. Theresa Willenbrink, a friend of coworkers Kathleen Stocker and Beth Schirmer, was valuable at the onset of the project when I needed assistance launching the draft.

I thank Dennis Janson, one of the great sports reporters in Cincinnati history, and former WCPO News Anchor Carol Williams for reviewing the manuscript and providing insight.

I also thank Jack Greiner, a noted First Amendment lawyer, and Stuart Kunkler, an avid photographer and design expert, for their help and guidance, and Judge Mark Painter.

I thank my friends Rock Robinson, Doug Raftery, Sherry Aune, Jeff Betz, Les Gunzenhaeuser, Tom Blinn, John Bogusz, Ron Majeski, Steve Byrnes and Beth Schirmer for their support and encouragement. Each contributed insight that was much needed.

Kevin Luken of the Findlay Market Association encouraged me to join the parade years ago. When I mentioned this project, he voluntarily spent hours looking for pictures of past parades and providing a valuable perspective on the growth of the parade from the early 1920s to today. His family and the Gibbs family have had perhaps the greatest influence in keeping the parade tradition alive on a strictly volunteer basis for the last half century.

Finally, this book would not be possible without Tony Brunsman and his staff of interns and designers at Cincinnati Book Publishing. They were particularly helpful to an author taking his first leap into writing a book unrelated to his day-to-day work as a lawyer. My previous two books involved subjects about which I had much more direct knowledge. This book was entirely different, requiring months of research and tackling design issues that were not necessary in my previous books. Tony was always professional, practical, and understanding.

I want to acknowledge last but not least the Cincinnati Reds Community Fund, headed by Charley Frank, a true man for others. Over the last several years, I have become familiar with the outstanding work he and his dedicated staff do for youth in Greater Cincinnati. That work involves participation in baseball and softball activities, such as the well-known Urban Youth Academy, but it is much more. The fund provides educational and life-skills support for the youths they serve that will benefit the community for generations. Brendan Hader, Communications Manager for the Reds, provided valuable assistance as well. For those reasons, I have elected to contribute a portion of the proceeds from this endeavor to the Community Fund.

Table of Contents

Introduction

What is this book all about? It's a blend of Cincinnati baseball's rich Opening Day history and some of the local and national historical events in America that surrounded, and occasionally directly impacted, those 150 years of Opening Days from 1869 to 2019. I wrote it because of my love for Opening Day and all the tradition and hoopla that have made Opening Day Cincinnati's most beloved institution.

My love affair with Opening Day began in the 1960s. I took part in my first Opening Day in 1967, when I was 10 years old. As a young boy, one of six children growing up in post-World War II Cincinnati, Reds baseball was what we did from April through September. We spent many summer evenings listening to the play-by-play on WSAI and later on the "50,000 watt, clear channel voice" of the Reds, WLW. The rest of our free time was spent playing baseball or dreaming of games in which we drove in the winning run. From October through February, we would rifle through the sports section of the *Cincinnati Enquirer* each morning to see if there was any news from the "hot stove league" about possible trades of players. We also wanted to make sure we were aware of any significant news about the players, such as whether they suffered any injuries during the off-season that would impact the next season. With the optimism of youth, we were perpetually certain that the team's record in the coming season would be better than the previous one. But until the first pitch was thrown, we waited anxiously for Opening Day.

> *Opening day is a state of mind, a rite of spring, a happening, unique in Cincinnati because only in Cincinnati does the home team open at home every year.*
>
> Jim Montgomery,
> Enquirer sports columnist

When Opening Day arrived, we would scour the entire paper to read about the buildup to the big game. The *Enquirer* often had special supplements devoted to the opening of the season, and various columnists—not just the sports columnists—would cover the events leading up to and surrounding the game. The editorial page contained cartoons and opinion pieces about this annual rite of spring.

Opening Day has always been a special day for the people of Cincinnati despite what might be going on in the world around us. A few years ago, my close friends and former Cincinnatians Joan and Doug Raftery suggested that I chronicle my Opening Day experiences in a book. They knew our family had religiously attended Opening Day, much as Joan's family had carried out their decades-long love affair with the Wisconsin Badgers. With their encouragement, I started writing my recollections, but before long I could tell my draft was missing something.

That something was how Opening Day was sometimes interwoven with historical events of the day. To satisfy my curiosity, I scoured newspaper archives to learn if anything significant was reported about the city or the world on Opening Day. I went all the way back to 1869, when the Reds played their first professional game. In my research, I primarily consulted the *Enquirer*, as it is the only daily paper that has existed in Cincinnati throughout the club's 150-year history. I wanted to find out what the headlines said on Opening Day during those 150 years. Was Opening Day affected by Prohibition, wars, the Depression, or local events such as Ohio River floods? Were there other interesting historical events that I remembered from school that coincided with Opening Day? Were fans filling the ballpark on every Opening Day? Did anything else affect the pageantry surrounding Opening Day?

What I have discovered in my research is that the one constant in Cincinnati since 1869 has

been baseball and, in particular, the unique spectacle that is Opening Day. Whatever else was happening in the city or the world in a given year, Cincinnatians enthusiastically celebrated the first day of the baseball season—that one special day when hope springs eternal. I have learned that the game is secondary to the affection people show for each other, the tradition, the city, and the Reds on the one special day that transforms our town.

This book describes the history of Opening Day traditions and some of the interesting historical events and customs that help place the opener in context. For a more detailed description of the actual games that took place on Opening Day, I recommend *Redleg Journal: Year by Year and Day by Day with the Cincinnati Reds Since 1866* by Greg Rhodes and John Snyder. Another great resource is *Opening Day: Celebrating Cincinnati's Baseball Holiday* by John Erardi and Greg Rhodes. I thank all three of these authors and the *Enquirer* for the enjoyment and information they have provided to me, first as a fan and, later, as the writer of this book.

As any Cincinnati baseball fan knows, sometimes our team wins and sometimes it loses, but what really counts is what brings us together on that one day every year—the day when we celebrate baseball, the arrival of spring, and the storied tradition of the Cincinnati Reds. We gather together to celebrate and to hear those words that are music to every fan's ears: "Play ball!"

Bob Freking and Esther Heithaus Freking

IT'S ALL IN THE FAMILY

Opening Day is a day baseball keeps its Little Boy promise. It's the one day when being unreasonably optimistic and hopelessly naive isn't just accepted; it's preferred. We sit in the sun and let a little spring wind give loft to all that might be.

Paul Daugherty, *Enquirer* sports columnist

Without a doubt, my fondness for baseball originated with my father passing along his love for the sport to me. My dad, a World War II veteran and an outgoing, enthusiastic salesman of the Yellow Pages—the free phone book of business listings delivered to residences and businesses—loved baseball. He coached our grade school teams as well as the youth teams we played on in our version of Little League, which was called Knothole Baseball in Cincinnati.

My parents, Bob Freking and Esther Heithaus Freking, married on Dad's birthday after the war. Mom learned to love baseball after delivering five boys into the world. She was a beautiful and spirited woman. I remember fondly how she banged pots and pans on our front porch after the Reds won the National League pennant in 1972 in their final at bat. I was 15 at the time. Unlike most playoff games today, the game ended around 7:00 p.m., so there was no risk of disturbing the neighbors, especially since they were likely rejoicing as well. We lived in Finneytown, a blue-collar neighborhood slightly northwest of the Cincinnati city limits. Her reaction seemed so normal. Why wouldn't you run to the kitchen, grab a couple of pots and pans, and bang them together on your porch after a playoff win?

The Prophecy

My parents were good-hearted, lower- to middle-class people who simply wanted their kids to enjoy their work and family life. Oh, and to enjoy baseball, too! Dad had a friend, Al Schottelkotte, who was the evening news anchor on Channel 9, the local CBS affiliate. Back then Channel 9 was one of only

Harold and Jeanne Freking

three or four TV channels. We all thought Schottelkotte had a Walter Cronkite air about him, and we watched him religiously at 6:00 p.m. Schottelkotte was beloved around town, and he instilled in me an interest in news that I regrettably never pursued beyond stints as a teenage reporter for a local newspaper and a contributor to high school publications. We also enjoyed watching Jack Moran, the Channel 9 sports anchor, who did double duty during baseball season by teaming with Hall of Famer Waite Hoyt on the Reds radio broadcasts.

My parents, along with Dad's brother Harold, and his wife, Jeanne, taught us to pay attention to local, national, and world events. Uncle Harold died young in 1969, but by then he had implanted the value of learning about history and current events through his annual tradition of "Queens and Commoners' Predictions" or, as we refer to it now, "the Prophecy." On January 1 of each year, the family's adults and teenagers would gather around Harold and Jeanne's kitchen table, usually at halftime of the Rose Bowl Game. Collectively, we would predict the events of the coming year. A couple of the perennial questions were, Will the Reds win the pennant? (I always voted "yes.") Will there be peace in the Middle East?

Aside from those, there were plenty of questions each year that required us to read the newspaper and to pay attention—at least a little. Topics ranged from who would win the Oscar for best actor to the nation's economic prospects, including predictions about the price of a gallon of gas on the next New Year's Day. Every four years, we would speculate about who would be the Republican and Democratic nominees for president.

Along with predicting the future, we would tally the results from the past year's Prophecy, and the winner would take home a few bucks. Unfortunately, Harold passed away just one year before the opening of the ballpark he had dreamed about: Cincinnati's Riverfront Stadium. In his honor, Aunt Jeanne upheld the New Year's Day tradition of the Prophecy, which I am happy to say is still going strong today. Jeanne's interest in current events was not limited to January 1, however; during the rest of the year, she loved to discuss national, statewide, and local politics with us. She also enjoyed recounting stories of days gone by, such as what it was like growing up during the Depression or about Uncle Harold's work as a pharmacist after World War II. My siblings and I owe Harold, Jeanne, and our parents a debt of gratitude for teaching us the importance of understanding both current events and history.

The Birth of Opening Day

Speaking of history, that brings me back to the topic of Opening Day, and specifically to my first Opening Day in 1967. But first, some background. Cincinnati holds the honor of being home to the nation's first professional baseball team, the Cincinnati Red Stockings. The Red Stockings, formed in 1869, later came to be known as the Reds. (For a brief period in the 1950s, the team adopted the name Redlegs to avoid the suspicion of Communist infiltration fostered by Senator Joseph McCarthy.) For many, though not all, years of the Reds' existence, Cincinnati has been accorded the privilege of hosting what is now known as Opening Day—a term used offhandedly by the *Enquirer* in 1895 to signify the launch of the professional baseball season. In the early years, Cincinnati won the honor largely because of geography. As the southernmost team in the league, spring came earlier to Cincinnati than it did where most of the other professional teams played. With one exception in 1888, the Reds have been the only team in Major League Baseball (MLB) to be granted the privilege of being scheduled to start every season at home. (Rain forced the Reds to start the season in Louisville in 1877 and 1885 and in Philadelphia in 1966, and a labor dispute resulted in the Reds traveling to Houston for their first game in 1990.)

We Cincinnati natives grew up taking pride in Cincinnati's unique role in Opening Day. Although we are one of the smaller MLB cities,

QUEENS AND COMMONERS PREDICTIONS 1972

Who will get Democratic nomination, President _Muskie_ X

" " " " " V-Pres. _McGovern_ X

" " " " " V-Pres. _Agnew_ ✓

" " " Republican " V-Pres. _Agnew_

THE WINNER: Democrats _____ Republicans _X_ ✓

Reds will finish in __1st__ place in their division. ✓

If first will they win a National League Pennant __Yes__ ✓

" " " " " the World Series __Yes__ X

Bengals will finish in __1st__ place in their division. X

If first will they win an ABA pennant __Yes__ X

" " " " " the Super Bowl __No__ ✓

Who will be the leading money winner in Pro Golf __Archer__ X

Any new babies? Julie Eisenhower __no__ (yes or no) ✓

Trisha Cox __no__ " " ✓

Will Princess Anne's engagement be announced __Yes__ (yest or no) X

Will Dean Martin remarry __Yes__ X

Will Ethel Kennedy remarry __no__ ✓

Predict the attendance opening day at Kings Island __30,000__ 11,541 X

Will there be any new grandchildren in our Club __Yes__ X

If so, who __Carolyn__ X

7

A Dream Come True

As a kid in the 1960s, I could only dream about attending an Opening Day game. Other people got to do that, but my family wasn't that lucky. So imagine my surprise when, on the morning of April 10, 1967, my brothers and I were awakened to the news that we were going to Opening Day! Somehow Dad had got tickets, most likely from his longtime friend, "Dinty" Moore, who worked at the local Hudepohl Brewing Company. We could not believe it. We were going to THE GAME! (I still don't know if my older sister Sue particularly cared that she was left out, but later in life she joined her husband, Glenn Showers, in having a love for Opening Day and the Reds.)

What a thrill when I learned my mom had dutifully advised our schools that we each had a "dentist appointment" and could not attend school that day. Thankfully, our schools simply overlooked her fib. (I was in grade school with two of my brothers; the other two brothers were in high school). Around 11:00 a.m., we proceeded to downtown Cincinnati to have an early lunch at the Red Fox Grill on Sixth Street so we would not miss the pregame festivities. "The Fox" was Dad's favorite lunch spot, and it still thrives today offering menu items such as double-decker cheeseburgers. No healthy salads are necessary at lunchtime for the Red Fox's regular clientele!

A sign at the Red Fox stated "no splitting of sandwiches," so each of us had to order a full-size sandwich, which we were all too excited to finish. Shortly after the noon bells rang next door at St. Francis Xavier Church, we were on our way to iconic Crosley Field in our Ford station wagon. After weaving through downtown traffic that had snarled because of the annual Findlay Market Parade, we arrived at the ballpark. Our eyes took in

The Freking Family Opening Day tradition starts at the Red Fox Grill

hosting Opening Day makes us feel special for a day. It is a day second to none in Cincinnati and has become an unofficial city holiday for baseball fans in a baseball town.

Al Schottelkotte

the new, bright-green Zoysia grass on the field just as the parade marshal entered through an outfield gate. My brother Robert saw some of his Roger Bacon High School classmates who, unlike us, did not have "dental appointments" that day but were legitimately off school. They were in one of the many marching bands entering behind the color guards.

The Reds beat the Dodgers that day, which kept our spirits high, but the score did not seem all that important when all was said and done. What mattered to us was the chance to be there and enjoy all the festivities surrounding the game. And just as Opening Day has always taken place within the larger context of local, national, and world events, 1967 was no exception. The morning *Enquirer* jubilantly announced the opening of that Reds season on the front page, but a smaller headline down below reminded the city that sober news was being delivered elsewhere. The headline read, "Faulty Wire Blamed in Apollo Fire." A blue-ribbon panel had issued a 3,000-page report about the tragedy that

had taken place at Cape Kennedy, Florida, just two months earlier. Astronauts Gus Grissom, Ed White, and Roger Chaffee had perished in a flash fire on January 27 while training in their Apollo 1 command module. The panel concluded that the fire, which had spread rapidly in the pure-oxygen environment, was started by a stray spark from bruised or broken wires. When we turned on the television that evening, Schottelkotte reported on the breaking news of the day, while Moran reported on the win, just as they had for years on end.

FAMOUS RED STOCKINGS OF 1869

IT ALL STARTED WITH A PARADE

However, at Cincinnati the first game is always played there. This is because the Citizens of this Ohio city do not consider Opening Day just as Opening Day. They consider it one small notch below Christmas.

Fred Schwed, Jr., *How to Watch a Baseball Game* (1957)

Like many traditions, the observance of Opening Day in Cincinnati has evolved over time, but the energy undergirding it has always stemmed from the pure joy of welcoming a new baseball season. From its humble beginnings of Red Stocking players marching to the first game, the celebration has grown to include cages of warbling canaries, a century of parades beginning at Findlay Market, citywide parties, a block party with music, beer, and food throughout "The Banks" entertainment district, and military planes performing flyovers to signal the season's beginning.

Activities of the first Opening Day bore little resemblance to the current state of affairs. On May 4, 1869, the first professional baseball team in history played its first official game. According to author Stephen D. Guschov in The *Red Stockings of Cincinnati: Base*

Ball's First All-Professional Team, the city of Cincinnati was in a festive mood, and the players themselves joined the parade to Union Grounds:

> Harry Wright's boys rode out to the Union Grounds in a caravan of fancy, ribbon-adorned carriages, behind which followed hundreds of merry cranks, eager to see whether their boys could measure up to the first real competition of the season. The Red Stocking players strode confidently into the Union Grounds and onto the emerald-hued field, resplendent in their crisp, white flannel uniforms and blazing scarlet hosiery, marching nine abreast across the field, like soldiers in formation on their way into battle.

Without knowing it, Wright and several hundred baseball fans launched a tradition that would become entrenched in Cincinnati's culture for the next 150 years: a parade to mark the start of the baseball season. Although the ragtag version of the first parade bears no resemblance to its current form, this public celebration of Opening Day became the hallmark of Cincinnati's spring celebration. And who were the merry cranks referenced by Guschov? They were baseball-crazed fans named after a local lawyer.

A Quiet Beginning

While the unofficial holiday known as Opening Day was not recognized until decades later, 1869 marked the beginning of Cincinnati's love affair with professional baseball. In the eight-page edition of the *Cincinnati Enquirer*, the May 4 game was previewed as follows:

> The Cincinnati and Great Western Base-Ball Clubs play the first regular match game of the season this afternoon at three o'clock, on the Union Grounds. Both clubs will send forth the whole of their first nines, and a very interesting game may be expected.

There was no marching band, no parade grand marshal, and no ceremonial first pitch as there would be later on. The fan base consisted of a small number of those "cranks," and the opposing team wasn't even from another city. The professional Cincinnati Red Stockings

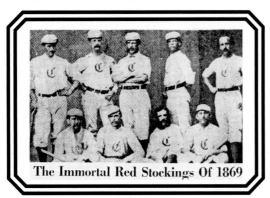
The Immortal Red Stockings Of 1869

beat the amateur Great Westerns of Cincinnati 45–9, with three inside-the-park home runs. (No player ever hit a ball over the fence at Union Grounds and, in those days, most baseball fields had no fences). The *Enquirer* apparently did not cover the game, as there was no mention of it in the newspaper the next day.

And who could blame the readers of the *Enquirer* for missing the brief announcement

of the first game? Page one detailed the trip to England that the US Ambassador to Great Britain, John Motley, was scheduled to take 15 days later. "Despite all the talk about war with England, … the instructions to be given [Motley] are yet subjects for future discussion and consideration by the President and his Cabinet," said the article. Farther down the column, concern was expressed about US citizens in Cuba, and the US Consul-General at Havana was cautioned not to "precipitate a quarrel with the Spanish authorities."

With professional baseball being a new phenomenon, the *Enquirer* was more concerned about events in Indianapolis, Columbus, and New York, as well as the doings of the Cincinnati city council the previous day. Local commerce concerns were of much greater interest to *Enquirer* readers than was baseball. On page seven, an ad appeared for "a good boot and shoe maker" promising "good wages" if one wanted a job in Boone County, Kentucky—about a ten-minute car ride today from Cincinnati but much longer by horse in 1869. The riverboat schedule showed 11 departure times for various cities along the Ohio River. And in other transportation news, the nation's first transcontinental railroad was five days from completion in Promontory, Utah.

But little did the bustling city of Cincinnati, and indeed the nation, know what had just happened. The game played at Union Grounds kicked off a cultural phenomenon that would come to be known as "America's National Pastime" for the next one-and-a-half centuries. Unlike this first Opening Day that was barely newsworthy, Opening Day in the modern age signals a generational feeling of rebirth for millions of baseball fans—so much so that Tom Boswell, the great sports columnist from the Washington Post, was inspired to write the book, *Why Time Begins on Opening Day*. Another great author, George Vecsey, explained in *A Year in the Sun* that "there is no sports event like Opening Day of baseball, the sense of beating back the forces of darkness and the National Football League."

The White House Pitches In

Opening Day has become such a national event that it is even a place for US presidents to show the world their stuff. President William Howard Taft, a baseball enthusiast from none other than Cincinnati, Ohio, attended Opening Day at National Park in Washington, D.C., on April 14, 1910, in a game between the Washington Senators and the Philadelphia Athletics. President Taft's ceremonial first pitch to Senators catcher Gabby Street continued a tradition in professional baseball whereby a guest of honor throws a ball to mark the beginning of a game and, on Opening Day, the beginning of the season.

Since Taft's first pitch, all but a few sitting presidents have similarly marked the beginning of the season. And, while later presidents followed Taft by throwing the first pitch from the first row of the box seats, President Ronald Reagan started a new twist on the presidential tradition in 1984 when he made an unscheduled appearance in Baltimore, walking out to the pitcher's mound and throwing the pitch to home plate! The overachiever of all presidents on Opening Day was undoubtedly Harry Truman. In 1950, he threw two opening pitches: one with his left hand; the other with his right! Over time, presidential appearances on Opening Day have only solidified the sport's honorary position as the nation's pastime.

President William H. Taft

Ad for first game in professional baseball history

THE RED STOCKINGS PLAY BALL

The Red Stockings, by winning 90 consecutive games between October, 1868 and June, 1870 also lay claim to being the sport's first great dynasty.

Stephen D. Guschov, *The Red Stockings of Cincinnati*

No story about Opening Day would be complete without significant mention of the first professional team, the Red Stockings. The team had actually been formed on an amateur level in 1866 as the Cincinnatis (or the Union Club), and it was referred to alternately as a cricket club or a "base ball" club. ("Base" and "ball" were not combined into one word until the mid-1930s.) The 1866 team played only four games. The 1867 amateur team quickly became the best of the local teams, winning 17 of its 18 matches in the first season, scoring an average of 55 runs per match! Compare that to today's great teams, which usually score an average of five to six runs per game.

The 1867 amateur season was noteworthy on a few fronts. On July 4, the Cincinnatis christened Union Grounds and, for the first known time by a Cincinnati baseball team, admission was charged (25 cents) to gain entrance. This game was also the first Cincinnati baseball contest reported in the *Enquirer*. This brief article appeared on July 6, failing to mention that Louisville had been soundly beaten, 60–24:

> They have laid out the grounds in elegant style, erected a spacious pavilion for the accommodation of ladies, and all the accompaniments to boot, so that the club can now boast of having the finest grounds west of the city of New York. Everything being in order for the inauguration, the club extended an invitation to the Louisville Base-Ball Club to play them a match, which was accepted, and on the 4th [of July] the game came off, in the presence of hundreds of spectators, not a few of whom were ladies. There was some splendid playing on both sides, the Union Club [the Cincinnatis] having the victory.

Uniforms Carry the Day

When the 1868 season opened, the Cincinnatis appeared in knickers and long, red stockings in an exhibition game on April 18, prompting the nickname "Red Stockings." This uniform was a departure from the full-length pants that had been worn by amateur baseball teams for decades. National newspapers then got into the nickname act, adding several more monikers, such as the "Scarlet Hose," the "Flaming Stockings," or the "Knights of the Crimson Hose." The popularity of the Red Stockings nickname prompted the team to make Red Stockings part of the team's official name. Other teams followed the lead of the Red Stockings and started wearing colored socks and knickers, too.

UNION GROUNDS: *1869-1870*

The Red Stockings were led by their player-manager, Harry Wright, one of two "Wright Brothers" on the team. Wright, who was born in England but came to the United States as a young child, learned cricket from his father. His cricket background made him a natural as a baseball player. Under Wright's management, the Red Stockings won 37 of 44 games in 1868. Widely regarded as the best team in the West already, the Cincinnati club decided that Wright should take charge of recruiting and signing the best amateur

ballplayers to professional contracts. Wright slowly began to put together a club for the upcoming season and made a dramatic public announcement to the nation's sporting press: the Cincinnati Red Stockings of 1869 would be the first all-professional baseball club in the history of the game.

Going Pro

The National Association of Base Ball Players (NABBP) had been established in 1858 to set standard rules and regulations and to uphold the sport's gentlemanliness. The NABBP prohibited professionals, but by the 1860s a number of teams had both professional and amateur players. The organization had no power to enforce the prohibition against players being paid. It looked the other way until 1869, when it conceded that its member clubs could have professional players. It divided its teams into two separate classes: amateur and professional.

The decision to allow teams to pay ballplayers was heavily criticized by the national press and by those in amateur baseball. Their concern was that professional baseball would make players into bloodless mercenaries and destroy the game just as it was beginning to gain nationwide popularity. (Note that the same argument was repeated more than one hundred years later when the courts outlawed the "reserve clause" that barred professional players from leaving teams and becoming free agents. To the contrary, the game has only increased in popularity, despite the players becoming "mercenaries.")

Harry Wright ended up signing ten players to contracts for the 1869 season. As injuries occurred, he signed other players on an as-needed basis. The highest-paid player was Wright's talented younger brother, George, who was paid $1,400 for the eight-month season, which ran from March 15 to November 15. The other players were paid between $600 and $1,200—extraordinary salaries by 1869 economic standards. In that year, the average skilled worker earned approximately $525 to $750 per year.

George Wright

Old-School Rules

The rules of the game in 1869 were far different from the current rules. While the eight position players were the same, the pitcher stood only 45 feet from home plate compared with 60.5 feet— the distance established in 1889, and still used today. Pitchers threw the ball underhanded, resulting in virtually no arm or shoulder injuries. Rather than crouching directly behind home plate, the catcher stood anywhere behind the plate he desired. The first and third basemen played very close to their respective bases, the second baseman played directly behind second base, and the shortstop played right behind the pitcher. For 20 or more years, the players did not use gloves or other protection for the shins, chest, and face. Four strikes constituted a strikeout, and it took six to nine balls to constitute a walk. (Three strikes and four balls became the rule in 1889.) Despite

many more possible pitches and many more runs being scored, professional games were generally one or two hours long in contrast to today's average of three hours.

The Red Stockings played their first game as a professional club in an exhibition game on April 17, 1869. Neither the public nor the newspaper reporters were impressed. As the *Enquirer* reported:

> The baseball season for 1869 was opened yesterday by a game between the first line of the Cincinnati club and the field. The playing on both sides was very poor. There was quite a large number of spectators present, but the enthusiasm of last summer was lacking.

One of the most noteworthy events of that first professional season occurred on June 26, 1869. President Ulysses S. Grant, an Ohio native, welcomed the Cincinnati club to the White House, making the Cincinnati club the first professional team to be received by a president. The day before, the Red Stockings had defeated the best Washington, D.C., club, the Nationals, by a score of 24–8 before a crowd of 10,000. The game set an attendance record in Washington at the time.

THE "UMPS" WERE **SOME** DUDES IN THOSE EARLY DAYS. BUT THEY CARRIED BATS TO EMPHASIZE THEIR DECISIONS.

Undefeated!

In what seems like an incomprehensible winning streak now, the Red Stockings completed their inaugural professional season without a single loss. The team's perfect record became official on November 6 when they beat the Mutuals of New York by a score of 17–8. Over the course of the season, the Red Stockings averaged 40 runs per game compared with their opponents' ten.

Although the Red Stockings indisputably notched an undefeated season, there was nonetheless controversy as to the number of victories attributed to the team. Harry Wright recorded 56 wins and one tie, as he included only games that lasted at least five innings, and only games against teams in the NABBP. He did not include wins in San Francisco, Sacramento, and Louisville that were against "Picked Nine" ball clubs put together on a temporary basis. Making matters really confusing, the *Cincinnati Commercial* reported 57 wins, the *Enquirer* recorded 58 wins, and the New York Daily Tribune tallied 61 victo-

ries. Each of these newspapers disregarded Harry Wright's recording of a tie because that game was marked by controversy. Cincinnati was widely credited for the victory because the other team, the Troy Haymakers, effectively forfeited after the ninth inning instead of agreeing to break the tie. There was speculation that Troy's manager wanted to avoid a loss in order to satisfy those who had made wagers on the game.

The team naturally won the first national championship, and the Red Stockings also earned the distinction of being the first team to play on both coasts. The Red Stockings were able to play games in California beginning in September after the first transcontinental railroad had opened on May 10. The railroad, a 1,912-mile continuous railroad line, connected the eastern rail network with the Pacific Coast at San Francisco Bay. The railroad revolutionized the settlement and economy of the American west by making the coast-to-coast transport of passengers and goods considerably quicker and less expen-

sive. Eight decades after the Red Stockings made their first West Coast swing, MLB put down roots in California when the New York Giants and the Brooklyn Dodgers moved to new ballparks on the West Coast.

1870: Winning Games but Losing the Team

In early 1870, advertisements in the *Enquirer* foreshadowed the special nature of the first game of the season. On April 15, just four days before the Red Stockings' home exhibition game, a notice appeared that tickets could be purchased that afternoon at the Gibson House (a local hotel) from 4:30 to 6:00 p.m. for the "Grand Opening Game of the Nine of 69." Only a small crowd showed up, as many others were put off by the ticket price increase to 50 cents.

The official season began six days later with an away game in Louisville, kicking off a two-week tour to the South. The winning streak from the inaugural professional season was extended with a 94–7 victory. The question remained as to how long the Red Stockings could continue their undefeated streak in the 1870 season.

The first home game on May 12 was described as the "First Grand Game of the Season of 1870." The next day, the club added to the hype by proclaiming the game as the "Second Grand Game." After that, the team headed east for another road trip. On May 20, the *Cincinnati Commercial* newspaper used the nickname "Reds" for the first known time in a Cincinnati publication. Though it was used frequently by the Commercial and other newspapers thereafter, the team did not adopt the shortened name until 1882. (The *New York Herald* had used the nickname in June 1869, but the Cincinnati press did not pick it up until 1870.)

After running the undefeated streak to 90 games, the Red Stockings lost to the Athletics of Brooklyn in a most unusual way on June 14. The game was tied after nine innings, and

extra innings were to be played only if both teams agreed. Since extra innings occurred so infrequently, everyone assumed the game had ended. Most of the 9,000 fans began to leave the ballpark, and the game's one umpire left the field along with the Athletics.

The Red Stockings manager, Harry Wright, wanted to have a perfect season in 1870 without any ties, and he convinced the Athletics to return and continue the game. The Reds scored two runs in the top of the eleventh inning to take the lead, but an error

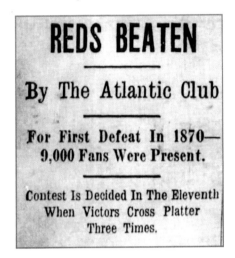

on a double play in the bottom of the inning resulted in an 8–7 victory for the Athletics. This first-ever loss for the Red Stockings came one year and 45 days after the first Opening Day.

The team would lose five more games that season, but it still finished with the best record in professional baseball with 67 wins to its credit. The season ended with a 27–6 victory over Cleveland on November 5. Because there was no professional league and there were no clear rules about how to crown a champion, several teams claimed the title. Ironically, the season finale would be the last professional game for Cincinnati until 1876. Despite its success on the field, the Red Stockings were a struggling commercial enterprise. During the 1869 season, the team had earned a profit of only $1.39 after meeting its $9,400 payroll. Revenues were not significantly higher in

1870. As a result, the club decided it could not afford to join the professional league that started to form after the 1870 season. With 1871 expenses projected to exceed $30,000, club president A.P. Bonte declared, "You can … talk about the Glory of the Red Stockings and the nine that knows no defeat, but you must put your hands in your pockets and pay the bills. You can't run the club on Glory."

The new league, known as the National Association of Professional Base Ball Players, was made up of nine teams from the East Coast to as far west as Rockford, Illinois. The Boston franchise, wanting to profit from the on-field success of the Cincinnati club, signed Harry Wright and several other of the original Red Stockings. Then, they rubbed salt in Cincinnati fans' wounds even more by doing the unthinkable: taking the name Red Stockings. Not having a professional team in Cincinnati was a bitter enough pill to swallow, but having to give up the team name was the ultimate insult. It would be five more years until Cincinnati would return to playing professional baseball. Of note during this period without a professional team was the dedication of Fountain Square in 1871, a site that would become the future site of many baseball celebrations.

Picture of first Red Stockings' loss

Charles Jones

BANK STREET GROUNDS: *1880, 82, 83*

OPENING DAY TAKES HOLD

Opening Day. All you have to do is say the words and you feel the shutters thrown wide, the room air out, the light pour in. In baseball, no other day is so pure with possibility. No scores yet, no losses, no blame or disappointment. No hangover, at least until the games over.

Mary Schmich, *Chicago Tribune* journalist

The Red Stockings were not alone in their struggle to make professional baseball a thriving commercial enterprise. The National Association of Professional Base Ball Players league faced financial challenges of its own and folded after five years of operation. Only two of its 25 franchises, Boston and Philadelphia, lasted all five of those years. No evidence remains of any special activities to mark each season's first game. Today, MLB refuses to recognize the National Association as a "major league."

From 1871 through 1875, the Cincinnati baseball club played as an amateur club and only reestablished itself as a professional team in August 1875. That team's opener on August 9 was against the Chicago White Stockings in Ludlow, Kentucky, just across the river from Cincinnati. A week later, the Boston Red Stockings came to the Ludlow Grounds, and an overflow crowd of 5,000 people watched an exhibition game in which Boston, the best team in the nation, won by a score of 15–5. The Boston team was captained by Harry Wright, the original manager of the Cincinnati team. The Boston Red Stockings easily won the National Association championship in 1875.

From the founding of the first professional league in 1871 until 1900, baseball in America was much like America itself—it was on the move. The country was expanding its footprint, spreading from the East to the "wild, wild West" as outlaws, the US Army, homesteaders, and Native Americans jockeyed for land. Seven states were added to the nation between 1871 and 1900: Colorado, North and South Dakota, Montana, Washington, Idaho, and Wyoming. Cincinnati, initially dubbed the "Queen City of the West," could hardly be considered west by 1900. Much like the nation that was stretching beyond its original borders, professional baseball was going through growing pains of its own. Leagues came and went, and professional teams were launched in one city only to die or move to another city. Throughout the latter part of the nineteenth century, professional baseball struggled for stability.

1876: The National League Beckons

In January 1876, Chicago businessman William Hulbert approached several National Association clubs with plans for a new league. He believed the National Association was poorly managed and was protecting the interests of the Eastern clubs at the expense of those in the West. His vision was to have stronger central authority and to include only teams from cities with a population exceeding 75,000. The four western clubs, Chicago, St. Louis, Cincinnati, and Louisville, met secretly in Louisville, Kentucky, to lay the foundation for the league. In early February, Hulbert then met representatives of four eastern teams in New York City and enlisted them to join. He launched the National League of Baseball Clubs (NL) with eight charter members, making an exception for Hartford, since its population was under 75,000:

- Chicago White Stockings
- St. Louis Brown Stockings
- Cincinnati Red Stockings
- Louisville Grays
- Philadelphia Athletics
- Boston Red Stockings
- Hartford Dark Blues
- Mutual of New York

The National League's formation meant the end of the five-year-old National Association, as its remaining clubs shut down or reverted to amateur or minor-league status. The first game in National League history was played on April 22, 1876, between the Philadelphia Athletics and the Boston Red Stockings. Boston won the game 6–5.

After joining the National League on February 2, Cincinnati's first league game occurred on April 25. The only mention of the game in the *Enquirer* that day was an ad announcing "Grand Opening Day." It contained a train schedule for the game with "cars reserved for ladies." The *Cincinnati Daily Star* reported the occasion under the simple headline "Base-Ball":

> The season of important base-ball matches commences to-day. The Cincinnati Reds and St. Louis Browns play this afternoon at the Stock-yard Grounds. … Our boys were the favorites in the polls shown at the Galt House and the Empire Saloon last night.

The previous evening's bettors were correct, as the Reds opened the season with a 2–1 victory thanks to "splendid playing," as reported by the *Enquirer* the next day:

> The prettiest and best game of base-ball played in Cincinnati since the disbanding of the old Red Stockings occurred on the new grounds of the new Cincinnati team yesterday. Our home club met the crack St. Louis Brown Stockings, and walked away with them to the tune of 2 to 1. There is not a bit of doubt in the minds of those who were present at the game yesterday that Cincinnati has a club this year that she may well be proud of. Its players are, with three exceptions, young and without a professional record. But they were picked out of semi-professional players and brought together by the same unfailing fellows who "discovered" the players of the famous Red Stockings of 1869, who went through the whole season that year without losing a game; and if the present club is not as strong as Harry Wright's old team, it is not far behind it.

The optimism of that report was not rewarded. The Red Stockings would finish in last place in the National League with a record of nine wins and 56 losses. It is the lowest winning percentage in the history of the Cincinnati Reds.

AVENUE GROUNDS: *1876-79*

1877: Rain, Rain Go Away

Heavy rains forced the Reds to postpone the opening series of 1877 that was scheduled to begin on May 3. Instead, they opened on the road in Louisville a week later. Under new player-manager Lip Pike, the major leagues' first Jewish player, the Reds opened their second National League season with a 15–10 win. The game was called after eight innings "owing to the lateness of the hour" after a three-hour game.

Four days later, the team opened the home portion of its 60-game schedule, losing 24–6 to Louisville in a game lasting three hours and ten minutes. It was probably the longest season opener in the nineteenth century, as later games tended to last one-and-a-half to two-and-a-half hours. (Some early box scores do not list "time of game.")

Although only 3,000 fans showed up for the game, the *Enquirer* described the crowd size as a "flattering attendance." Still, the local press was not impressed with the on-field action, calling it a "long tiresome game." As one reporter noted, "a few aching hearts will be relieved by the profoundly wise and philosophic reflection this morning that the

commercial prosperity and artistic progress of Cincinnati are not dependent upon the success of the combination of ballplayers that bear her name." The 18-run defeat is the worst Opening Day result in Cincinnati history. From a crowd standpoint, the opener was the high point of the season, as the Red Stockings would go on to draw fewer than 1,000 fans per game that season.

A month later, Red Stockings owner Josiah Keck decided to disband the team due to financial setbacks, proclaiming that "he had already lost as much as he intended to, and that he would now stop." The *National Associated Press* reported the sad news on June 18, 1877:

> Things are in a chaotic state, and it need not surprise the public if the announcement comes that the Reds as an organization are no more. The Club deserved the better fate, as there are excellent players in it, but they seem to have no pride in pulling together. Demoralization set in among them some time ago, and with no strong hand to hold them down to their work they have been going from bad to worse, until, as a team of good skillful and determined ballplayers, they have sunk far below any League Club in existence. When a Club dies, and from present appearances it is now suffering the pangs of disillusion, its epitaph will be 'died for want of a Head.'

Fortunately, new ownership headed by a prominent business executive, J.W. Neff, reorganized the team and the Reds resumed play three weeks later. They managed to make up nearly every game they had canceled during the hiatus. As the *Cincinnati Daily Star* reported on July 5, 1877:

> The interest in the game has taken a sudden advance in this locality, and if the Reds will but do as good playing in the future as they did yesterday, the Queen City will again be the center of attraction as regards the National Sport and regain the ground which has been lost in the last two years. Here's our compliments to the new syndicate and may the result yesterday [a win] be an earnest of what their friends may expect in the future.

The "new" Reds featured a new look. According to the *Enquirer*, "the Cincinnatis wear parti-colored caps with players wearing different hats: red, white, blue, green, white with a red stripe, red with a white stripe, blue and white, white and black, and yellow and black." The *Enquirer* reported that the players "look cute."

1878: Fans Turn out for the First Game

Compared to its 1877 season, Cincinnati baseball was considerably less chaotic in 1878. The Red Stockings spent 62 days in first place in the first half of the season before fading to second place with a 37–23 record. This strong start had been predicted in the *Enquirer* on May 1:

> At three o'clock this afternoon the League Season will open at 3 points—in Cincinnati, Indianapolis, and Providence. … It is not our province to prophesy how the three games will terminate. We can only give as a pointer of public opinion the sale of pools last night at the Arctic and other pool-rooms, where the betting was $10 to $7 on the Cincinnatis.

The optimism of the gamblers was rewarded with a 6–4 victory over Milwaukee. A local reporter also noted, "A lovelier day for out-of-door sports never shone more than our May day yesterday." The *Enquirer* described the large crowd in attendance:

> Before the days of turn-stiles the crowd would have gone down in newspaper history at about thirty-five hundred, but the turn-stiles counted sixteen hundred, and probably two hundred more came in through the carriage-gate. Both pavilions were comfortably filled, though four or five hundred more could have been squeezed in. About two hundred were in the grandstand, many of whom were ladies. The large collection of buggies and carriages in the lower part of the grounds bespoke a good tone for the crowd gathered there. There was plenty of enthusiasm as the game proceeded, though the game was slow and slogging.

The leadoff game in 1878 game was indeed another slow one, with the time recorded at three hours as a result of numerous delays. Reds' shortstop Joe Gerhardt was injured during the game, and the umpire threatened to quit after he was involved in two lengthy disputes.

The first game of this season appears to have received slightly more attention than previous opening games during the 1870s, at least from the standpoint of crowd size. The additional interest was probably the result of exhibition games being reported in the newspapers on a more regular basis. Another factor was nice weather for the "first championship game" of the season—a phrase often used to distinguish the first official game of the season from the exhibition games. The crowd size for the first game was rivaled only by attendance at games on holidays during the season, particularly July 4. Despite the strong turnout, there were no Opening Day festivities preceding the first pitch.

1879: Game? What Game?

Opening Day in 1879 almost went unnoticed. The May 1 *Enquirer* buried a small advertisement and one sentence on the last page of the eight-page newspaper announcing the season opener: "Base-ball opening of the League Season Today." Whether because of that single mention in the *Enquirer* or other factors, only 1,200 fans ventured out to Avenue Grounds

to witness a come-from-behind victory over Troy, New York, another new entry in the National League. Small crowds had been blamed for the Red Stockings' poor play in several exhibition games in Cincinnati prior to the first regular season game.

Despite the scarcity of coverage on the morning of the game, the Reds—as well as their opponent—received generous praise in the next morning's *Enquirer*:

> Yesterday the National League Base-Ball Season opened all along the line with games at Cincinnati, Chicago, Cleveland, and Buffalo. … The game between the Cincinnatis and Troy City Club in this city was one that, though not brilliant, was most exciting until the last man was out. The Cincinnatis, it was apparent to all, had no easy walk away. The Troy men are all young, athletic, and earnest ball-players. They are by no means the weak Club they are rated generally, and if the other new League Clubs show up equally well at the end of the year, they must play a good stout game. The visitors, by their quiet, gentlemanly behavior on the field, won friends by the hundreds, and their success at certain periods of the game was just as loudly applauded as was that of the home Club.

The article went on to comment about the facilities at Avenue Grounds, noting, "The shade of the Grand Stand and south pavilion was uncomfortable, and the sunny seats of the north pavilion were in demand." Pitcher Will White's off-season commitment to practicing was also duly noted: "Will White deserves credit for his fine pitching. He has certainly not lost any of his skill and seems to have profited by that hole in his brother's barn door." Finally, the *Enquirer* also reported the crowd's happiness over a game-winning catch:

> Troy's heavy batter stepped to the plate while the audience held their breath. He finally lifted a long foul fly to left field, which Dickerson captured on a dead run, making as pretty a play as was ever seen in the outfields of that ground. The crowd relieved themselves by a long and loud shout of applause and left the ground well pleased.

The *Cincinnati Commercial* encouraged the directors of the ball club to induce the attendance of ladies at the games, "as it adds to the respectability of the National pastime." The paper also noted that if the "old standbys" who had regularly attended games show

"like punctuality" in visiting churches on Sundays, it "would guarantee them front seats in the Celestial Choir and the ownership of a choice harp."

1880: Booted from the National League

The opening of the 1880 National League season was proclaimed on May 1 in the *Cincinnati Daily Star*, with no mention in the *Enquirer*. The *Daily Star* headlined the season opener as follows: "The League Season to Open Today Between the Cincinnatis and Chicagos." The article on page six of the *Daily Star* (then an eight-page newspaper, just like the *Enquirer*) started with a poem that portended future delight in the first game of the season:

Base-ball

Oh, hustle me out early, bright and early, mother dear,
This day will be the merriest of all the mad new year;
For the base-ball season opens, the League begins to play,
And this is the first of May, this is the first of May.

So scoot me off right early, for I want to see the fun,
When Carpenter comes prancing in upon his first home run;
And Smith and Andy Lenard, when their feet begin to fly,
I want to be on hand to shout and smell the battle cry.

And White, dear little Willy, with glasses on his nose,
I want to see 'em hustle when the first hot ball he throws;
For Johnnie Clapp, the catcher, I want to give a yell,
And raise a whoop and hurrah for Manning and Purcell.

Then let me have a good front seat, where I can get a sight
Of all the wondrous monkeyshines
of Mansell and Sam Wright;
When the base-ball season opens and
the League begins to play,
For this is the first of May, mother, this is the first of May.

Little did optimistic readers of the Daily Star realize what was going to happen that season: the Red Stockings would suffer through a mediocre record, there would be three changes in the club's presidency, and the team would finish last and be expelled from the league.

Nonetheless, until those events came to pass, the Reds christened a new ballpark on the north side of Bank Street called the Bank Street Grounds, replacing Avenue Grounds. The Bank Street grounds were closer to the center of the city. The new ballpark included a scoreboard that displayed the name of each player as he came to bat. (Identifying players by uniform number was not introduced until 1932.) The scoreboard also reported scores for games going on in other cities. Those scores were sent and received by telegraph.

Charles Jones

BANK STREET GROUNDS: *1880, 82, 83*

The opponent in the opening game was the eventual 1880 National League champion, the Chicago White Stockings. The Chicago team won the coin toss, earning the right to bat in the bottom rather than the top of the inning. (The home team didn't automatically bat in the bottom of innings until 1950.) This seemingly small victory in the coin toss was fortuitous, as Chicago scored two runs in the bottom of the ninth inning to win the game, 4–3. This was after the Red Stockings had scored two runs in the top of the eighth inning to go ahead 3–2:

> But the game was not yet won, for in the last inning Corcoran [of the White Stockings] opened for his side with a hit to right. Then Sam Wright got rattled and fumbled Burns' hit, allowing that young man to reach first. Quest's hit to right let in Corcoran, and Burns, who had kept booming right along to bring in the winning run for Manning, in trying to cut him off, threw the ball in home some six feet over [catcher] Clapp's head.

Despite the attraction of the new Bank Street facility and fine weather for the opener, only 2,038 fans came to the ballpark. Attendance declined from there, as the Reds averaged only 538 fans per game that entire season. When the Reds closed the 1880 season with a 2–0 win over Cleveland, only 183 spectators were present at the Bank Street Grounds.

The 1880 season is noteworthy for the establishment of the reserve clause in professional baseball. Each team was allowed to protect five players for the upcoming season, contrary to the previous practice, which allowed players to be free agents and switch teams from season to season if they so desired. The reserve clause was meant to help financially strapped teams from losing star players to higher bidders. Since most rosters contained only 11 or 12 players, the reserve clause protected nearly half of the team on the club's behalf. (In 1883, the reserve clause was broadened to include the entire roster.) The reserve clause remained in place until 1975. At that time, it was abolished by the courts, and limited free agency was returned to baseball through collective bargaining with the players' union.

A significant development occurred on October 6 when the league announced new rules prohibiting teams from renting their ballparks for use on Sundays. The rules also banned the selling of alcoholic beverages. These new rules were directed at the Reds, and the Reds declared their refusal to abide by them. They were then unceremoniously expelled from the National League.

The ban on beer sales was the death knell to the franchise. The German immigrants in Cincinnati who supported baseball expected that beer would be served at any and every event. Fans loved baseball, but not at the expense of giving up beer! A Cincinnati newspaper writer fumed: "Puritanical Worcester [one of the cities in the league] is not liberal Cincinnati by a jugful, and what is sauce for Worcester is wind for the Queen City.

Beer and Sunday amusement have become a popular necessity."

1881: A New League Comes on the Scene

The Red Stockings did not play in 1881, but a meeting at Cincinnati's Gibson Hotel on November 8 set the stage for competition between the seven-year-old National League and a new professional league, the American Association (AA). The founding of the AA meant that the two leagues had to compete for fans and the attention of the public. In part, this competition contributed to the fanfare that came to be associated with Opening Day.

The historic Gibson Hotel, the site of this momentous meeting, had opened in 1849 on Walnut Street between Fourth and Fifth Streets (southeast of Fountain Square). It was considered the "best house in the city" within a year according to the *Fort Wayne Times* and the *Zanesville Courier*. The hotel was named

after a Scottish immigrant, Peter Gibson, who provided financing for the hotel. It became the preferred venue for celebrations and banquets during the Red Stockings' first season in 1869. Fans of that team would escort the players to the hotel after home victories. Later, during the 1890s, the Gibson hosted both the Cincinnati team and its Opening Day opponent after both teams would parade through the city and then have a pregame luncheon at the hotel.

For the November 8 meeting, local sportswriter Oliver Perry Caylor convened representatives of six cities to form the American Association. By design, the founders intended for the new league to be distinguishable in many ways from what they considered to be the straitlaced National League. The new league established teams in what the National League derisively called "river cities": Cincinnati, Pittsburgh, Louisville, and St. Louis. (The Association also included Philadelphia and Baltimore.) The "river cities" label was intentionally meant to imply that there were low moral and social standards in those cities. In contrast to the NL, the AA offered its patrons cheaper ticket prices, Sunday games, and alcoholic beverages. Its ticket price of 25 cents compared favorably with the NL's standard 50 cents, which was a hefty sum for many fans at the time. With these fan-friendly policies in place, the AA was the world's first professional sports league designed to cater to a blue-collar fan base.

The Association soon became known as "the Beer and Whiskey League," another contemptuous label applied by NL owners. Despite the AA's popularity with fans, however, chaos reigned as to which cities fielded teams. As many as 25 different cities hosted AA teams, some for as short as a single season. Several teams disbanded or defected to the NL, including the Reds in 1889. As a result of the instability, the Association shut down after the 1891 season. The last physical remnant of the Association was Cincinnati's Crosley Field, which closed in 1970 but was built on the site of the ballpark that housed Cincinnati's Association teams from 1884 to 1889. Although the Association is not directly related to today's American League, the two-league structure formed in 1881 foreshadowed the major leagues in the twentieth and twenty-first centuries.

1882: "If at first you don't succeed, try, try, try again"

The first-ever American Association game was simply referred to as the "Opening of the American Championship" in the May 2 edition of the *Enquirer*. While this game received barely a mention, the paper devoted considerable attention to the opening games of the well-established National League that had occurred the day before. In describing the opening game of the new AA league, the *Enquirer* noted that the "Cincinnati and Allegheny [Pittsburgh] teams open the American championship race in this city … and the contest will undoubtedly be a very interesting one." This inaugural opener featuring the Cincinnatis attracted 1,500 spectators. In reporting on the game, the *Enquirer* dismissively reported its assessment of the team's play: "If at first you don't succeed, try, try, try again." The article continued,

> They are young and giddy, and need [some advice to try again]. It was the best thing that could happen to them to be beaten by the Alleghanys. It will prove to them that what is worth having is worth playing for. It was the opening game, and there were naturally several men quite nervous in the field … There is no use of singling out any one player and casting upon him the burden of the defeat of the team. It could in this instance be divided equally among the nine men.

The coup de grace was the gratuitous ad placed by the *Enquirer* in its own newspaper to declare its displeasure with the team's pitchers.

It is not known how many pitchers applied, but the starting pitcher for that first Association game, all-time Reds great Will White, ironically ended up as the winning pitcher in 40 of the team's 55 wins. The Reds got the last laugh when they won the first championship in the new league. Apparently, they were better judges of their talent than was the *Enquirer*.

WANTED—A PITCHER—For a base-ball nine Any body, aye, every body that has ever pitched a base ball; that thinks he can pitch a base ball; that believes he ought to pitch a base-ball; that is willing to try to pitch a base-ball; that never has, but sees no reason why he should not pitch a base-ball; that would not scruple, even if he knew not how, to pitch a base-ball; that may in time be made to pitch a base ball; that never saw a base-ball, but hasn't a doubt but if he did put his eyes upon one he could pitch a base-ball, may learn something to their advantage by applying at a base-ball grounds at the foot of Bank street. Do not hesitate to bring your brothers, your cousins, your uncles, and even your grandfathers along if you think they can pitch a base-ball; numbers no object; every thing goes.

The above advertisement, we regret to say, was not a few weeks ago inserted in the EN-QUIRER. Had the managers of the Cincinnati Club known as much then as they do now it would have gone in with the addenda, "keep in t. f." (till forbid.)

1883: "And they raised the flag!"

There was some hoopla surrounding the first game in 1883, but it did not necessarily concern the beginning of that season; rather, the celebration was all about the previous championship season. The ad in the May 1 morning *Enquirer* proclaimed not just that the Cincinnatis would play that afternoon against the "St. Louis Club," but that the "Cincinnati Champions" would be playing at the Cincinnati Base-Ball Park. Advance tickets could be obtained at Hawley's, a local store, after which patrons could take the Baymiller or Clark streetcars to the game. The story in the newspaper was short, but it highlighted the reason for the celebration:

> The championship flag pennant, which arrived last Saturday, will be flaunted to the breeze shortly after three o'clock. The flag-staff has been planted at the north end of the open seats, and the flag is already fitted to the balliards, ready to be run up at a moment's notice.

The paper predicted "a large crowd will undoubtedly be on hand to witness the first championship game of 1883." The festivities for the flag raising ("the price of so many hard-earned victories") went off as planned, and "a great cheer was sent heavenward from the throng of [spectators], who wished that it might remain where it is for another year at least." The game itself was a "picnic"

until St. Louis made the game closer, and errors revealed the "beautiful uncertainties" of baseball:

> When the Cincinnatis started in the majority the crowd was misled into thinking that the game would be transposed into a general picnic, for without special effort the home lads got in four runs, and with proper base-running could have added at least one more to their score, during the first three innings. … The picnic business was reversed a little after the third inning, and the Cincinnatis took their turn at making a series of provokingly bad errors, and those, combined with timely hits, enabled the visitors to tie the score, and to illustrate to the crowd the beautiful uncertainties of the national game.

> The Reds, however, sent the crowd home "amid great applause": The chances were 10 to 1 against the Cincinnatis when they went to the bat in the last inning, but they proved that they are able to pull out of a small hole by some hard rapping, which netted the requisite number of runs.

1884: Disasters of Several Kinds

The season opener in 1884 was hardly noticed, following on the heels of one of the worst floods in the city's history. The Ohio River had crested at 71¾ feet just two months earlier, causing thousands to be homeless in Cincinnati and across the river in Newport, Kentucky. The *Enquirer* covered the rise of the river for weeks, and the February 13 headline aptly summed up the despair: "DESTRUCTION …

The Unprecedented Tragedy of the River … Ruin and Desolation Sweeping Through the [Ohio] Valley."

When the waters began to finally recede two days later, the *Enquirer* declared "A brighter day has dawned":

> The long looked-for cold wave came and brought the desired results. Yesterday at noon the river reached the highest stage ever known. At half-past twelve and again at one it remained the same. An anxious populace stood breathless. The bulletin at two o'clock showed a decrease of a quarter of an inch. Hope was again revived. "The river is falling!" was the joyous cry that passed from lip to lip and was heard on every side.

The Reds had no championship flag to entice fans to come to the first game on May 1, but they did open a new ballpark called League Park at the corner of Findlay Street and Western Avenue, the same site that would later be home to Crosley Field. Many, if not all, of the 3,200 patrons who attended the game against Columbus likely wished they had stayed home, as a portion of a newly built grandstand collapsed, causing several people to be seriously injured. Others "made a narrow escape with their lives," according to the *Enquirer*. The Reds paid the injured patrons' medical bills.

The customary ad had appeared announcing the "Opening of the Championship Season," but there was no special mention of the Reds' first game other than noting it was one of six games that day to formally open the American Association season. Even before the grandstand collapse, the crowd did not enjoy much of the game because the dimensions of the new field caused balls to be lost when they went out of play. The *Enquirer* unleashed its sarcasm again in reporting on the game:

> The game was tiresome by reason of the fact that the ball was knocked over the fence so many times. The short right field and the little distance from the baselines to the buildings make such things possible on the new grounds. Lots of time was lost in this manner, and it took three balls to finish out the game.

… The Cincinnati American club will have to start a base-ball factory here, as it will require about an average of five balls to each game.

What would the *Enquirer* staff say if they only knew that today 60 to 70 balls are used in every MLB game, and that Rawlings Sporting Goods produces nearly one million "Official Major League Baseballs" each year?

As unhappy as the Cincinnati fans were about the season's first game, a much lighter mood prevailed in Columbus. A "Special Dispatch to the *Enquirer*" declared that "the city [of Columbus] is wild to-night over the success of the Columbus Base-Ball Club at Cincinnati. The Columbus boys made bets with Cincinnati men largely by wire to-day and are ahead more than they ever were before."

Betting on baseball, even among the players themselves, was commonplace until the 1920s. The practice was curtailed after the Black Sox Scandal of 1919 when certain Chicago White

WILDE'S CLOTHING HOUSE.

Twenty-One Hundred

BOYS' SAILOR SUITS

ON EXHIBITION

SATURDAY, MAY 3.

Grand Sailor Suit Day!

A SOUVENIR FOR THE LADIES.

A BASE-BALL EQUIPMENT (BALL, BAT AND CAP), OR FINE SET OF MARBLES,

Sox players were accused of deliberately losing the World Series at the behest of gamblers. If only the Reds' Pete Rose, baseball's all-time hits leader, had played in the nineteenth century rather than the twentieth! Rose was slapped with permanent ineligibility in 1989 after evidence surfaced that he had bet on baseball games as both a player and manager.

Even many diehard baseball fans are unaware that Fleet Walker was the first African American to play in the major leagues. Walker made his debut in Cincinnati on May 9, 1884. He played for Toledo, a new AA team. Jackie Robinson of the Brooklyn Dodgers is typically credited with breaking the color barrier in the big leagues, but Walker had actually done so 63 years earlier.

1885: Three Cheers for... the Umpire?

The April 18, 1885, *Enquirer* hyped the first game with its banner headline across the top of page 2:

CINCINNATI BASE-BALL PARK.
TO-DAY 3 O'CLOCK P.M.

FIRST CHAMPIONSHIP GAME!
CINCINNATI VS. LOUISVILLE.

No such banner had appeared in previous years, but this type of headline became commonplace on each day of the first game of the season thereafter. The only special mention of the first game in the newspaper that day concerned a well-known and beloved umpire, John Kelly, who was scheduled to oversee the game.

Unfortunately, rain postponed the game, and the "Falls City" team (as Louisville was known in those days) hosted the Reds on Sunday, April 19 instead. This was the second time the Reds had opened the season away from Cincinnati due to rain. A Sunday game was controversial, as some cities and states barred baseball games on Sunday if admission was charged; Louisville had no such law. The change in venue certainly benefited the Kentucky city, as a huge crowd of 8,000 turned out, largely to see the Reds. The April 20 write-up in the *Enquirer* noted, "The visitors from Cincinnati were loudly cheered when they made their appearance … and the Cincinnatis were liberally applauded at the conclusion of the game."

The Reds played their home opener on April 20 in front of a much smaller crowd. In addition to commenting on the team's uniforms, the *Enquirer* article the next day highlighted the fans' esteem for Kelly, the popular umpire:

> In the neighborhood of twenty-five hundred people witnessed the contest, and saw [the Reds] win a ballgame from the Kentuckians in a finely played though not very exciting game. Both teams shone resplendent in new uniforms. The old colors, red and white, which have always been the stand-bys with these two organizations, still continue in favor. … The reception of Kelly, the umpire, was in the nature of an ovation. He is very popular in Cincinnati, and as he stepped out to call the game most of the spectators stood on their feet, and hats and handkerchiefs were waved, while they cheered him to the echo.

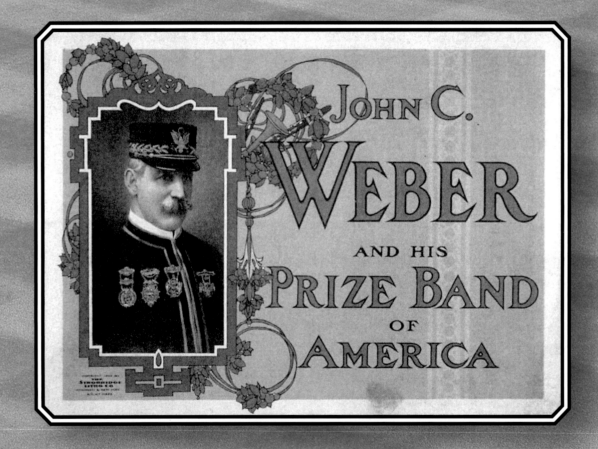

LET THE HOOPLA BEGIN

Frank Bancroft's Ten Tips for Opening Day:
1 Try to have at least one really good local player on your team, every year. **2** Pump in some new blood. **3** Introduce new spangles every year. **4** Give the fans—and the news fellows—something new to ponder on the grounds every year. **5** Invite some dignitaries, and some special guest, and notify the crowd of the latter. **6** Suffer the children. They are your future. **7** Design a special program for the opening game, as a keepsake. **8** Schedule some crackerjack exhibitions right there in the home Park for the days leading up to opening day. **9** Schedule a big parade, and pull in the players. **10** Always remember: Opening Day is "The Peoples Day."

As created by John Erardi in *Opening Day*

Between the first impromptu parade of Harry Wright's players in 1869 through 1885, no special attention was given to the first game of each season other than the appearance of small ads, headlines, and articles noting "the first championship game" of the year. That changed in 1886, when what would become a lasting tradition first came on the scene.

1886: A Concert and Canaries

Baseball fans opening their newspapers on the morning of April 17, 1886, were greeted by an ad announcing something special in conjunction with the first championship game: a 90-minute pregame concert by one of the great orchestras of the era, as well as a day dedicated to female fans:

CHAMPIONSHIP OPENING

Cincinnati Base-Ball Park,

TO-DAY AT 3:30 O'CLK

LOUISVILLES

——— Versus ———

CINCINNATIS,

Preceded by a Concert by the CIN-
CINNATI ORCHESTRA REED
BAND. Special Gala Day dedicated
to Lady Patrons.

The concert by the Cincinnati Orchestra Reed Band previous to the game was thoroughly enjoyed, especially by the ladies. The crowd was one of the most orderly that ever assembled at a ball game. The grandstand contained about two hundred ladies, and not an objectionable feature was apparent. The pavilion was densely packed with a well behaved crowd, which is saying a good deal. The brilliant plays on both sides were loudly applauded, and not the least bit of favoritism was shown by the spectators. … The umpire was way off in his decisions, and while they did not materially change the score, they were invariably against the Cincinnatis. If he wishes to succeed as an umpire he will have to change considerably from the way he began the season.

Cincinnati had a thriving music culture in 1886. In fact, a Cincinnati Music Center half dollar was minted in 1936 to commemorate the fiftieth anniversary of the city's musical heritage, though Cincinnati was known for its music community as far back as the 1870s. The well-known orchestra known as the Reed Band had played before games in the past but never on the first day of the season. The orchestra was very popular among both the socially elite and blue-collar fans. It became the Cincinnati Symphony Orchestra in 1895.

Another effort to delight the fans came in the form of greeting patrons as they passed through the turnstiles. But the greeting did not come from friendly attendants; instead, fans were treated to the melodious sounds of canaries in cages. Undoubtedly, this had to be one of the most unique welcomes in the history of sport. It is not clear why canaries were chosen, but the presence of warbling birds was certainly a welcome change from previous years when fans simply filed past harried ticket collectors.

The addition of the orchestra and the welcome given to ladies had the desired effect, as 5,460 fans attended the game—the Reds' largest home crowd ever. The next day's account of the opener focused not on the loss by the home team but rather on the pregame festivities, the presence of the ladies, and the umpire, who was clearly no John Kelly:

Unlike today, baseball sportswriters of the 1880s felt free to comment on the umpires' performance and to admonish them if their calls didn't measure up. Fans made sure to weigh in with their opinions on the umpires, too. But umpiring deficiencies aside, the success of the opener resulted in increased attention to the special nature of the day, and the seeds of traditions to come were firmly planted.

1887: Mayor in the House

The morning paper on April 16, 1887, screamed "Are You Ready! Then Let the Pennant Fight Begin," but the pregame festivities from a year earlier were missing from the inaugural game. The absence of the pregame music, coupled with extremely cold weather, resulted in an attendance of only 2,700--half the crowd that had been wooed by the concert in 1886. Ladies were again encouraged to attend, but a sign of the post–Civil War times appeared in the *Enquirer*: "Lady patrons will be looked after by a colored female attendant."

One noteworthy addition in the local press was the announcement that the city's mayor, Amor Smith, would "probably" occupy one of the private boxes at the opening contest. In subsequent years, a regular feature of the opening game would be the appearance of dignitaries—first, the city's mayor, and later the highest officials in baseball, governors, and indeed presidents of the United States.

Despite the freezing temperatures, the game was one of the finest openers played by the team from "Porkopolis," as Cincinnati was sometimes called. At the time, it was the largest pork-producing city in the world. Sportswriters appropriately dubbed the Reds the "Porkopolitans" in light of the city's nickname.

> The Cincinnatis played ball just as if it was a nice, warm, summer day. They batted the ball fiercely, ran the bases daringly, and fielded almost perfectly. … The Clevelands were defeated, and by a one-sided score at that, but their defeat is no discredit to them. … The game played by the Reds yesterday was a magnificent one and it would have beaten any club in the country.

1888: Starting the Season on the Road

One of the myths surrounding Opening Day in Cincinnati is that the Reds have always had the privilege of playing the first game of each season at home. Many believe this is an unwritten rule to commemorate the 1869 Red Stockings having been the first professional team. While the Reds have, in fact, been scheduled to begin at home every year but one since 1869, the rationale is betrayed by the 1888 schedule and the lack of a reaction to it. In that year, the American Association— gasp!—scheduled the Reds to open the season

What Best-Dressed Reds Wore In 1888

in Kansas City, followed by a trip to St. Louis. The Reds were not scheduled to play a game in Cincinnati for the first 13 days of the season. The lack of any protest by the Reds, their fans, or the press suggests that a home opener was not presumed as a guarantee.

And so, after opening the regular season in Kansas City on April 18, the Reds returned for their home opener on May 1. As in 1887, there was no pregame concert. Instead, the club instituted the "Centennial Register." The morning *Enquirer* announced, "All the patrons of the game and supporters of the club will be asked to register their names on books as they come in the gates."

With no pregame festivities scheduled, the Reds decided to create a sensation by outfitting each player in a different colored uniform. The nine starting players wore the following combinations: blue with black stripes; blue with a white collar and cuffs; red with white stripes; black with gold stripes; red with black stripes; maroon with a white collar and cuffs; black with blue stripes; blue with white stripes; black with white stripes; black with red stripes; and orange with blue stripes. All of the pitchers had white uniforms with a red collar and cuffs. The experiment was short-lived, and no photographs of the parti-colored uniforms exist.

Another clothing-related novelty that day was dreamed up by a local clothier, Fechheimer Bros. & Company. Fechheimer promised a new suit to the Red who hit the first home run of the season in Cincinnati. With cold weather and no pregame festivities being a factor once again, a crowd of only 2,200 was drawn to the opener.

Catcher Kip Baldwin won the suit in the home opener on May 1 by hitting the first home run, and the Reds vanquished their rivals in a "glorious" game resulting in a "Waterloo" for Louisville:

Last night there was not a man, woman, or child in Louisville who was willing to admit that they ever knew there was such an organization as the Eclipse Base-Ball Club [of Louisville]. … The Reds fell on the blue-ribbon team at the Cincinnati Park yesterday, and literally mopped up the grounds with the pride of Kentucky. … The weather was anything but auspicious for ball-playing. The air was cold and damp, and not once during the day did Old Sol favor Cincinnati people with one peep of his countenance. It was more like a cold February day than the 1st of May, and any of the patrons who forgot their heavy wraps had a very hard time keeping warm. In spite of this fact, a surprisingly large crowd attended the game. … They yelled themselves hoarse as the Louisvilles were being slaughtered.

Maybe because the club thought the opener itself was enough of a draw, the Reds instead promoted the second game of the home season as the "formal opening" by hanging banners

Many fans arrived at games on a horse-drawn trolley from the Little Miami Depot.

and inviting the orchestra back. Noted the *Enquirer*, "The Cincinnati orchestra will give an open-air concert. … They will render an excellent programme, and one of the features will be the cornet solos of Prof. Herman Bellstedt. The public would do well to come early to hear the music." The unique promotion worked, as the Reds attracted 2,600 fans for that second game—more than for the opener and far more than for the second home games in prior seasons.

1889: "Grand Preparation for the Opening"

On the morning of April 17, 1889, the *Enquirer* heralded the "Grand Preparation for the Opening," noting:

> Never in the base-ball history of Cincinnati has the opening of the season been observed as it will be at the Cincinnati Park this afternoon. With banners flying, music playing, with the loud huzzas of brave men and the encouraging words of fair women, the championship season of 1889 will be started in a way that will long be remembered by those who are there.

The article went on to say that "the decorators were at work at the Cincinnati Park into a late hour last night draping the boxes and stands with banners, bunting, and flags of all nations." The full Cincinnati Orchestra was invited for a 90-minute concert of "choice music" before the game, and the club announced that any lady accompanied by an escort would be admitted free of charge that afternoon. The Reds were to appear in their skintight uniforms for the first time, and they were said to be "undoubtedly the finest uniforms ever worn by an Association team."

As in 1886, making the first home game a special occasion was a resounding success, as 10,410 patrons attended—the largest crowd and the most festive day in Reds history:

> Cincinnati was base-ball crazy yesterday. … It seemed as if everybody were headed in the direction of Western avenue and Findlay street. All the street-cars were packed in suffocation. Car-load after car-load of humanity was dumped in from the gates. … The stands, which had been beautifully decorated with flags, banners and bunting, formed a splendid background for the gay spring bonnets and rich attires of the one thousand ladies in the grand stand. … Venturesome boys climbed to the roof of the pavilions, while a row of skirmishers held onto the fence by their fingernails. The telegraph poles on the outside, the roofs of the adjoining buildings and the tops of the box-cars on the side tracks west of the park furnished accommodations to bush whackers who had not made the acquaintance of the gentleman in the box-office.

A drawing in the *Enquirer* the next morning depicted the great crowd and "the grandest testimonial ever paid the National game in the Queen City."

The Reds announced after the 1889 season that they were rejoining the National League, and they would remain in "the League" for the rest of their history. A new rival called the Players League was formed, and many top professional stars (though none from the Reds) joined the new league. No Players League team was placed in Cincinnati as direct competition, and this league survived only one season.

1890: Players on Parade

A fan-friendly innovation occurred on April 19 to mark the Reds' return to the National League. Both the Reds and their opponent for the day, the Chicago Colts, paraded in uniform through the streets of downtown Cincinnati in horse-drawn carriages. When they arrived at the ballpark, they left their carriages and marched upon the field with "military-like precision." Their entrance followed a pregame

concert by the Cincinnati Orchestra. The park had been decorated the night before with banners and flags.

This was the most elaborate celebration of the Reds' opener in history, and despite poor weather, the crowd of 6,000 was exuberant:

> As the big Drum Major of the First Regiment Band strode through the carriage-gate, his baton aloft, six thousand pairs of eyes were on him. The crowd on the circus seats were the first to greet him with a feeble yell. Then the bleachers took up the refrain and gave more force to their welcome. Next the pavilion took a chance at the lung-testing business. The enthusiasm was infectious. The sedate and dignified grand-standers fell in line, while the private-box patrons added their little mite in the way of noise-making. … It was an ovation, and reached a climax with a great roar of applause. It followed when the players of each team lifted their hats in acknowledgment of the compliment.

Special celebrations also went on in other National League ballparks during the first week of the season. The league was well aware of the public relations challenge presented by the new Players League and the eight-year-old Association. League administrators knew they

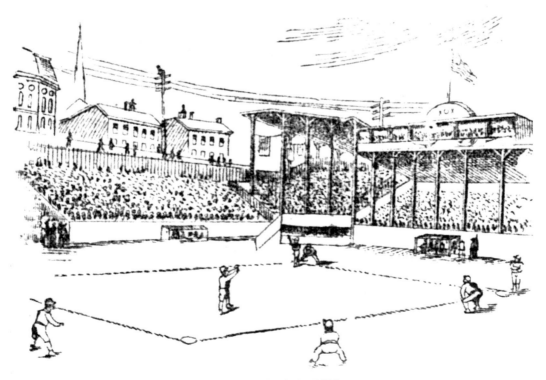

THE GREAT CROWD.

had to draw fans however they could. The morning *Enquirer* declared "The Grand Start To Be Made To-Day" and included a joke from the pages of the *New York Weekly* that revealed the public's admiration for the players:

> First College Boy: What are you going in for—wealth or fame? Second College Boy: Both. I'm going to be a ball-player.

The papers noted that the grounds were in excellent condition, adding that netting had been added behind home plate to protect fans from foul tips. The fans' hopes for a winning outing were dashed when the Colts beat the Reds, 5–4. The *Enquirer* reported that "stupid baserunning and loose fielding allowed the Chicagos to carry off the prize." Apparently, the sports writers were holding onto memories of a lackluster season in 1889, as they put their own sardonic spin on the loss:

> Brass bands, banners, flags, a multitude of people, old hollow-eyed defeat: in fact, all the usual accompaniments of the opening of a base-ball season in this city were at the Cincinnati park yesterday. Old hollow-eyed did not take up much space, but his influence was far-reaching and fell like a pall on the enthusiasm of the assembled spectators, who had come fully expecting to see [the] Chicago colts get a good dusting.

1891: Competing Parades

John T. Brush of Indianapolis bought the Reds after the 1890 season when the National League dropped Indianapolis from its ranks. He was a successful retail magnate whose years as owner were controversial. During his tenure, he tried to pass the "Brush Rule" that could banish a player for life if he addressed an umpire or a fellow player in a "villainously filthy" manner. This proposal failed. In 1903, Brush purchased the New York Giants while he also owned the Reds and the American League's Baltimore Orioles. Brush made controversial personnel transactions that preceded the sale of his Cincinnati and

Baltimore interests and positioned New York to be a juggernaut for the first third of the twentieth century. When the Giants ran away

> After an Exciting Struggle at the Cincinnati Park.
>
> A Great Crowd Out to Witness the League Inauguration.

with the National League pennant in 1904, Brush became responsible for the cancellation of the World Series because he viewed the American League as a minor league.

In his first season owning the Reds in 1891, Brush duplicated the parade of 1890 by having the players of both teams, the Reds and the Cleveland Spiders, parade for 90 minutes through downtown prior to the April 22 opener. They were led by Weber's Prize Band of America (a military-style band). In addition to leading the parade, the band also played a 90-minute concert at the ballpark before the game began at 3:00 p.m. On April 26, a new Association team called Kelly's Killers held a similar parade. For the first time, Cincinnatians were treated to two parades to kick off the baseball season.

The appearance by Weber's band at the Reds parade was indeed special. Weber's band was the main reason Cincinnati was recognized as the musical center of the United States at the time. The band's leader, John Weber, hailed from Cincinnati, and most of his players were recruited from the Cincinnati Symphony Orchestra. Music lovers thoroughly enjoyed the rousing music played by the band.

The morning paper announced that the new season would be inaugurated "in the appro-

THE OPENING

IN REVIEW

GENERAL FAN

GET YOUR MONEY DOWN
THEY'LL SOON BE OFF!

McPHEE'S KLONDIKE WONDERS MEET CLARKE'S PACKING HOUSE PIRATES IN A GAME OF
SNOWBALL—A COLD STORAGE OPENER.

1919 Pregame Concert by Weber's Band

priate manner" and declared that both teams were ready to begin:

> Both teams are in excellent shape. Both have passed through a hard course of preliminary practice, and will face each other this afternoon like two well-conditioned race-horses prepared especially for some rich prize. The Reds did their training at the best quarters known in America—Hot Springs, Ark., and are free from aches or ills of any kind. Indeed, the Reds had conducted their first out-of-town spring training trip in club history for the previous three weeks.

The festivities proceeded despite the most "miserable weather for its opening championship game" that the Reds had encountered in more than ten years. "Bucketfuls" of rain delayed the start for 39 minutes. The *Enquirer* reported that the field superintendent "and his corps of juvenile assistants" worked with brooms to sweep off the puddles before dumping "sundry and copious wheelbarrow-loads of sawdust around the pitcher's box, third-base, and home plate." Even the captain of the team, third baseman Arlie Latham, "rolled up his sleeves and lent a hand." The game was started "with the players standing ankle-deep in mud and water."

The new owner, Brush, had installed the first "press box" by placing a table at the end of the pavilion, anticipating increased press coverage of the Reds. Unfortunately, the weather forecast and the new rival Association team reduced the crowd to only 4,503, the lowest attendance for an opener since 1888. The Reds lost their third straight opener, 6–3.

One reason Kelly's Killers was able to attract fans related to the bold and entertaining personality of its star, Mike "King" Kelly. Kelly's Killers played at a site in the East End (near today's Schmidt Field softball complex) that was far removed from downtown and lacked public transportation. The team folded after one season, but not before King Kelly pulled an infamous stunt that led to a rules change. Kelly's teammate hit a foul ball out of reach of the Boston catcher. Kelly jumped from the bench and announced, "Kelly now catching for Boston" and caught the ball. The 1891 rulebook said a "substitute [was] allowed at any time during the game." Kelly confidently cited the rule to the umpire, who reluctantly agreed with him, and the hometown fans roared with laughter—even though Kelly got his own teammate out. A plaque in the National Baseball Hall of Fame describes Kelly as a "colorful player and audacious base-runner."

1892: "New Year's Day" but No Parade

The *Enquirer* announced that it was New Year's Day on April 12, 1892: "Well, another season is on us. Eighteen hundred and ninety-two opens this afternoon." The paper decided to give a history lesson in hopes that the Reds would regain their championship form:

> The opening game to-day takes one back just a decade. Ten years ago the Reds opened the first championship season of the American Association, and had the Pittsburgs for their opponents. On that memorable occasion the Pittsburgs larroped the Reds, but the Reds got their revenge that season. They came along and won the pennant of the Association. It was the only one Cincinnati has had since the wonderful record of the Cincinnati Reds of 1869, when Harry Wright and his men won every game they played. How will the local

team fare this afternoon? It is an even money bet, and take your pick. Both will have great teams.

For reasons unexplained in the local paper, the Reds abandoned the pregame parade through the city, but they retained the tradition of a 90-minute concert by inviting Bellstedt and Ballenberg's "grand orchestra." The club anticipated a large crowd, installing new turnstiles "so that there will be no jam or push in getting out" and adding a refreshment stand in deep right field. Owner Brush also decided that women would be admitted free of charge to the unreserved seats throughout the season, but "fifty cents will give them the best seats in the park."

Although there was no parade and the weather was cold, the opener drew the largest

THE DRUM TAP

Will Occur This Afternoon.

The Twelve League Clubs Get Of Together.

No One Will Be Able To Beat the Flag.

Grand Opening of the Base-Ball Season.

crowd (7,468) since the team rejoined the National League. But the fans were once again disappointed:

> It was a characteristic Cincinnati base-ball opening. … There was the same great crowd, the same concert by a grand orchestra, the same bright summer sky with a December temperature, and last, but by far the most undesirable, the same old hollow-eyed defeat. … Opening games are not the Reds' 'long suit.' Experience has shown it. It takes a time-tried enthusiast, with a memory like a college professor, to go back to the period when the Reds won their opening game.

The best news for fans at Opening Day in 1892 was the hiring of Frank Bancroft as the Reds' business manager. Bancroft would later be recognized as the "Father of Opening Day."

1893: Dignitaries and Front-Page Status

For the first 26 days of April 1893, there was not a single day in which it did not snow or rain in Cincinnati. Nonetheless, on the morning of April 27, the *Enquirer* declared that it was a safe bet that the first game of the season would go on. The paper noted that Frank Bancroft had superintendent Deiteh Oehler and the Can brothers (Louis and Snooks) "cleaning out the drainage outlets at the park and sanding the base paths."

Not only did Bancroft order that the field be in proper condition, he also began to put his stamp on the importance of the opener by inviting several dignitaries and a celebrity. The invitation list included Ohio governor William McKinley (who would be elected the twenty-fifth president of the United States in 1896), the governor's entire staff, Cincinnati mayor John Mosby, the city's police chief, many other city officials, and Jeffreys Lewis (a well-known actress). The guests were invited to witness a "splendid opening" to the season that again included the renowned Weber band for a 90-minute program of "popular music." And, just before game time, the Reds "tread across the field in jackets of dazzling red— redder than the reddest garment ever seen on the local ground."

The morning paper had announced, "Here is where friendship ceases. From now on everything will count, and for the next five months it will be 'everybody for himself,' and the devil take the hindmost." The Reds apparently agreed, beating the Chicago Colts 10–1 "in a whipping that they will remember for many a long day."

The next morning, the city was greeted by a first: the *Enquirer* reported the opener and the festivities with a front-page headline: "ALL READY."

Never before had either the Reds or the Red Stockings—or any sport for that matter—been featured on the front page of the paper. In the

past, baseball stories were usually relegated to a portion of a page in the eight- to sixteen-page newspaper that covered boxing and horse racing as well. But for a welcome change, in the far-right column on page one, the *Enquirer* gushed, "Cincinnati hasn't had an opening like it in years. Nothing was missing to make the happiness of local base-ball lovers complete. Their cup was brim full and running over the sides."

Some fans during the 1893 opener attempted to gain a free view of the game by sitting atop boxcars in the Baltimore and Ohio railroad yards. Unfortunately, "an engine backed up, hooked on and away went the freight cars and

spectators up Millcreek Valley. The thousands in the stands who put up their good money laughed loud and long."

Aside from the disapproval directed at those freeloaders, the only complaint about this opener concerned, of all things, the scorecard. The scorecard has been a tradition in baseball unlike in any other sport. It allows those in attendance to record each player's performance in the game. (In the radio era, scorecards were also used by those listening to the game over the airwaves.) For example, if a batter hits a ground ball to the shortstop and the shortstop throws the ball to first base and made an out, a fan writes "6-3" in the designated area on the scorecard. ('6' is the number assigned to all shortstops, and '3' is the number assigned to all first basemen). Later in the game, the fan is able to review the player's previous at bat and see that the player grounded out to the shortstop. In the early years of professional baseball, scorecards were simply part of the experience of attending a game. Ever the promoter, Bancroft capitalized on fans' interest by introducing and marketing a pictorial scorecard in 1893.

Baseball tradition at the time called for both teams to announce each of the nine players' field positions (from pitcher to right fielder), as well as the batting order, the day before the game. This allowed time for the scorecard publishers to print the players' names and positions on the scorecard. Patrons of the game could then purchase a scorecard on the day of the game that showed where each player was playing and when he would bat.

The Chicago Colts' captain decided to make a change in his batting order on the day of the game. This deviation from tradition annoyed the *Enquirer*:

> There should be a rule compelling the Captains of teams to play their men in accordance with the published batting order. It was an injustice to the patrons of yesterday's game that Anson [the Colts' captain] should have been permitted to change his batting order just

before "play" was called. After the change the score-cards were worthless, as the names were all changed around. To patrons who do not know the players by sight the change causes no end of annoyance. Every Captain should be able to tell twelve hours before the game how he is going to play his men. If he can't do it, there should be a rule compelling him to play his men as he sent in their names to the score-card publishers.

No such rule was ever adopted, and publishers eventually printed blank scorecards with both team's rosters. It was up to fans to pencil in the batting order and each player's position by hand. Over the years, fewer and fewer fans continued to use a scorecard, and today it is a rare sight to see someone with a scorecard at the ballpark even though the cards are still sold as a matter of custom.

1894: The First Pitch Arrives

The ceremonial first pitch is a long-standing ritual of baseball. The tradition involves having a guest of honor throw a ball to mark the end of pregame festivities and the start of the game. No one knows who started the ritual, but there are newspaper accounts about it dating back to 1890. In the years after 1890, the guest threw the ball from his or her place in the grandstand to the umpire, or in some cases to the pitcher. Today, the first pitch is often delivered from the pitcher's mound to the catcher behind home plate.

Cincinnati was scheduled to begin its own first-pitch tradition on April 19, no doubt as Bancroft's brainchild. Bancroft had planned a spectacular dedication and opening of the Reds' new ballpark at Findlay and Western avenues. Owner John Brush built a $12,000 grandstand topped by three turrets adorned with flags. Brush also changed the location of the diamond to take the sun out of the batter's eye. The field superintendent had sowed grass seed that had come from the World's Fair. All the dignitaries who had attended in 1893 were invited to return, and Ballenberg and Bellstedt's full band was scheduled to play. The parade route was published in the newspaper

so fans could choose their favorite viewing spot. Once again, the Reds and Chicago Colts players would ride in open carriages from the Gibson House throughout downtown. To the delight of fans, the Reds were scheduled to appear in their new white uniforms for the first time. Anticipating a sizable crowd, the *Enquirer* reported that "one great innovation this season will be the sale of single seats in boxes" that had historically been sold only to groups of wealthy fans.

After the Reds and Colts had ridden to the Gibson House in their carriages, "the rain again began to come down at a lively rate," and the game was postponed until the next afternoon. Wrote the *Enquirer*:

> When the game was called off the Reds were driven back to the park and took off their new uniforms, which they will again don this afternoon. That the city has a very severe attack of baseball fever was attested not only by the crowds of people in front of the Gibson House and all along the advertised line of march, but by the great number of people who journeyed through the rain to the Cincinnati Park, only to be turned back again by the sign "No Game." The city was full of excursionists yesterday, and the greater part of them stayed over for the opening this afternoon.

While 10,000 people were expected to attend the opener on April 19, only 6,285 attended

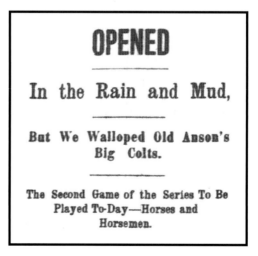

OPENED

In the Rain and Mud,

But We Walloped Old Anson's Big Colts.

The Second Game of the Series To Be Played To-Day—Horses and Horsemen.

the inaugural game in League Park the next day. The *Enquirer* opined that "the postponement took the edge off the opening in a measure, and the rain and mud kept thousands at home." The parade was canceled, as were the dedication ceremonies for the new park. Nonetheless, Governor McKinley made a few remarks after the band's open-air concert. He then tossed a brand-new baseball to the umpire, who shouted "play ball" to begin the first game in League Park. This ritual would be continued in subsequent years by the Reds, and by many other professional baseball teams. While the crowd could not foretell the historical significance of McKinley's pitch, the fans went home happy after left fielder Bug Holliday hit the first Cincinnati grand slam in an opener. With Holliday's help, the Reds beat the Colts 10–6.

The new ballpark was applauded for having the very best accommodations, including "roomy seats," but it was criticized because the new grandstand reduced the distances to the outfield wall so much that it was easier to make a home run. The players of both teams were complimented for looking "as clean and fresh as a nickel just out of the mint," but Reds captain Charles Comiskey "looked like a part of the present financial depression had located somewhere in his neighborhood. He wore a sweater that was faded and tattered and torn as badly as the colors of the forlorn hope. Commie should send his sweater to the old clothes man. It is overdue." Comiskey left the team after the season and helped to form a new minor league, which would become the American League in 1901. He is best known for owning the Chicago White Sox during the team's Black Sox scandal, and for presiding over the construction of Comiskey Park.

1895: Trolleys on Parade

Bancroft made other splashes before the opener in 1895 by having the Reds make a trolley car circuit of the city instead of riding in carriages. In a series of articles about the start of the season, the *Enquirer* invoked the phrase "opening day," though the term did not catch on until years later. One article compared the start of the baseball season to major celebrations in Europe:

> What the English "Darby" is to the land of roast beef and plum pudding, what the Prix de Paris is to Parisians, opening day in baseball is to about seven tenths of the citizens of this great and glorious country. … The opening of the championship baseball season is a matter second only in importance to the nation's great holiday, the anniversary of our independence. … The citizens of adjacent territory for miles around are wrapped up in the success of the team in their nearest big city. Cincinnati is particularly favored in this way. The grand old Queen City is the metropolis of the state, and most of the citizens of Ohio look upon its club as their club.

A drawing that accompanied the article depicted the parade that would take place that afternoon on the trolley, with Bancroft leading the procession.

The parade—perhaps because of its new twist—was an unqualified success, judging from the streets being full of fans shouting greetings from front doors and windows. When the team and the club's officers arrived at the Gibson Hotel for the annual luncheon, "the general verdict was that Cincinnati was 'all right.'" The crush of the crowd had been such that one man was killed at the Plum Street bridge, and another had a leg broken en route to the ballpark.

After the parade, the fans were treated to the now customary pregame concert and the introduction of the Reds' new player-captain, Buck Ewing. Ewing would go on to become one of the greatest players of the nineteenth century. In pregame ceremonies, Ewing was presented with a floral bouquet of roses in a horseshoe design. This gift to the popular player was a tribute from the tobacco merchants of the city. Ewing grew up in Cincinnati but played most of his career with the New York Giants. He was considered the "Johnny Bench" of his era. Bancroft understood that coming to Cincinnati would be a homecoming for Ewing. Although the bulk of his career was as a catcher, Ewing

OPENING DAY SCENES.

played first base while managing the team in that season opener. Ewing would end up being the team's captain for the next four years and in 1939 became the first catcher inducted into the National Baseball Hall of Fame.

In addition to hiring Ewing and inviting the customary political dignitaries, Bancroft also invited a "notable and historical baseball group" at the suggestion of Mayor John D. Caldwell. A. B. Champion, the president of the Red Stockings in 1869, was joined by three other officials from the "famous old team," along with the first baseman from the undefeated team, Charlie Gould. The *Enquirer* predicted that "many an enthusiast will cast his eye in the direction of this famous group during the progress of the game." Caldwell did the first-pitch honors, handing the ball to the umpire instead of throwing it as Governor McKinley had done the year before.

Bancroft had indeed delivered the most elaborate opener to date and was rewarded with attendance of 13,297, the largest in the team's history:

> It was like a coliseum loaded to the guards, and it is an even bet that the Olympic Games never drew a more enthusiastic crowd. It was not only an enthusiastic but a representative gathering. The best of the city's manhood and the fairest of her fair sex were in attendance. A glance at the pavilion reminded one of the first-class theater assemblage. It was a dressy affair as well, drawing into its folds the beauty and richness left over by a splendid Easter.

Buck Ewing led the Reds to a 10–9 victory, and hats, umbrellas, and cushions were hurled into the air. The victory cost the new captain "several dollars" because he had promised new hats to each player if they won the game!

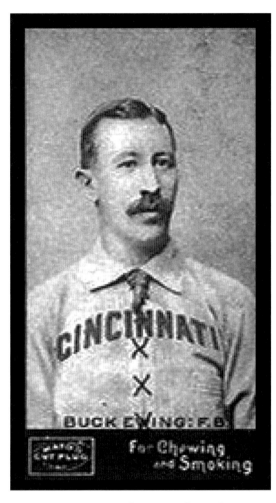

1896: Souvenirs, a Wild Pitch, and a Mascot

On April 13, Cincinnati, along with several other cities, hosted a tribute game to honor the passing of Harry Wright. Wright was recognized as the "Father of Professional Baseball" at the time of his death. The regular season opener took place three days later. In addition to the trolley car parade introduced a year earlier, the team gave away gender-specific souvenirs to all patrons. As the gates opened, every man and boy was given a "Rooters' Button," and every woman and girl was given a rudimentary photograph of the 1869 Red Stockings. It was the first time the Reds promoted the game with a giveaway, a practice that is commonplace throughout professional baseball today. The fans were also treated to a 90-minute pregame concert by Weber's Prize Band of America.

It was the warmest day ever for an opener at 87 degrees, but even Bancroft, the marketing genius, could not claim credit for the weather. The morning *Enquirer* reminded its readers of the importance of baseball in the nation's calendar:

> "Play Ball!" the most welcome words in the umpire's vocabulary, will tickle the ears of thousands of enthusiasts this afternoon. In six of the twelve most populous and most important commercial cities in America these two words will be followed by a burst of cheers, and the great championship baseball season will be started. … Yes, to-day is a day of all days in the estimation of the followers of America's national sport. Christmas, New Year's and even Fourth of July are second considerations in the minds of real enthusiasts when the opening of the season is mentioned.

Indeed, Cincinnati was the ninth largest city in the United States during the 1890s, with a population of 296,000. Located on the Ohio River, it was a major commercial center, so it was only fitting that the city be represented at the highest level of the nation's pastime. Among other reasons, Cincinnatians supported the Reds out of civic pride. Wrote the *Enquirer*, "with music playing, banners flying, with city and state officials present, with fair ladies and brave men to cheer and welcome, the Reds should play ball for all their individual and collective worth."

The now customary street parade of special trolley cars made its way from Government Square through the principal streets of the city. Henry Chadwick, who was a famous scorekeeper at the time, was a special guest during the parade. He had purposely remained in Cincinnati after attending Harry Wright Day to witness the opening game and to determine whether there was any truth to the charges made by East Coast teams that the "Western teams" were in the habit of indulging in rough play. Despite Chadwick's misgivings about the team's conduct, the players received a "continuous ovation" from fans along the parade route. The reports noted that at "the extreme points reached, such as Brighton, the foot of Price Hill, and the C., H., and D. Depot, the enthusiasm was not one whit less than at the start." No doubt the great weather helped encourage thousands to line the parade route.

After the concert, a monkey named Mose came on the field dressed in a costume that resembled the Reds' new uniforms, and each of the players petted him before the game for good luck. The team adopted Mose as its first mascot.

The team invited a number of dignitaries to the game once again, including George Wright, the legendary brother of the late Harry Wright and the star shortstop of the 1869 team. Mayor Caldwell was again given the honor of throwing the first pitch. After gathering the players and giving a short speech from the grandstand, Caldwell decided to throw the ball to the umpire instead of handing it to him as he had in 1895. That decision was a bad one, as he proceeded to make the first wild pitch in Opening Day history. His toss from the grandstand went over the head of the umpire!

Another record crowd (14,412) attended the game, but the fans were disappointed by the 9–1 loss to Pittsburgh. The *Enquirer*, however, found a silver lining:

> Yesterday's league opening demonstrated the honesty of the great national game. Financially it would be of great benefit for the home teams to win before the large crowds of their constituents that attend at every park. Cincinnati, Louisville, Baltimore, and Philadelphia all lost on their home grounds. This shows conclusively that the game is played on its merits, regardless of financial results.

Aside from the loss, the only criticism of the 1896 opener concerned the peanut vendor and the chewing gum vendor. In some cities, vendors in the stands had been abolished because they were viewed as a distraction during the game. The *Enquirer* even called them "loud-mouthed hawkers." Many fans wanted the Reds to institute a rule that the vendors only be allowed to peddle before the game or between innings.

1897: Where's the Mayor?

Even with threatening clouds and damp winds curtailing attendance, a "large sprinkling of new Easter hats" was conspicuous in the 1897 crowd of more than 11,000 fans, including the ladies who turned out in "goodly numbers." The fans were treated to a ten-inning, come-from-behind victory over the Chicago Colts. As in previous years, both teams took part in the pregame trolley car parade through downtown, followed by a light lunch at the Gibson House. The parade was scheduled to proceed along the main streets of downtown, but Reds captain Ewing persuaded the organizers to include Eastern Avenue on the route, close to his boyhood home.

The Reds introduced a new official scorecard for the occasion that was described as a "work of art." It featured pictures of every member of the team, the official scorers of the game, and club officials. Another new development was the team's announcement that bicycles could be checked inside the grounds and that a club official would keep an eye on the "wheels of patrons."

The biggest news out of this Opening Day concerned the master of ceremonies, again Mayor Caldwell. As had become the custom, there was a pregame concert. After that, the mayor was expected to address both teams' players from his grandstand box and then make the first pitch shortly after 3:00 p.m. However, Caldwell had not arrived by the appointed hour. The umpire and the players waited impatiently for several minutes. Exasperated, umpire Jack Sheridan, clad in his familiar blue uniform, walked to home plate and delivered the first pitch himself. This is the only time in Reds history that an umpire was accorded the privilege of a first pitch. The paper noted that "Weber's Band … subsided with a melodious sigh, and without more ado the season of 1897 on the local grounds was begun."

PLAY BALL! | TO-DAY, 3:15 Also Friday, Saturday. | Opening Championship of Season 1896. | Capt. Ewing's **CINCINNATIS** vs. Capt. Mack's **PITTSBURGS**

This photo of League Park is from sometime between 1894 and 1899. It shows the horse-drawn carriages bringing the players to the opener after their luncheon at the Gibson Hotel.

Was Caldwell missing because he was embarrassed by his wild first pitch the previous season? Perhaps we will never know. The mayor later explained that he had expected Bancroft to send a carriage to his office to take him to the ballpark. Caldwell waited in his office until 3:10, finally calling for a carriage himself. He did not arrive at the park until after two innings had been played and was said to be "very much grieved." Bancroft explained that he had ordered the carriage but "by some misunderstanding his orders were not executed, and the season of sport was opened without the usual pleasing formalities." Caldwell's three-year service as mayor ended that year, and he became the lieutenant governor of Ohio in 1900.

While fan complaints in 1896 concerned peanut vendors and chewing gum vendors, the 1897 crowd directed its ire toward the practice of sacrifice bunting. Sacrifice bunting is a weapon used by a batter to advance runners already on base to put them in scoring position—not by swinging to get a hit, but instead by tapping the pitch to fall several feet in front of home plate or down the baselines.

The player sacrifices one out in order to enhance his team's chances of scoring a run. The Reds' patrons expressed their displeasure with the tactic several times during the opener. Every time a batter tried to make a sacrifice bunt, there were vociferous yells to "hit it out!" or "smash the ball!" The *Enquirer* disagreed, stating that "the crowd should not influence a player from doing what he thinks is 'baseball.'"

1898: Talk of War and "Rowdyism"

The battleship USS Maine had inexplicably exploded in the harbor at Havana, Cuba, in February 1898, so there was talk of war when the season began on April 15. That morning, the newspapers announced that the entire regular United States Army was to be rapidly concentrated along the Atlantic and Gulf coasts, and the army was ready to embark for Cuba as soon as a declaration of war was issued. The 6th Infantry, stationed across the river from Cincinnati in Fort Thomas, Kentucky, was deployed to Tampa, Florida. The talk of war, however, did not dampen enthusiasm for Opening Day:

OLD GLORY

Raised Aloft By Willing Hands

For the Boys in Blue Have Orders at Last To Take the Field.

Entire Regular Army To Be Rapidly Concentrated Along the Atlantic and Gulf Coasts,

Ready To Embark For Cuba as Soon as a Declaration of War Is Made.

Arrangements Already Perfected and the Troops Will Begin Moving Southward To-Day.

Sixth Infantry, Stationed at Ft. Thomas, Goes To Tampa—Military Demonstration That Will Show Spain the United States Mean Business

WASHINGTON, April 15.—Decidedly the most warlike step taken by the Department in preparing for the possibility of an encounter with Spain was inaugurated to-day when orders were issued for the concentration at four points in the South of six regiments of cavalry, 22 regiments of infantry, and the light batteries of five regiments of artillery. At Chickamauga there will be six regiments of cavalry and the light batteries of five regiments of artillery; at New Orleans eight regiments of infantry; at Tampa seven regiments of infantry, and at Mobile seven regiments of infantry. Since the Civil War no such proportion of the army has been mobilized, and the movement itself is the best evidence of the

No other day in the year do as many people of this great and glorious country scan the weather predictions more closely than they do on the day before the opening of the baseball championship season. Hundreds of bedroom curtains will be anxiously drawn aside this morning and three of the most populous and important cities of the United States. If sunshine and fair weather promise greets the eyes of the watchers there will be joy over the land; if rain or dark and gloomy weather then sorrow will be the portion of the vast majority of the population of all three big cities and their contiguous boundary.

The good news for Cincinnati was that the forecast was for sunny skies and warm weather. At 9:00 a.m., the two finest "palace electric cars" of the Consolidated Street Railroad Company's Service left the big car barn in Brighton. One stopped in front of League Park to pick up the Reds, and the other traveled to the Gibson House to collect the Cleveland players. An hour later, the two palace cars were joined at Fountain Square by another car containing the members of Weber's band. The three cars then left Fountain Square and toured the city streets, which were lined with thousands of spectators, before returning the players to the Gibson House for lunch.

After the gates opened at 12:30 p.m., the eventual crowd of 10,000 people began to fill the park in anticipation of another concert by Weber's band. After the concert, new Mayor Gustav Tafel "deftly handled his opening remarks and tossed out the first pitch." Instead of throwing the ball to one of the two umpires (a new league rule required two umpires instead of one), Tafel chose to toss it to first baseman Harry Vaughn.

There had been some doubt as to whether the game would be played because the city had recently endured another flood, and five feet of water had covered the playing surface just one week earlier. The high-water mark of the flood was painted on poles under the grandstand, attracting much attention from the spectators. Despite the poor condition of the field, the Reds beat Cleveland pitcher Cy Young. Young went on to become the winningest pitcher in baseball history and the inspiration for baseball's coveted pitching award.

Cy Young

The *Enquirer* headline declared "WHOOPEE!" the next morning in celebration of the win. But much more newspaper ink was devoted to opinions about a new rule promulgated by owner John Brush after rowdy behavior by fans had marred the 1897 season. A new sign had been posted at the ballpark before the first game: "Any spectator who insults a player or umpire by use of profane or obscene language will be expelled from this ball-park."

The new rule apparently worked for all but one fan:

> Only one individual felt the force of the new law against rowdyism in the stands. A vaudeville artist from over the Rhine imbibed too freely before he came to the game. His enthusiasm and his big stock of liquid refreshments got him in trouble. The actor yelled some insulting remarks at Dusty Miller. The ballplayer didn't hear them, but some of [police chief] Happy Sam's minions did. They laid hands on the actor, yanked him along the entrance to the grandstand until they reached the gate, when they flung the misguided individual into the street. The actor put up 25 cents a few minutes later and got in on the bleachers. He didn't last any longer in the plebian seats than he did in the aristocratic grand stand. Once more the whisky got the best of him and he tested his voice yelling at Miller. Once more he was hauled to the gates and several of the number tens [police officers] of Happy Sam's squad were placed where they would do the most good. Those who saw the persistent individual yanked to the gate by the two able-bodied coppers won't care to emulate his example.

The *Enquirer* noted that the fans consisted of "all kinds and degrees of people," including ladies and gentlemen of what is known as the "better class." The paper complimented the "fair ones" who were "gorgeous with the colors of spring [and] were the most interesting part of the picture." What more could the management of the baseball club ask than to have such genteel patrons supporting it?

As for the war concerns:

> It was thought by some people that the war excitement might affect interest in the game, during the present uncertainty at least. All fear on this score was dispelled by the magnificent crowd that gathered at the park yesterday. It was a patriotic crowd, too, as the applause that accompanied one or two national [musical] airs attested.

A sign of a future tradition occurred when a professor at the Cincinnati College of Pharmacy adjourned school for the afternoon.

As a result, the students of the college "showed their loyalty to the national game by attending in a body." The *Enquirer* also noted that members of the faculty likewise celebrated the holiday as spectators.

1899: Running Afoul of the Rules

Bancroft was offended the day before the Reds' opener on April 15, 1899. Red Ehret, a retired ten-year player who had been with the Reds in 1896 and 1897, modestly asked Bancroft, "If I come out to the gate this season will there be any trouble about me getting in?" Bancroft replied:

> I ought to take a good, long swing right on your jaw for asking such a question. Was there ever an old professional turned down at the Cincinnati gate? You know better than that, Red. You are welcome any time you want to come. … The Cincinnati Club has always made it a rule to tender courtesies to every deserving member of the profession.

The fans who attended the 1899 season-opening game were witness to two violations of league rules. Neither impacted the eventual 5–2 loss to Pittsburgh, but the infractions were surprising since owner John Brush had always been a stickler for living up to the rules—not only to the letter of them, but to the spirit of them as well.

The first rules violation concerned the benches that the players occupied during the game. Before the season, the National League had ordered that the benches be covered by some kind of a roof to resemble what is now the modern-day "dugout." Apparently, the team's treasurer had not received printed instructions as to how the benches should be constructed until noon on the day before the game. His carpenters did not have enough time to get the work done. If the Pittsburgh team had complained, the plan was to cover the benches with canvas, though team captain Ewing was displeased at the prospect of sitting under canvas "with the sun beating down on it." Fortunately, the visitors either did not notice or did not care. Neither did league umpire Ed

Parade This Morning and Concert This Afternoon.

Swartwood, who was in a particularly good mood upon his arrival in Cincinnati. The *Enquirer* reported Swartwood's praise of the Cincinnati and New York ballparks for being the only ones with a private dressing room for umpires. He said, "This is as it should be. … It isn't right to ask an umpire to change his uniform where the players dress. It is not pleasant, especially after a losing game, to be with the players."

The second rules violation was more obvious to the fans. Home teams were always required to wear white uniforms, but circumstances forced the Reds to play with blue shirts and white trousers because they were the only uniforms available. Captain Ewing had sent the white uniforms back to the manufacturer a week before the season because they did not conform to the sample provided to the club. The manufacturer decided to send the correct uniforms by freight rather than by express delivery. The new uniforms did not arrive until April 16, a day late.

Neither of these issues affected the Opening Day festivities, but a forecast of cold temperatures and a potential for snow cut down on the number of fans who came out to view the trolley parade. The fans were not alone in having to contend with the "chilly blasts that came out of the north." The Reds players, who had spent spring training with "Old Sol" in balmy Georgia for the first time, shivered along with the fans. Weber's band again treated the ballpark crowd to a 60-minute concert of "popular airs." Mayor Tafel made the customary address before the game, wishing both teams luck in the upcoming season. He threw the first pitch to Ewing.

The *Enquirer* praised the turnout despite such a dismal forecast:

> Nine thousand one hundred and forty-eight people in overcoat weather is a championship opening worthy of even such a great baseball city as Cincinnati. … The shivering enthusiasts who filled all the stands and swarmed out on the field in large numbers stamped their feet to keep warm, and rooted with might and main for Ewing's men to get off in the lead, but their rooting was all for naught.

Until the bad weather started rolling in, the Reds had their largest advance sale of tickets for the opening game in history, but the actual game-day attendance was the worst since 1894.

As the Reds' popularity grew, so-called "rooters clubs" began to spring up in Cincinnati and the surrounding areas. On this particular day, 150 members of the "Wilmington Rooters" from Clinton County, Ohio (75 miles from Cincinnati) attended the opener wearing white string ties with large black letters announcing "Wilmington Rooters" on one side of the tie and "Reds to Win" on the other. One of the rooters' neckties was presented to the chief of ballpark police, "Happy Sam" Saffin, and the *Enquirer* predicted that other rooters groups would adopt similar neckties. The paper also noted that "there were a good many Pittsburg rooters scattered about in the grandstand."

> *"Many an aged grandfather will die today for the third or fourth time."*
>
> Enquirer Editorial

1900: Playing Hooky

After proclaiming the "Greatest of Outdoor Sports Starts To-Day," the morning *Enquirer* on April 19 summed up the city's excitement for the start of a new baseball season:

OPENING

Of Baseball Season.

Greatest of Outdoor Sports Starts To-Day.

This is a day when small boys will jump out of bed early to get a peek at the weather. The blinds shall be shoved aside from many a window this morning, and if nice weather seems likely all will be well with the future Congressmen. If the Weather Clerk furnishes rain there will be gloom at many breakfast tables. The pride of the household will be cross and surly, and will likely take a kick or two at the family cat for being denied an opportunity of witnessing his favorite sport. ... What a hold baseball has on the American people!

By now, Bancroft's traditions had been firmly established. A trolley car parade through downtown, followed by a luncheon for the players, a pregame concert by Weber's band, and a presentation of flowers. This year's recipient of "a nice floral piece" was new manager Bob Allen. Allen received the gift from "local admirers ... with becoming grace and [he] smiled a contented smile." But the greatest applause that afternoon during pregame ceremonies was for the idol of local fans, shortstop Tommy Corcoran, who had been reported to be ill during the previous days.

The presentation of flowers was followed by both teams lining up in front of the grand-

stand to hear Mayor Tafel's speech. The mayor addressed them from his private box "with uncovered head." The *Enquirer* quoted his address, in part:

Captains Corcoran and Ryan and Gentlemen of the Cincinnati and Chicago Baseball Clubs: I am glad to be able to address you on this auspicious occasion. To the members of the Cincinnati team I wish to say, on behalf of the people of the Queen City, that you are expected to not only make a good beginning, but to play well all year. You have trained faithfully and well for your duties on a diamond and it is the wish of all loyal Cincinnatians that you will be able to bring additional honors to the city, the home of the famous Reds of '69, in a baseball way. To you, gentlemen of the Chicago Club, I bid you a cordial welcome to Cincinnati. I order you to play ball.

Mayor Tafel then threw out a new ball to start the season. A crowd of 11,920 attended the game, many of whom had apparently left work early due to a sudden and unexplained illness. The *Enquirer* noted that a peculiar tradition had developed when baseball season opened, in that many businessmen became ill during the morning, only for each to be seen later at the ball game acting "anything but a sick man." Bookkeepers and clerks were said to have relatives who had suddenly taken ill or died, and many grandfathers seemed to die on Opening Day for the third or fourth time. The crowd was described as one of the most orderly in history—perhaps because all those playing hooky wanted to keep a low profile. The *Enquirer* reported that there were fans "of all classes" at the ballpark.

1901: Double Postponement

One of the worst weather systems surrounding the opening of the baseball season occurred during the week of April 14, 1901, causing two postponements of the opener due to rain, wind, and very cold weather. The scheduled April 18 game was postponed until Saturday, April 20, and it was one the coldest openers in Cincinnati history at 35 degrees. Only 4,800 fans witnessed the 4–2 loss to Pittsburgh. Perhaps the Pittsburgh team gained an advantage by having been permitted to use a large drill hall at the army post in Fort Thomas, Kentucky, the previous afternoon. In any event, the opening game was a frosty affair for all concerned:

> It was the coldest baseball opening that Cincinnati has experienced in years, and 4,800 fans shivered, sneezed, and coughed for one hour and forty minutes. … After sitting still and scoring yesterday's game one can easily imagine why people go to Alaska and are never heard of afterward by their creditors.

A cartoon the next morning portrayed the Reds' "Klondike Wonders" playing the "Packing House Pirates" in a game of snowball.

The trolley car parade was canceled due to the frigid temperatures, but the pregame concert by Weber's band and other celebrations of the new season proceeded as planned. Two Reds players were presented with bats courtesy of a company in Portsmouth, Ohio, and another player was the recipient of flowers. Mayor Julius Fleischmann threw out the ceremonial first pitch.

"Firsts" are often noted in sports, such as the first player to reach a certain number of runs batted in, yards gained, or points scored. The first day of the baseball season naturally brings a renewed interest in "firsts" for that year. In 1901, with little to talk about except the weather, the Sunday paper got carried away by listing 37 "first acts of the season." The tally included many firsts achieved by the ballplayers, such as hits, runs, or errors, but it also documented the first fan to buy a scorecard, let out a holler, or borrow a chew of tobacco. Never before had the *Enquirer* devoted so much attention to such unimportant facts surrounding the unofficial holiday.

Suffice it to say 1901 was one of the least memorable openers in Cincinnati history. The real story in baseball that year was the ascendance of the Western League from minor league status to the major leagues. The Western League reformed as the American League and became the primary rival to the 25-year-old National League.

McPHEE'S KLONDIKE WONDERS MEET CLARKE'S PACKING HOUSE PIRATES IN A GAME OF SNOWBALL—A COLD STORAGE OPENER.

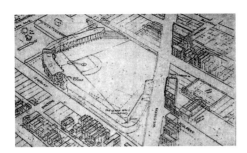

A drawing of the Palace location; Palace Grandstand; Rooters Row; Palace Bar

1902: "Palace of the Fans" Opens

On April 17, 1902, the *Enquirer* headline practically shouted: "'Play!' Fans' Palace Ready." The newly constructed Palace of the Fans was not really a palace at all, but rather a new grandstand to replace the one that had burned in May 1900. The Reds incorporated "Fans" into the name to show their ardent supporters that the park was renovated for them. The grandstand featured an extravagant façade with "CINCINNATI" inscribed in large letters behind home plate. The style of the park was a blend of Greek and Roman design, complete with 22 hand-carved Corinthian columns. The unique architecture created a feeling that the fans were at a special place. Nineteen "fashion boxes" in the front of the grandstand were built to accommodate the city's elite—an early precursor of "luxury suites." There was even easy access from the carriage stalls below the grandstand to the fashion boxes.

The grandstand was mammoth! It could accommodate 3,000 fans on wooden benches. Below the grandstand at field level was "Rooters Row," a rowdy, standing-room-only

area for 600 to 700 more spectators. Fans in this location were so close to the action that they could converse with the players. Rooters Row was strategically placed near a bar so fans could imbibe without missing any of the game. Spacious bleachers could accommodate thousands more, and the 10,000 fans who packed into the new ballpark for the season opener saw the most beautiful structure of its kind in baseball.

Although league personnel referred to the ballpark as the Palace of the Fans, fans continued to call it League Park. The Palace name was rarely referenced during the nine years the Reds played in front of the elaborate grandstand.

Bancroft's marketing mind was always at work, so he decided to tweak the Opening Day festivities by having the Reds ("garbed in their new uniforms of white and red") board the trolley car parade at League Park at 12:30 p.m. before meeting the Chicago Colts at Fountain Square. With Weber's band leading the parade, the special train chugged over the downtown streets for an hour before returning to the ballpark. Contrary to custom, there was no lunch with the day's opponent at the Gibson House. The band performed during the hour before the game. When it was almost game time, Judge William H. Lueders, standing in for Mayor Fleischmann, addressed the two teams from the president's box:

> The pleasant duty has fallen to my lot to open the season of 1902. Of the many things that Cincinnatians are proud of is the Cincinnati Baseball team. No matter where they play or when they play, no matter whether successful or otherwise, thousands and thousands of loyal Cincinnatians are with the club in person when you play here on the field, in spirit when away. … On behalf of the 400,000 inhabitants of the 'Queen City of the West,' I bid you play ball, play winning ball, play the gentlemen at all stages of the game, and when you do not win, deserve to win; and if you fail to bring home the pennant in October there will be a place reserved for each and every one of you out on Colerain Avenue, to spend six months to get in shape for 1903. Play ball!

With that exhortation, Judge Lueders tossed a new ball to umpire Bob Emslie, and the fans cheered the beginning of the 1902 season.

The *Enquirer* reported on the breadth of the Reds appeal in the geographic region by noting that "people from no less than 50 of Cincinnati's sister cities and villages in the three states [Ohio, Kentucky, and Indiana], and even as far away as West Virginia" had delegations in attendance. The newspaper also reported increased enthusiasm for the national game in the three other cities that held openers on the same day as the Reds, with a collective increase in attendance of nearly 100 percent over 1901.

The Reds' owner, John Brush, became chairman of a new executive board that was invested with full authority to act on behalf of the National League. The board issued instructions to league umpires giving them the authority to remove any player from a game, rather than imposing a fine, in order to enforce the rules of the game:

> The entire responsibility of presenting the game in a sportsmanlike manner and elimination of ungentlemanly conduct devolves upon you. If you succeed you will be endorsed; if you fail you will be condemned. … Never attempt to 'even up' after having made a mistake. … These rules are mandatory and not discretionary. If you allow them to be violated you become the chief culprit, and do not properly perform the duties of your position. … Compel respect from all and your task will be an easy one.

The new grandstand and the Rooters Row beneath it "were freighted with humanity and every stand on the lot held its full quota," but the Reds lost to the Colts 6–1. As reported in the *Enquirer*, "Fortune alone frowned on the Reds and reserved all her smiles for the gray-garbed tourists from the City of Wind."

Reds owner, John Brush

PEACE BETWEEN THE LEAGUES AND TALLYHO PARTIES

Whoever wants to know the heart and mind of America had better learn baseball.

Jacques Barzun, historian

Whoever wants to know the heart and mind of Cincinnati had better show up on Opening Day.

Tim Sullivan, *Enquirer* sports columnist

During the seasons of 1901 and 1902, the established National League was in a war with the upstart American League. The two leagues competed for fans, players, and franchises. Something had to be done to save the national pastime from itself. In stepped the president of the Cincinnati Reds, native Cincinnatian August "Garry" Herrmann, who had purchased the team from John Brush.

1903: "Cincinnati Peace Treaty"

Three months before the opening of the 1903 season, the rival National and American Leagues held a historic meeting at the St. Nicholas Hotel, which was located on the southeast corner of Fourth and Vine Streets just southwest of Fountain Square. Herrmann, the new owner of the Reds, hosted the other American and National League owners. Herrmann kept the owners at the hotel until agreements were reached on territories, rights of players, across-the-board playing rules, and nonconflicting schedules. A new governing body was formed called the National Commission, chaired by Herrmann, and it successfully established rules for the brand-new World Series. Because of what was dubbed the "Cincinnati Peace Treaty," the leagues agreed to be friendly rivals. If Bancroft is the "Father of Opening Day," Herrmann is the "Father of the World Series."

Perhaps because the treaty ended the leagues' rivalry, the Reds decided to forego the now customary downtown parade and simplify the official ceremonies on Opening Day. The morning paper on April 16 headlined the "Musical Festivities" to take place at League

August Herrmann

Park, and festive decorations of bunting were strewn over the grandstand railings to commemorate the occasion. The *Enquirer* featured a two-column-wide box that included some mild 1903 trash talk by Reds manager Joe Kelley and the Pittsburgh Pirates manager, Fred Clarke. The paper introduced the managers' letters by saying, "Neither Red nor Pirate manager was filling the night air with pompous boasts on the eve before the great clash, but both seemed to have a corner on confidence and a strangle hold on hope." Wrote Kelley:

> There is more than the usual element of luck in an opening game, and if Fortune will give us our share of the breaks to-morrow afternoon the Reds will have no complaints to make over the result. We are all in as good shape as it is possible to be at this stage of the game. If we don't win our opener, the other fellows will know they have been in a ballgame.

The Reds' opponents, the two-time National League Champion Pittsburgh Pirates, were said to be "full of sassafras tea and confidence." Said manager Clarke, "I don't say we are going to lick the Reds in the opening game, but I can promise you that we are going out there to do everything we can to win."

A crowd of 12,000 fans filled League Park under overcast skies. Weber's band started playing promptly at 2:00 p.m., and the band premiered a new march, "The New Cincinnati Ball Club." The only parade that occurred was when the Reds and the Pirates "marched in Indian file over the field" accompanied by "a midget athlete, garbed in Red uniform and carrying a big mitt." The teams' procession ended in front of Garry Herrmann's presidential box. A "great floral horseshoe," a "handsome Elk's pin," and a "diamond-studded watch charm" were presented to three of the players. Judge Howard Ferris gave a brief welcome that subtly referenced the fact that Herrmann, a native Cincinnatian, had purchased the team from outsider Brush. Brush lived in Indiana and owned two other major league teams:

> Gentlemen of the Cincinnati and Pittsburg Ball Teams: This is indeed a great day in baseball history. To-day we realize the hope and antic-ipation of years—a Cincinnati club owned by Cincinnati people, pulling for Cincinnati first, last and all the time. We hope that at the end of the season, Cincinnati will be first and Pittsburg second, and that our boys will at all times play pennant-winning ball. This is not the time for speech-making, but the time to—"Play Ball."

Judge Ferris then delivered the first pitch of the 1903 season, a season in which an average of 5,000 fans would attend games in Cincinnati, the third best attendance in the National League.

1904: "Not Much Fuss"

On the morning of the opener on April 14, the *Enquirer* headline held grim news: "Sister Ship of the Ohio Is the Victim of a Terrible Accident." Thirty-two men had been killed the previous day by an explosion in the handling

Thirty-Two Killed On U. S. Battle Ship By an Explosion.

room of the battleship *Missouri*. Unrelated to the accident, the paper reported, "There won't be much fuss and feathers about the go-off" of the baseball season, as only the pregame concert by Weber's band and an opening address by the vice mayor were on the agenda.

> by John C. Weber's Military Band, which will present this program between 2 and 3 o'clock:
>
> March—"The Cavalier"................Hall
> Medley—"Bedelia".................Jerome
> Gems—"Sultan of Sulu"......Ade and Walthall
> March—"Pan America".............Herbert
> Medley of late songs...............Mackie
> Indian Characteristic—"Navajo"........Alstyne
> Selection—"Prince of Pilsen".........Luders

The season started with the announcement of a new balk rule designed to limit the movements of pitchers. Umpire J. E. Johnstone explained the controversial new instructions to the Reds' pitching staff before the start of the season:

> There is nothing very complicated about the rules and as an old pitcher I am free to say that I believe the pitchers will like them after they get used to them. I do not look for as much trouble as some people seem to anticipate. Under the code to be enforced pitchers must cut every preliminary motion, many of which have simply serve to delay the game without adding to the pitcher's effectiveness. In the past, pitchers have been permitted to rub the ball on their trousers' leg two or three times; wriggle their bodies to get set in their places, and they often raised the ball over their heads a couple of times. All that has been cut out and will be penalized. A pitcher will be permitted to make but one pitching motion, and when he does that he must deliver the ball over the plate.

The new limitations on pitchers did not seem to have an impact on the game. The Reds won their first opener in five years when first baseman and manager Joe Kelley slid past home plate with the winning run in the ninth inning. "The field became immediately black with cheering enthusiasts [businessmen dressed in their dark suits and derbies], while

many of the 13,000 in the stands surrendered to the maddening joy which marks the first victory the Reds have won on get-away day for years." It was the largest Opening Day crowd since 1896 despite the grim news about the *Missouri* and the modest pregame activities.

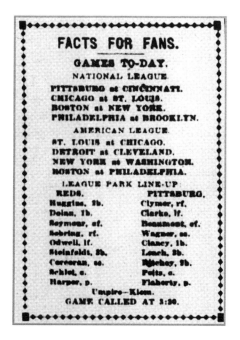

1905: No "Circus Parade"

In advance of the Reds opener on April 14, 1905, Garry Herrmann announced that the season would open without elaborate ceremony because "the game [is] the thing folks wanted to see, not a circus parade." The *Enquirer* agreed:

> The game will be the feature of the day. It has been wisely decided to have no big parade or any attention-distracting side issues. The gates of the park will be thrown open at 1 o'clock, and play will be called promptly at 3:30. For an hour before the game John Weber's celebrated Military Band will harmonize sound waves for the delectation of the great gathering.

Herrmann was either correct or lucky that nothing more special was needed, as a record-setting crowd of 15,118 turned out for the opener—or perhaps the sunny skies and 63-degree temperatures had something to do with the turnout! In fact, Herrmann had bet bandmaster Weber that the weather would be poor. Losing the bet meant the Reds had to pay "double price for the music."

Before the band performed, both teams came out on the field and gave the crowd an opportunity to "size them up, as they cavorted gaily over the green lot." The *Enquirer* added, "The Reds appeared for the first time in their new home uniforms of white, with white caps and all other trimmings of the glorious crimson that has made them famous." An *Enquirer* reporter described the eager crowd as representing "much of the wealth, beauty and fashion of the Queen City."

The huge crowd was described in the news as "a mass of tightly packed humanity." Five hundred fans sat in a new upper deck in left field that was still under construction. The rooters simply chose to ignore signs that the area was "off limits" for safety reasons. Without a doubt, League Park was the place to be for anyone who loved baseball. The *Enquirer* remarked how it was "imperative, in all decency, that office boys and other such steady toilers should be absent from their scenes of labor this afternoon." Anticipating the excuses that many workers had undoubtedly offered, the paper exhorted the Reds to remember their mourning fans: "Remember this, Reds, and bend your every effort to soothe the woeful breasts of the bereaved in the front rows of the benches."

Mayor Fleischmann made a brief and pointed address that echoed the sentiments of both Herrmann and the *Enquirer*: "It has always struck me that the least thing the professional baseball player cares about at the opening of the season is ceremony. Neither you nor the people came here to listen to me speak." The mayor hurled a brand-new ball at the group of players listening to his speech. Back-up catcher Gabby Street caught it and handed it to the umpire. After that, Umpire Klem "marched boldly to the plate, announced the batteries [pitcher and catcher for each team] as 'Harper and Schlei for Cincinnati; Flaherty

and Peltz for Pittsburg,' yelled 'Play ball!' in a rich, resonant voice with a Bowery accent, and the season of 1905 was on."

1906: The Joy of Anticipation

Jack Ryder, a sports reporter for the *Enquirer*, declared April 12, 1906, as the most glorious holiday of the year:

> To-day's the day. For many weeks the fans of eight great cities of this glorious land have been looking forward to April 12. For nearly two months the teams which represent those great cities on the field of baseball honor have been training for the long struggle which begins this afternoon. The eyes of the baseball world, which means all America, are turned to-day toward the fields on which will be fought out the opening battles of the season.

Once again, there was no parade through downtown, and Bancroft had arranged for only the simplest of ceremonies: the 60-minute concert by Weber's band "to soothe the anxious sensibilities of the waiting fans" and the address to the players by Mayor Edward J. Dempsey in front of his box.

The lack of fanfare did not diminish the enthusiasm of the city's baseball fans, as a record-setting 17,241 fans turned out for the game. The Reds owners added a wooden upper deck to accommodate booming attendance. Patrons arrived in carriages and horse-drawn wagons called tally-hos, in streetcars and "chugging auto cars," on bicycles, and on foot. "From 1:30 o'clock till after 3 the poor man's automobiles rolled on their iron tracks and steady lines past Findlay street, dropping their eager burdens there." The Palace was filled to capacity one hour before the game began, and the huge pavilions on either side of the Palace were packed with spectators as well. Ropes were even stretched around the outfield fence, where thousands of fans "chose the sunny earth for benches." (Accommodating large crowds beyond the outer reaches of the field was common in those days, resulting in special "ground rules" for balls that were hit past the ropes.)

A second consecutive opener featured wonderful weather. In fact, the day was so mild that "overcoats were a burden and the hundreds of ladies who graced the grandstand with their blooming presence were able to wear their lovely Easter finery, to the delectation of the masculine element."

After the fans had settled into their seats, Mayor Dempsey, who was a native Cincinnatian and said to be an ardent rooter, declared, "In the name of the people of the city of Cincinnati, I now open the season. Play ball!" Dempsey then joined the ranks of infamy in first pitches by hurling a wild toss that "went wide of its mark and rolled unimpeded over the diamond."

The Reds then dashed to the field to begin the season. Unfortunately, they came up short against the Cubs, losing 7–2. Wrote Ryder after the loss, "So there is more joy in the contemplation of the day, the throng, the refreshing balm of springtime breezes that fanned 16,000 heated brows, than in the sad perusal of the sorrowful score laid away in its neat box."

Players listening to Mayor's speech

1907: Tallyho Parties Replace the Parade

While the tradition of celebrating the first day of the baseball season was well established by 1907, the notion that Opening Day was a day for partying became firmly implanted on April 11, 1907. For decades, there had been "rooters groups" for fans, but the absence of an official parade opened the door for the rooters to take a more active part in planning festivities on their own.

These groups began to stage their own march through downtown on the way to the ballpark.

Their processions were led by tallyho wagons filled with fans dressed in costumes and blowing noisemakers as if it were New Year's

Eve. The tallyhos often carried bands that played along the way. Reliable reports indicate that the wagons stopped frequently at local drinking establishments along the route.

On the morning of the opener, Cincinnati seemed to have its interests divided between baseball and crime. The paper that day (and the next) devoted four pages of coverage to the "trial of the century" involving the husband of America's first "pin-up girl," Evelyn Nesbit. Nesbit's husband, Harry Thaw, was accused of murdering a wealthy architect in an open-air theater in New York City. The architect had sexually assaulted Nesbit when she was a teenager, and Nesbit's husband wanted to exact revenge. After a two-month trial, jury deliberations had begun the night before and continued for 47 hours before the jury announced it could not reach a verdict. Known as the "Thaw Trial," the city and nation were consumed with the murder case.

Despite the captivating theatrics of the trial, fans displayed their usual enthusiasm for the opening game. Noted the *Enquirer*, "The intense excitement which marks the opening of the new baseball season was eviden[t] last night in hotel lobbies, in cafés, on the streets and in every place of public resorts,

IDOLS OF THE FANS IN YESTERDAY'S GREAT GAME.

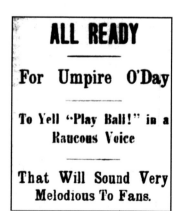

JOHN GANZEL.   MIKE MITCHELL.   JOHNNY KANE.

Captain John Ganzel won the game with his timely hit for Cincinnati in the ninth inning. Mike Mitchell made four hits out of four times at the bat, and little Johnny Kane was an all-round star, both at bat and in the field.

excluding all other topics of conversation." Baseball fans were not talking about the trial; rather, they were discussing who was going to pitch, whether it would be a good afternoon for a spitball, and every other detail of the upcoming contest.

ALL READY

For Umpire O'Day

To Yell "Play Ball!" in a Raucous Voice

That Will Sound Very Melodious To Fans.

Nearly 20 rooting parties paraded through the downtown streets in tallyhos and automobiles. One such group, called Spangler's Rooters, was described as "a grotesque looking lot in all sorts of absurd costumes with poke straw hats." The horse-drawn wagons were decorated with large, streaming banners. They were capable of carrying anywhere between six and 40 people. The fans were well equipped with megaphones, cornets, horns, and rattles. Even after the tallyhos began to arrive at the ballpark at 2:00 p.m., the revelers continued their party during pregame ceremonies and during the game itself. The crowd was so lively that the umpire's voice could seldom be heard.

As the party carried on in the grandstand, the two teams gathered near home plate according to custom. Vice Mayor Pfaff made a brief address before he "hurled a new ball into the diamond." The crowd was hushed during these proceedings, but the silence was broken when umpire Hank O'Day yelled "Play ball!" With cloudy skies and a 45-degree temperature, it was the smallest crowd for an opener since 1902, but it was no doubt the noisiest. The Reds won the game in their last at bat.

1908: The Crowd Keeps Growing

By 1908, the presence of rooters groups had become ever more pronounced in the mix of Opening Day activities. Dozens of rooting

WORLD'S CHAMPIONS MEET THE REDS THIS AFTERNOON AT LEAGUE PARK.

parties gathered at Fountain Square to make their way to the ballpark on April 15, and large crowds enjoyed watching them have their fun. Describing the spectacle the next morning, the *Enquirer* summed up the pregame partying as follows:

> But the most spectacular mode of going to the great game was in a tally-ho with some one of the many parties of organized rooters. Four and six horse vehicles were as thick as street cars on an ordinary afternoon. All were gaily decorated and full of excited fans, waving flags, tooting horns, singing popular songs and cheering for everybody, including themselves.

One big party of rooters from the bowling alleys were friends of Reds catcher Larry McLean, and they were given the honor of presenting him with "a handsome diamond pin of horse-shoe shape" in pregame ceremonies.

The rooting parties were greeted by the largest crowd in the history of the opener— 19,527 attendees! Five hundred fans were in line at the ticket windows a full three hours before game time, and by 2:00 p.m. every seat in the park was filled, as was the roped-off area in the outfield. The crowd was so large that Bancroft ordered the ticket windows closed—the first pregame sellout in the history of the opener for the Reds. Presumably, the intense interest in the game was attributable to Cincinnatians' long-standing love of the season opener, summerlike temperatures, and a visit from the world champion Chicago Cubs.

Weber's band again "discoursed popular airs for an hour before the game" before the players gathered around home plate. Mayor Leopold Markbreit had been invited to the game by National League president Harry Pulliam the previous day and, as was customary, he was asked to open the season with a short address. There was some question about whether the mayor would attend the game, because he had

never witnessed a professional ball game in his life! On short notice, he was reminded that he was expected to give an opening address to the ballplayers and to throw out the first pitch. As the *Enquirer* later reported, his toss "was not a mighty heave, and the sphere struck the ground and rolled lazily toward the plate, being corralled by umpire Hank O'Day … Hank let out an awful roar. 'Play Ball!'"

During the game, a number of "unlucky males" who sat behind women wearing "Merry Widow" hats complained that the city council should pass an ordinance forbidding the wearing of hats that block the view of the game.

After the game, the National League president praised the city's enthusiasm for the opener, declaring that "this town is one of the very best ball towns in the country, if not the best." He would find no disagreement among Cincinnati baseball fans!

1909: "Take Me Out to the Ball Game"

April 14, 1909, was one of the most noteworthy openers in Cincinnati history, mostly because it featured the first rendition of what would become the unofficial anthem of professional baseball. While the iconic song was first sung at a Cincinnati ball game, its roots were in New York City. Songwriter, singer, and vaudeville performer Jack Norworth was riding a New York subway train in 1908. A sign on the subway read "Baseball Today—Polo Grounds," and Norworth was inspired to write the now beloved song, "Take Me Out to the Ball Game." In the song, Katie Casey's beau invites her to a show. She accepts the invitation, but only if her date will take her out to a baseball game. As the lyrics went:

Katie Casey was baseball mad,
Had the fever and had it bad.
Just to root for the home town crew,
Every sou Katie blew.

On a Saturday her young beau
Called to see if she'd like to go
To see a show, but Miss Kate said "No,
I'll tell you what you can do."

Chorus

Take me out to the ball game,
Take me out with the crowd;
Buy me some peanuts and Cracker Jack,
I don't care if I never get back.

Let me root, root, root for the home team,
If they don't win, it's a shame.
For it's one, two, three strikes, you're out,
At the old ball game.

Katie Casey saw all the games,
Knew the players by their first names.
Told the umpire he was wrong,
All along, good and strong.

When the score was just two to two,
Katie Casey knew what to do,
Just to cheer up the boys she knew,
She made the gang sing this song.

(Repeat chorus.)

Norworth's words were set to music by Albert Von Tilzer. Not avid baseball fans themselves, Norworth and Von Tilzer finally saw their first major-league games 32 and 20 years, respectively, after writing the song. According to

John Erardi and Greg Rhodes in *Opening Day*, the pregame concert by Weber's band featured the catchy new tune. Decades later, the chorus would be adopted by every professional baseball team to be sung during the seventh-inning stretch of each game.

> *"There is not a single day in the year that is looked forward to in this city more than the opening of the baseball season."*
>
> Cincinnati Commercial-Tribune

On the morning of April 14, the headline in the morning *Enquirer* said it all—THE NATIONAL GAME BEGINS TO-DAY:

> The Reds, pride of the valley, are to clash with those desperate Pirates from the grimy hills of Pittsburg … There will be 153 other games before said season is completed, and each will count just as much in the standings as this one, but about the opener there is a breath of romance and interest which is absent in any other contest of the year. To win the opener is the hope of every patriotic citizen of Cincinnati, while the smoky bulletin boards of Pittsburgh will be watched with eager eyes as the contest progresses in the heart of Redland, 300 miles away.

By noon, three hours before the game, all the streetcar lines running to the ballpark were equipped with extra cars, and they were packed to capacity. Hundreds of fans traveled in private automobiles, but most of the attention was again focused on the rooters groups.

The rooters groups went out in tallyhos, "sight-seeing autos," and carriages. Each was furnished with flags, banners, and noise-making devices. The rooters paraded through the city and attracted an "immense amount of attention." One party of rooters needed 30 carriages to transport them. The organizer of these carriages had a huge bell to "toll the knell of the Pirates."

One particular group of rooters drew considerable attention before and after the game:

> Jack Sutthoff, the ex-National League pitcher who is now a bowling-alley proprietor in the West End, took out a crowd of husky rooters

on a load of hay. They were dressed up Weber-Fields fashion, and made a big hit by their funny sayings at the park. Two of the star rooters tipped the beam at 300 pounds or more. After the game, the driver of the hay cart tried to make a neat little turn in reverse English with his team, and the two fat men and one lean one rolled off the feed pile with a resounding whack. An attaché of the Coroner's office wended his way through the crowd expecting to get some work for his boss, but the Humpty-Dumpty boys were seen exhibiting signs of life, and within a few minutes were in the hay again and laughing as though they got paid to turn out that kind of stuff for the amusement of the public.

Weber's Prize Band was hushed "by the sound of the gong, promptly at 3 o'clock," and the players formed two long lines diverging from home plate. Mayor Markbreit, after his debut the previous season, deferred to Vice Mayor Galvin to deliver a brief address. Galvin had such a "strong arm" that he threw a wild pitch, winging it "clear over their heads so far that no one could catch it." It was the fourth wild first pitch at an opener.

The park was filled to capacity, with fans coming from as far away as Logansport, Indiana, which is 189 miles from Cincinnati but only 117 miles from Chicago, where the Cubs were playing the same day. According to the *Enquirer*, these distant fans were true baseball connoisseurs, noting, "These boys knew where they would be able to observe the real thing."

With automobiles gaining in popularity, the paper noted that "the smoke wagons were packed in so closely an hour before the game" that Bancroft had bars put up to prevent any more cars from entering the gate. (An exception was made for two big stockholders in the club who arrived in their sedans shortly thereafter.) On the field, the customary ropes had been stretched around the entire outfield for fans who could not find seats. Bancroft placed a row of benches immediately behind the ropes to keep the "standees from encroaching on the limit of the playing

field." It worked, and his solution was declared a "triumph of genius."

There is some controversy, however, as to whether 1909 was a record crowd. The *Enquirer* declared the attendance of 18,000 "the largest ever inside the yard" despite the fact that 19,257 were said to have attended the

game just the previous season. Regardless of the exact number of fans, big hats continued to vex spectators, as apparently the city council had not acted on the plea to ban the Merry Widow hats. As reported by the *Enquirer*, the "grandstand was a bower of beauty, marred in many places by the eccentric headdress of some thoughtless creature."

1910: "Lucky Seventh" and the Twenty-Seventh

The Cincinnati Traction Company, the operator of the city's vast streetcar system, placed 75 extra cars in service on April 14 in anticipation of another record crowd for the opener. The pictures below are examples of the streetcar lines that delivered fans to the opener.

Sportswriter Ryder had predicted the busy transportation scene as people would be journeying to the ballpark:

Business will be practically suspended in many sections of the city after the noon hour, and the entire populace, or as much of it as can crowd and jam its way into the sacred precincts of the yard, will devote the latter half of the day to the noble pastime. Every tallyho, omnibus, taxicab and seagoing vehicle of any description, or without any, has been engaged for the occasion and will be seen and heard wending toward the park ... The sidewalks and pavements will be worn smooth by the hurrying hoofs of the multitude of bugs [the nickname for fans in the late 1800s and early 1900s], dashing madly toward the scene of the great battle that is to inaugurate another baseball campaign. ... The opener is the large and ornate event because the public is crazy on baseball after its long winter abstinence from the sport.

All the reserved seats had been sold in advance. Bancroft had planned to open the gates at 12:30 p.m., but he was forced to open them 30 minutes early "in order to pacify the howling mob outside," and by 1:00 p.m. "all the choice locations were taken, but the people continued to pour in by thousands."

Shortly thereafter, the National League champion Chicago Cubs came on the field to "hearty cheering," but the noise did not compare to "the roar that went up to the firmament when the Reds, bravely clad in their new home uniforms of white, trimmed with red," began to practice 30 minutes later. Their arrival "was the signal for the breaking loose of all kinds of noise-making machines, the greatest and most popular of which was the human throat."

Weber's band played another concert, manager Clark Griffith and center fielder Mike Mitchell were presented with bouquets of posies, and first baseman Dick "Doc" Hoblitzell received a medal from his fellow students at the Ohio College of Dental Surgery before the players gathered in front of home plate. Mayor Louis Schwab delivered a flawless first pitch after giving a speech to welcome the players.

Neither team scored a run in the first six-and-a-half innings of the game, so "the crowd stood up in the lucky seventh, pulling for a run." The "lucky seventh" gave birth to the modern "seventh-inning stretch," which takes place in the middle of the seventh inning before the home team comes up to bat. It is the moment in the game when the home team hopes to experience a string of good luck. To encourage the team's good fortunes, fans rise, sing, cheer, and otherwise root the team on. The lucky seventh was first noted to have occurred in Cincinnati during this opener. While the good-luck charm did not produce the desired results right away, the Reds managed to score in the bottom of the tenth inning to win the game, 1–0. There were no lineup changes during the game, resulting in the game's swift completion in one hour and 51 minutes. Years later, the seventh-inning stretch would become a ritual at all MLB games, including the requisite chorus of "Take Me Out to the Ball Game."

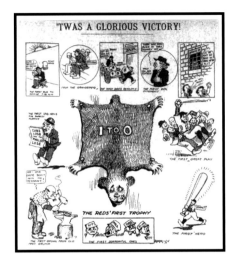

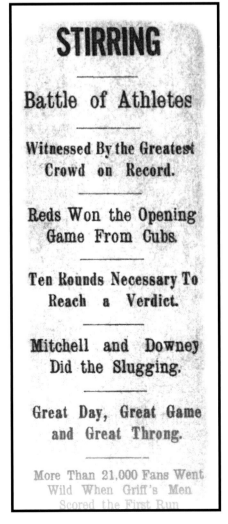

The official attendance for the game was 21,221, making it another sellout and the "greatest crowd on record." The ticket window that sold 25-cent tickets closed at 2:30 p.m. after 8,000 bleacher seats and standing-room-only tickets sold out. The crowd included 3,000 women, and to the apparent surprise of the *Enquirer*, they "displayed as much interest and enthusiasm as their male escorts." In the eighth inning, shortstop Tom Downey won a pair of Bostonian shoes promised by "the Race street shoe man" for hitting a triple.

In addition to reporting on the Reds' victory, the next morning's *Enquirer* devoted a column to another first in baseball history for an opening game. This one occurred in the nation's capital when Cincinnatian William Howard Taft, who had been elected the twenty-seventh president two years earlier, became the first president to throw out the first pitch on Opening Day:

> Catcher Street stood at the plate ready to receive the ball, but the President knew the pitcher was the man who usually began the business operations with it, so he threw it straight to Pitcher Johnson. The throw was a little low, but the pitcher stuck out his long arm and grabbed the ball before it hit the ground. The ball was never actually put in play, as it is to be retained as a souvenir.

The adoption of the seventh-inning stretch and the initiation of the presidential pitch tradition made 1910 one of the more memorable season openers across the nation.

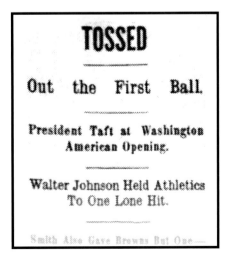

1911: Sad Disaster

Prior to the 1911 opener, Bancroft announced a number of rule changes for the opener concerning parking, paying, peanuts, and posting. In a sign of the times, the parking rule stipulated that no horse-drawn vehicles would be admitted to the ballpark; only autos would be permitted to park under the grandstand. Regarding paying, Bancroft complied with a National League directive that said boys could no longer be offered free admission to the game. They had to pay the regular ticket price and be registered at the turnstiles just like everyone else. Peanut vendors and other sellers were given only restricted access to the grandstand, because "the nuisance of waiters, candy butchers and peanut sharks crowding in front of people and annoying them after the game starts" would no longer be tolerated. Bancroft pledged that "people in the grand stand this season will be given the same protection that they get in a first-class theater." Finally, Bancroft announced that the number of each player would be posted on the scoreboard as he came to bat, matching the number given for him in the scorecard.

THE EARTH'S APPEARANCE TO-DAY.

Rooters were again in a partying mood for the opening of the season, and fans "dashed to the park in great numbers." However, a steady rain that began on the eve of the opener and continued throughout the morning of April 12 threatened to derail the "city holiday." Fortunately, the Reds had purchased a canvas tarpaulin the previous year to protect the infield from rain rather than relying on sawdust to dry out the field. As a result, the game was played without interruption. The Reds later regretted their newfound ability to keep the field playable, as they suffered their second-worst Opening Day loss in history and the worst defeat after 1900 by falling to Pittsburgh 14-0.

The next morning's *Enquirer* declared, "Opening Game Resulted in a Sad Disaster," but there was little mention of pregame ceremonies other than a paragraph about one rooters group:

> Lee Heine's Rooters, numbering 150, all arriving in six parlor cars of the traction company. They were headed by Weber's band and were one of the largest rooters groups. They presented the home team with an immense bunch of red carnations.

Losing the opener to Pittsburgh was not the only loss the Reds suffered on Opening Day in 1911. Cracked beams and weakened floors discovered by city inspectors began to reveal the deterioration of the Palace of the Fans. Then, when a fire destroyed much of the grandstand, the Reds decided to construct a new ballpark at the site after the 1911 season. The new ballpark would include an expanded seating area to accommodate the large crowds on Opening Day and on other holidays.

1912: "Glorious Opening of the New Ball Park"

Jack Ryder previewed the April 11 opening of what would later be named Redland Field:

> To-day's the day. With proper protection from the weather man the National League championship season for 1912 will be sprung open this afternoon under the shadow of the most magnificent grand stand yet devised in this country for the comfort of the baseball fans.

The new park was built with concrete and steel construction at a cost of $400,000. It consisted

Demolition of Palace of the Fans on November 14, 1911

of a double-decked grandstand that extended from third base around to first base, single-decked pavilions that stretched to the outfield walls, and right field bleachers that would later be referred to as the sundeck. Total seating capacity was 20,696.

The only problem with the new ballpark? It had no name. Reds president Garry Herrmann refused the request from many fans to christen the field "Herrmann Field," because "the Red Chief does not approve of naming the place after himself." Perhaps the *Enquirer* had a premonition, as the headline over a sketch of the ballpark proclaimed "Palace of Redland Fans." Sure enough, Redland Field was officially dedicated on May 18.

One 19-year-old fan, Mike Maxwell, took great pains to be present for the first game in the new ballpark. He arrived at the park at 8:00 a.m. to await the opening of the ticket booth at 11:30 a.m., prepared to purchase his 25-cent ticket. Meanwhile, other fans were doing their best to live up to the headline in the *Enquirer* that morning. It read, "This Is the Day of All Days for the Noisy Fans." Boisterous groups of rooters came out in force to begin their parades. Ben Deters's rooters from Upper Vine Street were "all fully equipped with the noise-making contraptions." They, along with

other groups, paraded through the downtown streets for several hours. The Storm Fishing and Outing Club was 110 strong, and its members proceeded to the ballpark in seven tallyhos preceded by their own band. This group did not tolerate absenteeism, as it fined about 90 of its members who failed to report for the parade. Their fine? Buying five rounds of drinks each at the chicken banquet held that evening to celebrate the opener.

The reserved seats in the grandstand were again all sold in advance, but "there was a big rush of the early birds for the front benches" when the gates to the new park opened at noon. By 12:30 p.m., "all the unreserved seats were alive with humanity," and 6,000 fans stood in the outer reaches of the outfield and in foul territory. The crowd enjoyed the pregame hitting and fielding practice of both teams, and they cheered "the clever stops and catches of the Reds." Weber's Prize Band performed its customary concert for one hour, and both teams lined up at home plate before marching in order to center field for the raising of a new American flag on the flagpole. The players then retreated to the area behind home plate in front of the private boxes. The speech by Mayor William Thomas Hunt was welcomed by the fans and players alike who were anxiously awaiting the start

PALACE OF REDLAND FANS.

of the game. The *Enquirer* writer was particularly enthused about the brevity of the speech: "Mayor Hunt's speech was a corker, lasting less than one minute. It may well be copied by some of the windjammers who delight in keeping a baseball crowd waiting while they exercise their vocal cords."

The mayor admired the "magnificent edifice" and congratulated the "Cincinnati Baseball Association upon the possession of a high appreciation of art, imagination and courage." Reds manager Hank O'Day was presented with a huge bouquet of flowers by a delegation of admirers, and "he walked from the plate to the bench with his nostrils buried in the fragrant blooms."

The mayor then tossed a new ball to Reds pitcher Frank Smith, who took his place in the center of the diamond. Bancroft brought an innovation to the infield by having a path cut out from the pitcher's mound to home plate. The groundskeeper also designed the mound in the shape of a shamrock, another novelty. Bancroft had arranged for the construction of a wire screen to protect the members of the press and the rooters directly behind home plate. The next morning's paper noted the amusement caused when two foul balls got caught in the screen, and one foul ball found its way through the screen. Luckily, a "gallant gentleman immediately rose to the occasion and, stabbing it with his mitt, saved a new Easter bonnet worn by one of the many lady bugs."

Speaking of women, in a special dispatch to the *Enquirer* on the morning of the opener,

THE OPENING

"Wasn't that a jolly dish to set before the King?

Mrs. Charles S. Havener explained how to run a baseball club. Havener was the new president of the Milwaukee minor league baseball team, and she thought a woman could be a success in baseball:

> I think any woman who will take the pains to master the game may thus equip herself to run a ball team. A woman seems especially adapted for it. She has above all other qualities intuition—this more developed than man has. Her intuition enables her to foresee things that a man never realizes could happen until they do. In baseball one must be constantly looking ahead. Then a woman has diplomacy, and it takes diplomacy to run a ball team, I can tell you. These two qualities give women an advantage over men. When you come to plain business ability I think women are just as capable as the men. I think that more and more women are going into business of some kind or another. Why shouldn't they?

Unfortunately for Havener, Milwaukee would not be awarded a major-league team until 1954, by which time she was deceased.

1913: Wettest Opener on Record

The third worst flood in Cincinnati history forced the 1913 opener to be delayed for two days until April 12. The rains began in March, and the flooding was so severe that the Reds remained in the South a week longer than expected. The field was in such poor condition that no practice could be held. A trench was even dug under the left field grandstand to hasten the flow of water out of the ballpark. The commissioner and inspector of buildings was called upon to inspect the ballpark to determine whether any damage had been caused to the structure of the grandstand. Fortunately, the commissioner determined that the grandstand was safe and the opener could proceed.

While the grandstand was in satisfactory shape, the Reds' clubhouse was destroyed, causing the team to move to the visitors' locker room. This forced that afternoon's opponent, the Pittsburgh Pirates, to dress at their hotel and travel to the field in full uniform. The Pirates did not mind the reason for the inconvenience, however, as shown by their declaration that they were better "mud horses" than the Reds and were confident of victory.

It was a good thing the Pirates felt confident because, when they arrived, they saw anything but the usual playing field. In order to make the field playable for the opener, the grounds crew had set bonfires the evening before to dry out the field. The fires had blazed through the entire night, resulting in a skinned, blackened diamond with no grass. Behind home plate was a "sea of slime," and the outfield was soft and slippery.

Despite the flood conditions, but perhaps aided by the earlier start time of 2:30 p.m. that still gave fans "plenty of time at the game to visit other places of amusement" (presumably local drinking establishments), 20,000 spectators celebrated the opener:

> Considering the uncertainty of playing and the poor weather and ground conditions, the crowd was a hummer. Though many reserved seats were turned back at the last moment, largely by speculators, who will never be favored with blocks of tickets again, the real fans held on and would not be denied. They came in autos, wagons, in street cars and on the hoof. They came provided with bands, which ground out popular airs that were pleasing to the excited multitude. They came adorned with streamers and with badges. They came in costumes and they came in their working clothes, right from the shop, the bench and the counter.

The gates opened at noon, and the crowd flocked in to hear Weber's band. The speculators (scalpers) referenced by the *Enquirer* were disappointed because they could not sell many of the reserved tickets they had purchased in advance. When they attempted to turn the unsold tickets in to the box office, Bancroft

DRYING THE BALL PARK FOR TO-DAY'S GAME

refused to accept them. Bancroft announced that the tickets could have been redeemed in the morning when there was a chance to resell them, but this "privilege" did not extend until game time. Bancroft told the scalpers to burn the tickets or keep them as souvenirs.

This opener featured members of the 1882 Reds as guests. A famous, former opponent of the Reds, Joe Tinker, served as the team's manager only for the 1913 season. Tinker was popular with baseball fans, having played 11 seasons for the Chicago Cubs as part of the famous double-play combination of "Tinker to Evers to Chance" that was immortalized in the poem, "Baseball's Sad Lexicon." There were no special pregame ceremonies except for the presentation of a gold watch chain to Tinker by the largest group of rooters, the "Tinker One-Two-Three Club," as the band played "My Hero" in his honor. Mayor Hunt then surprised everyone by leaving his grandstand box and throwing a pitch from the mound! The crowd was entertained by this first in Reds' history, and even more so by yet another wild pitch from a politician whose toss sailed over the batter standing at home plate.

The game itself featured a "sixth-inning stretch" when a band in the upper grandstand played "Hail, Hail, the Gang's All Here," prompting fans to rise to their feet in hopes of spurring on the Reds. The Pirates ended up being the better "mudders" and won the game, 9–2. Contrary to the tradition in those days of tossing foul balls back onto the field, four foul balls were kept by the fans who caught them. The *Enquirer* disapprovingly declared that "the price of horse hide is going up" because of such greedy behavior.

Despite the wretched conditions, umpire Bill Brennan called Cincinnati "the greatest town in the country for an opening game." Brennan said he had never witnessed such enthusiasm in his life, as the fans were "all good-natured and show no disposition to harshly criticize players or umpires."

1914: Lake Redland

There was no flood on April 14, but the conditions were worse for the fans than they had been the previous season. The morning

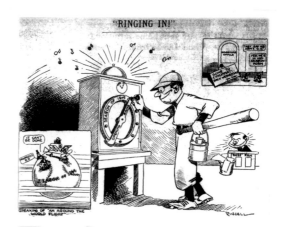

Enquirer announced that the opener would be a "Battle of Spit-Ballers," and it turned out that the hurlers had plenty of moisture to apply to their pitches.

After the bleachers had already filled, a steady rain caused a delay in the game and elimination of all pregame ceremonies other than the annual concert. The field was in such bad condition and the weather forecast so ominous that the game would have been postponed had it not been Opening Day. The Reds decided to proceed because of "the insistence of the crowd, which refused to go away, even when it rained the hardest."

The rain caused such comical and sloppy play that the Reds scored six runs during the sixth and seventh innings without managing a single hit. In the sixth, they scored three runs on an error, three wild pitches, two hit batsmen, a couple sacrifice flies, and a stolen base. In the seventh, they again scored three runs, this time on four walks, two sacrifices, and a wild pitch. It was only then that the drenched crowd of 15,728 began to head for the exits.

Since many fans who had bought tickets stayed away because of the steady rain, team president Herrmann announced "as a matter of justice" that any unused tickets would be good for the next day's game. The next day's Enquirer summed up the proceedings:

1915: Manager Nearly Chokes to Death

DROWNED

Cubs in the Drizzle

And Buried Them Under a Sea of Mud.

On April 10, an up-and-coming player named Babe Ruth made his first appearance in Cincinnati while pitching for the Boston Red Sox in an exhibition game. Four days later, when the Reds were scheduled to open their season, Reds fans encountered somber news when they opened their morning paper. Zeppelin war crafts had dropped bombs on England the previous day during the early days of World War I. But on the sports page, Jack Ryder gave the fans relief from wartime anxiety by predicting springlike weather—at last—for the opening of the championship season. A large crowd of over 20,000 was expected, as almost all of the reserved seats had been sold in advance. Large delegations of fans would be arriving from Dayton and Hamilton, Ohio; Lexington, Kentucky; Indianapolis, Indiana; and cities in between. Everything was in order for a perfect outing against Pittsburgh.

The arriving fans were not limited to those coming from within driving distance. An international flavor was added to the fan base in the form of Joe Massaguer, manager of the Havana Reds in Cuba. Massaguer was in town to see if he could secure dates to play other local teams after his team finished playing in Tennessee. The Havana Reds were said to be a first-class ball club composed of the best players in Cuba, but the team had made a mistake in coming to the United States so early in the year before the baseball season was underway. The team had already lost $1,200 by having to pay its expenses without any offsetting revenue. Senor Massaguer had placed an ad in the *Enquirer* four days previously.

GAMES WANTED

"HAVANA REDS" B. B. CLUB

Of Havana, Cuba. Address JOE SMITH, 17 E. Fifth St., Cincinnati, Ohio.

Long lines of rooters formed at the bleacher and pavilion entrances before the gates were even open. A soloist, Minny Hammond, later joined Weber's band to stir the crowd with her vocal selections, but her voice could not be heard in the bleachers or the upper grandstand because of the hum of the large crowd. The mayor, who was joined in his box by first baseman Charlie Gould of the 1869 Red Stockings, one of the few surviving members of the famous team, made the traditional first pitch without incident. The designated "megaphone man" announced the entire batting order, and the season was on.

The play of the Reds was so listless that the team almost lost its new manager, Buck Herzog, during the seventh inning:

> While the Reds were at bat, Herzie was chewing away on a big ball of gum, large enough to choke an ox. As man after man went out on easy chances the Red leader became so interested and excited, in pulling for something to happen, that the gum got the better of him and slipped in a sneaking manner down his gullet. It lodged in the windpipe, and the crafty manager was up against it for air to breathe. He was choking and gasping when Dr. Hines, the club physician, arrived on the scene and extracted the offending substance. Herzie became very ill and the game was delayed a few minutes while he was recovering.

Fortunately, Herzog was able to resume his position at shortstop, although "he was very unsteady on his pins for an inning." What started with news of war on a beautiful day ended with near tragedy and a loss for the Reds.

GENERAL FAN

II

BRAVES GIANTS

GET YOUR MONEY DOWN
THEY'LL SOON BE

PATRIOTISM AT THE PLATE

What's the rumpus in our nation? What's the cause of this sensation? If you listen you will note a joyful tune—For the very simple reason that another baseball season will be opened up Wednesday afternoon.

Cincinnati Commercial Gazette

World War I began during the summer of 1914. The United States stayed out of the war as long as possible, but by Opening Day of 1916, it was becoming increasingly clear that Uncle Sam would enter the turmoil. Patriotism was evident at games in 1916 and reached a fevered pitch during openers in 1917 and 1918. On April 6, 1917, the United States declared war on Germany. Traditional festivities took a back seat to public showings of support for the troops.

1916: Rotarians Mark the Occasion

As the April 12 opener approached, the Battle of Verdun in France was underway with what was described as the heaviest charges ever delivered in battle. On the eve of the opener, the United States was considering warning Germany of dire consequences if ships carrying Americans were attacked.

Establishing a tradition that would continue for years, the Cincinnati Rotary Club and the "Minute Men" of the Chamber of Commerce hosted the 1916 Reds at a luncheon to pay homage to their guests of honor. The president of the Rotary Club delivered the keynote address and announced that the business community was firmly in support of the team:

> The business men of Cincinnati are heart and hand back of every one of you ballplayers. We want you to feel that your interests are our interests. We want you to know that we are with you from the first inning to-morrow until the last out is made at the closing game of this season. Whether you win or whether you lose you are going to have our moral and financial backing. Never before have the business and professional men of the city taken an interest in any ball team as the men of Cincinnati have in you ballplayers this season.

The next morning the rooters groups parading through downtown were joined by 500

READY FOR THE FIRING LINE

Rotarians who marched from Third Street to Redland Field. Upon arrival, the Rotarians joined the other rooters and paraded around the diamond "headed by Hofer's Band" in what was hoped to be the liveliest event of the day. Each of the Rotarians carried a banner proclaiming "First Place or Bust." A sign in left field urged fans the vote for an upcoming bond issue to support a $6-million subway and above-ground commuter rail system that would make it easier for fans the reach the ballpark. (The bond issue passed and a 2.2-mile section was excavated to house a subway tunnel, but the project was never completed when the original source of funds was depleted.)

The Reds anticipated one of the largest crowds ever and stretched ropes around the entire outfield to accommodate the overflow from the grandstand and the bleachers. Extra chairs were placed in front of the Cubs bench for the 100 rooters arriving from Chicago. The *Enquirer* declared that Redland Field "is the finest park in the country for handling a big throng without cluttering up the playing field with a lot of rooters."

Weber's band received a standing ovation from the fans and players during its rendition of "America the Beautiful." And, after a single with the Reds trailing 7–1 in the eighth inning, the crowd of 24,607 "cheered as madly as if the hit had meant the turning of the tide." But the tide did not turn for the team that had not placed higher than seventh place for three seasons. Nonetheless, the *Enquirer* found a silver lining, noting that the large crowd was a sign that "the game is still the most popular and attractive of all outdoor sports."

1917: Patriotism on Display

In 1916, President Woodrow Wilson had threatened that the United States would no longer remain neutral if Germany attacked American ships. A year later, he was forced to carry out his threat after repeated attacks by Germany on US ships. But any theories that preoccupation with the war would diminish interest in the national sport were quickly dispelled across the country. Indeed,

in Cincinnati, the team announced that all grandstand and reserved seats had been sold, and only a limited amount of pavilion, bleacher, and standing-room-only tickets that were not previously available would be sold on the day of the game. Those tickets were sold shortly after the gates opened at 12:30 p.m., and then the entrance was closed. The *Enquirer*, after devoting most of its coverage that morning to the war, placed this headline on the sports page to reflect the feelings of baseball fans: "War, Get Off This Page! Give Baseball a Chance." The traditional cartoon

War, Get Off This Page! Give Baseball a Chance

that had become a hallmark of Opening Day in the *Enquirer* featured references to the war and the outpouring of patriotism.

April 11 marked the first-ever appearance by the St. Louis Cardinals at an opener in Cincinnati. What the Cardinals saw was an immense crowd of nearly 25,000 flush with patriotic fever. Redland Field was decorated with bunting and flags, and fans had been encouraged to wear the stars and stripes. Nearly every fan dressed accordingly, and at least 10,000 flags were carried and waved by patrons throughout the festivities. Hundreds of soldiers from all parts of the city and state, plus officers from the armory in Fort Thomas, Kentucky, dressed in full uniform. A recruiting station was opened at the park after President Wilson announced plans that morning for the draft that was needed to raise a large army. It was likely the greatest showing of patriotic fever in the city's history.

After the downtown parades had reached the park and the overflow crowd had settled in, Weber's band played a selection of patriotic songs, prompting several standing ovations. After the Rotary Club arrived through a special gate in the outfield, two bands played in harmony, and there "was a demonstration that lasted nearly five minutes" after the national anthem. The area around home plate looked like a conservatory as rooters bestowed bouquets of flowers on the teams. So many were delivered that the utility players

of the Reds were delegated the task of carrying them to the respective benches. One rooter presented each Reds player with an American flag, entirely overlooking the Cardinals, who were equally patriotic.

After one of the briefest opening remarks ever, the game was fittingly played in just an hour and 32 minutes—the shortest opening game on record to that point. The Reds won, 3–1, but it was clear that concerns about the war were on every fan's mind. The next day's headline referenced the preoccupation with war: "Reds Outplay Cardinals in Wonderful Combat."

National League president John K. Tener, who had been a professional baseball player in the 1880s and later a one-term congressman, summed up the feelings of baseball fans:

> Despite the unsettled condition of this country due to war, the baseball season was off to a good start, and I am pleased with the outlook. The national game of America has a wonderful hold on the baseball fans, and I think it is a grand thing to arouse the fighting spirit of Young America. Baseball will make athletes out of our youths, and athletes are bound to make good soldiers. Cincinnati put up a splendid article of ball.

The next day fans learned that Congress would pass a bill raising taxes and issuing bonds for $7 million to prosecute the war. There likely was little dissent about supporting the war effort among the Reds fan base.

SIX LONG MONTHS WE'VE WAITED FOR THIS DAY!

1918: Wartime Hysteria about Germans

While Uncle Sam and his allies appeared to be gaining ground in World War I by April 16, hysteria about all things German was reaching an all-time high in Cincinnati. Public schools could no longer teach German, the public library removed German books from its shelves, and the German-sounding names of 13 streets in the city were changed. Newspapers were dominated by war news, including reports of "tricks" by German soldiers, who would appear in front of the trenches and speak French or English to deceive the Americans. This hysteria spilled over to the pregame ceremonies on Opening Day.

Former Reds manager Hank O'Day was now a well-known umpire in the National League. He was assigned to work the opener with Pittsburgh. As Weber's band was playing "The Star-Spangled Banner" and fans stood with their heads "bared" in solemn respect, a German fan shouted "Hello, Hank" to O'Day. O'Day looked around to determine who was greeting him and spotted the man. He became angry and yelled back, "Take your hat off, you dirty brute." The man removed his hat, but O'Day continued: "Go sit down, you traitor. I wish I could kill you." The following day, the *Enquirer* recounted the incident under the headline "Umpire and Patriot." A city with a strong German heritage and thousands of German immigrants was on edge.

Although the United States had declared war against Germany five days before the 1917 opener, the 1918 opening game was the first since the nation's armies had been "actively hurled against the heartless Hun on the blood-stained and shell-bitten fields of France." The crowd was more somber and smaller owing to the absence of large numbers of young men. Ordinarily, young men would be leading the cheers, but now they were fighting overseas. Wrote *Enquirer* reporter Ryder: "It was a calm and peaceful crowd, evidently out to forget for the moment the worries forced upon the people by the operations of the brutal Hun and satisfied to observe a clever exhibition in a quiet manner."

Your Bond May Bring Him Home in Safety

The supreme tragedies of war are not enacted on the battlefield, but in the home.

Above the shouts of command and encouragement, the roar and shock of the great guns, and all the swelling tumult of battle which bear the husband and father to a hero's grave and a martyr's glory, there rise the weeping of the bereaved wife and the cries of little children deprived of a father's love and care.

American fathers are now on the battle fronts of France. Many must fall; how many depends upon us who remain safely at home.

A single Liberty Bond will help to save a soldier's life, YOUR soldier's life, and bring him home in safety to those who hold his life far more precious than their own.

Like the year before, the crowd of nearly 19,000 waved flags and listened to military music by Weber's band and the Base Hospital Band from Camp Sheridan, but the minds of many of the fans were "divided between the doings on the sunlit field below and the more strenuous battles being fought so nobly by our boys who are over there." The paper referred to the pregame ceremonies as "preceding the combat" and assuming "a strictly military and patriotic hue." The concert was performed with the display of a Liberty Bond banner, and the crowd stood with their heads "uncovered" and in silence as the bands played "America" and "The Star-Spangled Banner." Other patriotic songs included "Goodbye Broadway, Hello France," "Keep the Home Fires Burning," and "Stars and Stripes Forever."

The Reds players, while not serving on the battlefield, contributed to the war effort at the urging of club manager Christie Mathewson. Each member of the team bought stamps daily for the Liberty Bond and thrift stamp campaigns, and some purchased higher-priced war bonds as well.

Oh, the game? Pete Schneider threw the only one-hitter in Reds Opening Day history, a 3–0 victory over the Pirates, and "not one

of the enemy advanced as far as third base during the entire conflict." (There has never been a no-hitter on a Reds Opening Day.) Casey Stengel got the lone hit, a double. The game was once again played in short order, concluding in one hour and 20 minutes.

1919: An Aerial Show

The signing of the armistice on November 11, 1918 meant many star players returned from the battlefield and took their place on the ball field instead. The end of the war revived

Many of the Star Players Have Returned From War.

interest in baseball that had been eclipsed for the past two seasons. On the morning of April 23, the *Enquirer* reported on the tremendous progress in the Victory Loan Campaign to erase the nation's war debt, noting that Cincinnati had already sold a third of the loan subscriptions on the first day of the campaign. Fans were more than ready for the start of the baseball season without also carrying the anxiety of war. Despite the fans' excitement, the goings-on around the city were fairly tame. Absent from the morning of the opener were the rooters, their amateur bands, and fans dressed in outlandish costumes. "The truckloads of wild-eyed enthusiasts … were busy elsewhere," said the *Enquirer*.

Not that there was a lack of interest. Nearly all the reserved seats had been sold in advance, and more than 20,000 people were expected to view the opener. Weber's band was back for another performance, and a New York music publisher provided "a dozen cabaret singers … to warble ragtime for the fans." The customary speech and first pitch from the mayor were also on the agenda. The main attraction, however, was going to be stunts in the air by army airplanes. One of the smaller planes was scheduled to make a landing on the field. Reds

OH, BOYS! WE COPPED THE OPENER!

Reds Uniform 1919

president Herrmann accepted an invitation from Major P. H. Hemphill to accompany him in one of the flights above the park. Herrmann was expected to view at least part of the opener from the loftiest altitude ever attained by a member of the Reds organization.

When the appointed hour arrived for Herrmann to board the military plane, he decided that he would be better off riding in a vehicle that would remain on the ground:

> The expected attack of cold feet became very prevalent in President Herrmann's vicinity when the time arrived for his trip to the park by the aerial route. The Red Chief shied violently when Major Hemphill came to take him to the flying field. What had looked the evening before like a glorious little excursion assumed the proportions of a trip into the wilds of Africa, followed by a jaunt to the North Pole. Hiding his trepidation as well as he could behind a pale smile, and pleading unusual press of business matters relating to the game, Mr. Herrmann firmly declined the offer of the joy-ride and took the trip to the park in a vehicle guaranteed to remain on terra firma.

Although the crowd was eagerly anticipating the spectacular airshow, the promised exhibition never materialized. Nonetheless, the one plane that appeared delighted the fans when the pilot, who hailed from Dayton, Ohio, flew over the grandstand and dropped a baseball in center field. Herrmann graciously—or was it sheepishly?—threw out the first pitch.

The *Enquirer* reported that the other "tiresome preliminary ceremonies were wisely omitted" but that "seldom has there been more intense and earnest rooting than was heard in the later rounds when the Reds were struggling with all their power to come from behind and grab off the victory." The rooters were not partying as much as they had in earlier years, but a group of fans from Cuba got "so excited that the authorities [had] to put them in jail to cool off," and several of them "almost fell out of their seats" in the grandstand.

Why such excitement from the Cuban fans? The Reds had two Cuban-born players, Dolph Luque and Manuel "Potato" Cueto. Luque was the winning pitcher thanks to the Reds scoring five runs after two outs in the eighth inning. The flurry of hits secured them a 6–2 win over the Cardinals.

One innovation that greeted the crowd of 22,462 was the posting of the respective numbers of the pitchers and catchers of all the National League teams that were playing that afternoon. With a scorecard in hand, the fans could determine the identity of the "battery men" in any league game.

Despite a big win for the Reds in the opener, the team was not expected to compete for the championship of the National League. Little did anyone know on Opening Day that the team would finish with its first world championship, tainted as it was by the infamous "Black Sox" World Series gambling scandal. In that best-of-nine series, the Reds beat the Chicago White Sox five games to three.

Weber's Band, 1919 Opening Day

THE ROARING TWENTIES

···

Opening Day does funny things to people in this town. It is the one day of the year when everyone considers it his birthright to call in sick, to drink, and predict boldly.

Tim Sullivan, *Enquirer* sports columnist

Following the end of World War I, Opening Day in Cincinnati saw ever-increasing attendance, most likely a result of the World Series championship in 1919. The day remained a "half-day holiday," but the revelry that had characterized the openers before the war was somewhat subdued for several years. A number of developments in the early 1920s affected the course of Opening Day festivities. These included the beginning of Prohibition, the fallout from the Black Sox gambling scandal, labor strife, and the ever-increasing use of automobiles. Prohibition may have been the largest contributor to the decline in revelry, as rooters groups historically enjoyed stops along the parade route at local drinking establishments. Coincidentally—or not—reports of fights among fans declined as Prohibition took hold.

1920: Findlay Market's First Appearance

Three months after Prohibition started, readers of the April 14 *Enquirer* were greeted with extensive coverage of an ongoing "wildcat" strike by railroad workers that was opposed by the railroads and even by the unions representing the workers. The strikes had lasted a year already, and President Wilson's cabinet declared that they were "a direct, well-planned attempt to overthrow the United States Government by means of revolution." In response, Wilson had appointed nine individuals to serve on the newly created Railroad Labor Board, three of whom were from Cincinnati. The board was charged with the difficult task of settling the dispute.

On the eve of this Opening Day, snow was beginning to melt after covering the entire field a day earlier. A record crowd had been anticipated to honor the world champions. All the reserved seats had been sold months earlier, but the recent snow and cold weather kept some fans at home. The conditions did not prevent the attendance of one noteworthy fan, John D. Rockefeller, then the richest

FRANK C. BANCROFT
Manager Cincinnati Club

man in the world. After Reds pitcher Dutch Ruether delivered the first pitch, the ball was taken out of play, signed by Rockefeller, and presented to Reds president Garry Herrmann.

Among the missing fans for the opener was Ohio governor James Cox, a longtime attendee. But the person most missed by the team and the fans in attendance was the "Father of Opening Day," Frank Bancroft. "Banny" had injured his leg and was reported to be healing well, but his physician ordered him not to attend the game because he suspected Bancroft would attend to his varied duties at the gate despite his weakened condition.

In addition to the usual pregame ceremonies, fans were expecting to witness the raising of the National League pennant, the first ever won by a Cincinnati team. The large blue and red pennant had been delivered to the

Reds the previous day. The Reds decided to postpone the flag raising until a later date in the interest of attracting another large crowd.

The most significant happening on April 14 may have been the birth of a new rooters group based at Findlay Market. Founded in 1852, Findlay Market is a public market in Cincinnati's Over-the-Rhine neighborhood (now known simply as "OTR"). While no mention of the Findlay Market rooters is made in Cincinnati newspapers until 1922, the organizers conducted their first march to the ballpark on April 14, 1920. This first parade consisted of one band, one horse-drawn wagon, and the merchants of the market marching to Crosley Field. (Cincinnati newspapers reporting on the 1925 opener noted that the group had celebrated the opener for "many years.") Little did the organizers

ALL SET? SHOOT!

anticipate that the group would mark its one hundredth parade in 2019. Suffice it to say that 1920 was the start of an Opening Day tradition in Cincinnati that is second to none.

1921: Bancroft Dies

Two weeks before the opener on April 13, Frank Bancroft passed away. Bancroft surely would have liked to see the fruits of his nearly 30 years promoting Opening Day when a record-setting crowd of 29,963 packed the ballpark. He was missed by many fans:

> Many fans spoke with regret of the absence of Frank Bancroft, who had been at every previous opening game here for 29 years. His genial countenance was sadly missed by the regulars. And how Banny would have delighted in handling that big crowd!

The opener was short on hoopla, which would have disappointed Bancroft, but he would have delighted in the appearance of "Doc" Howard's Cabaret. Howard's group featured 15 singers who mixed harmony, jazz, and melody to entertain the fans along with Weber's band.

The record crowd was a testament to the popularity of baseball in Cincinnati despite dark clouds hanging over the sport after the Black Sox scandal. It took almost one year to prove that there had been illegal betting during the 1919 World Series. On the day before the opener, baseball commissioner Kenesaw Mountain Landis, speaking pointedly at a dinner for the two Chicago teams, warned MLB players that they were facing a hard proposition in regaining the confidence of the public:

> Never before in any activity in the United States has anything been scrutinized as will our activity be scrutinized this season … If a man gets caught off first; if he muffs a ball, there will be winks of eyes in the stands and "I told you so" whispered around. We must put up with that for a little while and the characteristics of fair play soon will snuff out that attitude.

The same day, a Cincinnati municipal court judge fined a Cleveland man $50 on the charge that he had promoted a baseball lottery in Cincinnati, and a warrant for his arrest was issued at the request of the US Department of Justice.

As if the passing of Bancroft and the taint of the gambling scandal weren't enough to dampen enthusiasm for Opening Day, the Reds were also faced with their first-ever contract disputes. Two of the three holdouts, Reds starters Edd Roush and Heinie Groh, would remain unsigned for weeks, and the third, starter Larry Kopf, retired over the dispute. Roush and Kopf nonetheless chose to attend the opener, buying seats in the grandstand. Their replacements for the opener, three relative unknowns, combined for five of the Reds' nine hits in a 5–3 win over Pittsburgh.

The big crowd was partly the result of a large delegation of fans that had arrived on a big river steamer. The steamer stopped at all the major towns on the Ohio River, enabling more than 600 rooters to attend the game from cities such as Huntington, West Virginia, and Portsmouth, Ohio. These fans applauded each player as he came up to bat for the first time, as noted by the *Enquirer*: "No favorites were played, but each of the boys was given a hearty

Ed Roush

hand." New Ohio governor Harry L. Davis also attended and was seen keeping his own scorecard and "watch[ing] every play from the standpoint of an expert."

1922: Two Hall of Famers

The April 22 opener featured two pitchers, Eppa Rixey of the Reds and Grover Cleveland Alexander of the Cubs, both of whom would go on to become Hall of Fame inductees. On this day, Alexander outdueled Rixey. (Only one other time in Reds history would two future Hall of Fame pitchers face each other in the opener, that being Tom Seaver and Steve Carlton in 1981.)

FEATURES OF THE GAME.

Long driving of Bohne and Fonseca.

Clever pitching of Luque with runners on base.

Excellent catching and throwing of Ivy Wingo.

Babe Adams knocked out of the box in eight innings.

Smart handling of thrown balls by Sam Crane.

Record-breaking opening-day crowd.

All of the reserved seats in the grandstand and pavilions were again sold months in advance. After the rooters' scarce showing a year earlier, they were back in force in 1922. The merrymakers were equipped with horns and rattles for their procession, while clown bands, other bands, and solo musicians also marched to the ballpark. Five thousand cars

BASEBALL
To-Day
REDS vs.
CUBS
2:30 P. M.
Concert, Weber Band, 1:30 to 2:30.
Ticket Office Open at 10 A. M.

were parked on nearby streets. The Findlay Market Association's rooters paraded through downtown until they arrived at the ballpark and presented an immense floral horseshoe for good luck to Reds manager Pat Moran. The rooters were joined by members of the Rotary Club, who arrived at an outfield entrance in 50 decorated automobiles. Members of the club circled the field before serenading the manager. Although there was a pregame concert, there was no speech and no first pitch. Ohio governor Harry Davis had wired Herrmann the previous day to inform him that the press of state business would make it impossible for him to attend. As noted in the *Enquirer*, "President Herrmann wisely called off all speeches or other exercises, realizing that the fans came out to see the ball game and not to listen to flights of oratory."

The local YMCA hosted the Reds on the eve of the opener, but that would be the last dinner attended by the full team in 1922. Herrmann and Moran announced that invitations to luncheons and dinners in the future would be declined because they believed the energies of the team "should be expended on the field of play and not in social activities." This plan proved to have some merit, as the Reds rebounded from a loss on Opening Day and a 1–10 start to the season to finish in second place.

The mammoth crowd of 27,095 was accommodated with temporary bleachers erected in left field that extended to the scoreboard in center field. Ropes were stretched in front of the bleachers in right field to accommodate the overflow crowd. Fans saw a playing field that was in perfect condition thanks to field superintendent Matty Schwab. Reported the *Enquirer*, "the athletes, clad in white or gray, tore madly over its brilliant surface." Despite the chilly weather and cloudy skies, it was an ideal afternoon except for the Reds' loss.

Away from the field, the Associated Press had reported earlier in the day that it had secured a confidential report from experts meeting in London. The report outlined a comprehensive plan to rebuild Europe and Russia in the wake of World War I. The Allies were willing to aid the Soviets in their recovery, but they insisted upon sweeping reforms, including granting rights to foreigners.

1923: First Opener over 30,000

The *Cincinnati Commercial Tribune*, the city's other daily newspaper from 1896 until 1930, reported that April 17 "was Christmas, Fourth of July, Yom Kippur, and St. Patrick's Day rolled all into one and with an added flavor only sensed on Cincinnati's day of days—the baseball getaway." As it happened, the temperature more closely approximated Christmas weather than what would typically be enjoyed on July Fourth.

Interest was so high that the entire grand-stand had been sold out four days before Thanksgiving, and only 6,000 bleacher seats remained for sale on the day of the game at a cost of 50 cents. Holders of reserved seats were encouraged to arrive early to avoid the crush of the crowd, which was expected to be the largest crowd ever for the opener. To accom-modate early arrivers, the gates were thrown open 90 minutes earlier than usual. By 11:00 a.m., 12,000 patrons had already arrived, bundled in overcoats and furs, and hundreds more poured in every few minutes. Cardinals manager Branch Rickey had invited ten local Prohibition agents as his guests for the game, but they were not on duty. Many of the chilly rooters were likely unaware of the agents' presence and showed remarkable foresight by having hidden the flasks they had brought to ward off the cold.

It was the largest crowd in Reds Opening Day history at 30,338. The fans sat in seats "shining with new paint" and received a souvenir poem penned by pioneering sports-writer Ren Mulford, known for coining the phrase "baseball fan." Twenty-five Boy Scouts passed out the poetic souvenir on behalf of the Community Chest. Flowers were presented to the members of both teams. Perhaps in a nod to the weather, there was no speech or ceremo-nial first pitch.

Special ground rules were established to allow for an automatic triple if a ball was hit into the outfield crowd in front of the grandstand and bleachers. The rules did not end up being needed, as no balls traveled that far on such a cold day. The teams were tied 2–2 through ten innings. Manager Moran, coaching at first base, realized that hits were scarce on such a chilly day, so he came up with a plan when the Reds had one out in the eleventh inning:

> Then manager Moran stirred up the old gray matter and evolved a clever scheme. It is not usual to send up a batter to sacrifice, with one man out and a runner on first. But Donohue, though a sensational pitcher, is not a whirl-wind at the bat. He had been up four times without striking a safe blow and the chances were that he would make it five if he attempted to drive the ball against the fence. So Pat instructed him to lay it down and put [Wingo] on second, whence a fair-sized single would bring him home with the winner. The plan worked out to perfection.

After Donohue was thrown out at first base and Wingo advanced to second, the next batter, Burns, singled. "[Wingo] was on his way with the crack of the bat, and how that Georgia boy did tear up the pathway home! He rounded third on the high gear and increased his speed as he came in to home and victory … Wingo started his slide 15 feet from the platter and shot over in a cloud of dust and the music of the wild cheering from 30,000 throats." The

Reds Take Opener, 3 to 2, Beating Cards in Eleventh

packed crowd surged onto the field "stamping its feet to restore the circulation, but warm and merry at heart."

After the game, the players of both teams were guests of the *Enquirer* at the Shubert Theatre near Fountain Square for a performance of "Up in the Clouds." The paper had invited the players that morning and they were simply told to show up at the box office and give their names, and they would be provided with choice seats.

While the Reds' National League season was off to a great start, another league, the League of Nations, was just getting underway. The League of Nations had formed in 1919 after the Paris Peace Conference, and it had two empty seats. Those seats were designated for the United States and Germany, though Germany's seat was not recognized until 1926 as punishment for their part in World War I. Lord Robert Cecil of England came to Cincinnati on Opening Day but had no plans to attend the game. Instead, he appeared at the Cincinnati branch of the Foreign Policy Association at the Hotel Sinton. "Lord Bob" argued that the League of Nations was a "league of victors" that America should support. Ultimately, he failed to convince the skeptics, and the United States never joined the league.

1924: First Radio Broadcast

On the eve of the April 15 opener, an apparatus was installed on top of the grandstand, and a special wire was strung from Redland Field to the broadcast facilities of radio stations WLW and WSAI. The next day, announcer Eugene Middendorf provided a play-by-play simulcast on both stations, broadcasting from the same roof where hundreds of fans were perched. It was the first Reds game broadcast by radio in Cincinnati. Thousands of baseball fans in Ohio, Kentucky, West Virginia, and Indiana tuned into the game. Northern Ohio cities reported that the cheering of the rooftop

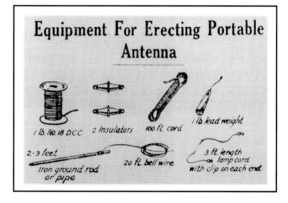

fans was so loud at times that the voice of the announcer could not be heard. Since this reaction was anticipated, the announcer often repeated descriptions of exciting plays.

Among the listeners were the workers at the Cincinnati Association for the Welfare of the Blind. Shortly before the game started, the workers were called into an auditorium, and the blind fans listened to the play-by-play. This was the only game of the season that was broadcast on the radio.

The 1924 opener was much anticipated in Cincinnati, as well as around the country. The Associated Press had reported the previous day that "Fandom East and West is keenly

Thousands Tune in To Opening Game

awaiting the opening shout of 'play ball' that will mark the close of the long 'off-season,' the end of the spring training grind and which will send the 16 American and National League outfits off to a battle for supremacy that will not close until last week in September." Most of the tickets were once again sold months in advance. A squad of deputies from the IRS was assigned to the game to apprehend any person who was scalping baseball tickets in violation of federal tax law. Only one person had properly registered as a scalper with the Collector of Internal Revenue. He no doubt realized that eight sellers had been penalized the previous year for failing to register and pay the government tax imposed on baseball ticket sales.

The "First Fan" honor was bestowed by the *Enquirer* upon George Awl, who anticipated the scarcity of tickets and arrived at the ballpark at 8:00 p.m. the night before. He was joined

by two 16-year-olds who arrived shortly after midnight. After they and a few thousand other patrons were able to buy tickets for the unreserved seats or for standing room only after the gates opened, "thousands were turned away, unable to force their passage into the enclosure." A record crowd of 35,747 squeezed into the ballpark under sunny skies and a nearly 80-degree temperature. Upon arrival, fans saw a "playing field of dazzling green [that] was as smooth as a table made to order for the swift cavorting of the merry athletes." Many unlucky fans who could not purchase a ticket were seen peeping through the iron gratings on the sloping runways to the park.

The Reds had a number of California players on their team. Friends from San Francisco sent an elaborate floral horseshoe that was presented to the team in pregame ceremonies after Weber's band played. The *Enquirer* reported that the entire Pacific Coast was rooting for the Reds "tooth and nail." Findlay Market's parade, which by now had become a well-entrenched tradition, eclipsed all former parades in originality. Each of the 400 members of the association, with flowers in their coat, wore a large white hat and carried a cane when they entered the ballpark through a special entrance. They marched around the field before presenting a "trophy" to manager Moran that was a bouquet of flowers in the form of an immense baseball resting on two baseball bats. The arrangement was so large that it had to be hoisted on the shoulders of four men after the presentation, who then paraded around the field to the accompaniment of the band.

The Reds rewarded their loyal fans with a 6–5 win when pinch runner Ed Hock scored the winning run on a sacrifice fly in the bottom of the ninth. Hock would appear in only one other game the rest of the season. The fans were ecstatic, including the "fair wearer" of a new Easter bonnet that was "smashed to smithereens in the third inning" by a foul ball

that reached the grandstand. After she scrambled for the prized ball and retrieved it, she exclaimed, "Why bother about a new hat?"

The only mourning that occurred on this Opening Day was for a family of six that had been struck at a railroad crossing the previous day. The *Enquirer* front-page headline announced the sad news: "Six Cincinnatians Are Killed in Indiana Crossing Wreck." The paper reported that the warning signal on the track had been flashing. The story was a painful reminder to new motorists unfamiliar with the rules of the road as automobiles were increasing in popularity.

1925: Police on Trial

On Opening Day eve, a stunning case of corruption began to play out in a Cincinnati courtroom. With Prohibition in force, police officers and federal employees known as dry agents were charged with monitoring the illegal use and sale of alcohol. But some agents and police officers were willing to take bribes to look the other way when liquor was being bought and sold. All told, 71 defendants had been accused of illegal dealings related to liquor sales, with 55 Cincinnati police officers and village dry agents already having pleaded guilty by Opening Day. Witnesses testified that they paid large sums of protection money to the police and even made liquor deliveries to the Fourth District station house. The April 14 front page of the *Enquirer* delivered the shocking news to the public: "Huge Graft Fund Admitted at Opening of Police Trial." Three detectives were charged with conspiracy by the United States government, a very serious offense.

While the law-abiding citizens of Cincinnati were outraged at the officers' brazen disregard for the law, the disturbing details of graft did not dampen enthusiasm for Opening Day. What bothered fans more than graft was the acute congestion that clogged the streets around Redland Field as cars of every make and model came from nearby towns,

REDS WHO ARE TO MAKE DASH FOR PENNANT

Top Row—Benton, Sheehan, Harper, Rixey, Bressler, Donohue, Pick, Carl Mays and Fowler. Middle Row—Hock, Dibut, Harris, Wingo, Hargrave, Luque, Sandberg, J. May, Bohne and Vines. Bottom Row—Begley, Fonseca, Caveney, Burns, Pinelli, Daubert, Manager Hendricks, Duncan, Roush and Priesmuth.

hilltop suburbs, and from across the river. The *Cincinnati Commercial Tribune* reported that working-class people from the long line of streetcars contributed to the congestion by knocking people down if necessary to secure a ticket.

Those lucky enough to attend the game on baseball's gala day joined in the celebration of the fiftieth season of the National League. The occasion was marked with a blue flag that said "National Jubilee" in gold letters. With the exception of the customary concert, Reds officials dispensed with all other official ceremonies. Noted the *Enquirer* on the day

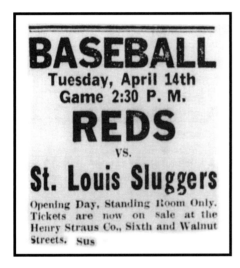

before Opening Day, "The Red officials realize that the fans want to see baseball and not listen to oratory." Joe Tinker, the manager of the 1913 Reds, was a special guest at the game. When the band ended its concert with the national anthem, the great crowd stood in unison. With no further ceremonies, the fans were said to be relieved because they "were hungry for baseball and spurned any other form of entertainment."

The game took only one hour and 26 minutes, the third shortest in history, and there was not as much wild cheering as in the past after the Reds took a comfortable lead in the first

inning. The fans "scented victory early and set themselves to watch the cool, smooth performance of [pitcher] Donohue and his backers in a calm and pleasant frame of mind." The

> ## Opening Day Ceremonies To Be Dispensed With—Enormous Crowd Expected To View Battle.

Reds beat the Cardinals 4–0 before 31,888 fans on a pleasantly sunny afternoon.

Fans retreated from the ballpark knowing that each game of the coming season would be played regardless of the weather. The game program read, "There will be a game played on these grounds on every scheduled day, despite rain storms. Rain cannot penetrate the cover we use for the diamond. It sheds water like a duck's back."

1926: Prohibition Politics

Patriotic fever that had begun with World War I continued to energize fans and players alike. The Reds won eight of nine Opening Day contests after 1916, prompting fans to gobble up, in just 72 hours, all the reserved tickets sold in November 1925 for the 1926 opener. Over the winter, the Reds' rooters were among the "wets" who unsuccessfully urged the federal government to modify Prohibition laws, citing statistics that the law had actually increased the amount of crime and drunkenness.

On the eve of the April 13 opener, women representing nine national organizations with an aggregate membership of 18 million stormed the US Senate committee hearing on Prohibition. As ardent supporters of Prohibition, they came to protest the wets' proposals. Of the 600 demonstrators, only

66 were able to squeeze into the small Senate committee room to voice their objections. They argued that any modification to the law should make it more, not less, produce, sell, or consume alcohol. Whether due to these protests or to the senators' overall reluctance to relax Prohibition, the wets failed in their efforts to loosen the limits on alcohol.

Despite the ideological controversy in the capital, baseball's senators—the Washington Senators baseball club—did something on the eve of the new season that every baseball fan could agree upon: the club decreed that President Calvin Coolidge would not have to pay for a ticket to the opening game, or for any other game of the season! The club presented him with an engraved season pass, and the American League mailed a similar pass to Mrs. Coolidge.

It seems likely that Garry Herrmann supported the women who favored Prohibition, as he announced before the opener that the team would crack down on the "rowdy element" of the vast throng expected for the holiday. Any disorderly fan at the park would be ejected and arrested.

Despite Herrmann's disdain for oratory during pregame ceremonies, Herrmann liked to have a surprise or two for the fans in addition to the customary events. This year, he "sprang a new stunt" by introducing navy blue caps for the players with a red "C" stitched in front. The traditional white caps had typically become dirty after just a few games, so Herrmann decided to discard them in favor of the darker color. The new look was an immediate hit.

Another modification that was less well received was a new ground rule declaring that a ball hit on the fly into the temporary left field bleacher seats would be a home run. Jack Ryder opined that it was a bad ground rule, "as no legitimate home run can ever be made in that direction unless the ball goes over the concrete wall." Ryder believed it was also inconsistent with the agreement that a ball hit over the ropes in center and right field was deemed a triple. Neither the umpires nor the managers explained why such a peculiar ground rule was agreed upon before the game. (The rule was abandoned before the next season's opener.)

WLW—CINCINNATI—422.3.

7:30 A. M.—Stradtman exercises.
8:00 A. M.—Y. M. C. A. devotion.
10:00 A. M.—Weather, river, police news.
11:55 A. M.—Weather, time.
12:10 P. M.—Hotel Gibson orchestra, directed by Robert Visconti.
1:00 P. M.—Opening National League baseball game; Cincinnati Reds vs. Chicago Cubs. To be announced by Powel Crosley, Jr.
1:40 P. M.—Spray service information.
4:00 P. M.—Sermon of Rev. Henry C. Koch, of St. Paul's Evangelical Church, College Hill.

The new blue lids turned out to be lucky hats, as the Reds once again came from behind in the opener for a dramatic 7–6 win in ten innings. The crowd of 32,304 was ecstatic. The cheering fans included two eighth graders who had huddled beside a bonfire from 10:30 p.m. the previous night until the ticket window opened. No doubt they were jubilant that their day of playing hooky ended in a win.

One noteworthy addition to the team on Opening Day was "The Original Spin Doctor," 22-year-old Ethan Allen. Allen had come from the campus of the University of Cincinnati to play for his hometown Reds. (Allen's .475 batting average is still a record at the school.) He remained with the Reds for four years, patrolling center field as a starter for three of those years. He later retired after 13 big-league seasons with a .300 batting average. After retiring as a player, Allen was the National League's director of motion pictures, and he wrote several instructional books about baseball. He was also the baseball coach at

Yale University for 23 seasons and named the future president, George H. W. Bush, as the team's captain in 1948. Allen was featured on the Wheaties cereal box in 1946 in a promotional gimmick connected with what is most remembered about him—his wildly popular board game, "All-Star Baseball." The game had

been conceived in 1933 when Allen was with the St. Louis Cardinals.

1927: Sacco and Vanzetti in the Headlines

Although the *Enquirer* was always generous with ink about the Reds on Opening Day, the Reds had to share the April 12 headlines with anarchists Nicola Sacco and Bartolomeo Vanzetti, who had been convicted in Massachusetts of robbery and murder. In their 1921 trial, this pair of Italian immigrants had received a death sentence from a judge who referred to the two men as "dagos" throughout the trial. The case attracted worldwide attention and drew protests for six years. On Opening Day in 1927, the *Enquirer*'s front-page story reported that after many appeals, the Massachusetts Legislature would be the final arbiter of the pair's fate. The efforts of many supporters were for naught, as the two men were executed later that summer.

After record season attendance in 1926 of 672,987, Redland Field underwent a nearly 20 percent expansion of the park's capacity. By Opening Day in 1927, seating capacity had risen to 26,000, including 5,000 field-level box seats on a wooden floor in front of the existing boxes behind home plate. To accommodate the additional seats, home plate was moved out 20 feet and turned slightly. Despite the expansion of the park, more than 8,000 of the 34,758 fans on Opening Day did not have seats, so they stood throughout the game.

The team also added more billboards atop the signs already adorning the left field wall, making this "billboard monster" 30 feet high. Herrmann had originally wanted to build a new, larger ballpark, but the city rejected his offer to buy the site of a nearby jail, and Herrmann refused to build in Bond Hill, an area north of downtown. The Reds remained at the intersection of Findlay Street and Western Avenue for the next 43 years.

"Shelve th' Ifs an' th' Ands," Real Thing Is On Today

Due To Increased Seating Greatest Crowd Ever To See Contest in Cincinnati Will Be on Hand.

Interest in the national pastime had never been greater. Two days before the opener, National League future Hall of Famer Rogers Hornsby sent a letter to American League future Hall of Famer Ty Cobb. Cobb was on his way to becoming the all-time hits leader (later eclipsed by the Reds' Pete Rose in 1985). Hornsby sent his observations about spring training to Cobb, speculating that managers would employ the sacrifice hit and stolen base more often because of a "slower ball." He said he had a feeling Cobb was going to have another big year, concluding with, "I certainly hope so." The *Enquirer* published Hornsby's letter in its entirety on Opening Day.

Like the rest of the nation, Cincinnati had a case of baseball fever. The Cincinnati Street Railway added extra cars to carry the anticipated record crowd, knowing fans would be eager to see the renovated ballpark. The early throngs were "favored with sparkling practice stunts by both teams" that kept the early arrivals amused before the concert. Despite the day being cloudy, Weber's "famous fair-weather band caused the clouds to blow away and the afternoon was perfect for the pastime." Radio station WLW recognized the fans' surging interest in the opening game and came on the air a full half-hour before

the first ball was pitched. The station's owner and future owner of the team, radio magnate Powell Crosley Jr. delighted listeners at home by interviewing several of the leading players and the two teams' managers before the game—another first for Cincinnati.

Many rooting parties paraded once again, but Findlay Market stole the show by marching around the field, headed by Esberger's Band, and presenting another large floral baseball supported by crossed bats to manager Jack Hendricks. (After the Reds lost that day, Jack Ryder speculated that the result might have been quite different if Pirates pitcher Ray Kramer had been forced to pitch with the floral ball.) Even the three umpires assigned to the game were not neglected; they were presented with flowers by their "fellow sufferers" of the Cincinnati Umpires Association. The umpires of local amateur games sympathized with the professional umpires, as they understood what it was like to bear the brunt of fans disappointed with calls against their team.

The Reds were handicapped that afternoon by the absence of first baseman Wally Pipp. Pipp is remembered for his quote that he had taken "the two most expensive aspirins in history" in 1925 when a headache sidelined him, and the Yankees inserted a rookie by the name of

ROSTER OF REDS, 1927

Following are the officials and members of the Cincinnati Ball Club: August Herrmann, President; Frank J. Behla, Business Manager; C. J. McDiarmid, Secretary; John C. Hendricks, Manager; Roderick J. Wallace, Coach; Grover C. Land, Coach. Trained at Orlando, Fla.

	Age.	Height.	Weight.	Bats.	Thrs.	Club in 1926.	Btg. Ave.	Fldg. Ave.
CATCHERS.								
Eugene F. Hargrave	34	5.11	170	R.	R.	Reds	.353	.988
Valentine Picinich	30	5.9	165	R.	R.	Reds	.263	.967
Clyde L. Sukeforth	24	5.10	155	L.	R.	Nashua	.367	.981
INFIELDERS.								
Hugh Melville Critz	26	5.7	148	R.	R.	Reds	.270	.981
Charles W. Dressen	28	5.8½	151	R.	R.	Reds	.266	.966
Horace Mills Ford	29	5.10	165	R.	R.	Minneapolis-Reds	.288	.972
George Lange Kelly	31	6.3½	193	R.	R.	Giants	.303	.989
Ralph A. Pinelli	30	5.8	155	R.	R.	Reds	.222	.978
Walter C. Pipp	34	6.2	180	L.	L.	Reds	.291	.992
Clarke A. Pittenger	27	5.10	160	R.	R.	Louisville	.312	.943
Harry A. Schwab	23	6.00	180	L.	R.	Seattle	.373	.990
OUTFIELDERS.								
Ethan Nathan Allen	23	6.00	175	R.	R.	Reds	.308	1.000
Raymond B. Bressler	32	6.00	187	R.	L.	Reds	.357	.970
Walter Christensen	27	5.8½	157	L.	L.	Reds	.350	.978
William Curtis Walker	30	5.9½	165	L.	R.	Reds	.306	.961
William A. Zitzmann	29	6.00	180	R.	R.	Reds	.245	.965
PITCHERS.							Won.	Lost.
Peter J. Donohue	26	6.1	170	R.	R.	Reds	20	14
Peter Jablonowski	22	5.11	180	R.	R.	Waterbury	7	6
Raymond Carl Kolp	29	6.00	175	R.	R.	St. Paul	18	11
Charles F. Lucas	24	5.10	155	L.	R.	Reds	3	5
Adolfo Luque	36	5.10	170	R.	R.	Reds	13	16
Frank Spruell May	30	5.8	162	R.	L.	Reds	13	9
Carl William Mays	34	5.10½	195	L.	R.	Reds	19	12
Arthur N. Nehf	34	5.8	170	L.	L.	Giants-Reds	0	9
Eppa Rixey	35	6.5	204	L.	L.	Reds	14	8

(Compiled by Charles J. Foreman. Copyright, 1927.)

Lou Gehrig into the starting lineup. Gehrig would go on to play 2,130 consecutive games at first base—a record that stood for 56 years until it was eclipsed by Cal Ripken Jr. For the 1927 opener, Pipp had a stomach ailment and was replaced in the lineup by future Hall of Famer George Kelly, but unlike in 1925, Pipp returned to the lineup after his brief illness.

1928: Where is Cy Young?

When Garry Herrmann stepped down as president of the Reds after the 1927 season, citing poor health and deafness, new owner Campbell Johnson ("C.J.") McDiarmid grabbed the reigns. He made an immediate splash, announcing that the retired star and future Hall of Famer, Cy Young, would toss out the first ball. Young would be the first former baseball great to be given the honor.

McDiarmid also invited several dignitaries, including the current and past governors of Ohio, Cincinnati mayor Murray Seasongood, and the MLB commissioner, Kenesaw Mountain Landis. The dignitaries' boxes were decorated with flags and bunting. Herrmann attended his first game as a fan in 25 years.

Although the reserved seats had not sold out as quickly as in previous years, they had all been bought by early March. According to Ryder, there was "no more pitiful sight outside of a hospital or an asylum than was furnished … by the spectacle of short sighted-fans rushing around at the final moment vainly begging for box scats down in front, or even a perch on the roof of the grand stand." The gates to the park opened earlier than ever before, at 10:00 a.m., to accommodate the bleacherites

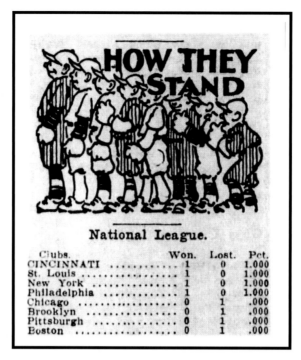

HOW THEY STAND

National League.

Clubs.	Won.	Lost.	Pct.
CINCINNATI	1	0	1.000
St. Louis	1	0	1.000
New York	1	0	1.000
Philadelphia	1	0	1.000
Chicago	0	1	.000
Brooklyn	0	1	.000
Pittsburgh	0	1	.000
Boston	0	1	.000

and the fans who would be required to stand, a total predicted to reach 16,000. The eventual crowd of 30,517 was lower than expected due to chilly weather, parking and traffic difficulties, and the emergence of radio as a substitute for attending in person.

WLW arranged with McDiarmid to place microphones in both dugouts, and members of both teams tried their hands at broadcasting during batting practice. After the band finished its concert, the crowd waited eagerly for the arrival of Cy Young. Everybody wanted to see the greatest pitcher of all time, who was now a farmer in Tuscarawas County, Ohio. His motorcade from Columbus encountered the heavy traffic around the ballpark and, like many others that day, he arrived late. The game was delayed for four minutes with the hope that Young would arrive soon, but the real first pitch of the game by Dolph Luque was delivered just as Young entered the park. He was a moment too late.

Less noticed in the crowd was ardent fan John D. Spilman of Clifton. He and his wife of 57 years celebrated their wedding anniversary at the opener and were lifelong Cincinnatians. Spilman's claim to fame was that he had attended every game played by the 1869 Red Stockings. Equally amazing was the story of Pat Rogan, from Wellston, Ohio, a small farming community approximately 100 miles east of Cincinnati. Rogan was blind, and 1928 marked the fortieth Opening Day game he had attended in Cincinnati.

The women in the crowd did not escape notice by Ryder, who patronizingly reported:

> In almost equal numbers with the rooters of the sterner sex appeared the beauty and grace of the city, for the ladies were there in full force and a birds-eye view of the various sections of the huge stand furnished a dazzling and colorful sight. The day was not ideal for the display of feminine finery, but the ladies were brave enough to make a merry showing, and their presence added much to the beauty of the scene.

A photographer from Chicago was no doubt clicking photos of some of these members of the fairer sex before he needed to leave to meet his deadline. His plane departing for Chicago circled the field in the sixth inning and surprised the crowd as the pilot banked over the grandstand in its final maneuver.

Speaking of planes, the next day's paper reported on the first attempt by three Germans, later dubbed "The Three Musketeers of the

Sky," who were taking off from Ireland and attempting the first successful transatlantic flight from east to west. (American Charles Lindbergh had flown west to east the previous year.) The trio successfully landed on Greenley Island, Canada, which is small, barren, and rocky. The crew was fortunate that the airplane landed in a peat bog, damaging the plane but likely saving their lives. Three hours after they touched down, the story was in all the newsrooms along the Eastern seaboard.

1929: The Expansion of "Reds on Radio"

At a campaign-style rally at Music Hall on the eve of the April 16 opener, the Cincinnati Community Chest launched its aggressive goal to raise over $2 million to serve the needy. The organization, founded in 1915, had recruited 7,000 volunteers to raise an average of $300 each. While the rally was in progress, 200 recruits from a small area north of town called Hartwell stayed home and raised more than their goal of $4,000 during a two-hour canvass; the results were announced at the rally, and the audience roared with approval.

Cincinnati baseball fans awoke on the cold, windy, and damp Opening Day the next morning to news that Babe Ruth, a New York Yankee, had obtained a license to marry Claire Merritt Hudson. The Sultan of Swat had denied that he had intentions to marry the actress, and when pressed by reporters for the exact date of their wedding, the Babe retorted, "I don't know myself just when it will be. Someday this week, probably. Remember, the baseball season opens tomorrow." The couple married two days later and remained together until Ruth's passing in 1948. Mrs. Ruth would live to see two of her husband's most famous records broken: the single-season record of 60 home runs, surpassed by Roger Maris in 1961, and the career record of 714 home runs, which was tied by Henry "Hank" Aaron in Cincinnati on Opening Day, 1974, and broken by Aaron just days later.

Why did the fans, and indeed all of the citizens, of Cincinnati care about the wedding plans of a player in the other league on Opening Day? The Babe, both figuratively and literally, was the largest sports figure of his day. In an era of relatively few home runs, Ruth captivated the

Learn to Pitch

Babe Ruth

Tells How In

The Enquirer

Every Monday, Wednesday and Saturday.

A remarkable set of articles by the King of Swat himself.

1929

A Happy Moment for Cincinnati baseball fans who could not make it out to old Redland Field, took place in 1929. Bob Burdett became the very first sportscaster to announce a baseball game from the grandstand roof where he could see all the action and give the listeners a really accurate account of the game.

nation with his ability to hit the long ball and pitch effectively.

The Reds, WLW, and little-known station WFBE warmed the hearts of Cincinnati fans by announcing that Opening Day would no longer be the only game broadcast by the station. In addition to hearing play-by-play for the opening game, fans would be able to tune in to hear 40 of the Reds' home games that year. WLW's Bob Burdette and Harry Hartman on WFBE became the first regular announcers to serve as the "voice(s) of the Reds." The chance to listen to the game from home helps explain why the attendance for April 16 was the smallest since 1919 at 24,822. The 42-degree temperature also kept pneumonia-fearing patrons away from the park.

The fans who did attend the game were treated to the customary pregame show and a new twist initiated by the Findlay Market rooters during their parade inside the park. The organization had chosen Tobey, a bricklayer from Oxford, Ohio, to lead the parade and throw out 18 baseballs to fans in the bleachers. Governor Myers returned to a tradition from the 1890s by throwing the first pitch to the umpire, who picked up the ball as it rolled gently toward the plate.

But for the fact that it was Opening Day, the game would have been postponed because of the miserable weather conditions. Like his predecessor, however, McDiarmid decided that the game should go on because so many people had looked forward to the occasion and had made sacrifices to be there. The Reds lost 5–2, partly because Cardinal left fielder Chick Hafey hit a ball that fell among the rear rows of the temporary "circus seats" in left field. By the time Reds outfielder Pid Purdy retrieved the ball behind the rooters, Hafey had circled the bases for an inside-the-park, two-run homer. The game was played in an hour and 17 minutes, tied for the shortest opener in history.

The next morning's *Enquirer* reassured fans that all was not lost for the season despite the disappointing opening. It featured a cartoon headlined "Sour Start May Presage Sweet Ending!" On the national scene, President Herbert Hoover had similarly calmed the nerves of the public by downplaying the economic effects of a farming crisis and a slowing construction industry. Hoover was of the opinion that the quieting of speculation after a small stock market crash in March was a healthy influence on the business cycle. Hoover's optimism was misplaced, as six months later, the stock market crashed on October 29, known as "Black Tuesday." Thank goodness, the Community Chest was ready to help those in need.

HARD TIMES FOR THE NATION

It moves in slowly / A quiet pause from years past / the restless timing, the restless March / Ah the waiting, the coming of April / Watching for the day the leaves come out / Listening for the dull roar of victories past / the surging crowds moving across the bridges / coursing alleys / plodding ramps / The quiet hopes, the anticipation, the exhilaration / the Reds are coming north / coming back to wed another spring / coming back to breathe another greening / another warmth / another race / for seasons past, and seasons to come.

Louise W. Borden, Cincinnati author and speaker

The stock market crash ushered in 15 years of struggle and heartbreak for many Americans. The Great Depression created record levels of unemployment, deflation, and homelessness during the 1930s despite President Roosevelt's controversial "New Deal" programs designed to stimulate the economy. The rise of the Nazis in Germany resulted in another world war, and baseball players joined the war effort during the early 1940s amid a period of sacrifice nationwide.

Through it all, interest in the national pastime ebbed and flowed, but one constant remained: the hope that came with Opening Day.

1930: Choice Seats Sold for "Christmas"

Cincinnati experienced a string of bank robberies in early 1930. On April 15, fans woke up to news of a particularly bold bank looting in the southeastern Cincinnati suburb of Amelia. Four masked robbers had grabbed all the currency in sight at the bank—$2,700—and had escaped. They eluded police officers, including several who searched for them from two airplanes. Other reports in the newspaper described the "depression" in American business and industry but focused on optimistic projections of an economic rebound. Most Cincinnatians believed the worst was behind them and that the successes of the Roaring Twenties would soon return.

And so, despite ripples of a recession at the very least, Mayor Russell Wilson proclaimed the return of spring in a letter published in the *Enquirer*:

> The opening of the baseball season resembles Christmas in that it comes but once a year. Of course, 'the flowers that bloom in the spring' herald the vernal season, and other manifestations of nature declare the glories of April. But to the average American the opening of the baseball season is a necessary confirmation of the advent of spring.

Jack Ryder followed the mayor's lead with the Christmas theme and reported that reserved seats "are as scarce as were bones and Mother Hubbard's famed cupboard," because "Christmas usually finds all the choice seats gone."

Predictions that baseball would begin to decline because of the increased competition from movies, golf, and radio proved to be false. Concerns that the automobile would cause fans to choose other pursuits likewise fell by the wayside. Baseball weathered the storm in each case. Interest in the national game among Cincinnatians was so high that

the *Enquirer* included a 60-page supplement devoted entirely to the Reds, their history, and the goings-on throughout the sport. The supplement contained more pages than the actual newspaper, and advertisers were eager to show their support for the team.

Indeed, the advent of automobiles only meant that more fans could motor to the park from nearly every city in Ohio, Indiana, Kentucky, and West Virginia. As fans entered the ballpark, they were entertained by music blaring from the loudspeakers. As game time approached, the Findlay Market rooters paraded around the field, preceded by a band, before they presented a United States flag to club president Sidney Weil and manager Dan Howley. Six Boy Scouts made a bow and then rushed to the flagpole in right-center field to hoist the flag. As the cheers of the crowd subsided, city manager "Colonel" Sherrill tossed the first pitch from the mound "in the general direction" of the mayor at home plate.

Included in the crowd of 30,112 were thousands of women, dubbed "fanettes," who now regularly attended games. Just before the opener, the Reds announced that there would be 14 "Ladies Days" during the upcoming season, at which they would be welcomed as guests of the team.

SCORE OF YANK MARINES SLAIN

1931: Simple Ceremonies

Construction of Union Terminal, one of the last great rail stations built in America, began in 1931. It was situated just blocks from Redland Field and provided thousands of jobs to Cincinnatians. Its railroad yards reduced the parking lot at the ballpark from 1,000 to 400 spaces, so the Reds offered free parking for the first 400 cars arriving for Opening Day on April 14. They would continue the policy throughout the season.

The optimism about the economy that had surrounded the 1930 opener was long gone. The Great Depression was beginning to take hold. Nearly 30,000 businesses and 2,300 banks had failed. Since bank deposits were not insured by the federal government at the time, bank failures were catastrophic for depositors. Unemployment rose to 16 percent nationwide, and soup kitchens became increasingly common. On the international scene, as if this grim economic condition wasn't enough to dampen the spirits of baseball fans, Nicaraguan rebel bandits killed 25 United States Marines and 10 civilians in Puerto Cabezas, Nicaragua, on the eve of the opener.

Not surprisingly, it was a subdued Opening Day. Most rooters groups took the day off, with the Findlay Market group and its band receiving the sole mention in the newspapers. They presented the Reds with their customary gifts. A band concert was held before the game, followed by one of the most unusual first-pitch ceremonies in history. Mayor Russell proceeded to the pitcher's mound and, to the crowd's surprise, there were two catchers at home plate, city manager Clarence Dykstra and Ohio governor George White. Russell threw two first pitches, and both were strikes. Despite the simpler ceremonies, the game still attracted nearly 30,000 fans. Nationwide,

more fans watched a major-league game on Opening Day than ever had before.

After the Reds lost 7–3 to the Cardinals, the *Enquirer* continued an odd tradition in its reporting that it had started years earlier. While it is common for sports pages to show the standings of each league, the win and loss totals for each team are not given much attention so early in a season. (At the time, the season consisted of 154 games; the number of games has risen to 162 games today.) The morning after Opening Day, the *Enquirer* took pains to note that the Reds were in "the second division" of eight teams, tied for fifth place. Four teams naturally had won their openers, and four had lost.

1932: Trading Places

Shrugging off increasingly difficult economic times, Reds fans were in the partying mood once again on April 12. Four weeks before the opener, the Reds and Brooklyn Dodgers pulled off a blockbuster trade, with the Reds receiving three players, including Ernie Lombardi. Lombardi went on to become one of the greatest catchers in Reds history. Not

Ernie Lombardi

finished, club president Weil negotiated for over 24 hours and announced another big trade on the eve of the opener: the Reds acquired the defending National League batting king Chick Hafey from the Cardinals for two players and an undisclosed amount of cash. The amount of cash was reported to be "liberal." After a last-place finish by the Reds in 1931, these trades offered a "concentration of heavy artillery" for a previously lethargic offense.

Reds fans were rejuvenated. Despite cold weather and cloudy skies that once again threatened a postponement, there was more enthusiasm for this opener than there had been for several years. Weil generously announced on the morning of Opening Day that fans who did not want to brave the cold to see his new sluggers could redeem their tickets until noon, and that any unused tickets for the game would be honored for reserved seats at any succeeding contest.

It appears few fans cashed in on Weil's offer, as Ryder reported that "the full seating capacity of the park was jammed to the limit, with a double line of standees in right field." The eventual crowd of 25,869 arrived early despite thermometers hovering around the freezing point. The loyal fans were not disappointed. Weil had arranged for a spirited pregame demonstration. The headliners included the Lower Cincinnati Business Men's Association marching with a band, followed by the famed drum corps of the Bentley Post of the American Legion. The groups played several stirring tunes in front of the grandstand and marched off the field to great applause.

After the music had died down, the Findlay Market rooters appeared, some with unique costumes such as a few that looked like stove pipes. After a rather elaborate presentation of gifts by these faithful fans, Mayor Wilson unintentionally entertained the crowd with a

wild pitch. The game that followed was one of the most thrilling in Reds' history, as the team scored four runs in the bottom of the ninth inning. They overcame a 4–1 deficit to win their first opener since 1928. The Reds succeeded despite the Cubs delaying the game "for a long time trying to figure out how to prevent the Reds from doing just what they eventually did." The next day's *Enquirer* gave a nod to the late flurry of hits, proclaiming, "Cubs Wound up Punch Drunk in That Ninth Frame!"

The National League president, John Heydler, spent an hour during the game trying to borrow a heavier overcoat to withstand the elements. Despite being chilled, he proclaimed, "Cincinnati is certainly the opening day city, par excellence." The only somber note for the

day was a show of respect for Louis Widrig, the popular treasurer of the team who had passed away. The Reds wore mourning bands on their sleeves, and the center field flag stood at half-mast, where it would remain for 30 days.

Earning an exciting win was a welcome relief from other news dominating Opening Day coverage. Stocks continued to be liquidated, and share prices descended to a new low. Wall Street's chief was peppered by questions from the United States Senate Banking and Currency Committee, and he denied that the stock exchange was a gambling center. Locally, three priests from St. Martin's Catholic Church were robbed at gunpoint by two bandits who were accompanied by a lookout and the driver of a getaway car.

The city was also anxiously following the continuing saga of the kidnapping of Charles Lindbergh's 20-month-old son, Charles Jr. The case was in its forty-first day on Opening Day, and the *Enquirer* published daily reports on the front page. Ransom money of $50,000 that had been given to the kidnappers was found in circulation in a Connecticut bakery, and a complete list of the serial numbers of the five-, ten-, and twenty-dollar bills that had been paid were published in the paper. The next day, it was reported that part of the ransom had found its way to England, and that the toddler's mother, Anne Morrow Lindbergh, had collapsed under the strain of the kidnapping. Other reports, later denied, claimed that Colonel Lindbergh was close to a nervous breakdown. Sadly, the body of Charles Jr. was found several months after he was abducted.

1933: Beer Here!

The Great Depression continued unabated into 1933, with the unemployment rate in Cincinnati at a staggering 30 percent. Franklin Delano Roosevelt was inaugurated as president on March 4, declaring, "The only thing we have to fear is fear itself." His inauguration took place just over five weeks before Opening Day on April 12. Roosevelt immediately declared a bank holiday for one week in response to renewed stress on major banks that threatened another round of bank failures. On the morning of Opening Day, Roosevelt began discussions with members of Congress to establish some modified federal insurance on bank deposits for the first time. At the same time, the Nazi Party won a narrow majority of seats in the German federal election. As Roosevelt was taking steps to improve the American economy, readers of the *Enquirer* learned the Nazis were proclaiming that capitalism was doomed.

Since fans had so little to cheer about, the headline on the sports page urged readers to show up in force, proclaiming, "Come On, Let's Go Out, to the Old Ball Park." Sportswriters wanted to counter pessimists who were predicting such a heavy slump in attendance at various ballparks that it "would make the magnates sorry that they ever started the season." At least for one day, the skeptics were proven wrong. Opening Day was celebrated as a major civic event as always. With schools closed for the day, students did not have to come up with phony excuses for their absence, prompting the *Enquirer* to observe that "the fatality among grandmothers was much less than usual." Adults had their own reasons to celebrate the holiday: On March 21, Congress had signed the Cullen–Harrison Act, which permitted the sale of beer and wine with low alcohol content. While the full repeal of Prohibition would not occur until December 1933, fans were elated that they could buy beer at the park for the first time in 13 years! The Cincinnati branch of the Ohio Liquor Control Commission granted a permit for Redland Field just days before the opener as it worked overtime reviewing applications for beer and wine sales.

"Come On, Let's Go Out," To Old Ball Park

A cartoon in the morning paper showed the picture of a beer tap coming out of a baseball labeled "1933 Season." Fans came from all walks of life and from all sections of the city, the county, and the state. The Reds set up a rathskeller-like area beneath the main grandstand for partygoers. The grandstands, pavilion, and bleachers were full, and an overflow crowd squeezed behind the ropes in right field. Local politicians and the governor attended as usual, and the pregame parades were said to be admirable. A columnist for the *Enquirer*, Lou Smith, disclosed the next day that the local politicians obviously enjoyed themselves right along with the fans: "After spending the entire winter teaching the citizens how to be refined, what do they do—go tearing up Western Avenue, whooping and carrying on like a band of collegiates out for a lark."

With school out and beer in, 25,305 patrons enjoyed themselves on a sunny day despite a loss to the Pirates. The *Enquirer* staff opined that the game that "dragged a bit," as it crossed the two-hour limit, "which is supposed to be the absolute boundary for legitimate contests."

1934: A New Name: "Crosley Field"

> *"All the schools were out yesterday afternoon, so the fatality rate among grandmothers was much less than usual."*
>
> Enquirer editorial

After owner Sidney Weil began to veer toward bankruptcy and defaulted on loans secured by his stock in the club in late 1933, a local bank known as the Central Trust Company took control of the Reds. (Weil continued as a rabid Reds fan and later rebuilt his fortune in the life insurance business until he died in a 1966 auto accident on Columbia Parkway.) Two months before the opener on April 17, Powell Crosley Jr. organized a syndicate to purchase the team.

Powell Crosley

Crosley had made his fortune in the automobile supply business and became a pioneer in radio. He manufactured sets for home use and became a broadcaster by establishing radio station WLW in Cincinnati. WLW became known as "the Nation's Station" because its signal, backed by 500,000 watts of power, was the most robust in the world. A private man, Crosley remained behind the scenes throughout his tenure as owner for 27 years, preferring instead to give his general managers control of decisions. On the eve of the opener, the club's directors decided to rename the field "Crosley Field," which remained the name of the ballpark until it was torn down after the Reds moved to Riverfront Stadium in June 1970.

After two of the most financially disastrous years in the history of professional baseball owing to the effects of the Depression, the National League hoped to regain some of its lost fan base by introducing a livelier ball in 1934. The league wanted to bring the ball's performance in line with the one used by the American League. (Thereafter, the leagues

THAT BIG DAY WE'VE ALL BEEN WAITING FOR IS HERE!

agreed to have a standard baseball for both leagues.) The ball was expected to be a real boon to hitters and to be "a pain" to pitching craftsmen "who had rival batsmen handcuffed most of last season."

The Reds had made improvements of their own in the off-season to attract more fans. They concluded that the ballpark was in dire need of renovation. The 30,247 fans who entered the ballpark on Opening Day saw that previously gray seats had been painted green and orange. They also marveled at a rebuilt scoreboard and noticed that ads had been removed from the outfield walls. Crosley believed that a plain green background for hitters would increase offense. The only advertising left in the outfield were two giant Crosley radio images on each side of the scoreboard with the dial set for WLW, even though Reds games were broadcast on rival stations WSAI and WKRC! Temporary stands were added in left field for the opener, and the ropes were again deep in right field to accommodate the overflow crowd. The Reds players were adorned in new uniforms with a touch of blue on the sleeves and stockings.

The pregame festivities included ponies joining the Findlay Market rooters and their band. In a new twist, the McTavern Bowlers from Bellevue, Kentucky, staged a burlesque act. Flowers and other gifts were presented to the Reds as well as Cubs manager Charley Grimm. Reds general manager Larry MacPhail, manager Bob O'Farrell, and team captain Jim Bottomley received suitcases. The newspaper speculated, "Maybe they think these boys are going somewhere this summer, and possibly they are."

Fans listening at home were introduced to the voice of legendary baseball broadcaster Red Barber, who at that time was beginning his rookie season as a play-by-play announcer.

Despite new ownership, a livelier ball, and radio announcing by "the Ole Redhead," the only thing that kept the fans in the ballpark was a no-hitter by Cubs pitcher Lon Warneke that lasted through eight innings. Sensing history, the large crowd became Cubs fans momentarily and cheered when the Reds' own Ernie Lombardi struck out to begin the last frame. Despite the unexpected fan support, Warneke lost his no-hit bid two pitches later. The Reds bowed, 4–0.

The other big local story of the day concerned the bitter divorce trial in Cincinnati of Leo "the Lip" Durocher. Durocher had played

Red Barber

for the Reds from 1930 to 1933 and later coined the famous phrase "Nice guys finish last" when he was a manager. After witnesses testified that Mrs. Durocher was seen "in the company of other men" at the Netherland Plaza Hotel during the marriage, the judge refused to order the former Reds shortstop to pay any alimony. Durocher had previously agreed to pay $25 per week to help care for the couple's son.

1935: Don't Steal Our Tradition!

Horror of horrors! The National League schedule makers decided that the Reds' monopoly on Opening Day had lasted long

> *"Why does this Opening Day and the game it represents have such a hold on Cincinnati? Because it is an heirloom, a thing passed from generation to generation to generation. It is a time-worn Bible, grandma's oaken China closet, the sepia-toned daguerreotype photograph of a great- great- grandfather who fought with the Union Army at Shiloh. It is a gift, from one generation to another—the gift of baseball, with all its pleasures and disappointments, it's heart-stopping moments and even its occasional tedium … A gift from one generation to the next. A gift of memories, to be shared by the old with the young."*
>
> Howard Wilkinson, Enquirer columnist

enough. The league released a preliminary schedule for 1935 showing the Reds beginning the season in Pittsburgh. Pittsburgh had long favored opening on the road in the belief that better weather could be expected at home a little bit later in the spring. The Pirates thought starting later at home would result in larger crowds for the first game in Pittsburgh. However, a new Pirate ownership group decided that 41 years without an opener at home was long enough, and the owners petitioned the league for the opportunity to host a real opening day of their own.

Volatile general manager MacPhail protested immediately. He argued that it was a matter of simple economics. The country was in the middle of the Great Depression, and the opener in Cincinnati was a guaranteed sellout, so both teams would benefit from their share of the gate receipts. Besides that, the Reds were financially strapped. Sports writer Tom Swope of the preeminent sports publication at the time, *The Sporting News*, made what is thought to be the first claim that the Reds deserved to host the opener because

Cincinnati was the city where professional baseball was born.

MacPhail's challenge proved to be successful, as the league relented by proposing a compromise. Yes, Cincinnati would be granted the privilege of hosting the first game, but they would have to travel the next day to Pittsburgh. Crosley and MacPhail had ensured that the tradition would continue. The 1888 away game in Kansas City remains as the only scheduled opener for the Reds outside of Cincinnati.

Securing the opener was one thing, but MacPhail could not control the weather. Columnist Lou Smith informed readers that "the weather man, in his usual elephant-hearted style, promises perfect football weather for the big affair." A thin coating of snow covered the field on the morning of April 16, but the team announced early in the morning that the sold-out game would proceed. Several thousand ticketholders with reserved seats decided to stay home rather than risk the flu. Even the bleachers were partially empty as the high temperature reached only 38 degrees.

The customary first pitch and the Findlay Market parade were the only special ceremonies for the 27,400 fans, some of whom stayed long enough in the frigid conditions to see the Pirates score seven runs in an unlucky seventh inning before putting away the Reds, 12–6. The Reds and Pirates then boarded a special

train at 10:00 p.m. for another Opening Day, which the Reds ruined for the Pittsburgh faithful, winning 4–0.

As the Reds opened Pittsburgh's home season, MacPhail was completing the contract for the new lighting system at Crosley Field that would illuminate the park for the first night game in major-league history in May. MacPhail was not feeling as generous as his predecessors, however, as there would be no refunds for unused tickets to the opener.

1936: Unsold Tickets Scooped up Quickly

The April 14 *Enquirer* announced that the Hamilton County sheriff had foiled a jailbreak plot. Sheriff George Lutz had placed five prisoners in solitary confinement in the county jail after their escape plans had been discovered. On the national scene, President Roosevelt was touting a new plan to boost employment. After securing the passage of the Social Security Act the previous November, Roosevelt floated a new idea that would limit jobs to people between the ages of 18 and 65. He announced, "The period of social pioneering is only at its beginning."

But with Opening Day at hand, the *Enquirer* editorial board shrugged off the worries of the day and reminded readers that baseball represented the true soul of America:

Lucky for the politicians that the World Series is timed before the elections next November! How else would the American citizen be able to fasten his mind on the momentous issues of the nation? Recovery? Well the news about that is that the clubs last year got out of the red. Surely that is something of an index, perhaps as good as bank clearings, the number of kilowatt hours, the postal mailings. Is not baseball nearest to the heart of the American?

The paper also confirmed earlier predictions of warm weather for Opening Day after fans had suffered through one of the most miserable openers the previous year.

Like many business enterprises during the depression, the Reds were struggling to make ends meet. The team had expressed its displeasure about holding spring training in Tampa, Florida, where they often played before fewer than 200 fans. With the economy still in decline, 9,000 tickets remained available when Opening Day arrived. Fans could purchase tickets at three price points when the ticket office opened at 9:30 a.m. on game day: there were 1,500 reserved-seat tickets for $1.25, 3,000 general admission tickets for $1.10, and 4,500 bleacher tickets for $.60. Enticed by the 76-degree temperature, a cross-section of the city's population quickly scooped up the tickets. A sellout of 32,643 was assured.

Given the mixed age of the crowd, one newspaper report surmised that only half of public school classrooms were filled in the afternoon. Fans young and old enjoyed taking in the sights and sounds of the day. Some seats had been freshly painted the color of salmon, others were a medium brown or chocolate color, and the rest of the park glistened in apple green and dark green. Said the *Enquirer*, fans soaked in "fresh vapors of green paint in the heady perfume of sun-baked clay and new mown grass."

Promptly at 2:00 p.m., Smitty's Symphonic Band led the annual Findlay Market parade as it entered Crosley Field, parading around the park before the Reds and Pirates took infield practice. Bombs were then dropped from the grandstand roof to signal the beginning of the official ceremonies, causing considerable excitement behind home plate as fiery fragments fluttered from the sky through the backstop screen. Women were again out in large numbers, and some "Easter finery" may have been scorched. Tobey the bricklayer circled the bases to the amusement of fans, followed by the Norwood, Ohio, post of the American Legion Drum Corps escorting the flag to the center field flag pole as the band played the national anthem.

The Reds and Pirates found themselves in a slugfest, with the Reds falling 8–6. Future Reds broadcaster and Hall of Famer Waite Hoyt was the winning pitcher for the second year in a row. He remains the only opposing hurler to win two consecutive openers in Cincinnati.

Meanwhile, at Opening Day in New York, Babe Ruth was celebrated for 15 minutes prior to the game before he settled into a box seat as a Yankees' spectator for the first time in 22 years. (The Reds had unsuccessfully sought to lure Ruth out of retirement a month earlier, at which point his legendary career officially ended.)

Crosley Field did double duty for several years, as the Reds shared Crosley in 1936 and 1937 with a Negro American League team, the Cincinnati Tigers. The Tigers used the discarded uniforms worn by the Reds in the prior season.

1937: Worst Flood Ever Retreats Just in Time

The April 20 opener was especially welcome relief for a city recovering from the worst flood in Cincinnati history. The flood caused widespread suffering in a city already hurting from the Great Depression. The Ohio River crested at 79.9 feet in late January, completely submerging buildings in the neighborhood surrounding the ballpark. At the high-water mark, 21 feet of water stood at home plate, and the lower grandstand was underwater. Groundskeeper Matty Schwab's underground drainage system had betrayed him by allowing water to backflow into the park. The water so overwhelmed the park that two Reds pitchers and Schwab hit a "home run" by rowing a boat over the center field wall. Newspapers around the country published pictures of the escapade.

The ballpark suffered significant damage to the playing field and the concession stands. Fortunately, the river subsided over the ensuing weeks, and Schwab was able to repair the damage and prepare the field for Opening Day. So, when the holiday finally arrived, fans were ready to enjoy a spring day and take their minds off their troubles. A temperature of 73 degrees assured there would be a full house. The largest crowd since 1927 arrived at the ballpark early, with a number of rabid fans camping out overnight. The sundeck in right field began to fill at 10:30 a.m. The unreserved seats were packed by noon, with holders of reserved seats taking a more leisurely approach. More tickets could have been sold to make it a record crowd, but the Reds heeded the warning of the city's safety department and closed ticket windows just before noon. Charles Reickel of Cynthiana, Kentucky, made sure he arrived on time, as he had not missed an opening game in 50 years! At age 101, he was accompanied by his grandson. Reickel was featured in the next morning's paper as the winner of a "Memory Derby," because he recalled attending the 1867 opener of the amateur Cincinnati Red Stockings!

The attendance of 34,374 was the largest since 1927 and the third largest opener in Reds history to date. It was the most watched game in the National League that day. As fans entered the ballpark, they noticed that beams supporting the grandstand had markers on them to indicate the height of the flood waters. The flagpole had a line on it in center field pointing out that the water had been higher than the center field wall. After the Findlay Market rooters paraded from Over-the-Rhine to march around the field, and Tobey the "Wild Bricklayer" from Oxford circled the bases and strutted in front of the stands, one of the players who had rowed over the scoreboard, Charlie Grissom, jumped in front of Henry Fillmore's band, grabbed a baton, and danced to "The Organ Grinder's Swing." Perhaps fearing he could not top those antics, Mayor Wilson then decided to throw the first pitch from the stands instead of from the mound. His toss sailed wide of the mark. For the first reported time, airplanes flew over Crosley Field carrying banners for stoves and beer.

The Reds lined up along the third baseline for the national anthem to the delight of the crowd. The fans were excited not only because of the dawn of a new season but because they approved of the team's new attire. The *Enquirer* made known its observation that the Reds clearly showed up their opponents in the fashion department:

> Our boys, dressed in their flashy new outfits, presented a striking contrast with the Cards when the two teams lined up at home plate before the game. The Reds looked as sparkling as a crowd of overstuffed jockeys in riding colors in their new red satin jackets, white trousers, and black caps with red peaks. The Gas House Gang looked just like that in their sweat jersey material jackets.

Pitcher Chuck Dressen then started the official proceedings for the home team. He was described in the paper as "a fighting mad nag that can chew 'em all up. Only too much Rhineland [as Cincinnati was nicknamed] beer can stop 'em." He was good, but St. Louis star Dizzy Dean won the duel, completing a 2–0 shutout.

Opening Day folklore in Cincinnati includes the myth that, because the city has bragging rights to the first professional team in baseball, the team is always accorded the privilege of having the first big-league game of each season. But 1937 is one of many examples of why this is a myth. By April 20, Boston and Philadelphia had already played two games in the National League, and Philadelphia and Washington had played the American League opener the previous afternoon. There was no reported protest from the fans in Cincinnati at the time, confirming that the real tradition is simply that the Reds are the only team that is scheduled to open at home every year.

The dominance of the pitchers in 1937 likely precipitated action by the major leagues.

Club owners decided to take steps to offer the baseball public a better "show" by making accommodations to allow for more night games and by "deadening" the baseball. Balls that are deadened are softer, thereby reducing the distance the ball can travel off the bat.

In less important news for fans, President Roosevelt announced in a special budget message that there would be a larger-than-expected deficit coupled with new taxes. His counterpart on the world stage, German Reichsfuhrer Adolf Hitler, then made a surprise announcement that he would be willing to attend an international economic conference if President Roosevelt convened such a summit. Roosevelt declined to do so.

1938: Strange Numbering

By the time the Reds departed for Tampa for spring training, the April 19 opener was sold out. An *Enquirer* editorial summarized the importance of the game to Cincinnatians under the title "Play Ball":

> The soldiers, the statesmen, the aviators, the economists, the politicians, the ax murderers, and all of the folk who customarily bathe in the public spotlight are escorted to back seats on the news rostrum today, so far as Cincinnati is concerned. For today is the opening game of the 1938 season at Crosley Field. To this baseball-minded community, it is an event much like the day the cherry blossoms bloom in Washington, or the day the ice goes out at an Alaskan seaport.

Taking a back seat to the game was news that morning that city manager C.O. Sherrill had proposed a vast public improvement program to the city council. Cincinnati was eligible for over $1 million in federal aid as part of another New Deal proposal in Congress. Sherrill's plan included a joint armory and municipal auditorium, a new city hall, conversion of the rapid transit system to accommodate buses and trucks to take them off the downtown streets, expansion and improvement of the waterworks system, and extensive street and sewer projects.

"Opening Day is for dreamers. The slate is clean and the first ball has yet to be scuffed. Hundred possibilities hang on every pitch in a nation pauses to look for a pattern in the first acts of a new season."

Tim Sullivan, Enquirer sports columnist

The Reds must have thought that they, too, could receive federal funding to pay for their pet project. For reasons otherwise unexplained, the team announced that it was adopting new uniforms that would eliminate all player numbers from 1 to 34! A sellout crowd entering Crosley Field learned that star catcher Ernie Lombardi was now number 35, and coach Ed Roush was assigned the highest number, 67. Perhaps the Reds simply wanted to make sure that patrons purchased scorecards. In any event, it was the strangest numbering system ever used by a major-league team. (The novel plan lasted only one year.)

For the first time in its history, the Cincinnati Street Railway chartered every available bus operated by the company to accommodate the sellout crowd of 34,148, largely because of an acute parking situation at the ballpark. After arriving at Crosley, a large part of the crowd was ushered to their seats by athletes from Hughes, Purcell, Roger Bacon, and Western Hills high schools who wore their monogrammed sweaters for the occasion. Noted the *Enquirer*, "Everybody and his brother was on deck: from the boys and girls who chase foxes in redcoats to those who still eat dinner at noon and supper in the evening."

Once the fans were settled, the traditional pregame ceremonies proceeded as expected. One addition was the presentation of a birthday cake to a new Reds outfielder, Harry Craft, and a players' parade. After Craft blew out the candles and the flag was raised in center field, the Reds and Cubs paraded across the field with the band playing "Happy Days Are Here Again." After the umpire sternly ordered the removal of several thousand dollars' worth of camera equipment that he referred to as "high-priced flicker boxes," the season was on.

Under sunny skies and warm temperatures, the Cubs won 8–7, but only after the most controversial game-ending play in Reds' Opening Day history. With two outs in the bottom of the ninth, pinch hitter Willard Hershberger scored the apparent tying run on an infield single, sending the crowd into a wild frenzy. But umpire Larry Goetz, who had been presented a floral bouquet in the pregame ceremonies, pointed to third base and signaled that the runner behind Hershberger should have been called out for running more than three feet out of the baseline to avoid a tag before Hershberger crossed the plate. Reds manager Bill McKechnie was apoplectic, but his protests fell on deaf ears. The game was over. It would be the last game witnessed by 102-year-old Charles Reickel, who is believed to be the oldest fan to have attended Opening Day in Cincinnati.

1939: Another Flood Threatens the Opener

Storm clouds were gathering worldwide on the eve of the April 17 opener. As Germany appeared to be planning to expand its empire into Eastern Europe, President Roosevelt had directed an open message of peace to Hitler and Italian prime minister Benito Mussolini. Roosevelt called for the two nations to pledge at least ten years of nonaggression to 31 nations and to participate in a world conference working toward peace, disarmament, and better trade relations. On Opening Day, the United Press reported that Mussolini had violently denounced the proposal, accusing Roosevelt of being ignorant of history, and he encouraged Hitler to follow suit. The United States was already on edge after reports of the continuing war between China and Japan, which had begun in 1937. The Associated Press reported that Chinese officials had asked a Minneapolis, Minnesota, manufacturer for a quote on the production of 50,000 artificial legs and arms for crippled war victims. The Chinese had been using bamboo to make temporary legs.

Cincinnati fans were anxiously awaiting the 1939 season, promoted as the one hundredth anniversary of the beginning of baseball. Mother Nature and "Old Sol" appeared not to be in a mood to cooperate just two years after the 1937 flood that had jeopardized Opening Day. This time, the pair waited until the weekend before the game to unleash torrential rains on the city. By the morning of April 17, the Ohio River had surged 20 feet to the flood stage of 52 feet. The river was expected to rise a steady quarter foot per hour. Fans, and no doubt Reds officials and players, were advised by forecasters that, if the river surpassed 54 feet, the dugouts would begin to flood; at 56 feet, "the outfielders must use pontoons. At 58 feet the hottest pitcher will have watercooled feet." The headline that morning ominously guessed that the river "May Touch 58."

Nature relented, however, and the "Reds nosed out Ol' Man River and the elements in a photo finish," observed the *Enquirer*. The rain subsided before noon, just a few inches of rain invaded the dugout, and the players and photographers made an improvised bridge from the playing field to the bench by laying boards over the water. Honoring his promise of the previous day, the grounds superintendent somehow had the playing field in excellent condition after the infield had been wearing its "canvas jacket" for three days. The outfield drains were operating perfectly.

No doubt as a result of the impact of the flood on their homes and workplaces, the closing of major highways leading into Cincinnati, and the uncertain weather forecast, fans did not turn out in their usual numbers. By game time, the smallest attendance (30,644) in almost a decade had streamed into the ballpark for the battle with Pittsburgh. When the huge tarpaulin was rolled up at 1:00 p.m., the crowd let out a cheer when they could see that the playing field appeared to be in "splendid shape." The customary parades still took place, and flowers were presented to the managers of both teams by local politicians. Mayor James

Garfield Stewart had the honor of presenting a bouquet to the Reds manager, proclaiming, "Because we love you and have confidence in you we present you these flowers." After Stewart waved the American flag and delivered a sizzling strike to Honus Wagner, one of five inaugural inductees into baseball's Hall of Fame just three years earlier, the sun miraculously broke through the threatening clouds.

Reds Uniform 1939

The Reds managed to set a record that still stands today, but it is one they would rather forget. They lost to the Pirates for the seventh consecutive time on Opening Day. The most talked-about event marring the opener was when the Redlegs (as the Reds were often referred to in the 1930s) shortstop Billy Myers was hit in the head by a thrown ball as he hustled down the first baseline for a single in the second inning. Time was called as the team physician hurried out of the stands and performed an examination. The doctor ordered Myers rushed to a local hospital, and he was carried to the dugout by four teammates. National League president Ford Frick, watching the game from the press box, thought Myers should have been carried on a stretcher from the field rather

than in the players' arms, but a stretcher was at least brought for his journey to the waiting ambulance. Myers regained consciousness soon after arriving at the hospital. He did not recall what happened and insisted he be permitted to leave the hospital and return to the game. Given that he was diagnosed with a concussion, his request was denied. In probable noncompliance with today's concussion protocols, he was allowed to return to action the following Sunday for the second game of the season after the Reds had sustained three consecutive postponements due to rain in Cincinnati and snow in Chicago.

The next day's coverage focused on the weather conditions, Myers's injury, and the "colorless" though vocal crowd. In her column "Skirting the Field," *Enquirer* writer Sue Goodwin gave this description:

> Well, it's all over but the shouting, and that goes on and on even if we did lose. In Hollywood they'd say it was colossal, stupendous, and magnifious! Usually the grandstand is a riot of color on opening day, but the rain and Old Man River had us all in our hip boots and the seething mass was colorless, but only as to togs. A throatier 30,000 could be found nowhere.

The international storm clouds turned more ominous throughout the summer, and World War II began on September 1, just four weeks before the Redlegs clinched their first National League pennant in 20 years in the third-to-last game of season.

VOL. C. NO. 8—DAILY   Entered as second-class matter Post Office, Cincinnati, Ohio.   ***** WEDNESDAY MORNING, APRIL 17, 1940   26 PAGES   THREE CENTS In Hamilton County and Campbell and Kenton Counties   FIVE CENTS ELSEWHERE

HOMERS BY REDLEGS BEAT CUBS, 2-1

1940: Where's the Championship Flag?

The morning *Enquirer* said it all: "It's Opening Day for the National League Champs of 1939." After the Reds' first World Series appearance in 20 years the previous fall, albeit a losing outing, Cincinnati fans eagerly anticipated the raising of the 1939 National League pennant in center field on April 16. When the club announced they would delay that celebration until the following homestand (to boost attendance), it served as the only disappointment

of the day as the Reds won their first opener since 1932, beating the Cubs 2–1. The winning run scored in the bottom of the eighth inning.

Prognosticators of the sport had established the Reds as the favorites to repeat as league champions. Fans also felt optimistic about the season, and the team welcomed its then fourth-largest crowd (34,342) in Opening Day history, grossing $50,000 for the team's business office. The early-arriving fans were treated to a home run exhibition during batting practice, and they saluted the darling of Redleg fans, Ernie Lombardi, forgiving him for his oft-criticized fielding gaffe (known as "the Snooze") in Game Four of the 1939 World Series. Lombardi's error did not affect the outcome of the game, as the Yankees were already about

to sweep the Reds when Lombardi missed a tag on Joe DiMaggio at home. Some analysts even say Lombardi had been knocked unconscious by the previous baserunner, coming to just in time to attempt to tag the oncoming DiMaggio. In any event, Reds fans were ready to cheer on their favorite catcher by the time the 1940 season rolled around.

The Findlay Market Association winded its way from Elder Street to the ballpark, led by Mayor Stewart and Smitty's band. These rooters were armed with miniature baseball bats and canes. At the ballpark, they were met with the sights and sounds of new hot dog stands and vendors selling championship pennants. The rooters presented their traditional flag and floral display, and Tobey the bricklayer ran the bases as usual. The only other deviation from the traditional festivities of recent years was that the honor of the first pitch was bestowed upon Ohio governor John Bricker instead of Mayor Stewart. Disdaining his topcoat in the chilly breeze, the governor bounced the ball from his box seat alongside Cincinnati's dugout to fan favorite Lombardi.

Meanwhile, up north in Chicago, Bob Feller of the Cleveland Indians pitched the first and only no-hitter on Opening Day in a 1–0 victory over the White Sox.

1941: Championship Rings amid Winds of War

By April 15, the world war in Europe and Asia was becoming what would become the deadliest conflict in human history. Germany now controlled much of continental Europe, and battles were being waged primarily between the European Axis powers (Germany and its allies) and the coalition of the United Kingdom and the British Commonwealth. Air and sea battles were also taking place in Africa and the Atlantic Ocean.

Attack Coming, Nazis Warn; Line Reinforced, British Say

The United States was providing aid to Great Britain, but the official policy of the US government was to remain neutral. Cincinnati fans woke up on Opening Day anxiously awaiting the celebration of the Reds' first world championship since 1919. Their enthusiasm was tempered by news of increasingly likely involvement of the United States in the war. Henry Stimson, secretary of war, revealed that the army had spent more than $6 billion on military contracts during the previous eight months. He added that the nation's armed forces needed to be trained "for the possibilities of war in many and varied terrains."

Given the threat of war, Major League Baseball found itself in a state of mixed emotions ranging from worry about the war to gleeful optimism about the coming season. On the one hand, there was "fresh" money in circulation from the boom in defense contracts; on the other hand, there was an underlying fear that players would enlist or be drafted. The dean of baseball, Connie Mack, predicted that "folks will be wanting to go to ball games and relax." Lou Smith of the *Enquirer* advised readers to put their worries aside: "Our town, rated the tops in all baseball, has gone completely mad. Let the rest of the world worry about wars, dictators and revolutions; we have this little matter of our Reds to concern us."

Indeed, preparations had been made for one of the largest Opening Day celebrations in the city's history. In 1940, the Reds had become the first team to ever win 100 games. In light of the club's thrilling seven-game World Series victory over Detroit, including winning the final two games at Crosley Field, fan interest was high. Tickets were in short supply, and fans who were intent on attending the opener but did not want to stand in line for bleacher seats were forced to pay scalpers a hefty premium: $5.00 for reserved seats with a face value of $1.75!

Many dyed-in-the-wool fans were willing to stand in line for many hours, so the bleacher seats sold out shortly after those gates opened at 10:00 a.m. The Findlay Market parade began in Over-the-Rhine, accompanied by Tobey, the bricklayer from Oxford, who sported a new Uncle Sam outfit. He would later perform his usual antics before the game. When the fans and partygoers entered the park, which was decorated in patriotic fashion with bunting and flags, they could not help but notice the new red, white, and blue sign along the left field line: "Our Country, in her intercourse with other nations, may she always be in the right, but Our Country right or wrong."

After the traditional parade around the field, Schmitty's Band, the Findlay Market Band, and a group of Boy Scouts circled the pitcher's mound to witness the presentation of World Series rings to the Reds by Commissioner Kenesaw Mountain Landis. The fans responded with wild applause. Powell Crosley and National League president Ford Frick then marched four abreast across the field with the players from each team to watch the world championship pennant be hoisted below the American flag on the center field pole. The celebration then became more somber with the playing of the "Star-Spangled Banner," as the fans were well aware that ominous war clouds were looming throughout the land.

The all-star cast of VIPs included the mayor of Cincinnati and a longtime Reds fan, Senator

A. B. "Happy" Chandler of Kentucky. Ohio governor John W. Bricker officially started the season with a toss from Box 149. The Cardinals dampened the crowd's enthusiasm with a come-from-behind, 7–3 win. Although attendance fell short of the "announced crowd" record set in 1924, club secretary Gabe Paul announced "with a big proud smile" that the paid admission count of 34,947 was an all-time record for Opening Day. (There remains skepticism as to whether the 1924 figure was padded by team officials.) The *Enquirer* highlighted the attendance of three women who had missed "but few games in the last two seasons," one of whom was the owner of the cowbell known for its familiar "clang, clang, clang" at the games.

Eight months later, Congress declared war on Japan following the December 7 bombing of Pearl Harbor. On December11, Congress also declared war on Germany and Italy. For the next four years, Opening Day and baseball took a back seat to the war.

128

1942: World War II Takes Center Stage

Worried citizens had wondered since the Pearl Harbor attack whether the baseball season should proceed at all. However, those concerns were diminished after President Roosevelt issued his famous "Green Light" letter to Commissioner Landis on January 15. Roosevelt advised that it "would be best for the country to keep baseball going" and suggested more night games be scheduled so hard-working people could attend. In an editorial on Opening Day, the *Enquirer* agreed with FDR, reasoning that baseball is an "eminently worthwhile public entertainment" and, while many of the game's most talented players were joining the armed forces, the time had not yet come for baseball to become one of the major war casualties. But the editorial concluded rather ominously: "Let's 'play ball' while we can, and for however long we can."

As 1942 unfolded, Japan was marching forward in its conquest of Southeast Asia and, five days before the April 14 opener, the United States had suffered one of its most embarrassing defeats in the peninsula of Bataan in the Philippine Islands. General Douglas MacArthur had unsuccessfully attempted to defend the last Allied stronghold. War anxiety was at its peak. An official from the Veterans of Foreign Wars warned a Rotary Club in Newport, Kentucky, that "we are losing the war as fast as is possible." He even began to advocate for a 60-hour work week, stating that many of the citizens living in the Midwest, including Cincinnati, did not fully appreciate that the nation was in a war it could lose. He went on to say the unthinkable: "It would be a very simple matter for Cincinnati or Northern Kentucky to be bombed with modern equipment … such as incendiary bombs."

The Associated Press seemingly confirmed those fears by reporting on the morning of Opening Day that four American ships had been torpedoed off the Atlantic coast by Axis submarines, with shelling occurring within sight of hundreds of "spectators" on North Carolina's shores. President Roosevelt tried to calm nerves by confidently explaining that the United States would triumph in two or three years. He said, "I shudder to think of what would happen to any part of the hemisphere that came under German domination." Colonel Eddie Rickenbacker, an American flying ace from World War I, predicted that the war would last five years, maybe ten. Just a day earlier, a Justice Department official described prewar agreements between General Electric and German companies as amounting to the defense contractor "holding hands" with Hitler.

Reds officials were well prepared for this most unusual opener. Fans were greeted upon arrival with signs on the outfield wall that read "Remember Pearl Harbor," "For Victory, Buy Defense Bonds and Stamps," "Avoid Waste," and "Keep Fit." Foul balls could no longer be kept as souvenirs, and spectators were instructed to return them to be donated to the recreation departments of the armed forces. (The policy remained in effect throughout the war.) Commissioner Landis and the league presidents instructed umpires to be more sparing about tossing out new baseballs to replace those damaged during play. Although fans understood that slugging might be curtailed by pitchers who took advantage of scuffed baseballs, they did not complain.

The wartime opening proved to be a solemn affair. Realizing that the crowd was more concerned about what was happening on the various battlefronts and in the country's defense plants than on the baseball field, the Findlay Market Association chose to discard its tradition of presenting flowers to Reds officials and players. Instead, the head of the organization presented Reds manager Bill McKechnie with two war bonds after the band "whipped the crowd into the proper pregame spirit" with repeated renditions of "Deep in the Heart of Texas," a popular song that had just been released. The rooters requested that the first war bond be awarded to the Reds players batting in and scoring the first run.

The *Enquirer* reported on the crowd's reaction during the national anthem:

> It was a solemn-faced gathering that stood yesterday as the Stars and Stripes were being raised on the center field flag pole. It was a quiet, serious, and attentive crowd that listened to Smitt[y]'s band play the National Anthem. There was no haphazard jostling or muffled talking during the ceremony. The men, with their hats held reverently over their hearts, stood in military fashion. They then simply hold their hats and stand—first on 1 foot, then the other or with their backs to the flag. The women were just as attentive and solemn.

Bucky Walters and Ival Goodman won the war bonds, but the Pirates won the game 4–2. A sellout crowd of 34,104 left the park disappointed with a loss but hoping this would not be the last Opening Day.

Bucky Walters

1943: A Marine Throws out the First Pitch

April 21 dawned with newspaper coverage focused on promising war news from around the world. President Roosevelt and Mexican president Avila Camacho proclaimed the solidarity of the two neighboring countries in the war. There were also reports of multiple aerial blows to Japanese shipping interests under the direction of General MacArthur. A US lieutenant was quoted as predicting, presciently, that "Two years from now is just about the time we will be doing to Tokyo what's being done to Berlin today—in other words, we will be blasting the daylights out of Hirohito's sunspot …" At the same time, the Ohio Legislature was voting to relax restrictions on the employment of women during the war.

On the morning of the opener, the *Enquirer* headline reassured readers: "Yes, Ball Clubs Are Going to Play Today." Lou Smith informed readers that another war was starting in "this second year of all-out war": a war for the championship of the National League. This second war was one that fans had patiently waited for since October.

Fittingly, the Reds chose Private John Decker of the United States Marine Corps to deliver the first pitch on Opening Day. Decker became a war hero after engaging in hand-to-hand combat with Japanese soldiers during the Battle of the Solomons in August 1942. The successful encounter helped the United States gain a strategic and tactical advantage in the navy's campaign in the Pacific.

There were radio broadcasts on two stations, as the Reds had not yet granted exclusive rights to a single station. Only 27,709 fans—the smallest crowd since 1935—were there to witness Decker's first pitch, which followed his appeal for the purchase of war bonds. Meat,

butter, cheese, flour, canned goods, coffee, shoes, and heating fuel were rationed during World War II. It was a good thing coffee was not on the ration list until later in the year, as fans needed it to stay warm in 37-degree temperatures. It was so cold that some fans lit a bonfire in the left field stands.

Future Reds Hall of Fame pitcher Ewell Blackwell was missing from the roster because he was a mess sergeant with George Patton's Third Army. Blackwell went on to win two battle stars. Rumors circulated that starting pitcher Johnny Vander Meer, the only pitcher in history to throw consecutive no-hitters, was possibly to going to be inducted into the service by May 8. Reds fans put those worries aside and watched Vander Meer pitch an 11-inning

Ewell Blackwell, top, and Johnny VanderMeer

On a more serious note, the morning after Opening Day, the Associated Press reported the disturbing final words from a secret Polish radio station that had suddenly gone off the air: "The last 35,000 Jews in the Ghetto at Warsaw have been condemned to execution. Warsaw again is accurate echoing to musketry volleys. The people are murdered. Women and children defend themselves with their naked arms. Save us …" It was a grim reminder of Hitler's murderous ways and his contempt for Jewish citizens in his homeland.

1944: Joe Nuxhall Joins Club at Age 15

One of the most beloved players and broadcasters in Reds history is Joe Nuxhall. Nuxhall was little noticed by the fans when he was signed to a contract just days before the April 18 opener. Only 15 years old, Nuxhall was a student at Wilson Junior High School in Hamilton, Ohio. Nuxhall was granted an excuse to attend the game like many youngsters, but instead of occupying a bleacher seat, his seat was on the Reds bench. He was recruited after 27 players had been called to serve in the armed forces, four others had passed physical examinations and were waiting for their call, and three others were classified 1-A, meaning they could be subject to early

masterpiece, a 1–0 win over the Cardinals. The shutout was no surprise, because the Reds general manager, Warren Giles, had anticipated less scoring given the league's adoption of new balls. The new balls were supposed to be 25 percent livelier than those used in 1942, but Giles conducted a test prior to Opening Day that proved otherwise. He climbed to the roof of the grandstand and dropped 12 of the new cork and balata-center baseballs to the concrete pavement 50 feet below, as well as 12 balls used the previous year. The old balls bounced four feet higher than the new, deader balls. Not coincidentally, every game in both leagues that day ended in a shutout!

Joe Nuxhall

calls during the season. The Reds' participation in the war was not extraordinary. The draft, which required every American male between the ages of 21 and 36 to register for

12 months of military service, affected every profession and occupation. During the war, more than 500 major league players and 4,000 minor league players saw military service. Thirty-two of the 44 minor league circuits that operated in 1940 were shut down during the war years. In an *Enquirer* piece, General Brehon Somervell of the US Army opined that baseball was an important factor in helping to win the war:

> It has been said that the successes of the British Army can be traced to the cricket fields of Eton, and I may say that the sandlot's and big league parks of America have contributed their share to our military success. … Help your Army and your Navy by employing your skill and your knowledge in the maintenance of morale both at home and among our troops. It is your power to encourage both the workers and the fighters to give all they have to achieve the victory.

As the 1944 season was about to begin, there was less anxiety about the war outcome than there had been a year before. Russian troops, aided by air attacks from the Allies, were advancing in Eastern Europe. In Great Britain, all the communications of key diplomats were being censored. Why? The Allies were protecting the secrets of the coming invasion of Europe. A Bern, Germany, radio broadcast predicted that the Allied invasion "will not be long delayed" and "zero hour" was near.

> *"The playing of baseball games offers a needed recreation for those at home. News and radio reports of the game are greatly desired by men in uniform in this country and abroad. We inaugurate the 1944 National League season with this in mind."*
>
> Cincinnati Reds

Fans were prepared for the substandard play of nervous athletes who were either new to the big leagues or were concerned about their overseas teammates. They also found out that even the baseball record book was affected by the war effort. Commissioner Landis reported on the morning of the opener that the War Production Board would not grant an allotment of paper for publication of the 1944 edition of the sport's official record book.

With the anticipated successful conclusion of the war, MLB expected a bump in attendance, and Cincinnati fans proved this assumption true. On Opening Day, the city fulfilled national predictions that the leagues' largest crowd for the opener would be at Crosley Field. The Reds had painted and decorated the stands for the third wartime season, and the customary ceremonies took place. When the teams paraded across the field to the cheers of 30,054 patrons and the strains of martial music, they did so "without the rigidity of military carriage, or the precision of military step, with President Powell Crosley, Jr., General Manager Warren C. Giles, and Deacon McKechnie striding jauntily at their head." The game, though, was played with military precision in record-tying fashion. The 3–0 win by the Cubs took only one hour and 17 minutes.

Although patriotism was surging nationwide and throughout the baseball world, *Enquirer* writer Lou Smith expressed cynicism about whether owners, managers, fans, and indeed the players truly wanted to sacrifice for their country at the expense of their teams. He speculated, "As one key player after another drops through the trap door into khaki or blue, the season will turn into a summer-long mystery story. 'Who's next?' will be the $64 question." Smith added that the fear of being drafted would undoubtedly affect the quality of play:

> The performances of athletes who are nervous in the shadow of the draft will doubtless be affected, and in turn they'll affect the pennant race. How can a fellow run bases when he's weary from dodging the mailman, and how can he pitch with his fingers crossed?
>
> A broken leg, a sore arm … Accidents like these have decided past pennant races. This year the draft boards will really write the standings of the teams in both leagues, from week to week.

Oh, yes, the owners, managers, and players will have to do their screaming strictly in private, of course. They must utter the conventional "We're happy to see Ol' Joe serve Uncle Sam," and poor Joe will say: "I'm happy to go," but we all know it'll be a tough break to surrender those fat pay checks when a deferment until September would be so very, very sweet. So look for a lot of quack quotes, a lot of bologna from that quarter.

1945: FDR Remembered; Radio Rights

War conditions have made inroads on playing personnel, park, office and concession personnel and otherwise restricted our general operations, as has happened to many other businesses during war time.

Even though the play may not always be of the high standard you have seen at Crosley Field during the past six or seven years, and even though the park services may not be of the standard we desire and have had in the past, we feel sure you will understand our problems.

The typically American game of baseball is being offered for your diversion, fun and healthy relaxation in these trying times, and we will earnestly strive to make the games as attractive as we can.

The Contest Is The Thing
PLAY BALL

CINCINNATI BASEBALL CLUB

Five days before the April 17 opener, President Franklin Roosevelt died suddenly of a cerebral hemorrhage at Warm Springs, Georgia, after 12 momentous years as president. The country went into mourning just as the Allies appeared on the verge of victory in Europe.

On the eve of the opener, several developments foreshadowed victory over Germany under the new commander in chief, President Harry Truman. General Dwight Eisenhower proclaimed that "V-Day" would not be declared until all important enemy forces on the Western front had been knocked out and all major resistance ended. British Field Marshal Sir Harold Alexander announced that "the last battle, which will end the war" was started that day to drive the Germans from northern Italy. Troops from the U.S. Fifth Army joined that assault. Truman pledged to Congress that he would carry out the peace ideals of Roosevelt: there would be no terms short of unconditional surrender, and all war criminals would be prosecuted. The *Enquirer* continued its front-page tradition of listing the names of local servicemen killed or wounded in action, known as "the Day's War Heroes." On Opening Day, eight servicemen from Greater Cincinnati were listed as having been killed, along with 15 who had been wounded. But the newspaper also reported much-welcomed good news: 13 local soldiers had arrived home from German prisons.

The Reds made it a point to acknowledge the passing of FDR as well as the sacrifices made by so many families in the war effort. Each person within the crowd of 30,069 could no doubt claim a loved one, friend, or neighbor who had been or was involved in the fighting overseas. The game was another sellout, with the last of several hundred reserved "jury box" seats in the right and left field corners sold shortly after the gates opened in the morning. As guests of the team, 550 uniformed service members were sprinkled throughout the stands.

After 15 minutes of martial pageantry, the giant American flag was lowered to half-staff during the playing of the national anthem. The capacity crowd then stood reverently at attention for 30 seconds out of respect for the

U. S. AND RUSSIAN FORCES REPORTED JOINED

memory of FDR. Flags on top of the grand-stand were also lowered to half-mast, where they remained for the next 30 days. New Ohio governor Frank Lausche tossed a ball from the stands to his defeated opponent from the November election, Cincinnati mayor James Stewart. Stewart then delivered a wild pitch from the mound over the head of the city manager. Other customary traditions took place, but the crowd was subdued throughout both the ceremonies and the game until the Reds scored a run in the bottom of the eleventh inning to beat the Pirates, 7–6.

For Cincinnatians unable to secure a ticket, the voices of Lee Allen and Waite Hoyt called the action on radio station WCPO. Earlier in the year, the Reds had granted WCPO the exclusive rights to broadcast Reds games. Hoyt began with WKRC in 1942 and became one of the most revered color commentators in the team's history until he retired in 1965. He continued to live in Cincinnati until he passed away in 1984.

It was fitting for the winning pitcher to be 44-year-old Hod Lisenbee, the oldest player in the major leagues, as teams were dotted with older players and rookies while many of the sport's stars were still in service for the country. All told, there were 120 rookies on Opening Day rosters! The quality of play may have left something to be desired, but there was optimism that the return of the stars after the war would result in a tremendous boom for baseball. Baseball had weathered the threats to its existence as a form of public entertainment.

Three weeks later, the war in Europe concluded after Western Allies and Soviet troops invaded Germany, culminating with Berlin being occupied by the Russians, Hitler committing suicide, and Germany surrendering uncon-ditionally. Five months later, Japan formally surrendered after Truman ordered the dropping of atomic bombs on Hiroshima and Nagasaki in August. World War II was finally over!

Waite Hoyt

POST-WAR BASEBALL BOOM

It was sort of a tacit understanding, at the parochial schools, anyway. If you had an Opening Day ticket and could show it, the nuns wouldn't say anything if you missed school and went to the ballgame.

Jim Schottelkotte, *Enquirer* sports editor

With the war over, baseball fans in Cincinnati and elsewhere were ready to get back to business as usual. It was a welcome relief to be able to enjoy the prospect of baseball without worrying about friends and family who were serving in the war.

1946: Normalcy Returns

The Reds opened spring training in February, and it was clear from the outset that 1946 baseball would be far different from the past five wartime seasons. Thirty-three Reds players who had spent the entire 1945 season in the military reported to Tampa for spring training, and eight of them reclaimed their regular positions. Especially noteworthy were Eddie Lukon, who returned to left field after suffering a case of badly frozen feet in the famous Battle of the Bulge, and pitcher Millard Howell, who had been a prisoner of war in Germany. With the seasoned players regaining their form, only ten of the 34 players who had played for the team in 1945 made the team in 1946.

Eddie Lukon

When fans awoke on the morning of April 16, they were reminded of the horrors of the war. The Associated Press reported that a German commandant had admitted during war crime trials in Nürenberg, Germany, that he had supervised the slaughter of 2,500,000 Jews at the Auchwitz concentration camp in Oswiecim, Poland. The report included grim details of the use of poisonous acid crystals in the gas chambers to increase the "efficiency" of the camp's killing capacity. Cincinnatians read the news with distress while fully appreciating that the Allied victory had saved millions more who would have died in the Holocaust had the war continued.

Of lesser importance, the Reds anticipated a boom in attendance by war-weary fans. To accommodate the increase, they renovated Crosley Field, adding seats in front of the right field bleachers. They also added "sort of an orchestra pit" that would house the band for night games but afforded 150 additional seats for Opening Day. Club officials were pleased to occupy a new box at the back of the grandstand. The entire park was freshly painted, including the light towers. Adding seats in right field eliminated the need for temporary seating in the outfield for the opener, but the seats reduced the distance down the right field line from 366 feet to 342 feet.

The April 16 game-time temperature was 51 degrees, and fur coats and blankets were abundant enough that the 30,069 fans resembled a football crowd. The customary ceremonies ended with Mayor Stewart nearly throwing another wild pitch. In a major departure from past years, the ranks of the Findlay Market Association parade had dwindled to a dozen participants. More disappointing to fans was the Reds' announcement that beer would not be sold by vendors in the stands. It was only available at concession stands under the grandstand because of a beer shortage. This inconvenience may not have mattered at the cold opener, but it would rankle fans later in the summer.

The game turned out to be one of the most disappointing contests in Opening Day history, as the Reds blew a three-run lead in the ninth inning and lost to the Cubs, 4–3.

1947: Strikes of a Different Kind

As the postwar economy continued to grow, so did labor unrest. On April 15, fans read updates about an eight-day-old nation-wide telephone strike by 340,000 telephone workers. The central issue in the walkout was the union's demand for a wage increase of $12 per week. Secretary of Labor Lewis Schwellenbach had intervened and proposed to both AT&T and the National Federation of Telephone Workers that they agree to submit their ongoing dispute over working conditions to an arbitration board and negotiate a host of local issues.

On the local front, 300 workers returned to work at two plants of the Drackett Company, a maker of cleaning fluids and a soybean processor. The strike lasted two weeks before the union secured a wage increase and agreed to various concessions. Several other strikes at private companies were in process or had started the previous day, and 29 teachers at North College Hill High School resigned the previous evening after three school board members were accused of religious bigotry. Tensions were so high that two of the three accused board members were "mauled" by angry citizens at the conclusion of an otherwise orderly and peaceful meeting about the strike.

In more pleasing news, Milton Reynolds, a Chicago fountain pen manufacturer, was aboard the "Reynolds Bombshell" that was on the last leg of a record-breaking flight around the world. Reynolds was accompanied by a pilot and an engineer. The plane made three unscheduled stops (for a total of nine stops) due to minor mechanical difficulties, and it finally touched down at LaGuardia Airport in New York City about seven hours after the opener ended. The 79-hour flight broke the previous record of 91 hours set by Howard Hughes in 1933.

After the cold-weather affair in 1946, 72-degree temperatures greeted the early-ar-riving sellout crowd of 33,383 at Crosley Field. More students than usual were in attendance, as public school authorities recognized the importance of Opening Day by starting classes one hour earlier, at 7:30 a.m., and dismissing students at 1:00 p.m. Those grateful students were no longer forced to tell fibs about their grandmothers' demise or their need for urgent dental care.

One noteworthy attendee was Thomas Baker, one of 12 jurors seated for a second-degree murder trial, who had disclosed in pretrial questioning that he had a ticket to the opening game. As game time approached, the jurors were engaged in deliberations over whether to convict a woman for the slaying of her common-law husband. In homage to Cincinnati's dearest institution, Judge Alfred Mack ordered the jurors to stop their deliberations so Baker could attend the game, because the opener "supersedes virtually all else."

> *"It's Wednesday, but the day of the week is irrelevant to most people's conversation at the office water cooler. It's Opening Day—a ritual of spring observed in Cincinnati, the birthplace of professional baseball, through rain, snow and even player strikes. Better yet it's a perfect excuse to play hooky from wherever it is you're supposed to be."*
>
> Ellen Brown, Enquirer reporter

The crowd was treated to a pregame concert by Smitty's band and to a reenergized Findlay Market parade after the group's disappointing showing the previous year. Five hundred partygoers participated in the parade from downtown and around the ballpark, each carrying a balloon that was released during the ceremonies. The balloons contained a coupon redeemable at the Findlay Market store, and the weight of the coupon caused many of the balloons to land in the grandstands and the bleachers. The marchers were led by Mayor Carl Rich, who had engaged in a game of toss with his chauffeur the previous day in order to prepare for the honor of throwing the first pitch. The mayor lamented, "I haven't thrown a baseball for 10 or 15 years." Carrying on a tradition that began two years earlier, Rich received a "first toss" from the Ohio governor standing in his box next to the Reds dugout.

The two-hour-and-15-minute game could have been played in less time, but there was a delay in the top half of the fifth inning. A group of 12 youngsters had situated themselves on top of the center field fence as if they were sparrows on a telephone wire, and play was suspended while the umpires instructed them to return to their seats. There was another slight delay later in the game when two fights broke out in the right field bleachers. The crowd did not seem to mind the interruptions, as the Reds were already leading 3–0 on their way toward an eventual 3–1 win. Fans were happy to have the four-year Opening Day losing streak come to an end.

The next morning the *Enquirer* explained why Opening Day crowds, though sellouts, would sometimes be eclipsed by larger crowds later in the season. In the article, Reds general manager Warren Giles noted that all seats, except 4,800 in the bleachers, are reserved on Opening Day, and many fans chose not to miss work to stand in line on the morning of the game for a chance at bleacher seats. Later in the season, large blocks of unreserved seats in the grandstands were held back until game day, and fans hoping to secure those seats often remained to buy standing-room-only tickets when the grandstand seats were gone, resulting in crowds up to 36,000 later in the season. The biggest attendance usually came on Sunday afternoons or for night games, when work duties did not interfere.

1948: My Word, What A Nice Party, Powell!

While federal judge T. Alan Goldsborough was making history with his decision to hold legendary John L. Lewis guilty of civil and criminal contempt for ignoring a court order to end a coal strike, Jane Finneran, the *Enquirer*'s society editor, decided to attend her first Opening Day. Finneran regularly oversaw coverage of more sophisticated gatherings such as the symphony, the opera, and other celebrations attended by the elite citizens of Cincinnati. Her April 19 Opening Day experience exposed her to a different slice of Cincinnati life.

In her detailed account of Opening Day, Finneran described her journey through the city's picturesque and historic West End to Crosley Field or, in her words, "Mr. Powell Crosley's rambling estate." As she made her way into the park, she joined closely packed lines of men, women, and children of all ages and sizes as they squeezed through the turnstiles with "long-treasured tickets clutched in excited hands."

Upon entry, she noted that the various officials in attendance added dignity to the occasion, including the assistant chief of police with "his silvered leaves of office glistening on his blue uniform. "Flags, whipping in the breeze, topped the tiers of animated pin-pointed faces," she wrote. Finneran was directed to the "alfresco stands" (the bleachers, as they were known by fans), where a "diplomat" (usher) advised her "You gotta havaticket" to enter the "sun parlor." Her press pass was an acceptable substitute. Clearly, Finneran was more of an observer than an enthusiastic fan, as noted by this observation: "The rhythmic crunching of peanuts, the gurgling of amber-colored liquids formed an undercurrent to the shrieks of approval or condemnation, as all 32,000 spectators—minus me—took a hand in directing the game."

Finneran described how Smitty's band led the "grand march of honor guards of soldiers," along with representatives from the U.S. Navy, the Marine Corps, and the Findlay Market rooters with their massive sign "tastefully edged in tissue paper fringe." Finneran marveled at the precision of the ceremonies that were carefully planned, the presentation and raising of the American flag, and the attentive players as they lined up along the baselines to the delight of the crowd.

Finneran went on to describe the flowered hats and coats that were peeled off as the 81-degree temperature made them unnecessary, and the ushers who shrieked "siddown" during the proceedings. She watched men with portable radios pressed to their ears to hear Waite Hoyt describe the play on the field; the omnipresent vendors hawking peanuts, drinks, ice cream, pennants, and souvenirs; and fans who were recording movies of the game. Finneran also reported on the cheers of the crowd, such as, "Get in there and swat 'em" and "What's the matter Dixie, can't you steal?" The game Finneran saw was the year's largest gathering for an opener in the National League, with 32,147 in attendance.

Ms. Finneran was a fine journalist, but not a true fan. After five innings, she found that the gates were securely locked as she tried to leave, offering her proof that this was truly an exclusive event for ticket holders only. She reminded readers that "Climbing fences is not my customary method of leaving a party!" after she successfully scaled the barrier.

If only she had remained! Ms. Finneran missed an altercation three innings later that certainly would have shocked her: an umpire pushed a photographer away as he moved to take photos of a skirmish at second base. A rumble ensued as a fan jumped over a box-seat railing to help the photographer. Meanwhile, the Reds and Pirates were jawing about the hard slide into second base. Other photographers and the managers were soon escorted back to their respective places and the game resumed, resulting in a second consecutive victory for the Reds on Opening Day. Only then did the fans leave Powell's party.

1949: Most Fans to Ever "See" A Game

In February 1949, Cincinnati sports fans welcomed the area's second major sports venue when the Cincinnati Gardens debuted with an exhibition hockey game featuring the Montréal Canadiens. The Gardens facility was modeled after Maple Leaf Gardens in Toronto, Ontario, though it lacked a dome. Upon its opening, it was the seventh-largest indoor arena in the country. Over the next seven decades, it would be the site of minor-league hockey teams, other sporting events, concerts (including the Beatles and the Rolling Stones), stage shows, circuses, and political rallies. From 1957 through 1972, it was home to the Cincinnati Royals of the National Basketball Association and its star player, Oscar Robertson. The arena eventually became outdated and was demolished in 2018.

Just two months later, there was another big development for Cincinnati sports fans. For the first time, the Opening Day game was

televised, making it possible for loyal fans to see the game whether they had a ticket or not. Although the attendance inside Crosley Field did not set any records, the game was the most watched Opening Day game ever. Because of the growing availability of black-and-white television sets, fans without tickets were elbowing their way to choice tavern seats or were gathering in crowded living rooms throughout a 100-mile radius of the city to watch the game on TV. At least 20,000 television sets had been sold in the area, and it is a safe bet that tens of thousands of fans were able to see the opener through the new medium. It was a transformational time in the history of live sports in Cincinnati, as it was in most of the country. The first televised major league game had occurred ten years earlier on August 26, 1939, featuring a doubleheader between the Reds and the Brooklyn Dodgers. Since television was not yet a commercial enterprise, few people saw those games. World War II delayed the growth of television dramatically, but by the late 1940s, more and more games began to be televised. In fact, the 1947 World Series was the first championship that fans across the country could view live in the comfort of their homes or at the local watering hole. 1949 was the first season in which multiple Reds games were televised.

Viewers at home were able to witness the pregame ceremonies that they might only have read about in newspaper accounts if they had not attended an opener in person. The Findlay Market Parade around the ballpark featured Grand Marshal James Gibbs, the owner of Gibbs Cheese and Sausage at the market. Gibbs's father had helped organize the parade when the family business moved to the market in 1922. (James Gibbs's son, Jeff, has continued the family tradition by serving as a

longtime organizer of the pregame event.)

Not televised was the array of airplanes that advertised an upcoming championship boxing fight; a Dayton, Ohio, spaghetti house; and the Galley Food and Bar restaurant that still operates today at nearby Lunken Airport as Sky Galley. A sellout crowd of 32,118 enjoyed a 3–1 victory over the Cardinals for the Reds' third consecutive Opening Day win.

1950: A New Tradition Is Born; Another Passes

On the eve of the April 18 opener, United Press sportswriter Carl Lundquist, who would later become an esteemed writer for *Sports Illustrated*, declared that Opening Day "is H-Day when Americans play hooky everywhere from the White House down to public school No. 69 to open the baseball season. Kids, old men, housewives, office and factory workers—even President Truman will make it out to the old ball game." The national news on the morning of the opener included the widening of Senator Joseph McCarthy's probe of alleged communist supporters inside the United States State Department.

The weather on Opening Day couldn't have been better, and one condescending writer noted that the women were dressed in "their most colorful finery, [as] they filed into

Crosley Field with their men to see and be seen … [but] the feminine contingent couldn't have told the starting pitchers if their best spring bonnets depended upon it." The fans of the fairer sex were part of another large crowd of 31,213, but 1,500 bleacher seats went unsold—most likely due to the Reds' string of second-division finishes. One of the diehard fans who remained loyal was 83-year-old J. T. Lambert of Wayne, West Virginia, who had attended every opener since 1888 except one. Another out-of-towner, 70-year-old W. H. Ruppert, of Portsmouth, Ohio, was attending his fiftieth consecutive Opening Day in the Queen City.

The festivities included a "first toss" by the highest-ranking government official to perform the honor in Cincinnati's history, Republican senator Robert Taft, who was the eldest son of President William Howard Taft and a lifelong Reds fan. Taft showed off his grin as he tossed a "good, true ball" to the Democratic mayor of Cincinnati from his colorful bunting-draped box, and the mayor then delivered the official first pitch.

Missing from the celebration was the colorful performance of the Oxford, Ohio, bricklayer, Harry Thobe, who was reported to have strutted and danced for 56 straight years on Opening Day. Known to fans as "Tobey" because of the way his name was pronounced, Thobe was arguably the biggest Reds fan ever. He had passed away just 20 days before the opener, appropriately buried in his familiar red-trimmed white suit with a red tie embossed with the Reds logo. Thobe was a famous gate-crasher, and his attire enabled him, Thobe claimed, to gain admission without paying to 20 World Series games (one more than the Reds had played) during his 80-year life. "I just march in with the band—any band," he explained in a 1948 interview. "The men who throw the gates wide open for the band usually think Thobe, in his clownish attire, is part of the act," noted the interviewer. "Baseball players, umpires and newspapermen

often escort Thobe through the press gate if there is no band present for the occasion."

The Reds decided to add what would become a fan favorite to Crosley Field: a new organ. The morning *Enquirer* told excited fans that "there will be more music than you get at a hillbilly jamboree, including organ music between innings." The debut of the organ "came through in great style," according to *Enquirer* reporter Charles Warnick: "As the Chicago lead gained and gained, the organ played faster and louder, as though it hoped to stave off defeat with its own deep voice. It looked for a moment as if it might succeed until [Reds pitcher Eddie] Erautt threw that fat pitch in the ninth." This entertaining innovation that the team borrowed from Brooklyn's Ebbetts Field would become a mainstay at Crosley Field and, indeed, throughout professional baseball.

The "fat pitch" referenced by Warnick that quieted the organ music resulted in a mammoth, three-run home run in the ninth inning by Andy Pafko of the Cubs, vaulting the Cubs to a 9–6 win. Another improvement made by the Reds, this one intending to help players field the ball, was having the grounds crew smooth out the infield dirt at the end of the fifth inning, a practice that was quickly adopted throughout the major leagues. And on the national baseball scene, the St. Louis Cardinals made history by hosting the first-ever Opening Day game at night.

1951: Miss America!

April 16 news was dominated by the return of General Douglas MacArthur. MacArthur, who served as Supreme Commander of Allied Powers in the Far East after the war, had been fired by President Truman five days earlier for making public statements against the administration's stated policies. Relieving MacArthur of his duties was one of the most controversial decisions of Truman's time in office, rivaled only by his decision to drop atomic bombs on Japan. Ironically, MacArthur had become a hero in Japan as he helped guide that nation's rebirth as a democracy. The *Nippon Times* sent good wishes to the general from 83 million grateful Japanese people and called him a "statesman-administrator without peer."

MacArthur's route to the Tokyo airport was lined by millions of Japanese, and a 19-gun salute was fired before MacArthur boarded the Bataan with his wife, Jean, for the flight to the United States, a home she had not seen in 14 years. MacArthur was similarly welcomed when his plane touched down in San Francisco, and he was scheduled to address a joint session of Congress two days later.

At the same time, Senator Harry Kane of Washington announced that he would introduce a resolution the next day calling for a declaration of war against Communist China, which was supporting North Korea in the Korean War that had erupted the previous June. Kane conceded that his move could lead to World War III, and a war-weary Congress never adopted his resolution. As such, the Korean War remained geographically limited.

Cincinnatians woke up to the coldest Opening Day weather in years, and thousands boarded streetcars for the last time to make the trek to Crosley Field. Streetcars stopped running in Cincinnati just 13 days later in favor of motor buses. The Reds had anticipated one of the largest post–World War II crowds in history and had installed extra seats in the outfield, but the cold weather limited attendance to 30,441. Even the all-night vigil by some fans was abandoned, and the line for bleacher seats did not form until 8:40 a.m., just two hours before bleacher seats went on sale. The Reds and Pirates took pregame batting practice amid snow flurries.

> *"This is a golden opportunity for everyone to get out after being stuck inside for the winter."*
>
> Stephen Prince, Reds Fan

The highlight of pregame activities was the introduction of Miss America, Yolande Betbeze, of Alabama, to an excited crowd. Betbeze, an opera singer, was a trailblazer for women's rights. She had reluctantly posed in a swimsuit during pageants but refused to do so after she won the title. The Miss America organization claimed that Betbeze was pivotal in directing the organization away from its focus on beauty, instead focusing on intellect, values, and leadership abilities.

Joining Betbeze for pregame ceremonies was William "Dummy" Hoy. Born in Cincinnati in 1862, Hoy became deaf at age 3 after suffering from meningitis. He graduated as class valedictorian from the Ohio State School for the Deaf. After opening a shoe repair store in Cincinnati and playing baseball on weekends, he went on to become the most accomplished deaf player in major league history, playing for the Reds between 1894 and 1897, and again in 1902, as a center fielder. Although "dumb" was the acceptable way at the time to describe a person who could not speak, the epithet unfairly came to connote stupidity. Despite the pejorative label, Hoy was regarded as one the most intelligent players of his era. He was inducted into the Cincinnati Reds Hall of Fame in 2003.

Hoy joined future Reds Hall of Fame pitcher Ewell Blackwell on the mound before the start of the opener, appearing in a vintage 1876 red uniform, to throw the first pitch—underhanded. He could see, if not hear, the standing ovation he received. He would make another appearance at the age of 99 when the Reds invited him to throw out the first ball before Game Three of the 1961 World Series. After a life of enormous accomplishment and unique abilities, Hoy passed away two months after his World Series toss.

Blackwell had his shortest appearance ever on Opening Day, being lifted in the third inning by manager Luke Sewell after allowing the only runs Pittsburgh would need to secure a 4–3 win. During the game, the manager of Sports Service, Inc., the concessionaire of the ballpark, complained that the fans were more interested in keeping warm then seeing a winner. "Usually I hear 'em yelling 'We want a hit', but today all I get is, 'We want coffee.'"

1952: Jingle Bells and an Overnight Guest

Cincinnatian and Republican presidential candidate Robert Taft was fuming about President Truman as another season opened on April 15. Just 15 months earlier, Truman had unilaterally proclaimed a "limited" national emergency, resulting in the United States entering the Korean conflict without a Congressional declaration of war. Taft had called Truman's actions a usurpation of the power to make war, but when Truman seized the nation's private steel mills a week prior to the opener, Taft reached his limit. He compared Truman to Hitler and warned that his policies would lead to a totalitarian government. Truman replied to the criticism by telling Taft and other critics of his unilateral actions to "read the Constitution … The president has the power to keep the country from going to hell."

The frigid relationships in the nation's capital were equaled by the cold weather in Cincinnati for the second consecutive opener. It was the Findlay Market Association's one-hundredth anniversary, so the rooters were eager to celebrate the auspicious occasion. They marched into the ballpark behind Judge Ralph Kohnen, who served as grand marshal. As the parade circled the field in weather that was more conducive to skiing than baseball, Smitty's band played "Jingle Bells," followed by their rendition of "Wait Till The Sun Shines, Nellie." The cold weather even affected the first toss from the governor and the first pitch from the mayor, as both men uncorked wild throws that eluded their targets. The *Enquirer* suggested, "A little more practice, Mr. Mayor" when the mayor's pitch missed home plate by six feet.

> "Some people want every day to be Christmas. Not me. I vote for Opening Day. (No one will pine for snow today when the Cincinnati Reds start their 2013 season.) Plus, the baseball season lasts longer. There are only 12 days of Christmas. The Reds play 162 games."
>
> Cliff Radel, Enquirer columnist

Fur coats and flowered hats dotted the crowd, with the majority of fans bundled up in scarfs and blankets. Fans retreating to warmer areas under the grandstand could enjoy a new "fish fry" for Easter week, competing in popularity with the perennial ballpark favorite, the hot dog. The weather was so biting that 12 separate bonfires were set in the temporary outfield seats, the bleachers, and the right field grandstand. The Cubs danced up and down in their dugout in order to stave off the cold on their way to a ten-inning, 6–5 victory. The cold was such a factor that one fan, 30-year-old James McElhaney, went to a bathroom to keep warm during the game. He fell asleep and was overlooked by the cleanup crew. In the middle of the night, he awoke to find all the gates locked, prohibiting his exit. The police eventually helped McElhaney escape the ballpark by tossing a ladder over the left field fence.

The next morning, fans learned that President Truman had signed the Japanese Peace Treaty, formally restoring independence and full sovereignty to Japan after the discord that began with Japan's attack on Pearl Harbor in 1941. A related security pact gave the United States the right to station military forces in and around Japan to protect Japan from the communist forces of China and Russia.

1953: Redlegs

"McCarthyism," meaning the practice of making accusations that communists within the United States were guilty of subversion or treason, was rampant in the spring of 1953. Communists, and even those suspected of being communists, were known as "Reds" to reflect their allegiance to the Soviet Union's flag. Terms and phrases such as "the Red Scare" and "Better Red than dead" became part of the national lexicon. There were even ads in newspapers saying, "Americans … Don't Patronize Reds!!!!" Government employees, entertainers, educators, and labor union activists were targets of the campaign, resulting in loss of employment, destruction of careers, and, in some cases, convictions that resulted in imprisonment. (Some convictions were later overturned.) Even J. Robert Oppenheimer, the scientific director of the top-secret program that developed the world's first atomic bomb, the Manhattan Project, was accused of being a communist sympathizer.

Cincinnati team officials were so concerned about the anti-communist sentiment that the club changed its nickname from "Reds" to "Redlegs" four days before the opener. The new and previous official name of the team had been used interchangeably since the mid-1930s anyway. (By 1960, after McCarthyism had waned, the club returned to calling itself the Reds.)

Al Schottelkotte was once the youngest journalist for any major American newspaper when he was a student at Cincinnati's St. Xavier High School during World War II. By 1953, he was the *Enquirer*'s "Talk of The Town" columnist. On the morning of the April 13 opener, Schottelkotte wrote a column titled "Here We Go Again":

> It's pushing and shoving to get through the crowd. It's standing silently with **30,000** others with a tingle inside as they run up the flag. It's home runs, hot dogs … and peanuts. It's frenzy, glumness, glee and disappointment. That's right, it's Opening Day. It's been going on for many a year, but every time it's a brand new thrill. Here, like no other place, it's a corny and wonderful tradition.

Schottelkotte would go on to become "The Voice of Cincinnati" as he anchored the Channel 9 (WCPO) TV news broadcasts for 27 years. Schottelkotte's newscasts consistently had the highest TV ratings from 1960 to 1982.

He was unseated as Cincinnati's news leader by Nick Clooney on Channel 12 (WKRC), a longtime talk show favorite and father of actor George Clooney.

April 13 saw the debut of the Milwaukee Braves, who had moved from Boston, in the National League. It was the first time since 1898 that Chicago, St. Louis, or Pittsburgh did not serve as the Reds' Opening Day opponent. On the eve of the opener, the new rivals were welcomed to Cincinnati as dinner guests of the Redlegs and Chamber of Commerce officials at the Cincinnati Country Club.

Milwaukee rooters wasted no time in taking part in Opening Day traditions. A six-foot-long bat engraved with the words, "Presented by the Milwaukee Association of Commerce with all good wishes" was presented to Braves manager Charlie Grimm before the game. As was customary, the Findlay Market Association presented a floral display with similar wishes to new Reds manager Rogers Hornsby. Ohio governor Lausche then gave a short speech in which he hoped for an all-Ohio World Series in light of the state celebrating its sesquicentennial. He and Mayor Rich must have heeded the *Enquirer*'s advice from the previous season to practice, as both the first toss and the first pitch were perfect strikes.

For the third consecutive Opening Day, fans were disappointed to experience both cold weather and a loss. The Braves won 2–0 in a game that took slightly less than two hours. A hearty 30,103 fans braved cold temperatures with a windchill of 41 degrees; fortunately, many in the crowd "had taken the necessary anti-freeze precautions by raiding the family cellar before reaching the ballpark," according to the *Enquirer*.

Reds manager Hornsby had to use a "special telephone-intercom system" between the dugout and the bullpen only one time. This was the first game in which the Reds had a bullpen telephone that also allowed the manager to report lineup changes to the press box, the scoreboard operator, and the public-address announcer. (According to the *New York Times*, the origin of the bullpen phone is unknown, although the paper found a reference to dugout telephones being used at Yankee Stadium as early as 1930.)

1954: Breaking Barriers

Fans on April 13 witnessed history. During the customary pregame ceremonies, Governor Lausche made another first toss from his flag-draped box next to the Reds dugout, but the ball was not delivered to a man. Instead, the ball was tossed to Vice Mayor Dorothy Dolbey so she could throw out the first pitch—the first woman ever to do so on Opening Day. Dolbey had been asked to do the honors by Mayor Edward Waldvogel, who had become ill and insisted that Dolbey assume his official duty.

Dolbey, wearing a skirt, reluctantly marched to the pitcher's mound and, contrary to fans' expectations, hurled a 60-foot pitch to city manager C.A. Harrell. The hurl, low

and arguably on the outside corner of home plate, caught Harrell by surprise, and he was assessed with a passed ball when it eluded his glove. Dolbey became the city's first female mayor a month later when Mayor Waldvogel passed away. She served as acting mayor for six months until the city council elected former mayor Carl Rich to fill the position of mayor.

Jackie Robinson broke the color barrier in 1947 by becoming the first African American to play in the major leagues, but full acceptance of minorities evolved slowly. It took the Reds several years, but integration began to increase in the mid-1950s. Shortly after Dolbey's pitch, the players from both teams were introduced, with the African American players lining up with their respective teams. First, Hank Aaron, who was promoted to the Braves' major-league club only after Bobby Thompson fractured an ankle during spring training, trotted out during player introductions. Aaron was said to have led the South Atlantic League in 1953 in every category except for hotel accommodations! When the Reds were introduced, African American Chuck Harmon and Nino Escalera, a Puerto

Chuck Harmon, left, and Nino Escalera

Rican of African descent, joined their teammates on the field. Harmon would have a four-year career with the Reds and Cardinals, but Escalera played only the 1954 season. The Reds became the ninth of the 16 clubs in MLB to integrate the roster. Each of these players was subjected to discrimination despite the team being integrated, often being required to stay in different hotels and eat at different restaurants than the rest of the team. In 1959, the Boston Red Sox was the last major league team to add an African American to its roster, a full 12 years after Robinson broke the color barrier in the modern age.

While not as consequential as the "firsts" in gender and race, this opener offered a new ballpark twist for Reds fans. Fans in the right field bleachers learned they were sitting in the newly named "Sun Deck," complete with a sunburst painting on the rear wall at the top of the bleachers. As the season went on, the painting was covered with a sign reading "Moon Deck" during night games.

In a different ballpark modification, three painters in left field worked feverishly to complete a new beer sign above the left field wall even after fans had entered the park. They paused in their work while "The Star-Spangled Banner" was being played, but as soon as the anthem concluded, they turned back around to keep painting. They finally completed their work by the second inning. Their hard work paid off when they got to take a seat under the shade of the roof, allowing them to enjoy the game from the best seats in the house.

The weather conditions were perfect, with sunny skies and 81-degree temperatures, making it the Reds' second-warmest opener in the twentieth century. Cincinnati hosted the largest crowd for an opener in the National League with 33,185 fans. Before the first inning, players were reminded of a new major-league rule: they could no longer leave their gloves on the field between innings. The game was the first opener to break the three-hour barrier, largely because of impressive offense for both teams during a thrilling, 9–8 win by the Reds.

The crowd became more subdued in the eighth inning when Braves right fielder Andy Pafko fell victim to a "beanball" pitch to the head by Joe Nuxhall. Although Pafko was carried off the field on a stretcher and writhed in pain at home plate, the plastic insert inside his baseball cap was credited for Pafko escaping serious injury.

Ted Kluszewski

1955: "Mr. Muscles" Honored

"The Opening Day Carnival," as the *Enquirer* described the events of Opening Day, usually began 24 hours in advance of the opener. Many organizations and groups held their own parties and get-togethers. Out-of-town followers of the team poured into the city on the day before the game and celebrated well into the evening. "It is near dawn before Cincinnati goes to bed," wrote one columnist. The *Enquirer* described Opening Day as a Queen City institution:

> Opening Day in Cincinnati is a festive event that has created nation-wide attention. In no city in the country is there the holiday spirit that prevails in Cincinnati on that day … Many cities are famed for their particular celebrations—New Orleans' Mardi Gras, New York's St. Patrick's Day Parade, Inauguration in Washington, Philadelphia's Mummers, etc. But none is more universally accepted than Cincinnati's Opening Day. Other cities have tried to copy Cincinnati but they have been unsuccessful. There is no substitute for genuineness. No promotion can create a duplicate of Cincinnati's opening day traditions.

Cloudy, rainy skies had prevailed during the

week before the opener, so not surprisingly, festivities on the morning of the game were affected by the inclement weather, to the point of causing the Findlay Market parade to be rained out. The rain-soaked field, made worse by a steady drizzle, resulted in batting practice being canceled. A tarpaulin kept the infield covered until game time. When the sun finally came out for the first time at 2:09 p.m., the opening ceremonies began.

The main focus of the ceremonies was the coronation of Reds first baseman Ted Kluszewski. Known as "Mr. Muscles" and the "Crunch King," "Big Klu" was famous for needing to wear a sleeveless jersey because his biceps were too large for a regular uniform. During the previous season, "Big Klu" led the major leagues in home runs (49) and runs batted in (141). Before a sellout crowd, the Findlay Market Association presented Kluszewski with a crown and scepter. The crown identified Kluszewski as the king of hitters, and the scepter, in the form of a huge bat, contained inscriptions of Kluszewski's 1954 achievements. As it turned out, the game played second fiddle to the pregame celebration, with the Reds losing to the Cubs 7–5.

The next morning's paper featured coverage of the coronation, as well as a paragraph that likely went unnoticed by most readers. It noted that seventeen-year-old Bernie Stowe had begun his sixth year of service as a batboy for the Reds. The paragraph did not

Bernie Stowe

mention that Stowe had had the privilege of serving as a batboy at the 1953 All-Star game at Crosley Field. Stowe would go on to work another 61 years for the Reds, working his way up to the club's senior clubhouse and equipment manager before retiring in 2013. He was one of the team's most beloved employees, and on May 19, 2018, the Reds and the Reds Community Fund dedicated a renovated ballfield on Cincinnati's west side in his honor, appropriately named Bernie Stowe Field.

On the national front, the US Navy unveiled a six-foot-wide flying machine that defied the laws of gravity. Officially named a "Flying Platform" by the navy, some described it as an airborne manhole cover with a man standing on top. It was kept aloft by two counter-rotating fans. The *Enquirer* speculated that the unusual contraption "may ruin Superman."

1956: The Today Show

On the eve of the April 17 opener, Cincinnati welcomed Dave Garroway and his cast from NBC-TV's The Today Show to a celebration on Fountain Square. The cast's appearance on the Walter Phillips Show, a local radio program, was broadcast in front of a live audience beginning at 7:00 p.m., preceded by 30 minutes of music by Cliff Leah's band. Garraway's mascot, a chimpanzee by the name of J. Fred Muggs, was by far the most popular star on the set. The next morning, a special three-hour Today show originated from

Fountain Square in honor of Opening Day. To Cincinnatians, the national attention proved what they already knew: Cincinnati was the epicenter of Opening Day festivities in the United States.

With hopes high for a championship season, the Findlay Market Association pulled out all the stops by arranging a unique means of arrival for Mayor Charles Taft: he was delivered to center field via helicopter. The spectacle this created was duly noted by the *Enquirer*. "What with a helicopter buzzing and television wires streaking the grass," wrote the *Enquirer*, "the players risked decapitation or electrocution during pregame warmups." Mayor Taft left the helicopter in a fall jacket, with 48-degree temperatures making it "good television viewing weather." Clowns entertained the fans while he made his way to the mound.

Smitty's band tried to warm up the chilly crowd with "oompah" music, but it was to no avail. Governor Lausche delivered his ninth and last Opening Day toss to Taft. Perhaps the mayor needed more of a warm-up in the cool weather, as the *Enquirer* was less than complimentary about his throwing prowess: "Hizzoner … was … charged with the season's first wild pitch, an underthrown curve that bounced far in front of the plate and rolled by catcher C. A. Harrell, in private life the city manager." The sellout crowd enjoyed the mayor's unusual manner of entrance and laughed at his pitch.

Included in the crowd of 32,095 was James M. Josten, a retired soft drink manufacturer from Athens, Ohio, who was attending his fiftieth consecutive Opening Day game. Josten's streak began in 1906 when he made the 156-mile trek each way on a Baltimore and Ohio train. In the early years, his $1 round-trip would begin at midnight the night before the game. He would arrive in the Queen City at 6:00 a.m. and make the return trip after the game at 6:00 p.m.

The 1956 opener featured the addition of air-conditioning in the dugouts and the debut of a future Hall of Famer, 20-year-old Frank Robinson, who appeared in the new sleeveless uniform that the Reds adopted for the 1956 season. While the sleeveless look was designed with Ted Kluszewski in mind, neither the air

Frank Robinson

conditioner nor the uniforms were designed for the cold weather that so regularly accompanied the opener!

Fans were entertained during breaks in the action by organist Ronnie Dale. Dale would become the first big-league organist to lead the crowd in choruses of "Charge!" He also holds the distinction of being the first organist to be thrown out of a game by an umpire! His offense? The umpire was irked by the "Charge!" fanfare.

The crowd remained in a jovial mood for eight innings as Joe Nuxhall pitched a gem, and the Reds entered the ninth tied with the Cardinals. However, Nuxhall bobbled a two-out, inning-ending ground ball, and then he served up a game-winning home run to future Hall of Famer Stan Musial.

As previously noted, many fans erroneously believe that the Reds have long been guaranteed the privilege of having the earliest opener each year in the National League. The 1956 schedule of opening games should have squashed that misperception. In 1956, there were two other National League games scheduled an hour before the Cincinnati opener, plus three games in the American League. In fact, no teams that year began their opener later than the Reds!

In local news on the morning of the opener, the *Enquirer* headlined the end of school segregation in rural Hillsboro, Ohio. Eleven

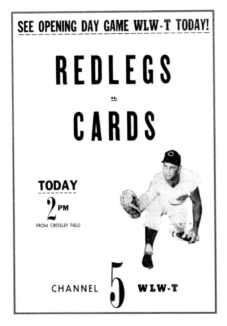

African American mothers had enrolled their children in the public schools of the small town southeast of Cincinnati. School officials assigned the students to grades lower than those for which they were qualified, resulting in a "stand up" strike for several hours in the school halls. The integration of that school eventually went into effect, with seven of the students accepting their assignments and four others receiving "promotions" to their rightful grade. Segregation of schools had been declared unconstitutional by the United States Supreme Court in its landmark 1954 *Brown v. Board of Education* decision, but schools in the Cincinnati area, like others throughout the country, were slow to enforce the ruling.

1957: A 55-Foot Scoreboard

Cincinnati's three daily newspapers, The *Enquirer*, the *Post*, and the *Times-Star* almost

did not provide coverage of the April 16 Opening Day festivities and game. The three papers were threatened with a strike that would have stopped the presses just before the opener, but the shutdown was averted by a last-minute settlement.

"Operation Front Page" was a remarkable joint endeavor by the three papers that, when the strike seemed inevitable, called for the staff and management of eight Cincinnati radio stations and three local television stations to undertake 24-hour coverage of local and worldwide events utilizing the news-gathering facilities of the newspapers. An *Enquirer* editorial explained:

> The facilities mentioned are natural competitors, and ordinarily the rules of competition apply rigorously, but in an hour of evident public need, all concerned were willing to forgo their rivalries, subordinate their differences, and join together in keeping the public informed, to the exclusion of all other considerations.

The strike was averted at "zero hour" and the presses kept rolling, as did the competition between the papers and the TV and radio stations.

Fans who had long relied upon the newspapers to keep them informed about the Reds were relieved that the strike did not take place, particularly because hopes were running high for a possible championship season. In 1956, the Reds had tied the National League home run record (221), a record that stood until 1997, and they had surprised experts by battling the Dodgers and Braves in a fierce pennant race that lasted until the final weekend of the season. The Reds ended up throwing a million dollars' worth of preprinted, unused World Series tickets into the boilers of the Superior Towel and Linen Service, located behind the Crosley Field left field wall and known as "the laundry."

As always, tickets for the opener were at a premium. The manager of the Cincinnati Art Museum, Philip Adams, reported he had unsuccessfully applied for tickets the previous November, and all he could get were tickets in the thirty-seventh row of the bleachers by standing in line that morning. But obtaining a ticket for the game was not the only concern for eager fans. In his column on the morning of the opener, Al Schottelkotte reassured automobile drivers that they could park safely at Crosley Field without worry. In previous openers, vandals had offered to "watch your car for a quarter," and the automobiles of owners who rejected the watchers were often vandalized. The police decided to crack down, so they added additional officers on motorcycle to patrol the ballpark area. Schottelkotte advised fans they would not need "insurance" at the ballpark with this enhanced patrolling underway. The lots were packed to capacity as another overflow crowd of 32,554 came early despite a dark, gloomy sky and a temperature of 52 degrees.

The downtown rooters preparing to march in the Findlay Market parade, as well as the many spectators, were treated to something special from the Union Central Life Insurance Company. The company's bells regularly echoed throughout the downtown section of the city, but for Opening Day the chimes played "Take Me Out to the Ball Game" at 9:00 a.m. and again at noon.

> "As mother-nature awakens from her winter slumber, nothing signifies the onset of warmer times ahead than Opening Day. A Cincinnatian day of celebration where grandparents, parents and children put aside the troubles of the world for three or more hours and bask in the marvelous game of baseball!"
>
> Michael J. Wolber, Reds Fan

Fans took in a new sight as they hurriedly rushed through the portals leading to the grandstand and the bleachers. A newly constructed, 55-foot-high and 65-foot-wide scoreboard replaced the original model that had been used since 1912. The new scoreboard was the first in baseball to display each hitter's batting average. Because its larger size would interfere with the path of balls headed its way, a new ruling deemed the entire scoreboard to be in the field of play, including the 40 feet that extended above the outfield wall in left center field. Balls that would easily have been home runs before became doubles when they bounced off the scoreboard instead of sailing over it. So much for breaking the home run record the Reds had tied the previous season! The scoreboard was even more impressive during night games when glass panels were backlit and blue neon lights outlined the hands of the huge clock. The addition became an iconic feature of Crosley Field.

In pregame festivities, the perennial Smitty's band entertained the crowd, followed by the Findlay Market band. There were three brief speeches by the newly elected governor of Ohio, William O'Neil; Mayor Charles Taft; and Judge Ralph Kohnen. Kohnen represented Findlay Market and made presentations to Roy McMillan and Johnny Temple as "baseball's greatest double-play combination" and to Frank Robinson, who was National League Rookie of the Year in 1956.

Also in attendance was a longtime fan and Opening Day attendee, Kentucky governor "Happy" Chandler. The Reds were in a quandary. With two governors present, who would receive the honor to toss the first ball to Mayor Taft? Chandler, ever the gentleman, solved the dilemma by offering to be the umpire for the mayor's first pitch. Fortunately for the hitters, Chandler would return to his regular occupation after the game. He bellowed "Strike!" even though Taft's pitch was so far off course that the real umpires and the managers preparing to discuss the ground rules "headed for cover to avoid being struck by the misguided missile."

A special treat for the fans was the stirring rendition of the national anthem by Marian Spelman. Spelman was an icon in Cincinnati as a regular on the popular "Fifty-Fifty Club," a live morning show on WLWT. She was known for her work with the Cincinnati Playhouse, the Cincinnati Symphony Orchestra, and the Cincinnati Pops Orchestra. Her signature songs were "Soon There Will Be Christmas," "Christmas Lullaby," and "There's No Time Like Christmas Time," lyrics specifically written for her by her friend and fellow Cincinnati icon, Ruth Lyons. She became the regular singer of the national anthem at Crosley Field openers as well as the early openers at Riverfront Stadium.

Marian Spelman

Despite the Redlegs hanging a gold-plated horseshoe for good luck in the dugout, the Cardinals carried the day by trouncing the Reds, 13–4. During the first inning, a fan hurdled the low fence next to the Reds bullpen and had a brief visit with Frank Robinson in left field before returning to his seat.

Though Redleg fans were discouraged by the result of the opener, they showed their passion for the team throughout the season by electing five of their favorite players to the starting lineup for the All-Star game. Balloting for the midsummer classic was unsophisticated at the time, with newspapers put in charge of distributing the votes nationwide. There were no restrictions on how often fans could vote or how many ballots could be printed. Proving Cincinnati's love of all things baseball, the 500,000 votes that came from Cincinnati were more numerous than votes from the rest of the country combined! MLB commissioner Frick was not impressed with the fans' efforts, choosing to replace three Reds in the starting lineup with Stan Musial, Willie Mays, and Hank Aaron because of the "over balance of Cincinnati votes."

1958: Baseball in California?

Although baseball had indisputably been the national pastime for nearly a century, there was no major-league team west of the Rocky Mountains until the New York Giants and Brooklyn Dodgers stunned their heartbroken fans by moving to San Francisco and Los Angeles, respectively, before the 1958 season. The teams had made history for 67 years as beloved rivals in the Big Apple.

The expansion of the National League to the West Coast was controversial, to say the least. In Cincinnati, fans were concerned that night games in California would not start until 11:00 p.m., Eastern time, making it difficult for them to watch games when they had to get up for work the next day. In addition, it was expensive to install transcontinental lines for television lines, so the still-young television industry was largely limited to local programming. Even radio would be affected, as broadcasters Waite Hoyt and Jack Moran would not actually attend the West Coast games. Instead, as was the practice prior to 1956 for road games, Hoyt and Moran fashioned a "live" broadcast from Cincinnati based on teletype reports from Seals Stadium in San Francisco and Memorial Stadium in Los Angeles.

Given the dramatic moves made in the off-season by the Giants and the Dodgers, Reds fans became extremely nervous when Powell Crosley Jr. threatened to move the Reds if the city council did not purchase and clear additional land for 2,600 parking spaces near Crosley Field. Newly elected council members were well aware of the betrayal by the New York franchises, so they quickly approved the request. In return, Crosley signed an agreement that committed him to keep the team in Cincinnati—but only through the 1962 season. (As it turned out, the new parking spaces were not available for almost two years, so talk of a new location for the Reds began as early as 1959 when Carthage, a neighborhood in the city's Mill Creek Valley, offered its fairgrounds location.)

With the Reds committed to staying at Crosley Field—at least for the next four years—they invested their energy in improving the ballpark. The unpopular inner fence in right field that reduced the distance for a home run from 366 to 342 feet was removed. The fence,

along with seating inside of it, had been added in 1953 to increase the home run chances of Ted Kluszewski. When "Big Klu" was traded to the Pirates in December 1957, there was no reason to keep the fence. And the ballpark received another paint job, with venerable steel beams and some seats sporting a bright orange-red look. The portals that fans passed through to find their seats were painted in robin's egg blue. To add to the color changes, the Reds donned new uniforms for home games: white with red pinstripes and red raglan sleeves.

The Findlay Market rooters, wearing their now traditional cardboard hatbands, arrived on the field with colored balloons. They joined in a march with Smitty's band, the members of which were decked out in black uniforms with gold braid. Powell Crosley Jr. took the microphone and thanked the fans for their support. Crosley appeared to gaze to the heavens for support, and he was rewarded with a bright peek from the sun that warmed the temperature to 68 degrees, allowing patrons to sit on their raincoats for the remainder of the day.

Cincinnati Hotel Rates

Hotel	Rooms: Single		Double		Twin	
Terrace Hilton...	$10.25-$18.25				$16.50-$22.50	
Netherland Hilton	7.00-	17.00	12.00-	15.50	13.00-	21.00
Sheraton-Gibson .	6.50		10.00		11.00	
Sinton	5.50		8.00		10.00	
Fountain Square.	4.50-	7.50	6.50-	9.00	8.50-	11.00
Metropole	5.00-	7.50	7.50-	9.00	8.50-	11.00
Broadway ....⎫ Kemper Lane.....⎭	4.50-	7.00	6.50-	9.00	8.00-	12.00
Alms	7.50-	9.75	10.50-	12.25	11.00-	13.25
Vernon Manor....	6.00 up		9.00		10.00-13.00	
Carrousel Motel..	10.00-	15.00	15.00-	18.00	15.00-	18.00

Marian Spelman returned to sing "The Star-Spangled Banner" as part of the customary pregame ceremonies. As she sang, attendants were pulling on the flagpole's rope attempting to unfurl the huge, new flag presented by the Findlay Market Association. It "finally flapped away in the wind at full length." The appreciative crowd gave Spelman a warm round of applause. With their attire, fans contributed to the splashes of color that had been added throughout the ballpark. Wrote one *Enquirer* reporter, "With a goodly number of red hats and suits, the red jackets of the ushers and the red jackets of the Redlegs, the giant crowd looked from the upper stands as if a flock of red birds had flown in for the game."

The Phillies came to town for the first time ever on Opening Day, and the game turned out to be one of the most controversial in Opening Day history. With the Reds leading 4–3 after six innings, the Phillies' Richie Ashburn was on first. Granny Hamner hit a frozen rope down the left field line, rolling into the Reds bullpen area before a fan reached out and touched the ball. Ashburn scored from first to tie the game, and Reds manager Birdie Tebbetts stormed from the dugout for a lengthy dispute with the umpires, unsuccessfully arguing that it was a ground rule double. He asserted that the fan had interfered with play and that Ashburn should return to third base. The umpires declined to reverse the call, and the otherwise good-natured crowd lost its collective temper during the uproar. The fans were displeased again when the Phillies scored the game-win-ning run in the eighth inning on three undisputed singles. After the game, Tebbetts filed a protest with the National League office that put the final outcome in doubt. The next morning's paper even wondered whether there were 153 more games to play in the season or 154! (The League office later overruled the appeal, making a replay of the game unnecessary.)

At the time of Tebbetts' tirade, the game was already two hours old, and the Dodgers and Giants had just begun their historic opener before 23,448 new fans in San Francisco's Seals Stadium. Some diehard fans at Crosley Field began to wonder how many hours of sleep they were going to miss in June when the Reds played night games in California!

1959: "Happy Days Are Here Again"

April 9 was the earliest Opening Day ever, and Reds fans were hoping the team could reverse its recent misfortune in openers and come away with a winner. The morning *Enquirer* focused its news coverage on the other Reds—the communists of the Union of Soviet Socialist Republics (USSR). The USSR was commonly referred to as "Russia" because Russia was by far the largest of the soviet republics. West and East Berlin were at the center of a controversy between the Western powers and Russia, as Russia's Nikita Khrushchev threatened to prevent all communication between Western countries and East Berlin. (The threat was later carried out with the construction of the Berlin Wall in 1961,

7 U. S. Astronauts Are Ready For Flight Into Space

which sought to prevent out-migration from East Germany to the West.) On Opening Day, the *Enquirer* reported on FBI director J. Edgar Hoover's warning that American "Reds" who had attended a Communist Party Congress in Moscow had received instructions for renewed activity in the United States. The Cold War was escalating.

Meanwhile, Americans were introduced to NASA's "Mercury Seven" as part of the Cold War's "Space Race" between the United States and the Soviet Union. This element of the Cold War began in 1957 when the USSR success-

fully launched Sputnik 1, the first human-made object to orbit Earth. The "Mercury Seven"— the seven astronauts who were part of an experiment to determine whether humans could survive space travel—were introduced in Washington, D.C., on April 9 and became immediate heroes. *Time* magazine compared the seven men to Columbus, Magellan, Daniel Boone, and the Wright Brothers. Americans were buoyed by the excitement created by the seven, especially since one of them would be chosen to circle the earth in a space capsule.

Although the Cincinnati Reds had changed their name to Redlegs in 1953 to avoid the

appearance of being associated with communism, the team's traditional name of "Reds" had survived and had even regained prominence in the late 1950s. Prior to the opener, the team's general manager, Gabe Paul, conceded that either name could be used when referring to the city's baseball team.

> *"Gone to the funeral at Findlay and Western Avenues. Grandma died again. Bob and Art."*
>
> Sign in window on Opening Day at a barber shop in Clifton.

Prior to the opener, 738 box seats had been added to Crosley Field down the left and right field foul lines. Temporary seats were being sold in the outfield for the last time. Although additional cooling was hardly necessary on the 53-degree, cloudy day, the team had installed large fans in the rear of both the upper and lower grandstands, making the park the first in the major leagues to be "air-cooled." As of Opening Day, the team was in the process of repainting the wall behind the right field stands, but the work was only one-third complete. Fans could still see part of a famous quote by President Herbert Hoover that had been painted on the wall: "The rigid rules of right and wrong in sports are second only to religious faith in moral training." Newcomers—if there were any in the crowd of 32,190—were likely confused by the few words that remained: "the rigid rules of right and wrong in sports," as the rest of the saying had been covered with fresh paint.

The pregame festivities were highlighted not by parades or music, but rather by the return of Ted Kluszewski and the theatrics of A. B. Chandler, the Kentucky governor. "Big Klu" had been traded to the Pirates in 1957 after a disappointing season, but he remained

A Perfect Opening Day!

popular in Cincinnati. The early arriving fans were enthralled with watching Kluszewski take batting practice. Governor Chandler attracted the fans' attention, too, as he was a popular politician in the bordering state of Kentucky. He was chosen to make the first toss of the season when new Ohio governor Michael DiSalle decided not to attend because of pressing business in Columbus. (Apparently such business never let up, as he cited the same reason for not attending the next three years.) Flashing his irrepressible grin that earned him his nickname of "Happy," Chandler put on a show when it came time to make the first toss. Standing in his box next to the Reds dugout, Chandler acted like a pitcher who was shaking off signals from his catcher. He shook his head several times and instructed his catcher, Cincinnati mayor Donald Clancy, to "get back, get back" before he threw a perfect toss. Clancy, with the honor of the first pitch, then strode confidently to the mound before throwing a high, wild pitch that hit the screen designed to protect patrons in the boxes behind home plate from foul balls.

The game with Pittsburgh was of special interest because the two clubs were involved in the biggest trade of the off-season. Pirates' third baseman Frank Thomas had signed with the Reds, and Reds third baseman Don Hoak joined the Pirates. Despite the hype surrounding these two players, neither one played a significant role in the Opening Day outcome, as the Reds won an opener for the first time in four years (and only the second time in ten years), notching a 4–1 triumph. After the victory was secured, Crosley organist Ronnie Dale appropriately sent the fans home to the tune of "Happy Days Are Here Again."

1960: The Outfield Belongs to the Players!

Finally, baseball purists received the gift they had requested for decades: Reds management decided to play the game on Opening Day using the field dimensions that were used in every other home game of the season. Historically, the Reds had accommodated the large demand for tickets by allowing fans to occupy the outer portions of the outfield and parts of foul territory on Opening Day. This practice helped to swell the crowd, but it caused problems: there were no nearby restrooms, and fans—who were actually seated on the playing field—were rowdy and sometimes interfered with play. Worst, at least for the purists, was the fact that some batted balls that landed beyond the ropes and were ruled ground rule doubles would otherwise have been caught for outs. Many felt those doubles simply were not earned, and some went so far as to call them a joke.

Reds management finally relented to increasing public pressure and eliminated the seats for the April 12 opener, reducing the park's capacity. In addition, rather than holding back bleacher seats for sale on the day of the opener, the Reds sold every ticket in advance except for standing-room-only tickets in the grandstand.

Smitty's band, the longtime official band of the ballpark, trumpeted the start of the Opening Day celebration precisely as the gates were opened at 12:30 p.m. There was the traditional onslaught of early birds, some of whom brought their picnic baskets, to enjoy every moment. Mert Gusweiler, an *Enquirer* columnist writing in jazz jargon of the day, described the ballpark atmosphere and the "katts" (i.e., fans):

The katts turned up en masse to orbit 'round the park. … If the game was a gasser and it was, it had a neat send-off. A parade like wow put the audience in the mood. Balloons, flags, horns, signs and all that jazz made its way from right field to infield. This parade … was really swingin'. And then there was Smittie, the coolest, who really got the message even before the parade, and played, "You Are My Sunshine." A little taste of the coming holiday made its way on the field, too. A real beat bunny, man-size, with tails, checkered, carried on a little chat with some clown, also man-size.

Sunny skies and 75-degree temperatures brought out fans wearing Bermuda shorts, Easter bonnets, and hats of every variety— black derbies, velvet berets, green felt tops, and straw hats. Pregame ceremonies featured an 11-year-old Knothole Baseball player, Carl F. Tuke Jr., who was garbed in a facsimile of the club's red and white uniform. He presented a bouquet of flowers to Reds general manager Gabe Paul at home plate. The "katts" went home happy after a rather easy 9–4 win over the Phillies.

1961: Powell Crosley Jr. Remembered

For the first time in 20 years, Cincinnati celebrated a national championship, but the winning team was not the Reds. On March 25, the University of Cincinnati won its first NCAA basketball crown. Three days later, the euphoria came to an abrupt halt: Powell Crosley Jr. died of a heart attack at the age of 74 after owning the Reds for 27 years. A family foundation took control of the team.

Powell Crosley Jr.

All the experts had predicted that the Reds would finish no better than fifth place in 1961. The local papers on April 11 were consumed with swirling events from around the world. After Nazi leader Adolf Eichmann had been captured in Argentina, his day of reckoning began when he was put on trial in Israel. He was accused of being the mastermind in the extermination of millions of Jews by Hitler's Third Reich. Seated behind bulletproof glass, the prisoner was called the "brains" of the horror operation by the prosecution, while his attorney painted him as no more than a tool of the Nazi state. The trial consumed people around the world and, in Cincinnati, WSAI radio began special reports that were carried Monday through Friday at noon, 6:00 p.m. and 10:00 p.m. Eichmann was found guilty of crimes against humanity and was executed in June 1962.

Welcome, Reds! Jim O'Toole Will Pitch Opening Game Today

166

Meanwhile, in the Cold War, the USSR's official press spokesman claimed he knew nothing about rumors that the Soviets had launched a man into space. The next morning, London's Communist paper, the *Daily Worker*, reported that Yuri Gagarin had, in fact, been launched into space orbit on April 6 and had orbited Earth three times. President John F. Kennedy, who had been inaugurated less than three months before, was forced to acknowledge Russia's advantage in the space race, lamenting, "We are behind." He congratulated Soviet premier Nikita Khrushchev on Gagarin's accomplishment.

SOVIET ORBITS MAN, CHALLENGES WEST
Time Needed To Catch Up In Space Race--Kennedy

As it bemoaned the Russian space victory, the *Enquirer* also expressed optimism that the 27-month-old dictatorship of Cuba's Fidel Castro might be coming to an end. Cuba had long been seen as a communist ally of the Soviet Union. The paper reported that exiled Cuban dissidents in Florida who had escaped Castro's regime were declaring, "By summer, we hope to be able to go swimming again in Cuba."

The weekend before opening day, the Civic Garden Center of Greater Cincinnati had announced a two-month program to "Buy a Flag—Fly a Flag." Downtown streets were replete with American flags on the morning of April 11. With little hope for a championship flag at Crosley Field, the parades from downtown slowly arrived at the park with less than a third of the park full an hour before the game. And yet, what marchers saw as they neared the park was the realization of Powell Crosley's dream: increased parking that he had lobbied for three years earlier. Buildings in the adjacent blocks, including the famous laundry behind the left field wall, had been cleared for the construction of the parking lots as well as I-75, a new highway skirting the western edge of downtown.

The outside appearance of the park was drastically changed, with the entire brick exterior now painted white. Gone was the famous "Win a Siebler Suit" sign that had been perched on top of the laundry building since 1939. Jack Siebler of the Siebler Tailoring Company joked during pregame ceremonies that Reds player Wally Post would now have to buy his own suits. In just over two decades, the company had given away approximately 225 suits to players who had launched home runs that hit the sign. With the laundry building demolished, the Reds erected a 41-foot-high screen from the left field grandstand to the scoreboard to protect cars in the new parking lot from balls hit over the wall.

Reds Uniforms 1961

Though the game was a sellout, actual attendance was the lowest since 1952 with only 28,713 fans filing through the turnstiles. Perhaps fans stayed away because of the

CINCINNATI REDS...1961 NATIONAL LEAGUE CHAMPIONS.
Won 93, Lost 61.

SITTING: Ed Kasko, Wally Post, Coach Reggie Otero, Coach Jim Turner, Mgr. Fred Hutchinson, Coach Dick Sisler, Coach Otis Douglas, Coach Pete Whisenant, Gus Bell, Frank Robinson, John Edwards.
MIDDLE ROW: Don Blasingame, Elio Chacon, Dick Gernert, Jerry Zimmerman, Jerry Lynch, Gordy Coleman, Leo Cardenas, Darrell Johnson, Vada Pinson, Gene Freese, Dr. Richard Rohde, Trainer.
TOP ROW: Jim Brosnan, Ken Johnson, Bill Henry, Bob Purkey, Ken Hunt, Jim Maloney, Sherman Jones, Joey Jay, Jay Hook, Jim O'Toole.
Players with the club sometime during the season but not appearing on photo: Claude Osteen, Hal Bevan, Bob Schmidt, Cliff Cook, Pete Whisenant (player), Jim Baumer, Howie Nunn, Ed Bailey, Willie Jones, Marshall Bridges, Joe Gaines and Harry Anderson.

construction issues surrounding I-75, or maybe they were put off by the cloudy, chilly weather. Nonetheless, as described by columnist Lou Smith, they missed what had attracted them in the past:

> There is something thrilling … about the first look at a baseball diamond after the long winter. The grass isn't as green as it's going to get, but it's still green enough that a white baseball bouncing on it provides a contrast that is sheer beauty to the man who understands such things.

The fans who chose to stay home also missed something truly remarkable. Dummy Hoy, who was 98 years old and the oldest former major leaguer alive, was given the honor of delivering the first toss of the season. Though 50 years older than Mayor Walton Bachrach, who threw the first pitch, Hoy still had good control and made a perfect toss, while Bachrach's pitch fell 20 feet short of the plate. Hoy would be honored for the last time in Game Three of the 1961 World Series just prior to his death.

After Marian Spelman's golden voice sang "The Star-Spangled Banner," the ceremony became more somber when a moment of silence was observed in tribute to Powell Crosley Jr. The flag was lowered to half-mast, and the Reds took the field with black armbands in honor of the late owner. In a departure from a long tradition, head umpire Dusty Boggess did not yell "Play ball!" He told a reporter, "Naw, we don't do that anymore. The home team runs out on the field and, after the 'Star Spangled Banner,' they start playing ball."

The fans were treated to a surprisingly strong showing when Jim O'Toole pitched a masterpiece to lead the Reds to a 7–1 win over the Cubs. In contrast to the predictions of the pundits, Lou Smith described the players as "dashing" and "power-laden." The Reds continued to surprise the experts by winning the National League pennant in a championship run referred to as the "Miracle on Western Avenue." (The self-proclaimed experts also believed Babe Ruth's record for home runs in a season was not in jeopardy even after the American League expanded the schedule by eight games to 162. The Yankees' Roger Maris broke the record in the last game of the 1961 season.) And the Cuban exiles who hoped to be swimming in Cuba were wrong, too; Fidel Castro remained in power until his death in 2008!

1962: John Glenn in Orbit

Everything seemed to be going well prior to the April 9 opener. Ohioan John Glenn had recently circled the globe as the first American in space; Reds general manager Bill DeWitt had bought the team from the Crosley family, promising to keep the Reds in Cincinnati and build a modern, municipal stadium; and the University of Cincinnati had won its second consecutive NCAA basketball championship. An on-field development was that the Reds had added a mechanical device that allowed coaches to shelve the "fungo bats" used during practice to loft balls to outfielders. Instead, they simply pulled a trigger on a new contraption that did the job. Cincinnatians were in high spirits!

Opening Day was cold and blustery, with winds averaging 18 to 20 miles per hour, including gusts up to 40 miles per hour. Despite the game selling out and the fans wanting to cheer for the defending National League champions, a good 2,500 ticketed fans decided to stay warm at home. The actual attendance was 28,506. The weather was so bad that *Enquirer* staff writer Libby Lackman noted that fans were not dressed in their usual attire. "It was not a fashionable crowd," she wrote. "Looking down from the upper grandstand, an occasional flowered headpiece could be seen among headscarves on the women, hats on the men." Said an assistant chief usher of the cold conditions, "I've been here for 27 years, and it's one of the coldest crowds I ever saw. They're nonchalant—indifferent."

The game was scheduled to start at the earliest time in memory, 1:30 p.m., because the Reds needed to fly to Los Angeles right after the game. They were set to christen the National League's newest and fanciest ballpark, Dodger Stadium. In an effort to stay warm as long as possible, fans were slow to arrive at the stadium. When they did arrive, they were

Doris Day

entertained by a new musical treat: four six-piece bands from the well-known Barney Rapp group. The sextets were stationed at four different spots in front of the box seats. Rapp had been a famous jazz musician and orchestra leader from the 1920s to the 1940s. His group was known as "Barney Rapp and his New Englanders" before moving to Cincinnati and opening a nightclub called "The Sign of the Drum" in Bond Hill. (A singer in his 1940s band was Cincinnatian Doris Kappelhoff. Rapp suggested she change her name because it was "too long for the marquee." She changed her name to Doris Day and went on to have an award-winning career as a recording artist and actress.)

Rapp had formed the Reds Rooters Fan Club in 1956, and parts of his group became a mainstay at Crosley. They were invited to play alongside Smitty's Band, which had paraded from downtown with the Findlay Market Association. Rapp's four bands then made their way into the stands to make music during the game—a tradition that would continue for years.

> *"Of all the places I played in either league, Crosley Field was my favorite. It was a unique, quaint ballpark."*
>
> Frank Robinson

The Reds took the field with their vest-type uniforms that had added a second dark stripe. They had worn a mourning band the previous season out of respect to Powell Crosley Jr., and a reporter asked a fan why the uniforms now had dark stripes. The response? "Probably because of the World Series!" (The team had lost the 1961 World Series to the Yankees.)

The game went poorly, so the "boo birds" came out by the third inning—in all likelihood many of the same fans who had cheered the team to the National League pennant just six months before. The crowd began to work its way out of the park early as the Reds were drubbed by the Phillies, 12–4. On their way out, the fans may have been discussing the latest rumors about actors Richard Burton and Elizabeth Taylor, both box office stars who were rumored to be lovers while married to other people. The *Enquirer* had followed the lead of the tabloids that morning by spreading the gossip. Burton and Taylor later divorced their spouses and became married to each other two different times during the 1960s and 1970s, finally divorcing for good in 1976. Ironically, they starred in in the film, *Divorce His, Divorce Hers* in 1973. At least new owner DeWitt promised that the Reds would not divorce Cincinnati!

Pete Rose with Knothole Baseball Player Tom Linz, Opening Day 1963

A ROSE-Y OUTLOOK

Today is a day when Cincinnatians—baseball fans or not—can kick off the winter drabs, throw open the doors and windows, and take a deep breath of renewal. It's about more than baseball. It's about nostalgia and hope, tradition and youth. It brings us together—people of all ages, ethnicities and backgrounds. For one day everyone's a kid again, peeking through the slats in the outfield fence. Or at the real-time updated tucked behind the spreadsheet on your computer screen.

Enquirer editorial

Opening Day 1963 will be remembered as one that changed the Reds forever: fans met Peter Edward Rose for the first time. He would become the face of the franchise for most of the next 27 years, and his style of play—gritty, hustling, never giving up—was admired by blue-collar and white-collar fans alike. Without question, he was the most popular player during those years.

The Rose years would see the Reds consistently compete for championships. Was it because of Rose? Certainly he was the heart and soul of the franchise that excited an already loyal fan base. The holiday of Opening Day grew larger and more festive as a result.

1963: "Charlie Hustle"

The April 8 morning *Enquirer* delivered good news to Cincinnati sports fans. Several leading industrial accountants had declared Cincinnati "America's Best Baseball Town." The accountants drew the conclusion by considering the total attendance at games and dividing it by the population of the area in which teams played. Cincinnati easily outranked all the other major-league cities. In professional basketball, the Cincinnati Royals were continuing their Cinderella season by having evened their playoff series with the Boston Celtics the previous night at Cincinnati Gardens, 3–3. (The Royals would lose the seventh and deciding game.) Without a doubt, the fans were in a good mood, as many experts had predicted the Reds would be the class of the National League in 1963.

Pete Rose

Many would say that Pete Rose was and is the most beloved Red of all time. Rose was a hometown boy, and he had been the talk of spring training because of his spirited play. He won the competition to start at second base over incumbent Don Blasingame. Rose would go on to be named Rookie of the Year en route to his career record of 4,256 career hits in the major leagues.

Unnoticed by the fans was the new groundskeeper, Mike Dolan, though his work in preparation for the game was apparent upon entry to the park. Dolan replaced Mathias "Matty" Schwab, his grandfather, who was the Reds' superintendent from 1903 until 1963. Matty had worked at League Park, the Palace of the Fans, and Crosley Field. Matty had succeeded his father, John, who was superintendent from 1894 to 1903.

Under Matty Schwab's tutelage, Dolan supervised the resodding of the field by bringing in sod from—of all places—Gate of Heaven Cemetery just north of Cincinnati. The fans noticed that the field had never looked better. There were no bare spots, and the field looked like a green, wall-to-wall carpet. Patrons also noticed three new painted billboards that stretched across the left field wall—the first time the club placed advertising signs on the outfield fence since the early 1930s. The signs presented a sharp contrast to the green center field wall. Outfielders noticed and appreciated Dolan's work as well, as padding was added to lessen the blow if they hit the hard rock fence trying to make a catch.

An early morning rain that did not subside until 45 minutes before the game put a damper on the annual parades, but the pregame ceremony included a particularly poignant moment. The Reds selected Susan Schroeder, a 1963 Easter Seal child, to toss the first ball. From her box seat normally reserved for political dignitaries, the disabled girl stood on her crutches and tossed the first ball to Governor James Rhodes.

The fans soon learned that the day belonged to Rose. In his first major league at bat, Rose took four consecutive balls and promptly sprinted to first base. He would soon score the first run

Jim O'Toole

of the season. The fans had read about Rose during spring training, when he was clocked running to first at 4.1 seconds after a walk, but this was the first time they witnessed it. Mickey Mantle, a New York Yankee legend, famously gave Rose his new nickname after he watched Rose run to first base after a base on balls during a routine exhibition game: "Who does he think he is, Charlie Hustle?" The Reds scored four runs early, and the Pirates never seriously threatened to ruin a complete game victory by Jim O'Toole.

Even as a rookie without a hit in his first game, Rose dominated the next day's coverage of Opening Day. Beloved manager Fred Hutchinson praised Rose for his defensive play in the field, calling it "good glove work." *Enquirer* staff reporter Libby Lackman declared, "It was almost as much 'Pete Rose Day' as Opening Day." *Enquirer* executive sports editor Al Heim devoted a full column to the new star:

> Rose is always in a hurry. It's not because he's excited or nervous. It's just the way he plays baseball. He drew applause from the capacity crowd in the first inning when he drew a walk and ran to first base with the vigor of a man trying to beat out a bunt.

On the national front, Cuba remained a grave concern. For 13 days during the previous October, the world had been seemingly poised on the brink of nuclear war, hoping for a peaceful resolution to the Cuban Missile Crisis with the Soviet Union. On the morning of the opener, fans read that Senator Barry Goldwater had stoked latent fears. He advocated a blockade of Cuba, support of Cuban exiles, and an invasion of Cuba if necessary to destroy communism on the island. The same day, a committee was formed to draft Goldwater as the 1964 Republican presidential candidate.

1964: Hutch Diagnosed with Cancer

Reds fans excited for another season had heavy hearts as they prepared for the April 13 opener. Manager Fred Hutchinson had learned on Christmas Eve that he had a malignant growth that was later diagnosed as lung cancer. Fortunately, his brother William was a physician involved in radiation research, and radiation was a new procedure available only in Seattle. Hutch underwent two months of radiation treatments in Seattle before joining the Reds to direct spring training. The players decided to dedicate the season in his honor.

Fred Hutchinson

The *Enquirer* opined in a morning editorial that Opening Day "is the desk-bound or bench-bound or stove-bound fan's first chance to renew the fresh-air acquaintance with a game that is engrossing for so many months of the year." The editorial board advised the team to just "Play!" after reminding readers that Official Rule No. 4.02 stipulated that the umpire shall say "Play," not "Play ball" nor "Batter up." Not that anyone really cared—the season was on, and various civic groups had already planned victory parties.

Although rain and gusty winds ensured the smallest crowd since 1943, the spectators resembled a large family reunion in Cincinnati. An *Enquirer* writer noted that "28,110 sisters, brothers, fathers, mothers, cousins, nephews, nieces, grandmothers, grandfathers, friends, and neighbors gathered at the big Crosley Field shelter house." The fans spent their time greeting friends, drinking gallons of beer, gobbling thousands of bratwursts, and strolling around the grandstand and Sun Deck during the game.

The customary pregame activities entertained the patrons before the Reds were introduced. Fans noticed something curious about the team's jerseys: the Reds had added players' names on the back of their uniforms for the first time, but they were under the number. No other team ever placed the name of a player under the number! The team discarded the practice after three seasons.

The unique uniform style did not provide enough motivation for the Reds, losing 6–3 to the Houston Colts. As an *Enquirer* writer noted, "What the heck, one couldn't have everything—every picnic has a few problems." And one problem that persisted was Hutchinson's cancer. After the opener, Hutch boarded a plane for Seattle for a routine

Leo Cabenas

examination. He would coach his last game on August 12 after a birthday party in his honor, and he died three months later.

Meanwhile, the fans were debating civil rights issues. The city's civil rights leader, the Reverend Fred Shuttlesworth, had paid tribute to a Cleveland minister who died under a bulldozer the previous Tuesday during a civil rights protest. Shuttlesworth spoke to a somber group of some 150 persons gathered in Garfield Park downtown. At the time, Congress and political candidates were debating the merits of the Civil Rights Act proposed by President Kennedy before he was assassinated by Lee Harvey Oswald in November 1963. (Cincinnati congressman Robert Taft Jr. was a strong supporter of the legislation despite some public resistance, and the bill passed in the summer of 1964.)

1965: Rosie Reds

April 12 was a beautiful day for Opening Day. It was sunny and 76 degrees, and the opener attracted rooters from such points as Louisville, Kentucky; Huntington, West Virginia; Muncie, Indiana; and Portsmouth, Ohio. Wrote *Enquirer* sports reporter Bill Anzer, Opening Day was like "a premier showing of a movie. A one-day World Series. And to have an opening day [ticket] is a status symbol."

One particularly enthusiastic group of fans was known as the Rosie Reds. Formed the previous June, the group was made up of local women who reacted strongly to Bill DeWitt's recent threat to move the team to San Diego. The members encouraged women to show support for the team by attending both home and away games. "Rosie" was an acronym for "Rooters Organized to Stimulate Interest and Enthusiasm" in the Cincinnati Reds. The women adopted a mascot that had a woman's face on a large baseball head. The mascot wore a white, skirted uniform trimmed in red.

Everything's Comin' Up Rosie Reds

Club management credited the Rosie Reds with being influential in the decision to keep the team in Cincinnati. As such, they decided to throw their support behind the group. The highest recognition for the fledgling group was the extension of an invitation by the Reds for the Rosie Reds to participate in the pregame ceremonies on Opening Day. Club president Jeanette Heinze presented a huge baseball to manager Dick Sisler, and vice president Marge Zimmer presented a bouquet of red roses to Milwaukee Braves manager Bobby Bragan. Their historic presentation—the first ever by an exclusively female rooters group—was preceded by the traditional music by Smitty's band and the Saint Clement School band that had led the Findlay Market parade. The bands entertained the crowd of 28,467 with popular songs, including, appropriately enough, "Hello Dolly" and "Happy Days Are Here Again." As the season went on, the Reds continued to support the Rosie Reds by donating regular season tickets to club members, sending speakers to club events, and encouraging women to join the organization by promoting it during games. The philanthropic group continues to be active today, donating scholarships and supporting youth baseball.

A relief pitcher of sorts was called on to handle the traditional first pitch. Governor James Rhodes, scheduled to take the mound, was forced to skip the game because of violent tornadoes that tore through the Midwest from Iowa to Ohio on the eve of the opener. Deaths totaled 91 throughout the region, including nine in the tiny city of Pittsfield in northern Ohio. That community had been reduced to rubble by the tornado. Cincinnati mayor Walton Bachrach performed the honor in Rhodes's place. Prior to the national anthem, the Findlay Market rooters recognized the team's late manager, Fred Hutchinson. They presented owner Bill DeWitt with a plaque honoring "Hutch," and the crowd then stood for a moment of silence.

Reds great Tony Perez, platooning at first base with Gordy Coleman, was introduced to Reds fans for the first time. The game was a pitchers' duel, with both starters completing nine innings in the 4–2 loss for the Reds.

Tony Perez

A noteworthy event in baseball occurred on Opening Day, as the newly named Houston Astros played the first major-league game indoors. The team, which had begun as a 1962 expansion team known as the Houston Colt .45s, occupied the brand-new Astrodome, the nation's first domed sports stadium. As noted in the *Enquirer*, "Sportswriters and sportscasters will be wrestling whether to call the thing a ballpark, a baseball building, a ball hall, or the Astros capsule, or something."

Opening Day occurred just five weeks after the first United States combat troops arrived in Vietnam. The United States had taken a defensive position in the war by providing support to the South Vietnamese, along with other anti-communist allies. President Johnson, given the power to launch any military actions he deemed necessary by Congress's Gulf of Tonkin Resolution, deployed 3,500 ground troops. On the morning of the opener, the official Hanoi newspaper Nhan Dan promised that the North Vietnamese would "resolutely fight to the end" in response to LBJ's offer the previous day to engage in peace talks to end the ten-year conflict. China, an ally of North Vietnam, called Johnson's offer "a hoax." The United States would commit another 200,000 ground troops by the end of the year, and the war soon became the most unpopular conflict ever engaged in by the United States.

1966: Rain, Rain, Go Away!

Reds fans were optimistic before the scheduled April 11 opener. The club was "pitching rich," and national experts had pegged the Reds as the favorites to win the National League. As was customary, the first thing fans checked in the morning *Enquirer* was the weather, always questionable with ever-earlier Opening Days. There was good news: the paper reported that "the weatherman had co-operated with the Reds for the big show. The forecast was for fair and warm today." The game was on!

Well, the weatherman was as wrong as he could be. Rain began to fall early, and the Findlay Market parade never left the corner of Vine and Elder Streets. The players, waiting in the dugout to begin batting practice, departed for the clubhouse at 11:45 a.m., never to return that afternoon. Most of a near-capacity crowd waited in the stands with ponchos and umbrellas before the game was finally canceled at 3:18 p.m. and rescheduled for the next afternoon.

When fans awoke the next morning, the weatherman predicted intermittent rain and a chance for a few thunderstorms with colder weather. He was wrong again, as the steady rain began in the morning, stopping only for brief intervals. The club was forced to postpone its home opener until April 22. The Reds would open the season on the road for the first time since 1888!

Mr. Red

The disappointment of the rainouts was compounded by news that seven Americans had been killed by a mortar attack, and 155 others had been wounded in southeast Asia. In the space race, Soviet cosmonauts launched a space vehicle trying to determine whether a moon landing would be possible. Cosmonaut Gherman Titov predicted that "builders and assemblers will soon appear in space," eventually leading to building small towns on the moon. Meanwhile, NASA reported that a $50 million Stargazer satellite failed in its mission to obtain new data about the universe. The mission was lost after the satellite's batteries went dead. The United States was losing the wars on Earth and in space.

After the double rainout, the Reds announced that Opening Day tickets could be exchanged for any regular season home date on the schedule, which turned out to be a gracious decision that went wrong. After a disastrous road trip with six losses in seven games, the fans were not very interested in attending the Friday night opener even though the Reds promised souvenir water tumblers and a fireworks show after the game. Only 10,266 fans bothered to show, making it the worst attendance at a home opener since 1907. The usual pregame festivities were held, but they seemed out of place under the lights before a small crowd.

The game was equally disappointing. After the Reds took an early lead, the Phillies scored five runs in the final three innings to win 9–7. The boo birds came out in force in the eighth inning.

Previously that day, House Republican leader Gerald Ford charged that Secretary of Defense Robert McNamara was mismanaging the war. The Associated Press reported that 3,047 GIs had lost their lives in combat in Vietnam. Protests were mounting on college campuses throughout the country, and "draft dodger" became part of the nation's everyday language.

1967: Hello, Mr. Howsam!

The April 10 opener was preceded by good news. The Reds signed a 40-year lease with the city of Cincinnati to occupy a new stadium on the riverfront. The stadium would have an enclosed circular design, and it would appropriately be called Riverfront Stadium. Fans breathed a sigh of relief as the cloud of a potential move to another city disappeared. At the same time, an investment group headed by the publisher of the *Enquirer* bought the team and hired a new general manager, Bob Howsam. Howsam would become the architect of the Big Red Machine, which would dominate the National League during the 1970s.

Cincinnati fans always enjoyed being in the baseball spotlight on Opening Day. This year, they were in the mood to celebrate the continued presence of the Reds in Cincinnati while, at the same time, reminiscing about Crosley Field. The *Enquirer* editorial page screamed "Happy New Year!" and highlighted a fan, William Clawson, who was planning to attend his seventy-second consecutive opening game. George Palmer reflected on the sentiment of those who saw the days of Crosley Field coming to an end:

Bob Howsam

Today will be one of the last. The death of Crosley Field as the home of the Cincinnati Reds is predictable. Within two years the great festivities that always attend a Reds opening day will be moved downtown to the new riverfront stadium. Crosley Field will then be an empty ghost on that early April opening day; and the plot of land that has witnessed the heroics of the baseball great of all time for 83 years will be retired to a new purpose.

As fans arrived at the park, they saw bright green grass imported from Asia, known as Zoysia. It was known to hold up better in hot weather than traditional species of grass used in ballparks. When the Reds took the field for batting practice, the early arrivals saw that the vest-style uniforms had been replaced with the traditional shirt and sleeves. The Findlay Market rooters arrived as usual, led by a parade marshal and color guards. The parade also featured the Roger Bacon High School Band, a Boy Scout troop, and baton twirlers by the name of the Linkettes. With new owners, new uniforms, and new grass, the spectators were in the holiday spirit.

The Reds rewarded their faithful fans with a convincing 6–1 win over the Dodgers. It was a perfect day for baseball, which caused meteorologist Bob Brumfield to breathe a sigh of relief after the previous year's forecast was off the mark. "Well, the heat is off me for a couple of days, anyway. The forecast for the Reds opening day weather was accurate."

The opener was a welcome relief for the citizens. They read bad news from all around earlier in the morning. First, there was the

> *If Opening Day happened every day, Cincinnati would be the most hopeful and happiest place on earth."*
>
> Cliff Radel, Enquirer columnist

report from a blue-ribbon board of review that blamed faulty wiring for the deaths of three Apollo 1 astronauts in a January 27 fire. Next, union representatives rejected a proposed truce by President Johnson that threatened to pile a nationwide railway strike on top of an already existing trucking shutdown. Worse, spreading racial riots around the country jolted Nashville, Tennessee, when police exchanged gunfire with rioting students.

On the war front, the Pentagon issued its biggest draft call of the year by asking for the induction of 19,800 men into the army by June. Meanwhile, a federal appeals court judge declared that the burning of a draft card was protected by the First Amendment of the Constitution. The Vietnam War was increasingly unpopular, and the Rev. Dr. Martin Luther King Jr. called on all draftees interested in civil rights to become conscientious objectors and not serve their country. Senator Barry Goldwater accused King of treason.

As students protested the war, other students decided to engage in acts of love. College students from the Boston area splashed around in a frog pond in Boston Common experiencing what they called a "Love In"—a protest against nothing.

1968: Mourning Dr. King

Dr. King, the most visible leader in the civil rights movement, was assassinated by James Earl Ray on April 4, just four days before the scheduled April 8 opener. King, inspired by the nonviolent activism of Mahatma Gandhi, had tried for 14 years to advance civil rights through nonviolence and civil disobedience. He had famously told Don Newcombe, an African American who was a longtime Dodgers pitcher, "Don, I don't know what I would've done without you guys setting up minds of people for change. You, Jackie [Robinson], and Roy [Campanella] will never know how easy you made it for me to do my job." Newcombe had played for the Reds in 1959 and 1960.

Guard Moves On Rioters; Curfew Slapped On City

Following King's death, riots occurred in many cities throughout the country, including in Cincinnati's Avondale community. President Johnson announced a national day of mourning on April 9, the day of King's funeral. His casket was carried through the streets of Atlanta on a mule-drawn cart in a tribute that was unprecedented in the nation's history. His marble crypt was inscribed with the words, "Free at Last."

The Reds and the rest of MLB, except the Los Angeles Dodgers, quickly postponed their openers. (Los Angeles later backed down when Phillies players said they would refuse to play on the day of the funeral.) Opening Day in Cincinnati was delayed until April 10 when all teams would open the season.

On the day of the funeral, Reds president Francis Dale hoped that baseball "could bring a smile back to our citizens." He stated his belief that there is a time for mourning and a time to return to the job of day-to-day living. Sports columnist Lou Smith poignantly explained why the postponement was necessary:

> It seems to me that it was fitting that the baseball season, opening day of America's favorite sport, should be postponed out of deference and respect for Dr. Martin Luther King Jr., for wasn't it baseball that first put into

action, so to speak, the philosophy of Dr. King? It was baseball that first acknowledged the ability of those other than the white players. Perhaps before too long all men will be judged, as Dr. King said, "not by the color of their skin, but by the content of their character."

For the Opening Day game, plainclothes police officers, plus a dozen extra uniformed police, circulated through the ballpark. The Avondale riots had occurred just two nights earlier, and curfew had been lifted that morning as fans entered the ballpark. Although every seat had been sold in advance, only 28,111 spectators attended the 10–4 win over the Cubs. Both the ushers and the ballpark sported a new look: the ushers were dressed in new Palm Beach red jackets, and the grandstand roof featured pennants identifying each National League team. To the delight of fans, a beer garden was added under the stands behind the third baseline.

Joe Nuxhall, 1968

Preceding the game, the Findlay Market Association made its traditional pilgrimage from Vine and Elder streets, and Marian Spelman sang the national anthem. As it did in some years, the association crowned a queen of Opening Day. Mayor Gene Ruehlmann, described as the "No. 1 Reds fan," threw out the first pitch to future congressman Willis Gradison. The annual festivities provided a welcome relief from the sorrows of the day.

1969: A Birthday Party

April 7, the earliest Opening Day in history, marked the one hundredth anniversary of the Cincinnati Red Stockings, the first professional baseball team in America. Cincinnati was ready to celebrate despite the club saying it would officially celebrate the birthday before the second game of the season. As it had done before, the team pushed a big celebration into the regular season in order to boost ticket sales later on. The fans, however, decided to blow out the candles on April 7!

Cincinnatians are proud of their baseball heritage dating back to 1869 and their status as trailblazers in the sport. After all, the Reds were the first to have a ladies' day, the first to host a night game, the first to have a farm system, the first to travel by air, and the first to be televised. But the historic season of the 1869 Red Stockings is why most baseball fans in Cincinnati believe the city deserves to open the season.

"It's Centennial Year for the Reds!" announced the *Enquirer* on the morning of the game. The day was made to order: 87 degrees and sunny. Not surprisingly, the game sold out, and the shirtsleeve fans who began to stream in at noon were rollicking. They welcomed the annual Findlay Market parade, which entered through Crosley Field's right field gate at precisely 1:55 p.m. as scheduled. The color guards of the combined armed forces led the Linkette Baton Twirlers and the Roger Bacon High School Band into the ballpark. Following close behind were the Boy Scouts carrying flowers to present to club officials. The local Knothole rooters brought the best present of all: a five-foot-tall, four-layer birthday cake! The only things missing were 100 candles to mark the occasion.

It's Centennial Year For The Reds!

In addition to the local politicians, Paul Brown, the founder and coach of Cincinnati's new franchise in the National Football League, the Bengals, appeared on behalf of the team. Mayor Ruehlmann presented an American flag to Bob Howsam and declared, "Under this flag stands the greatest country in the world."

The white grandstands were draped with colorful bunting, and the fans were sporting red vests, ties, hats, dresses, and jackets as they waved banners and flags. An *Enquirer* reporter spotted a Catholic nun wearing a "Go Reds Go" button. The reporter also observed, "Hearty matrons came in red knit suits, Easter chapeaux, and corsages—and gripped score-cards in their teeth as they applauded Pete Rose." Barney Rapp's strolling musicians entertained the crowd between innings, often featuring Jerry McDermott on the trombone. During the seventh-inning stretch, Sports Service, Inc., reported record sales of hot dogs and cold drinks. Veteran usher John Allen called it "the best opening day in years."

The crowd of 30,111 had barely settled into their seats when Pete Rose and Bobby Tolan led off the bottom of the first inning with back-to-back home runs. It was the last standing ovation of the day, as Dodger starting pitcher Don Drysdale recovered and pitched a gem. The Dodgers won 3–2.

Reds fans were nonetheless optimistic about the 1969 season, which saw the addition of four new teams to the major leagues and the splitting of each league into two six-team divisions. The Reds were expected to win the National League Western division title. (They did not, though they did win it in the next five out of seven seasons.) Reds catcher Johnny Bench was rumored in the morning paper to be baseball's first $200,000 man. Fans left the ballpark unsure of whether they had witnessed the last Opening Day at Crosley Field. The new stadium on the riverfront was projected to be ready for the full 1970 season if all went well.

Two nights later, the new MLB commissioner, Bowie Kuhn, was on hand with 34 all-time greats who were guests of the Reds. They had gathered to commemorate 100 years of professional baseball. The crowd gave Kuhn a loud, long cheer when he commented in pregame ceremonies that "you have one of the finest teams in baseball over in that dugout."

Secret Peace Offensive Under Way

On the national front, the increasingly unpopular Vietnam War was continuing. *The New York Times* reported that newly elected president Richard Nixon had set in motion secret peace talks in Paris. The talks were designed to extricate the United States from Vietnam. At the same time, the Army charged and tried 14 soldiers for mutiny after they had participated in a sit-down protest at the Presidio stockade in San Francisco. The soldiers objected to the cramped living space at the stockade.

In Ohio's capital city of Columbus, women's rights were being debated. The Ohio Senate was threatening to bar the press from the Senate floor. Why? The journalists refused to tell one of their colleagues, 25-year-old United Press International reporter Betty Work, to quit wearing thigh-high miniskirts while working at the capitol. Senate president John Brown claimed it was his responsibility to maintain "dignity and decorum." Work was eventually allowed to do her job.

Sparky Anderson

12

THE SENSATIONAL '70s

The one constant through all the years ... has been baseball. America has rolled by like an army of steamrollers. It's been erased like a blackboard, rebuilt, and erased again. But baseball has marked the time. This field, this game, is part of our past ... It reminds us of all that was once good and could be again.

James Earl Jones, *Field of Dreams*

The 1970s are etched in the minds of Cincinnatians old enough to have experienced the Big Red Machine, and often in the minds of younger fans who have heard the many stories passed down from their parents and grandparents. It is the decade that solidified the festivities of Opening Day. Why not celebrate a new season when times are really good, there are superstars on the team, and the players are local and national celebrities?

1970: Crosley Field Bids Adieu

April 6 was the debut of new Reds manager George "Sparky" Anderson. Between getting a new manager and playing their last Opening Day game at Crosley Field, the Reds made it a point to put on a good show. The prospect of having no more Opening Days at Crosley Field marked the end of an era: the team had played at the Findlay Street and Western Avenue site since 1884. The original home plate was located in what was now deep right field, where fans on this day filled the Sun Deck. To mark the occasion, the current and former presidents of the National League, along with other local and state dignitaries, came to pay their respects. The Reds planned to move to their new stadium in June.

It was a sad day for many fans who had come to love the quaint, little ballpark. It was the only one they had ever known, and they hated to say goodbye. The gloomy, chilly weather—complete with occasional rain showers—suited the occasion. Fans who arrived early to take in the festivities were greeted by 40-degree temperatures and two different rain showers. A reporter from Montréal, Quebec, covering the Red's opponent that day, the Expos, remarked, "S'ils parviennent à jouer ce match, ce sera un miracle!"! ("If they get this in, it'll be a miracle.")

Beer consumption had long been a hallmark of Opening Day, and this one was no different. The occasion of celebrating the final Opening Day at Crosley Field allowed beer-loving fans to temporarily forget that 807 workers at three local breweries—Hudepohl, Burger, and Wiedemann—had begun a strike earlier in the day. Beer was served at the park despite the strike.

The pregame ceremonies were remarkably unsentimental. There was little mention of the game being the last opener at the historic ballpark. It was as if club officials and patrons wanted to avoid the subject. The celebration focused more on marking the fiftieth anniversary of the Findlay Market parade. The fans witnessed the usual pomp and circumstance involving the crowning of the group's queen and the performance of the high school marching band. Marian Spelman sang her last national anthem at the park.

The team had been nicknamed the Big Red Machine the previous Fourth of July by Bob Hunter of the *Los Angeles Herald Examiner*. The team easily won this opener 5–1, defeating the Expos in only their second season. The victory was the first in a decade that would

see the Reds put together the best record in baseball and dominate the National League. They would win the National League in 1970 before losing the World Series to Baltimore.

The real goodbye to Crosley took place on June 24, described as a "happy wake." During a pregame ceremony, *Dayton Daily News* sports editor Si Burick concluded his remarks with "rest in peace," but there was one last game to play. Fittingly, Johnny Bench and Lee May hit back-to-back home runs off the Giants' Juan Marichal in the Reds' last at bat for a 5–4 victory. The crowd remained after the game to reminisce and watch a helicopter arrive to transport home plate by air to Riverfront Stadium. Tears were shed by many of the 28,027 fans who attended the finale. (Tens of thousands more claim that they were there!) Park officials were expecting trouble, so 60 police officers were stationed around the ballpark to prevent fans from taking a seat or running onto the playing field to grab a souvenir such as a base or a clump of grass, but there was no trouble. Mayor Eugene Ruehlmann proclaimed, "And now it is time to say 'farewell Crosley Field, hello Riverfront

'Another Opener . . . Another Show'

Stadium.'" Pete Wagner's Dixieland Band played "Auld Lang Syne" as a final salute. In what seems like an ignominious end for the grand old stadium, the iconic ballpark would become an auto impound center before it was demolished to make way for an industrial park in 1972.

Riverfront Stadium is Reds Country

1971: A New Parade Route

Although the Reds had settled comfortably into Riverfront Stadium during the summer of 1970, April 5, 1971, marked the first Opening Day at the new location. Parade participants had to follow a different route than they were accustomed to taking. Instead of proceeding west from Findlay Market, the grand marshal led the marching bands and floats south on Race Street and then west on Fifth Street past Fountain Square. As fans lined Race Street in Over-the-Rhine, they were able to see buildings that are the nation's largest collection of nineteenth-century Italianate architecture. The area was the former home of Cincinnati's German-speaking residents and their many breweries. Thousands of cheering spectators watched as the parade made its first-ever trek to the new riverfront ballpark. From there, they entered through a center field gate to an ovation from the largest crowd (51,702) ever to attend a baseball game in Cincinnati. The Pete Wagner Dixieland Band, the Roger Bacon High School Band, the Wright Patterson Air Force Base Band, and the Queen City Drum and Bugle Corps provided the music for the festive atmosphere.

The pregame ceremonies mirrored those conducted at Crosley. Reds manager Sparky

Anderson accepted a floral display from the Findlay Market Association, and local politicians, team officials, and National League president Charles Feeney made speeches. Sportscaster Al Michaels was introduced as the new voice of the Reds, joining Joe Nuxhall in the radio booth. The biggest roar of the day came when the National League pennant was raised on top of Riverfront Stadium to recognize the Reds' league championship the previous year.

The game-time temperature of 46 degrees fell throughout the game, so Reds reliever Clay Carroll joked that pitchers would be throwing snowballs by the sixth inning. After the Reds committed six errors and were beaten by the Atlanta Braves, manager Sparky Anderson warned reporters not to make a big deal about the result: "If this game had been played in July, nobody would have thought anything about it. But here, Opening Day is like the World Series."

In Washington, the Vietnam War continued to stir controversy. Representative John Flynt Jr. of Georgia was a Bronze Star medal winner after serving on the beaches of Normandy during World War II. He had voted without hesitation for every defense and draft bill for 18 years, but he announced in a dramatic speech on the House floor that he was opposed to extending the draft: "My conscience will not let me vote to continue to conscript young Americans to fight a war which most Americans do not want, and a war which the U.S. government apparently lacks the courage to either win or stop."

President Nixon was also being criticized for his reaction to the discipline meted out to Lieutenant William Calley Jr. A week earlier, Calley had been found guilty of premeditated murder of 20 Vietnamese civilians during the My Lai massacre of an estimated 400 unarmed people by the US Army in 1968. Nixon announced on April 4 that he would personally review the conviction and life sentence. He ordered that Calley be released from armed custody at Fort Benning, Georgia. This decision was roundly criticized by opponents of the war who believed that the "Mere Gook Rule" had encouraged soldiers to err on the side of killing South Vietnamese civilians. Supporters of the president believed that soldiers accused of killing civilians should be granted blanket amnesty. Calley's conviction was upheld, but his punishment was reduced to 20 years. He was paroled in September 1974.

1972: Does Anyone Still Care?

By 1972, labor unions had been a force in the United States for more than a century. In 1954, baseball players unionized by forming the Major League Baseball Players Association, but the new union was barely noticed until the players hired Marvin Miller in 1966 to head the organization. Hiring Miller sent shock waves through baseball's ownership circle. Miller was an acclaimed union man and had been a labor official in the Kennedy administration. In 1969, a nine-day strike at the start of spring training coordinated by Miller served notice to team owners that players would unite behind him.

Talks for a new collective bargaining agreement continued through spring training in 1972. The primary request from the players was for an increase in their pensions to match three years' worth of inflation. To the amazement of the owners, who wanted to break the fledgling union, 47 out of 48 player representatives voted to begin a strike just four days before Opening Day. Openers were canceled, and 74 other games would never be made up until the owners blinked and agreed to

Marvin Miller

increase the pension fund. Opening Day was postponed ten days, until April 15. By most accounts, the fans felt that the big leaguers had abused their privilege of being professional baseball players who were handsomely paid to do something they loved.

Enquirer columnist Dick Forbes blamed Miller for the strike, and he predicted the fans would soon forgive the players, just as Americans seemed to do often with former enemies. *Enquirer* sports reporter Bob Hertzel summed up the feelings of Reds fans: "If there's anyone left who still cares, Opening Day 1972 has arrived at last." The annual pregame parade went on as scheduled, but it was much easier to find a place to plant a lawn chair on the city's sidewalks than in past years, as many spectators boycotted the event. When the color guards, bands, and Rosie Reds entered the stadium, the applause was muted. More than 14,000 fans lodged a silent protest by not coming to the game against the Dodgers, but the 37,895 who did show were anything but silent.

> *"When you say strike today, say it softly!"*
> Jerry Dowling cartoon, 1972,
> of conversation between two umpires

The only two players to receive a warm welcome by fans were Frank Robinson, the former Reds star who was now a Dodger, and Pete Rose. Otherwise, the players from both teams were booed as they were introduced along the baselines. The fans reserved their heartiest catcalls for pitcher Jim Merritt, who was the Reds' union representative, and Johnny Bench, who was an outspoken

supporter of Marvin Miller. (Unbeknownst to the fans, Merritt had resigned as union rep two hours before the game and was replaced by Bench.) The game proved to be a disaster for the Reds, as they collected just three hits and lost 3–1. The game mercifully ended in two hours and 13 minutes. The demolition of Crosley Field began four days later. Around the nation, other teams also received a cool reception from fans. Some teams had fewer than 10,000 fans at their openers.

JIm Merritt

Johnny Bench

On the same day, Americans seemed equally ambivalent about the nation's space program, according to an *Enquirer* editorial. Despite the pride the nation felt upon Apollo 11's first lunar landing in July 1969, NASA's critics asserted that the space program wasted resources that could be better directed toward economic and social problems. As Opening Day was underway, three astronauts were preparing for the United States' fifth lunar landing. John Young, Charles Duke Jr., and Thomas Mattingly II launched from Cape Canaveral, Florida the next day. Their launch began an 11-day journey aboard Apollo 16, landing for the first time in the middle of the moon's mountains. During three days on the moon, they collected 211 pounds of lunar material to bring back to Earth.

The Reds would go on to win their second National League championship in three years, but lose again in the World Series, this time to the Oakland A's in seven games.

1973: Vietnam POW Honored

Just over two months before the April 5 opener, the United States signed the Paris Peace Accords to officially end direct American involvement in the Vietnam War. United States forces were withdrawn over the next 60 days, and prisoners of war were released by North Vietnam. Fittingly, the Reds invited fighter pilot Edward Mechenbier to throw out the first pitch on Opening Day. Mechenbier, whose home was in nearby Dayton, Ohio, had spent 2,076 days as a POW after his plane was shot down over North Vietnam during his eightieth combat mission. As controversial as the war had become, Mechenbier received a hero's welcome and a standing ovation from the 51,179 fans in attendance. Fans were still excited after another National League championship, so they turned out despite game-time temperatures of 42 degrees. The game was a sellout, and the *Enquirer* announced that it was "SRO"—Shivering Room Only!

Opening Day was much anticipated in 1973 as the Big Red Machine was expected to dominate the league again. Aureal Imfeld of Hamilton, Ohio, attended his sixtieth consecutive opener. The entire senior class from Grant County High School in Kentucky played hooky, as did representatives of the Goodyear Tire & Rubber Company and the United Rubber Workers. They were engaged in important national contract negotiations in Cincinnati, but the negotiators could agree on one item: they would hold their talks in abeyance so their representatives could attend Opening Day.

The opener followed the team's second World Series loss in three years, and Reds officials announced that the game would be held "in World Series atmosphere." Dignitaries, including Ohio governor John Gilligan, U.S. senator Robert Taft, and Cincinnati mayor Theodore Berry, welcomed Mechenbier, a lifelong Reds fan. The day began with the traditional opening game festivities and the fifty-fourth edition of the Findlay Market parade, but the downtown streets were lined with fewer people in the cold, damp weather. Coming off their World Series appearance, the Reds had anticipated the largest crowd in history, but thousands decided to stay home. The Reds lost 4–1 to the Giants.

Another freed prisoner of war, Lieutenant Commander John McCain III, made news that morning. He credited his father's role as commander of US forces in the Pacific as saving his life. The North Vietnamese had beat him mercilessly for refusing to meet with anti-war activists Jane Fonda and Tom Hayden. McCain told the United Press International that his captors agreed to take him to a hospital after telling him, "Your father is a big admiral." McCain would later become an esteemed senator from Arizona and the Republican candidate for president in 2012.

> *"As baseball spectacle, this could hardly be topped."*
>
> Pat Harmon,
> Cincinnati Post sports editor

The April 4 opener in 1974 was likely the most unusual one in Reds' history. The focus on the event during the off-season had always been the anticipation of another season, the festivities planned for Opening Day, and the unofficial beginning of spring. For five months, however, the sports world and Cincinnati fans had been consumed with Henry Aaron. Aaron had hit the 713th home run of his career at the end of the previous season, which put him one shy of Babe Ruth's all-time record of 714 home runs. Naturally, Atlanta Braves fans wanted to see this record tied and then broken in Atlanta. Fans, journalists, and baseball officials debated whether having Aaron sit out the first three games that were scheduled out of town was in keeping with the integrity of the game. The question was still unresolved on the morning on April 4, with Braves manager Eddie Mathews publicly stating that Aaron should wait to play until the Braves had their home opener four days later.

Although the game had long been a sellout, ticket scalpers wanted to know the answer to that question. If Aaron played and tied or broke the record, game tickets would increase in value as souvenirs. Fans who had tickets wanted to know. If he played, they knew he would bat fourth and it was possible his first chance to tie the Babe could be in the first inning. No fan anticipating the historic occasion wanted to arrive late! Reds pitcher Jack Billingham wanted to know because he anticipated a protracted standing ovation before Aaron's first at bat and wanted to be prepared for the delay. He admitted, "I'll be

191

thinking about the [possible record-tying] home run."

Whether or not Aaron should play had become an issue not just for the Braves but for the league overall. MLB commissioner Bowie Kuhn had "ordered" the Braves to play Aaron in at least two of the three games. As such, the Braves announced after a morning meeting of the team's brass that Aaron would start that afternoon. The decision was welcomed by the 250 members of the press who had arrived in Cincinnati to cover the event, as well as the commissioner and Vice President Gerald Ford. Ford had been given the honor of throwing out the traditional first pitch, although everyone was clearly more interested in Billingham's first pitch to Aaron.

The pregame pageantry featured more dignitaries than ever before, and the first-ever Opening Day appearance by the Miamisburg High School Marching Band and Stan Piatt's Band. The downtown parade was expected to be the largest in history. In addition to an unidentified number of Secret Service personnel, more than 50 uniformed and plainclothes police officers roamed the standing-room-only crowd. The officers were present because of Ford's appearance and the prospect of history being made. Some even feared harm to Aaron. After all, he was an African American chasing a hallowed record.

The parade route was crowded but less so than anticipated. The previous afternoon and evening, tornadoes had struck eight states in the Midwest and South before swirling across Canada. More than 100 persons were killed, including 85 in Ohio, Kentucky, and Indiana. In the Cincinnati area, five people were killed, hundreds were injured, and property damage was estimated at over $30 million. The natural disaster replaced Opening Day on the front page and dominated news coverage.

But back to baseball. Reds pitcher Jack Billingham was correct: the largest-ever Opening Day crowd of 52,124 gave Aaron a

huge standing ovation as he stepped in the batter's box in the top of the first inning. After looking at the first four pitches, Aaron smashed the next pitch over the left field wall (but not into the stands above) to tie the record. Stationed behind the wall, Cincinnati police officer Clarence Williams retrieved the ball and, knowing $2,000 had already been offered for it, briefly hesitated before placing the ball in a brown bag. Moments later, the center field wall parted dramatically. Williams and another officer, along with "a plump civilian in a red jacket and baseball cap," strolled onto

Jack Billingham

the field and delivered the prize to home plate. The game was stopped for seven minutes while the vice president and Kuhn congratulated Aaron, presenting him with the ball and plaques to commemorate the occasion. Ford said, "I congratulate you, Hank, on a great day, which is also a great day for baseball, and I hope you have many more." (Later that day, as Ford traveled back Washington, he reminisced with reporters about watching Babe Ruth hit two home runs over the fence in an exhibition game in Grand Rapids, Michigan, in "about 1922 or 1923.") Aaron would also play in the

third game of the series, but he left Cincinnati still tied with Ruth and promptly broke the record in Atlanta's opening home game.

The radio call of the historic home run was made by 31-year-old Marty Brennaman. Amazingly, it was the first game for Brennaman as the play-by-play announcer, having been announced in January as Al Michaels' replacement. A newcomer to MLB, Brennaman (simply "Marty" to most Reds fans) became a Hall of Fame announcer best known for his signature line of, "And this one belongs to the Reds!" at the conclusion of winning games. With Joe Nuxhall at his side, "Marty and Joe" were the most beloved announcing team until Nuxhall's retirement in 2004. (Nuxhall continued on a part-time basis for three more years.)

While still concerned about the tornado victims, Reds fans were giddy leaving the ballpark after the Reds rallied from a 6–1 deficit to win 7–6 in 11 innings. It was a remarkable day for baseball fans, notwithstanding the spectacle of a 24-year-old man being arrested in the left field stands for "streaking," which was something of a craze at the time. The fan had undressed in the restroom and walked naked back to his seat while smoking a cigar!

For Gerald Ford, the day was memorable in several respects. When he arrived back in the capital, his thoughts quickly turned away from baseball. That morning, the Associated Press had reported that his boss, President Nixon, had agreed to pay income taxes of nearly $500,000 that he had failed to pay during the first four years of his presidency. While Ford was in Cincinnati witnessing baseball history, the Judiciary Committee of the House of Representatives had issued an ultimatum to the White House to turn over presidential tapes that were necessary in an impeachment inquiry by Congress. Four months later, on August 9, Ford became the thirty-eighth president of the United States. Nixon had resigned in disgrace as a result of his cover-up of the Watergate affair.

1975: Rivals Meet Early

April 7 did not seem like spring at all. It was not because it was a chilly day that required three hibachi grills in the Reds dugout to keep warm. Instead, it was because the Reds were scheduled to play their archrival, the Dodgers, and the hype made it seem like a fall World Series game. The teams had battled fiercely for the Western Division championship the two preceding seasons. The last nine regular season encounters had been complete sellouts. The Dodgers were anticipating their best home opener attendance the following week when the Reds would continue the rivalry in Los Angeles. Six of the first nine games of the 162-game season would seem like a playoff series. (In total, the two teams would only play each other 12 more times in the 153 games after the opening two series.)

Fans always waited impatiently for Opening Day throughout the winter because they were eager for the start of another season and the first sign of spring. But fans anxiously awaited this one more than usual because of the rivalry between these two teams. *Enquirer* sports reporter Bob Hertzel put it aptly: "The 1975 baseball season begins today and the match had to be made in [commissioner] Bowie Kuhn's heaven. … It is the World Series in April." Sparky Anderson continued a long tradition by writing a column in the paper on the morning of the opener, and in the column, he declared that the current team was the best one in his six-year tenure. Anderson's hunch bore out, as the Reds would again win the National League and also notch a historic World Series win against the Boston Red Sox. (Most baseball people remember the iconic, game-winning home run by Carlton Fisk in

Game Six, but they sometimes forget that the Reds won Game Seven. Mark Frost wrote an outstanding account of the captivating Game Six and its participants in Game Six.)

The Findlay Market Association organized the largest parade in Opening Day history to date. Cincinnati mayor Ted Berry presided over a special program at Fountain Square. The party on the square was designed to give people who did not have tickets some kind of show after the parade and before the game. Grand marshal Waite Hoyt, the retired but still revered radio announcer, continued the party by leading a big brass band and other musicians to the stadium a short time later. A horse-drawn wagon carried market officials and other dignitaries to and around the field.

The teams did not disappoint the 52,526 fans lucky enough to have a ticket. In the longest Opening Day game ever played in Cincinnati, the Reds won 2–1 in the fourteenth inning. George Foster was declared safe at first on a

controversial play that allowed the winning run to score. Few fans had left the ballpark despite the long duration of the game, and the crowd erupted. Pete Rose had correctly predicted before the game that "50,000 people will warm this place up."

In other significant sports news, Lee Elder played a practice round at the Augusta National Golf Club while the Reds and Dodgers were battling in Cincinnati. Elder was preparing to become the first African American to ever play in the Masters golf tournament the following weekend in Georgia. His wife told reporters, "All he asks is to be left alone." He would end up missing the cut and not contending for the title, but the importance of his presence in the field was a major milestone in the sport of golf.

1976: World Champs Toasted on Bicentennial

As Americans everywhere were gearing up for the nation's Bicentennial celebration on July 4, 1976, Reds fans prepared to celebrate the first opening game in 35 years that would toast the team as the defending World Champs. Spring was in the air.

Bill Lindenschmidt of Acme Hardware was the president of the Findlay Market Association, and he was responsible for the largest parade ever organized in Cincinnati. More than fifty groups participated in one

> "The Opening Day parade will never be confused with the Rose Bowl parade or the Macy's Thanksgiving Day parade. No, this is a Cincinnati affair spanning back for generations. These are pickup trucks with flatbeds behind them for the most part. The marching bands serenade the city, but most people just waved to the crowds and have a good time."
>
> John Faherty, Enquirer sports columnist

way or another. Participants included five marching bands, local politicians, and cartoon characters from the local entertainment park, Kings Island. Uncle Al, the host of a long-run-

ning local television show, performed on one of the trucks to entertain the children who regularly watched him on TV. Lewis Crosley, the brother of Powell Crosley Jr., served as the grand marshal. One fan in attendance, Jack Murphy of Kettering, Ohio, displayed his team pride in grand fashion. He wore a red sport coat, pants, shirt, shoes, and red hat—and briefly showed off his red mesh underwear! His flashy costume was a bold departure from the early twentieth-century style of fans wearing suits and dresses.

When the parade reached Fountain Square, popular radio personality Jim LaBarbara of WLW radio hosted a rally for fans. Downtown Cincinnati had an atmosphere of Christmas, Fourth of July, and Mardi Gras all wrapped into one! The rally lasted for an hour, after which the fans headed to the stadium. On their way, they passed Peanut Jim Shelton. Peanut Jim was working his forty-fourth of an eventual 49 openers. (He missed one opener when he had his leg amputated because of a circulatory problem.) Dressed in his trademark costume of a black coat with tails, a black bow tie, and a stovepipe top hat, Shelton was hawking his specialty: barbecued peanuts from his coal-fired handcart. At age 86, Peanut Jim had no intention of retiring, and he worked alone. "Wanna buy a peanut?" he would ask. "They're cheaper out here!"

In 1983, Cincinnatian George Metzner remembered meeting Peanut Jim:

You have to understand who "Jim" was.

He was a black man who attended every Reds game, wearing a top hat and tux, and sold peanuts. To me, at that time a ten-year-old boy, he appeared to be a millionaire, and proved it when he produced a ticket on opening day when there were none to be had.

My uncle George won six tickets to the bleachers for opening day. Because he had to work, he couldn't go, and gave them to me. My popularity soared among my friends suddenly—the task of choosing only six accomplished, we began plans to "skip school" the afternoon of the big day.

Excitedly, we made our way to Crosley Field,

arriving before 1 p.m., waiting anxiously in the long line. The usher began taking tickets and to my dismay, mine was gone. Would my friends leave me behind? We got out of line and had a talk and decided that they would go in, hoping to be able to borrow enough money to get me in … I was leery, but there was nothing else to do so—they went ahead.

Already near panic, my heart skipped a beat when I saw what had to be the richest man alive approaching me. He asked what was wrong. I was afraid at first but finally spilled out what happened. He told me to stay right where I was until he came back.

More waiting. Here he comes the black man in the top hat and tux! He didn't forget me, and and … He had a ticket to the bleachers (he really must be special for they were sold out). He gave me the ticket and told me to find my friends—then he gave me a bag of peanuts and told me his name was "Jim."

Later on in life, Jim didn't remember me, but I did him. I never failed to buy a bag of peanuts from him.

God bless Peanut Jim, wherever he is.

There were fewer students than usual among the throng, thanks to superintendents and principals unpersuaded by custom. The Cincinnati school district had announced that it would refuse to excuse students from class to attend the first game of the season. Any student who skipped class would be marked with an unexcused absence. Teachers and principals were given discretion as to whether the student could make up his or her missed work. Another local school district, Mariemont, "sympathized and envied" students with tickets. However, they took the position that the Ohio legislature had failed to take Opening Day into consideration when writing school compulsory attendance laws, so they planned to uphold the laws. Most other school districts, however, simply turned a blind eye to students' absence on game day.

For officers of the law, working Opening Day was more of a respite from usual duties than a chore. Cincinnati police officer Gerry Thomas escorted the parade to Riverfront Stadium on his motorcycle, dismounted, and directed traffic under sunny skies. In an *Enquirer* interview, he commented that he enjoyed his assignment because the opener is "a party day" and he liked "the gaiety, the festivity and the fact that people are in a happy mood." Once inside the park, 52,949 fans—the largest ever to see a regular-season game in the city—listened to the introduction of national and local government dignitaries and stood reverently as Gwen Conley sang the national anthem. Louis Nippert, the Reds chairman, threw out the first pitch. A Xavier University student from Finneytown, Bob Thurman, had fun selling local Hudepohl beer: "Get moody with a Hudy!" The revelry continued throughout the game as the Reds trounced the Houston Astros 11–5. The Big Red Machine would go on to win another World Series, this time sweeping the New York Yankees to

cement their place in history as one of the greatest teams of all time. They became the last National League team to win two consecutive world championships.

Once the party was over, fans leaving the ballpark were debating the news of the morning. Did Georgia governor Jimmy Carter really win the Wisconsin primary? ABC and NBC had goofed two nights earlier by declaring that Morris Udall of Arizona

was the winner, but final tallies on the eve of Opening Day revealed that Carter had won by 7,000 votes. And was it really Howard Hughes, the magnate known to be one of the most financially successful individuals in the world, who died in a plane crash earlier in the week? Treasury Secretary William Simon was seeking fingerprints from the corpse. He wanted to confirm it was indeed Hughes before the IRS began tax proceedings on his estate.

Seven months later, long after Hughes was officially pronounced dead, Carter surprised the world by becoming the thirty-ninth president of the United States. Peanut Jim had his president, a former peanut farmer.

1977: Can They Re-Pete?

In January 1977, Americans were fixated on an ABC miniseries called Roots. The show won nine Primetime Emmy Awards, a Golden Globe, and a Peabody Award. Roots was the second-most-watched series finale in US television history. Reds fans likely were among those watching, but at the same time, they had spring and baseball on their minds.

All winter, listeners debated on Bob Trumpy's popular WLW Sports Talk show about whether the Reds could become the first National League team to win three straight World Series. As spring training opened, that topic was quickly displaced by talk about Pete Rose. Rose was in the midst of a contentious dispute with the Reds, and he sought a staggering $400,000 per season. (That amount is less than the required minimum for any major leaguer today.) Opening Day had been sold out since early February, but no one knew whether the local hero would be in the starting lineup.

The negotiations were emotional. They reached a climax when the club took out half-page ads in the *Enquirer* and the *Dayton Daily News* to explain its stand in the holdout. Controversial general manager Dick Wagner admitted that the team purchased the ads reluctantly "in an effort to get our story to the fan." The fans did not buy the team's rationale and began to make signs to express their support for Rose. Would some go further and boycott the opener? Rose had the full support of fans.

The fans' anxiety was relieved as they opened the morning paper. Hertzel announced the good news:

> Nighttime is still dark. Stars still twinkle in the sky. Spring still means love. And Pete Rose is still a Cincinnati Red. Opening day and all is right with the world. The captain and his bosses compromised, reaching an 11th-hour agreement before Rose's ultimatum took effect.

In the end, Rose and the Reds reached a compromise. He signed a two-year contract for $375,000 a season. Spring was here and it was time for baseball. Or was it? Reds fans should have had a premonition that a "three-peat" would not happen. The season was not starting out as they hoped. Snow was falling, and four inches of it already covered the field. Marchers on the parade route were dodging snowdrifts in 38-degree temperatures with 15 mile-per-hour winds. Fans wrapped themselves in quilts. Patrons from Portland, Indiana, drove 105 miles through a blizzard. An editorial cartoonist had a picture of Reds manager Sparky Anderson telling the coach of the Cincinnati Bengals NFL franchise that he should have taken his snow with him when he left the stadium after the football season. Ironically, a California team was the opponent on this frigid Opening Day. The Padres' Doug Rader built a small snowman outside the team's dugout.

Wagner was prepared for the foul weather. An expanded staff of 60 pushed, shoveled, and hauled snow off the field with the aid of a tractor and a dump truck. By game time, the field was cleared—to the dismay of some fans who believed the game should have been postponed. The main problem with a one-day delay? Adult ticket holders would have needed to explain the coincidental death of their other grandparent, and students would have had to update forgeries to their teachers.

When the parade entered the stadium and the dignitaries were introduced, the oratory was short. Mayor James Luken answered his

Jim Scott

own question. "Who else would go out and play baseball on a day like today except the Reds? This day is almost a religion [to the Reds]." Cleveland Browns football player Neal Craig, attending his first opener, claimed he saw an elderly woman "out cold … probably frozen." Charles Taft, a retired city councilman for whom the city council had renamed the stadium in February (a vote that was later rescinded) wished he was the grand marshal some other year when it was warmer.

Players often get blamed for demanding more money. Rose was treated differently, however. When the players were introduced, he received the loudest ovation. Fans did not care that his new salary meant he would be paid $225 per inning. *Enquirer* reporter Mark Purdy explained that Rose had successfully won the fans over in a host of local media interviews. Rose had spoken to seven television stations, 11 radio stations, and eight newspaper reporters. Perhaps the fan who was toughest on him was his own wife, who, when hearing that he had negotiated a compromise, asked, "What did you do, give in?"

The day began with the good news of Rose's signing and ended that way, too: the Reds prevailed 5–3 before 51,937 hearty souls. Rose went hitless in four at bats. Although the club went 88–74 on the season, there was no "three-peat" to be had.

1978: Rain Delay

April 6 was one of the wettest openers in history. Thousands lined the parade route from Findlay Market to Fountain Square with raincoats and umbrellas. As a result, the crowd was smaller than in the previous couple of years. There was a steady drizzle until game time, albeit at a warmer temperature than in some years. Cincinnatians and much of the Midwest had endured the Great Blizzard of 1978, also known as the "White Hurricane," that resulted in 71 deaths, including fifty in Ohio. President Carter had declared a state of emergency, mail deliveries were suspended,

and schools were closed for a week. Some likened the effect on transportation to a nuclear attack. It was the worst blizzard in Ohio history.

CBS was creating a comedy series called *WKRP in Cincinnati* about a floundering radio station switching from staid, middle-of-the-road music to rock 'n roll. During the week of the opener, CBS had invited Cincinnati mayor Jerry Springer to make a guest appearance in a future episode of the show. Springer arranged for the lights of the city to be turned on for a night skyline scene, and the producers video-taped Cincinnati and Riverfront Stadium. WKRP premiered later in the year; during its four-year run it was nominated for ten Emmy Awards. The series became one of the most popular sitcoms in syndication throughout the 1980s and early 1990s.

After a disappointing 1977 season, Reds fans were eager to witness the Opening Day debut of future Hall of Fame pitcher Tom Seaver. The Reds acquired Seaver from the New York Mets in the middle of the 1977 season. On the morning of the opener, Seaver claimed that he would never admit being nervous on Opening Day, but then confessed, "I am more nervous on opening day. You can't admit that to yourself. You have to have your emotions under control. You must discipline your mind to say 'No, there are no nerves.'" So inquiring minds want to know: was he nervous or not?

The pregame activities featured the return of radio personality Gwen Conley to sing the national anthem. (Conley was rumored to be in a relationship with the star left fielder for the Reds, George Foster.) The rain stopped just in time for her stirring rendition, but precipitation returned three more times during the game, resulting in delays of one hour and 39 minutes. Seaver had his worst Opening Day pitching performance ever, allowing five runs before he was removed in the fourth inning. The Reds managed to win the game against the Astros 11–9, but only 10,000 of the 52,378 spectators in attendance remained in the park when the game concluded after nearly five hours at 7:07 p.m. Ironically, the team had just been given permission by the city to install two clocks on the stadium's façade, so fans were well aware of the game's long duration.

Tom Seaver

THE MACHINE DISMANTLED

The rest of the country observes the beginning of spring time on March 21, and Cincinnati, in deference to the science of astronomy, gave lip service to that date. Now that the rules of common courtesy have been observed, however, Cincinnati can demonstrate its true feelings: baseball, more than planetary motion, determines the real start of spring.

Enquirer editorial

The economics of baseball were changing. The courts had outlawed the reserve clause that allowed teams to bind players to the same team year after year. Players and owners had negotiated that players could become free agents after six years of major league service, meaning they could then sell their services to the highest bidder. They had also negotiated provisions requiring arbitration of salary disputes between teams and players with greater than three years of service. No longer were so-called small-market teams such as Cincinnati on the same level as big-market teams such as those in New York or Chicago. It was now classic capitalism, and teams were more able to compete against each other for players.

The changes were despised by the owners of the Reds. They had relied on their farm system and their ability to identify potential stars when they were young. Once they signed players, they could keep them for their whole careers. Now, the farm system would still be important but only for the first six years of their major-league tenure. Howsam and Wagner believed the Reds were at a competitive disadvantage, and the owners said they could not afford high-priced stars. The Big Red Machine could not remain together.

211 Of course, all this is debatable. Just because a particular owner controls a team in a small market does not necessarily mean that owner has fewer resources than an owner who operates in a larger market. Owners are not required to be from the city in which they operate. Plus, the owners still share revenue equally from national television and radio rights fees. The only real differences are the revenues teams can generate from local media deals and from ticket sales. Baseball has witnessed smaller market teams be incredibly successful while larger market teams, such as the Chicago Cubs and the New York Mets, have had long droughts with no championships. Even the New York Yankees have experienced some periods of mediocrity. The highest paid players are not always the best players once they sign lucrative deals. (In professional football, where there is much more salary parity, the same teams seem to compete in the playoffs year after year, much more so than in baseball.)

As a result of the labor negotiations, the Reds looked in their crystal ball and decided they could not afford all their stars. They had been in seven World Series in the 37 years between 1939 and 1976, but they would be in only one during the next 42 years. Is that because they have been disadvantaged since the 1970s, or has their business strategy been wrong? After all, the sport has always been a business.

1979: Sour Moods

It was a winter of discontent. Dick Wagner had replaced the architect of the Big Red Machine, Bob Howsam, as president and chief executive officer of the Reds. Wagner was a familiar face in Cincinnati, as he had worked for the Reds' front office since 1967. But after the Reds made a lengthy tour of Japan at the end of the 1978 season, Wagner made the hugely unpopular decision to fire manager Sparky Anderson. Anderson had guided the Reds to five division championships, four World Series appearances, and two world champion-

Dick Wagner

ships in nine seasons. This decision was extensively criticized by Reds fans, and Anderson himself blasted Wagner on the eve of the opener. Anderson charged that Wagner deliberately delayed his firing until late November in order to prevent him from securing another managerial job. Vacant manager jobs were and are typically filled in October.

To make matters worse, Wagner did the unthinkable. He refused to sign free agent Pete Rose, resulting in Rose signing a four-year contract with the Philadelphia Phillies just a week after Anderson was fired. Rose's 1978 season had been noteworthy in several respects. He achieved his 3,000th hit, joining an elite group of 12 other players to ever reach that milestone. He also had a memorable 44-game hitting streak as he chased the all-time record of 56 games. A disgruntled fan took action on behalf of all Reds fans by hanging Wagner in effigy on Fountain Square. These two moves by Wagner—by far the two most controversial of his tenure—led him to become the most hated man in Cincinnati by the time he was relieved of his duties four years later.

The weather on the morning of the opener mirrored the mood of the fans. It was gloomy, damp, and cloudy. The rain stopped an hour before the fifty-ninth annual parade began. The lead vehicle in the parade was supposed to be a truck, but somehow it was replaced by a police officer on a three-wheeler. Carrying on the zany antics that had long been part of Opening Day, six marchers dressed as six-foot-tall beer cans swerved through the downtown streets while a high school band played "Disco Inferno." A group of women marched as representatives of the DOWN movement—"Dispose of Wagner Now." Thousands of fans lined the streets, but most were discussing whether the Reds could win without Anderson and Rose. When the marchers made their way to Riverfront Stadium, they were greeted by protesters. Twenty striking umpires outside the ballpark wore signs that read "Baseball Unfair to Umpires," as they sought increases in their annual salaries that ranged from $17,500 for rookies to $40,000 for veteran umpires. Fans had signs of their own, reading "Trade Dick Wagner."

During pregame ceremonies, Mayor Bobbie Sterne took the microphone near home plate, but the mic went out. When her voice could finally be heard welcoming the crowd and introducing dignitaries and club personnel, Wagner was loudly booed by the crowd as Sterne said his name. City councilman Ken Blackwell, standing nearby, said what everyone (except Wagner) was thinking: "It's a shame that Rose is not here. It [Rose being here] was a Cincinnati tradition." Perhaps to take the fans' mind off their discontent, they were treated to a most unusual first pitch. Six men had paddled

three canoes for 200 miles from Morehead, Kentucky, by way of the Licking River. They carried a ball stuffed in a waterproof bag tied to the crosspiece of one of the canoes. Their objective was to publicize Morehead's drive to raise money to erect lights on a baseball field. The ball was used for the traditional first pitch.

The game was officiated by Paul Pryor, one of only two MLB umpires who had signed a contract for the season. Three amateur umpires, Roger Grooms, Les Treitel, and Mick Sharkey from the Queen City Umpires Association, were recruited to cross the picket line. They were referred to as "10-centers," as if they were worth only a dime. However, there was little controversy about any of their calls during the game after the San Francisco Giants scored eight runs in the second inning on their way to an 11–5 victory. A total of 52,115 fans left the park as they had entered: dismayed. (The team recovered enough to win their division but lost in the National League championship series to Pittsburgh.)

In addition to worrying about whether the Reds could return to their days of glory, fans were concerned about their families' safety. A nuclear power station was scheduled to start up near Cincinnati the following year, and federal officials and Ohio governor James Rhodes were trying to reassure the public. Just a week earlier, a nuclear meltdown had occurred at Three Mile Island near Harrisburg, Pennsylvania. It was the most significant accident in the country's nuclear power plant history.

1980: Marathon Man

On April 9, the Reds continued a unique tradition concerning the first pitch. In 1979, the first ball had been delivered from a canoe. This year, the Reds would rely upon land transport. Keen Babbage, an employee at Cincinnati-based Procter & Gamble, carried the first-pitch ball during a two-week, 430-mile walk from St. Louis. When he arrived in Cincinnati, he joined the march to the stadium from Findlay Market—as if he hadn't walked far enough already!

When Babbage made it to the Queen City, he couldn't help but notice that the pomp and circumstance of Opening Day pleased anyone with a fancy for tradition and celebration. Among the favorites were the Jazz Butchers, who serenaded spectators along the route. The red-uniformed East Central High School band from tiny St. Leon, Indiana, cranked up "Take Me Out to the Ball Game." Three other high school bands marched as city council members waved from their convertibles. Vehicles carrying baseball enthusiasts honked their horns, and "amateur entertainer and free-lance dancer" Addel Rettig boogied alongside the fifty other entries. Rettig was dressed in a red sweater, silver boots, and silver shorts over her bright red leotards. Bringing up the rear was the crowd favorite, eight Anheuser-Busch Clydesdale horses pulling their signature beer wagon.

After long-distance walker Babbage arrived at the park and the customary pregame celebration ended, he delivered the first ball to five-year-old Jason Edwards, March of Dimes poster child for the Cincinnati area. From behind his walker, Jason tossed the ball to Reds catcher and future Hall of Famer Johnny Bench. Bench reciprocated with an autographed ball as a souvenir of the occasion. The boy beamed, and the season was officially on. Babbage looked on, ten pounds lighter than when he began his pilgrimage.

After his lousy performance a year earlier,

Tom Seaver was expected to start once again, but he caught the flu. Twenty-two-year-old Frank Pastore learned of the illness at 10:15 a.m. when he arrived at the clubhouse, and Reds manager John McNamara informed him that he was to be the Opening Day pitcher. With his father in attendance and Braves' owner Ted Turner grimacing, Pastore pitched a complete-game shutout. The Reds waltzed

Frank Pastore

to a 9–0 win. Reds right fielder Ken Griffey went 1–4 using a teammate's bat. The bats he had ordered for the season never arrived at the stadium. They were sent to the wrong location, but no one knew where. Griffey's young son, "Junior," played in the clubhouse before the game and would go on to become one of baseball's legends during the 1990s.

In national news on the morning of the opener, Iran's young radicals holding fifty American hostages in Tehran threatened to burn the United States Embassy and kill the captives. The terrorists had held the Americans since November 4, 1979. The Iran hostage crisis spawned ABC's Nightline just four days after the Americans were captured. Roone Arledge, ABC News president, wanted to compete against NBC's The Tonight Show Starring Johnny Carson. His show was originally called The Iran Crisis–America Held Hostage: Day "xxx", with xxx representing the number of days that the Americans had been held hostage in the US Embassy. Ted Koppel soon took over the duties of hosting the program, and late-night America was captivated by the Iran saga.

President Jimmy Carter was hinting at a possible naval blockade if the hostages were not freed, but instead he decided diplomatic efforts would be more successful. Iranian Foreign Minister Sadegh Ghotbzadeh told a Tehran news conference that his country had "decided to overthrow" Iraq's government headed by President Saddam Hussein. He also confessed to American television networks that his government likely could not stop the militants if they decided to kill the hostages.

The crisis would last another nine months before the fifty Americans were released on the day of Ronald Reagan's inauguration in January 1981. The hostage crisis likely contributed to Carter's reelection defeat.

1981: No First Pitch

Shortly after Ronald Reagan became president, brothers William and James Williams purchased stock in the Reds from Louis Nippert and became principal owners of the team. They soon arranged for the first pitch to be delivered by Ronald Reagan, the country's newly inaugurated president. It was an honor for the city, as no sitting president had ever thrown out the first pitch at an opener in Cincinnati.

Adding to the excitement of Reagan's attendance was the anticipation of a pitching matchup made in Cooperstown, the home of baseball's Hall of Fame. Tom Seaver of the Reds was scheduled to face Steve Carlton of the Phillies. Never before had two more distinguished pitchers opened the season in Cincinnati. (Hall of Fame pitchers Eppa Rixey for the Reds and Grover Cleveland Alexander for the Chicago Cubs faced off in the 1922 opener, but they were in the middle of their careers and were not yet as accomplished.) "It's great for the fans, but I don't like to think

about it that way. I'm not pitching against Carlton. I'm pitching against the Phillies," said Seaver. Long after Reagan would serve up the first pitch, the pitches thrown by Seaver and Carlton would likely be most remembered by baseball enthusiasts.

Tickets were sold out early in the winter. History would intervene, however. On March 30, John Hinckley Jr. shot Reagan as he was leaving the Hilton Hotel in Washington, D. C. Secret Service agent Timothy McCarthy, of the Cincinnati suburb of Finneytown, hurled himself in the line of fire between the gunman and President Reagan. McCarthy's willingness to absorb the bullet intended for President Reagan likely saved the president's life. Press secretary James Brady was also seriously wounded in the shooting, as well as Washington police officer Thomas Delahanty. Two days later, the White House announced that Reagan would not be well enough to make an appearance in Cincinnati for the April 8 opener.

Mr. Red

Supreme Court justice Potter Stewart, a Cincinnati native, was in his hometown on the eve of the opener. He was there to attend a ceremony for the formal unveiling of his portrait that would hang in the main court-

An Opening Day fit for a Queen City

room of the federal Sixth Circuit Court of Appeals located next to Fountain Square. (Later, the courthouse would be named in his honor.) Stewart acknowledged that the assassination attempt was traumatic, but he also reminded his audience that it was a "tremendous unifying event" for the country. The morning Enquirer noted the gravity of the assassination attempt with the headline, "This Opening Day Has a Dark Cloud on the Horizon." At the opener, fans wore sweatshirts bearing the message "Together We Can" while wondering who would replace Reagan in making the ceremonial first pitch. As the first pitch was about to take place, 30-year Reds public-address announcer Paul Sommerkamp introduced the Roger Bacon High School Band as they played their signature tune, "This Is My Country." Sommerkamp then made a somber announcement:

> Ladies and gentlemen, had certain events of nine days ago not taken place we would be honored to introduced to you a very good baseball fan who was to have thrown out our ceremonial first pitch. ... He is not here today in person, but we are sure he is with us in spirit. Ladies and gentlemen, there can really be no appropriate relief pitcher for the President of the United States and we have decided that it is most appropriate in 1981 to have no ceremonial pitcher.

He then asked the crowd to observe a moment of silence "as we give thanks for the physical recovery of Ronald Reagan." Sommerkamp almost choked up at the end of his announcement.

Moments before Sommerkamp's announcement, the crowd was introduced to two honored guests. Bert Moore from Mount Vernon, Ohio, and Army colonel Leland Holland, whose three children resided in the Cincinnati neighborhood of Hyde Park, were presented with lifetime baseball passes from Commissioner Bowie Kuhn. Why? They were two of the fifty hostages released by their Iranian captors three months earlier. Moore told a reporter that he did not find out who won the 1980 World Series until two months after it happened when a letter from his wife reached him in Tehran. Apparently, the Iranian terrorists were not baseball fans.

The parade that morning was rated as a "nine-bander," because the nine bands that lined up for the march exceeded the previous record of participating bands by three. Outside the park, Stan Piatt's Dixieland band played "Down by the River" to the delight of the early arrivals. Tuba player Jim Thorpe remarked, "Troubles? Problems? It all takes a backseat on Opening Day. People come here in a festive spirit." Fan Jack Moran (no relation to the Channel 9 sports announcer) was attending his sixty-third straight opener at age 73. He was conscious of his feat, saying, "People do talk about it. I drive carefully, much more carefully, to get here. I come early." His streak started in 1919, three years before the Rixey-Cleveland duel. And the first-pitch ball? This year, it arrived by bicycle. Burt Meyer and Peter Kutschenreuter of the Cincinnati Cycle Club biked 13 days and 788 miles from the Red Cross National Headquarters in Washington, D.C., to Riverfront Stadium.

Oh, yes, the game. The Seaver-Carlton matchup lived up to its hype, as each hurler surrendered just one run. The Reds won a thriller in the bottom of the ninth, 3–2. The locals were also pleased by Cincinnati native Ron Oester's first-ever appearance in an Opening Day game. He had been on the team since 1978 but had never appeared in an opener. This year, he started at second base. Oester defied the odds and fulfilled the dreams of many young ballplayers from

Ron Oester

Cincinnati. He went to his first Opening Day game at the age of 12 at iconic Crosley Field and vowed to become a major leaguer. Twelve years later, he was starting for the home team on Opening Day. Oester confirmed what native Cincinnatians knew:

> It's really a holiday … Here, the people go crazy. I know a lot of people take off work for the game. I remember my friends taking radios to school on Opening Day so we could listen to the game. I skipped class in grade school a couple of years to stay home and watch the game on television. My parents let me do it. It's a real special day.

Oester went hitless, but the thrill of playing that day was the fulfillment of his lifelong dream.

1982: Grand Marshal "Peanut Jim"

Cincinnati fans considered themselves baseball's number-one victims of an unfortunate turn of events in 1981. They were hoping for better things in 1982. In 1981, MLB had endured a players' strike during the middle of the season, and Commissioner Kuhn decided to split the season into two halves. The teams with the best records in each half of the season would proceed to the postseason. For the Reds, that spelled disaster. The Dodgers won

the first half of the season by one-half game, and the Astros beat out the Reds by one-and-a-half games in the second half. Even though the Reds had compiled the best record in baseball, they were excluded from the playoffs. Fans were outraged. Three law students from Ohio State University sought an injunction to halt the playoffs, but the school's dean and a federal judge forced them to drop the matter. The ardent fans felt their cause was not worth ruining their careers.

Reds supporters believed they were robbed, but hope springs eternal in baseball winters. The fans recovered and expected the team to be successful in 1982, this time with the long-standing playoff rules being honored. If you had the best record in either league, you should certainly have a chance at capturing the world championship.

Dick Wagner was still in charge, and he proceeded to remove another spark plug in the Big Red Machine: power hitter George Foster. Again, the trade was sparked by a salary demand. Wagner tried to convince the fans that new outfielders could fill the void.

A HOLIDAY OF OUR VERY OWN

His rationale did not hold up, and he could not have been more wrong, as the Reds ended up losing a team-record 101 games and finishing in last place for the first time since 1937.

The festivities were as special as ever on April 5 despite the return of bad weather. It was 44 degrees when the parade started at 11:30 a.m., and heavy rain or possibly snow was in the forecast. Sports fans in Cincinnati had endured the "Freezer Bowl" in January when wind chills during a Cincinnati Bengals playoff game were as low as 61 degrees below zero. Fair-weather baseball fans rationalized that it was 100 degrees warmer than that for

Opening Day. They came out in force for the morning parade, and 51,864 fans would later fill the ballpark.

Peanut Jim

The parade featured "Peanut Jim" Shelton as the grand marshal. Shelton had sold roasted peanuts from his cart for 49 of the last 50 openers, and he had just retired. Once again, he wore his familiar black stovepipe hat and bow tie. Instead of pushing his handcart to the riverfront, this time Peanut Jim rode to the ballpark in the back seat of a Cadillac convertible leading the largest parade in history. The parade consisted of 80 units and 3,000 marchers. Mike Luken, parade chairman, had constructed a 28-foot float in the form of a shrimp boat, and he gave himself the best float award. Appearing stylish in red crushed velvet with an emblematic white C, a participant by the name of Mai Thai joined the parade in progress from an alley near Seventh Street and Race Street. Her pace was somewhat slower than the others, as she was a 14-year-old elephant from the Cincinnati Zoo! (The zoo had planned to bring other, smaller animals, but the cold weather put a

damper on that plan.) "Mr. Spoons," 70-year-old Joe Dippong of Mount Healthy, marched in the parade and later played the spoons on the plaza outside the stadium. Although he had been entertaining fans for the last seven years dressed in his Reds cap, red jacket, and red slacks, he confessed that he had never attended an opener.

At the ballpark, the Reds continued their recent, and unique, tradition. The ceremonial "first pitch" consisted of two pitches. First, Air Force colonel Joseph Engle threw a strike, and then Navy captain Richard Truly followed suit. Engle and Truly had brought the two balls with them as they piloted the Columbia space shuttle, the first vehicle in NASA's space shuttle fleet. Engle told the crowd "We enjoyed flying this ball around." Some patrons were skeptical after reading Enquirer sports columnist Mark Purdy's view that morning. He demanded proof that the ball had actually been aboard the shuttle. He asked in jest, "Did anyone see these men play catch during the flight? Did anybody see them taking grounders?"

Happy Chandler

There was one thing Purdy did not question. A. B. "Happy" Chandler, former Kentucky governor and former baseball commissioner, had been elected to baseball's Hall of Fame. The standing-room-only crowd gave him a rousing ovation as he was introduced. Terry Cashman, a singer-songwriter best known for his 1981 hit, "Talkin' Baseball," entertained the crowd with his new composition, "Baseball's Red Machine."

While at the stadium, patrons were finally able to buy Cracker Jack so they could follow the suggestion in the song, "Take Me Out to the Ball Game." Riverfront Stadium previously had been one of the few major-league ballparks that did not offer Cracker Jack for sale. Hungry patrons would have been wise to purchase the new item before the eighth inning when heavy rain began to fall. A 51-minute rain delay ensued, and the game was officially declared over with only 42 fans left in the stands. One highlight of the day was the unveiling of the "Mr. Red Race" video game that would become a fan favorite for years to come. It was a race in black-and-white between the team's official mascot, Mr. Red, and two other mascots, Rosie Red and Mr. Redlegs. Portending the rest of the season, the Reds lost 3–2.

The game was officiated by major-league umpires who had reached agreement on a new four-year contract earlier that morning. John Kibler, the crew chief for the opener in Cincinnati, only learned at 3:00 a.m. that he would be working the game. Salaries for the umpires increased by 60 percent from the previous levels. Fans, meanwhile, were suffering through some of the harshest economic times since the Great Depression, with home mortgage rates averaging 17.52 percent

1983: *USS Cincinnati*

The combination of the club having its worst season ever in 1982 and fans' universal loathing for Dick Wagner resulted in the team's failure to sell out the April 4 opener. Fans continued to blame Wagner for dismantling the Big Red Machine and causing the Reds' performance to plummet. Only Johnny Bench and Dave Concepcion remained from "The Great Eight" of the 1970s. Thomas Boswell, a famous syndicated columnist for the Washington Post, did no favors for Reds officials who were eager to sell more tickets. He agreed with the disgruntled fans: "The Reds losing 100 games is the work of Dick Wagner. Wagner sold the Reds down the river for the sake of making a quixotic stand against the free agent era."

Only 42,892 fans attended the game, leaving 9,500 empty red seats in eight sections of the upper deck. It was a bad day for ticket scalpers, as there were tickets galore at regular, face-value prices. Las Vegas oddsmakers established the Reds as 100 to 1 underdogs to win the pennant. Oh, how times had changed!

Among the no-shows on Opening Day was announcer Paul Sommerkamp—his first absence in 2,470 home games. The flu sidelined the longtime public-address announcer,

Paul Sommerkamp

who was a Reds fixture and a fan favorite. Sommerkamp had first set up his microphone next to the visitors' dugout at Crosley Field in 1951. This opener would be the first and only home game he ever missed before retiring in 1985. Fans always loved Sommerkamp's signature introduction of hitters: "Now batting, third baseman, Pete Rose … Rose! Sommerkamp would pause just long enough for people keeping score to write down the player's last name. Veteran fans regularly pulled a bit of a joke on a newcomer to the ballpark. After Sommerkamp would announce the player's full name, such as "Now batting, second baseman Joe Morgan," a veteran spectator would yell "Who?" after which Sommerkamp would call out "Morgan!" The rookie attendee would be amazed that Sommerkamp had seemingly answered the spectator's question!

Along with missing the game, Sommerkamp missed the largest parade ever. There was an elaborate "Wizard of Oz" float. Another entry in the pageant was based on the popular comedy film, "Smokey and the Bandit." Float builder Dave Crist of Goshen, Ohio, who bore a striking resemblance to the movie's star, Burt Reynolds, dressed as the Bandit driving a Trans Am car. The perpetually enraged sheriff, Smokey, followed with his wrecked cruiser in tow. One solo marcher, providing no explanation, dressed as an oyster. The Roger Bacon High School Band was back, along with the Lakota High School Chorale.

USS Cincinnati

In keeping with tradition, the Reds had come up with a fresh and outlandish idea for the delivery of the first ball. They had chosen a nuclear submarine appropriately named the USS Cincinnati. Months before Opening Day, team officials had provided the crew with three baseballs, one that would be the official ball to use at the opener and the other two as backups. The balls were carried more than 50,000 miles into the Atlantic Ocean. Master Chief Jim Brewington was a bit sheepish after he threw the ceremonial first pitch to begin the season. It turned out that the original ball designated for the opener was still somewhere in the Atlantic. Brewington explained that the

crew had fired the balls out of the torpedo tubes in waterproof containers, but the divers could not find the designated ball. Fortunately, the backups were located. The choice of the submarine was ironic after the club's finish at the bottom of the league in 1982. As Enquirer sportswriter Mark Purdy snidely remarked, if the players wanted to look down any further in the standings, they would have needed to climb inside a submarine.

Marines

Despite the disappointing size of the crowd, the Reds staged a comeback and beat the Braves 5–4. Sommerkamp resumed his duties before the next game. When the Reds again fell into last place on June 5, the Williams brothers gave fans what they wanted: the firing of Dick Wagner. The club replaced him on an interim basis with the architect of the Big Red Machine, Bob Howsam. Wagner defiantly told the press he had made no mistakes, and Howsam promised "a new beginning."

1984: Shhh ... Fireworks

Sportswriter Purdy previewed the April 2 opener by giving advice to fans attending their first Opening Day:

1. Claim you love the rotten weather.

2. Pretend you recognize the songs of the bands in the parade are playing.

3. Act as if you're playing hooky and your boss actually cares.

4. Lie about the ugly back black shoes and low stirrups [on Reds uniforms].

5. Give Tony Perez a standing ovation when he's introduced.

6. Even if it's 28 degrees and a glacier is forming on your nose, order a beer and eat peanuts.

7. At least once every 15 minutes say, "How about that bleeping [pitcher]?"

8. Pretend the game actually matters.

9. Invoke the name of Pete Rose and/or Sparky Anderson.

10. Tell everybody what a great time you had.

What Purdy neglected to mention was that there were new sheriffs in town. Bob Howsam and his son Robert, vice president of marketing for the Reds, had decided to mix things up for the 1984 season. The first innovation was one that the father-son duo kept secret. On the day before Opening Day, firing tubes were set outside the stadium, fuses were wired, and circuits and batteries were checked. A senior Federal Aviation Agency official peered down the muzzles and approved the Howsams' plan to shoot off fireworks after each Reds home run and every victory. Cincinnati-based Rozzi's Famous Fireworks was hired to applaud the Reds with four smoke shells and six noisemaker rockets every time a home run was scored.

Other enhancements to the fan experience had been made public. Opening Day fans enjoyed the debut of a new beer garden behind the left field fence. Cincinnatians, with their rich German heritage, could sit there and view the game from long picnic tables while enjoying their brew. The garden, surrounded by a bed of flowers, came complete with an authentic Wurlitzer Military Band Organ. The organ would serenade beer drinkers with polkas and songs such as "Roll Out the Barrel." (The songs were to be played sparingly during the game so as not to distract the players.)

The younger Howsam also installed a new Baldwin organ in the camera pit behind home plate. He explained, "Baldwin [a piano and organ company based in the city] is Cincinnati, so we're staying with the local flavor." Unlike the Wurlitzer organ, this one could rise 15 feet from the ground. The organist was on tap to play traditional baseball songs and rousing pop songs.

Fans who wanted to be active while listening to music or watching the game could test their throwing arms with a new radar gun behind right field that gave a digital readout of their pitch speed. Howsam predicted that the radar gun would destroy some egos. (During the opener, the speed of fans' pitches was clocked at between 35 and 84 miles per hour.)

On the playing field, the club had taken a hacksaw to the outfield walls. The walls were lowered from 12 to 8 feet to enable outfielders to make leaping catches at the fence and to encourage home run production by the Reds. Of course, the risk was that the visiting team would gain the same advantages. With all these changes, it was going to be a whole new ball game in 1984.

With Howsam and his son in charge, fans began to grow optimistic. They turned out in droves for the parade. The Findlay Market organizers outdid themselves by arranging for 100 units to participate in the parade, including the Clydesdales and six marching bands. Best of all, a member of the Big Red Machine, Johnny Bench, served as grand marshal. Bench had retired at the end of the 1983 season. He led the parade in a vintage red and white Corvette. Dressed in a purple sport

Honor Guard

In the second inning of the one hundredth National League opener for the Reds, Reds center fielder Eddie Milner hit a home run. While the crowd was cheering, Robert Lutz of Rozzi's famous fireworks touched a button, causing rockets to explode above the outfield seats. It surprised both the fans and the players. Milner said, "It kind of scared me at first. I thought they were shooting at me." Instead, the fireworks had been shot for Milner, and they were launched again in the seventh inning following another home run and after the game. The Reds waltzed to an 8–1 win. At least for a day, the team made good on its new slogan: "Getting Back to Fun."

Eddie Milner

jacket, soft lavender shirt, and designer jeans, Bench was the focal point for the crowd's attention. "JB, JB, JB" was a continuous chant from the thousands lining the route. Several fans ran out and shook his hand and presented him with red carnations. Cincinnati mayor Arn Bortz joked that no one noticed him as he followed behind Bench. Observing the fans' adulation, Bortz told Bench, "I hope you never run for mayor!"

As 46,000 spectators arrived for the game, they were warmly greeted by the ticket takers and ushers. This too was somewhat of an innovation. Howsam had schooled stadium employees to offer every courtesy, acknowledging that the team had gotten away from that approach in recent years. Once fans settled into their seats, the traditional ceremonies and introduction of dignitaries were highlighted by the introduction of Tony Perez, another member of the Big Red Machine. Howsam had signed Perez in the off-season. Perez received a thunderous, 30-second standing ovation—the loudest cheering of the day. Emphasizing Howsam's point that the "fan experience" was more important than ever, the traditional first pitch was heaved by an excited patron. No dignitary was needed.

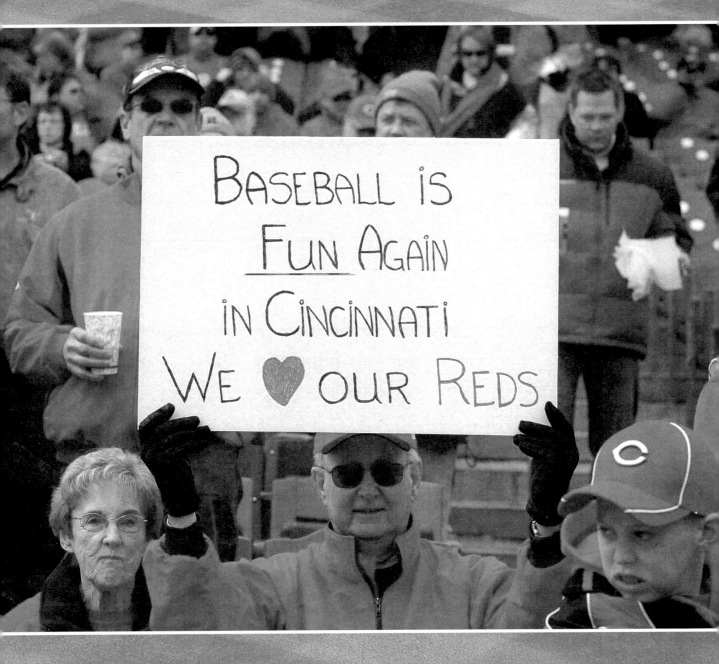

M·A·R·G·E
The Woman In Reds

14

THE EARLY SCHOTT YEARS

Cincinnati winters pass slowly. The nights are long, the weather disagreeable, the landscape drab and lifeless. The great out-of-doors is anything but great. Suddenly it is spring. The tri-state begins to come alive again. And just like that, everything turns ... CINCINNATI RED! It's Opening Day!

Enquirer editorial

1985: Wearing Red

April 8 was easily the most anticipated Opening Day in recent history. *Enquirer* columnist Camilla Warrick explained that there were "53,000 reasons for Opening Day fever." (52,971 fans had bought tickets.) For fans, however, there were two primary reasons: Pete Rose and Marge Schott. Rose had returned to the Reds the previous August and was now a player-manager chasing the base hit record of the legendary Ty Cobb. (He would break the hallowed mark in September.) Schott, the owner of a car-dealership empire, became the new owner of the team. Her love of the team was well known, and she championed the traditions of Opening Day. Her pet Saint Bernard, "Schottzie," was

practically a club mascot. When baseball commissioner Peter Ueberroth received his invitation to the opener, he laughed when he saw that it had come from Schottzie. The invitation included pictures of the dog in both a Reds cap and an Olympics hat. Ueberroth had organized the 1984 Olympic Games in Los Angeles. Shottzie's invitation said, "I'm keeping my paws crossed" that Ueberroth would attend.

Ueberroth accepted his first-ever invitation to an opener, a coup for Schott. "I attended the opener in Cincinnati because this is baseball. This is tradition ... Plus, I wanted to encourage Marge. She's a courageous lady." As for Rose, he asked, "How many people do you think are going to watch what he does every day all year

Peter Ueberroth

long? I think millions will … More than check the stock market, they're going to check the box score in the newspaper every day to see what Pete Rose does." *Enquirer* reporter Tim Sullivan wrote, "If it seems as if the season has become a sideshow, blame it on the lady with the dog and the guy with the Grecian Formula. They've captured our hearts and most of the headlines … Today's Standing Room Only sale can only be attributed, then, to the personal charisma of Marge, her manager, and her mongrel." The media took note of the team's new energy, with 285 press credentials being issued to interested news outlets.

> *"It doesn't matter how many games you're in, Commissioner. On opening day in Cincinnati, you get butterflies."*
>
> Pete Rose to Commissioner
> Peter Ueberroth

Shortly after 7:00 a.m. on Opening Day, CBS Morning News interviewed Ueberroth live from the lobby of the Hyatt Regency Cincinnati. Cold weather and snow were in the forecast, but Ueberroth predicted a great Opening Day nonetheless. Schott had encouraged fans to wear red, and the hotel lobby and streets outside were overflowing with crimson-covered bodies and scarlet faces. The whole town was wearing red. Despite 39-degree temperatures, spectators were four deep along the 15-block route from Findlay Market to Fountain Square. Three children— Madrigel Fields (age 15), Tammy Stegbaer (age 10), and Chris Eberhart, (age 14)—were selected to be the grand marshals, giving them the thrill of their lives. Schott and Bob Howsam Jr. rode close behind the grand marshals, waving to supportive fans. Elephants and horses, politicians and marching bands, and convertibles and dressed-up trucks clogged traffic for three hours. Streets were closed beginning at 10:00 a.m. and were opened only after the parade passed Fountain Square. With the full support of the club's new owner, the parade had never been more colorful. Kevin Luken, one of the longtime parade organizers, credits Schott for making the parade what it has become today.

The largest crowd for a regular-season game turned out to witness the historic occasion featuring the first female owner of the Reds. In fact, the other dignitaries who were present were largely overlooked. The Roger Bacon band lined up and even spelled "Good Luck Marge" in formation. A plane flew over the stadium with a banner arranged by the new owner: "We're Coming Alive in 1985. Love, Marge." Ueberroth then escorted Schott and her Saint Bernard to center stage. Standing in front of the pitcher's mound, the first lady of the Reds delivered a high and outside pitch to catcher Dann Bilardello. The spectators rose in unison to offer a standing ovation. Schott, attired in a cream-colored pants suit, a cranberry-red sweater, and loafers, waved gleefully to the crowd. On one side of her sweater, a button read, "I'm Reds Hot"; on the other was her name tag—as if she needed one.

Prior to the game, Rose read a letter to his players from the new owner. She urged them to win. Despite two snow delays, the team delivered with a 4–1 victory over the Montreal Expos, which had been Rose's second team during his five-and-a-half-year exile. Fittingly,

22 years to the day after his debut at Crosley Field, Rose hammered out two hits and drove in three runs. He was now 93 hits shy of breaking the all-time record for career hits. He left the game to a storm of applause. The classic was missed by Si Burick, the sports editor and columnist of the *Dayton Daily News*. It was the first Opening Day game in Cincinnati that he had missed in 56 years. He was being inducted into the National Sportscasters and Sportswriters Association Hall of Fame, the only writer ever to be honored from a city that did not have a major-league franchise.

> *"Opening Day is like spring itself. It's excitement. After New Year's, what else is there to look forward to?"*
>
> Jim Magoto, Reds Fan
>
> *"Opening Day in Cincinnati is the ultimate of sporting events. This is in a class with the Rose Bowl, the Kentucky Derby, the Indianapolis 500, OSU home games and all games played by the Cleveland Browns."*
>
> Rick Spriggs, Reds Fan

It may have snowed on her parade, but Schott needed to choke back the tears when asked about the importance of her first Opening Day. "I'm afraid I'll cry … The whole town is wearing red. They're in the spirit of it. All along the parade route, people were saying, 'We're with you! We're backing you all the way!' The people have joined with us. Everybody is together on this."

On the world stage, the Cold War between the United States and the USSR continued. The United States was deploying missiles in Western Europe that had been requested by NATO to counter a Soviet missile buildup. The morning paper reported that the new Russian leader, Mikhail Gorbachev, agreed to a summit meeting with President Reagan. Seven months later, the two men met in Geneva for the first of four high-level meetings between the two countries during the Reagan administration. (Reagan famously told Gorbachev to tear down the Berlin Wall months before their second summit occurred in Reykjavik, Iceland, the next year.)

1986: Sparky's Revenge?

The annual rite of the parade almost didn't happen on April 7. Organizers historically relied upon volunteers associated with Findlay Market, so as a result, the march did not have a significant budget. When the market received a liability insurance bill for $4,000, the organizers announced they could not afford to pay the premium. The streak of consecutive parades since 1920 was in jeopardy. Fortunately, a local lawyer, Stan Chesley, and health insurer Blue Cross/Blue Shield saved the tradition by donating the needed funds. (The $4,000 seemed trivial when the chamber of commerce later estimated that the Reds pumped $60 million into the local economy.) The parade ended up being somewhat smaller than in previous years.

> ## smile
> **Without going out on a limb, we can predict the Cincinnati Reds will be in either first or second place after today's opener.**

After the Reds finished in second place in 1985, Schott made several expensive additions to the team. She virtually demanded a pennant in return. She was willing to open her pocketbook significantly, a departure from the most recent ownership groups who were more frugal, but she expected a payback. Reds fans believed several prognosticators who picked the Reds to win the league championship. Tim Sullivan of the *Enquirer* echoed those favorable sentiments: "The good old days are back, disguised in red shoes and high stirrups in a generation of players who were battling acne when the Big Red Machine was laying waste to the Yankees. A decade in the dark has ended and a season of light lies ahead."

After the parade was salvaged, the main controversy surrounding Opening Day involved the MLB's schedule makers. For the first time in many years, the American League scheduled the Detroit Tigers to open their season 35 minutes before the National League got underway with the Reds against the Phillies. What were they thinking? Did tradition count for nothing? The Tigers were managed by erstwhile Reds manager Sparky Anderson, so the early start came to be called "Sparky's Revenge." Kenneth Blackwell, Cincinnati's vice mayor, orchestrated a tongue-in-cheek campaign against the American League for upstaging Cincinnati. He suggested that the Greater Cincinnati International Airport should suspend all landing rights for planes from the Detroit area.

Of course, Blackwell and other city council members overstated their argument. The Reds had not always been granted the privilege of beginning the major-league season. When Washington had a team in the American League, they often started their season before the Reds, but Cincinnatians had developed a case of amnesia about that. While Reds manager Rose supported the idea that Cincinnati should start the major-league season, he commented, "Who cares if they play a half hour before us? Maybe they'll get a rain delay." Marge Schott also brushed off the controversy, joking, "We're going to set our clocks back. We have so many things planned, I don't know when we'll start the game."

Schott reserved stronger feelings for the issue of players' facial hair. She refused to relax the team's rule that all players have a clean-shaven face. The rule resulted in free agent reliever Rollie Fingers not receiving a tryout with the club when he made it clear that he would not shave his trademark handlebar mustache. Fans called the rule "ridiculous" and "outdated." One fan quoted in the *Enquirer* said, "It's stupid, an invasion of privacy. This

isn't a monastery." Added another, "This isn't a military academy. If Pete Rose can have his little tail [miniature ponytail] the others should be allowed to have moustaches." General manager Bill Bergesch took the opposite view, asserting, "A clean-shaven face says something about personal discipline."

Hair controversies aside, Opening Day was a perfect day for baseball, with 77-degree temperatures and sunny skies. A new Opening Day attendance record was set by the 54,960 spectators. They cheered for the Clydesdales when they entered the stadium and for Ohio governor Richard Celeste, who wore a Schottzie cap. Ohio secretary of state Sherrod Brown hid a Cleveland Indians hat under his seat and predicted that the World Series would "be the battle of I-71." (Interstate 71 connects Ohio's two major-league teams, located only 225 miles apart.) National League president Charles "Chub" Feeney threw out the first pitch. The Reds went on to win their fourth opener in a row, 7–4, as Mario Soto outlasted the Phillies' Steve Carlton.

Earlier that morning, in the state capital of Columbus, the first trial began concerning the collapse of the Home State Savings Bank of Cincinnati a year earlier. The closure of the savings and loan had set off a series of similar savings-and-loan closures in Ohio and across the country. Investigators had discovered that Home State, owned by tycoon Marvin Warner, had invested approximately $140 million in a nonexistent securities firm. Depositors sought to withdraw all their savings when it was clear the bank was about to go under. Governor Celeste ordered that all of Ohio's savings and loan companies be closed. They remained closed until they could secure insurance from the federal government, and some of them never reopened. (Savings and loan associations in Ohio and other states were not previously required to have federal insurance.) The crisis cost American taxpayers more than $130 billion when state and federal governments agreed to repay depositors. Warner was eventually convicted on nine counts of fraud, and he spent nearly two-and-a-half years in jail while prosecutors sought to seize his assets, many of which were never found. Many suspected his assets were hidden overseas.

In international news, two leading newspapers in South Africa reported that Winnie Mandela had called for other countries to impose immediate sanctions on the South African government. In so doing, the newspapers ignored the government's 11-year ban on quoting Mrs. Mandela. She had also been barred from political activity for most of the previous 23 years while her husband, Nelson Mandela, was imprisoned for opposing the government's policy of apartheid. The Durban Sunday Tribune quoted Mrs. Mandela as saying, "The time of white privilege and power is gone." The next day, a consumer boycott crippled white businesses in Port Elizabeth, an industrial city on the Indian Ocean. The events led to the eventual release of Nelson Mandela in 1990 and the end of apartheid.

1987: A Mickey Mouse Start

The New York Times reported on April 6 that the smallest planet in the solar system, Pluto, was having an identity crisis. Some astronomers were suggesting that Pluto was not a planet at all! Many people wrongly believed that the heavenly body was named after the Walt Disney character named Pluto, a dog that first appeared in a Mickey Mouse animated cartoon in 1931. Ironically,

Pluto's friend Mickey Mouse served as grand marshal of the 1987 parade and later delivered the ceremonial first pitch before another record crowd of 55,166.

> *"There is spring in the air, happy chatter on the streets … it's Opening Day in Cincinnati and, on that account, all is right with the world."*
>
> Enquirer editorial

Unfortunately, the day's weather was inclement, as steady drizzle and 40-degree temperatures soaked and chilled parade watchers. Nonetheless, the parade route was packed with umbrella-covered spectators. At the start of the mile-and-a-half spectacle, residents of the urban Findlay Market neighborhood crowded the sidewalks. They also leaned out of third- and fourth-floor windows on pillows. In addition to seeing Mickey Mouse, they got to see Miss Cincinnati, the University of Cincinnati Bearcat bands, and a repeat appearance by "Mr. Spoons." The procession also included the East Central High School Band from Indiana, a beer carriage pulled by the Clydesdales, politicians who waved at anyone who would wave back, and truck drivers who liberally honked their horns. Pete Rose's look-alike brother, Dave, carefully steered a giant beer-can car down the streets. The optimism of spring was once again in the air as Dave Rose tipped a cup of brew to the cheering spectators, saying, "We get some pitching, we're gonna be all right." In total, there were 125 parade entries, including color guards and bands. Neither snow nor rain nor heat nor gloom of day could keep Reds fans, like mail carriers, from their appointed rounds at the annual parade!

Inside the ballpark, the Reds commemorated the fortieth anniversary of Jackie Robinson breaking the color barrier in the major leagues. His jersey number, 42, was painted on the second base bag. National League president Bart Giamatti had been scheduled to throw out the first pitch, but he was replaced at the last minute by former baseball commissioner and Kentucky governor Happy Chandler. Giamatti was forced to remain in New York negotiating an end to another threatened strike by umpires, and the agreement was not finalized until 10:00 a.m. on Opening Day. First base umpire Paul Runge later confessed that he was tired after being up most of the night in his Cincinnati hotel room keeping track of the bargaining. A local union dispute did affect the day's events, as private security officers patrolled the stands because the team was involved in a labor dispute with members of the Cincinnati Private Police Association.

The Reds would score 11 runs, tying the club's record for most runs on Opening Day, beating the Houston Astros 11–5. It was their fifth opening win in a row and the twelfth in their last 14 openers.

While the party was going on on the riverfront, Donald Harvey was being arraigned ten blocks to the north on a charge of aggravated homicide. The case would alarm and captivate the city. Harvey was an orderly at Drake Hospital. He was charged with giving a dose of cyanide to a helpless invalid, killing him. Hamilton County assistant prosecutors Joe Deters and Mark Piepmeier led the team that discovered Harvey was a serial killer. Ultimately, Harvey claimed to have murdered 87 people—some at the hospital, supposedly to ease their pain, and some that he knew in his personal life. He labeled himself the "angel of death." Harvey was convicted of 36 murders between 1970 and 1987 and was beaten to death in prison in 2017.

1988: Cincinnati's Bicentennial

Cincinnati was founded in 1788 when Matthias Denman, Colonel Robert Patterson, and Israel Ludlow arrived by boat on the northern bank of the Ohio River. They were opposite the mouth of the Licking River. The original surveyor, John Filson, named the area "Losantiville." It means "the city opposite

the mouth of the (Licking) river." The name was derived from four terms from different languages. "L" stood for the name of the river, "os" was taken from Latin for "mouth," "anti" was from Greek for "opposite," and "ville" was from French for "city." Two years later, the governor of the Northwest Territory, Arthur St. Clair, adopted "Cincinnati" as the name for the settlement in honor of the Society of the Cincinnati, an association for former officers of the Revolutionary War. The society took its name from Cincinnatus, a Roman general credited with saving the city of Rome. A disproportionately large number of Revolutionary War soldiers' descendants still call Cincinnati home. Their forefathers were granted land in the city. With its nickname of "The City of Seven Hills," Cincinnati still has a connection with Rome and its seven hills.

> *"Today is a day of the annual Findlay Market Parade. There will be Reds baseball in Riverfront Stadium again. And on television and radio. The street vendors will be back selling peanuts and souvenirs. The downtown streets will be thronged with happy people all decked out in Cincinnati red. Move over, Mister Robin. These are the signs that spring really has come to Cincinnati."*
>
> Enquirer editorial

The Opening Day parade on April 4 included signs marking the bicentennial. Traffic was again snarled as streets around the route were closed beginning at 9:00 a.m. It was a beautiful day under sunny skies. On Central

Parkway, halfway along the route, nearly 2,000 friends of the Hudepohl-Schoenling Brewing Company gathered for their annual party. (The Hudephol and Schoenling breweries had merged in 1986.) Under a large white tent in a parking lot, guests enjoyed beans, hot dogs, and samples of Hudepohl's trademark 14-K beer. Guest Al Armeene fondly remembered his youth. "Years ago, before Opening Day was this big, we used to skip school and make up excuses that our grandmother died. Mine died four years in a row, and I don't think any of the teachers believed it, but they never really said so." By the end of the party, creative fans had gathered up the 14-K boxes that had decorated the tables. They removed one end, tore a space for their nose and mouth, punched out eyeholes, and turned the boxes into square-headed masks.

As fans made their way to the park, vendors were busy selling hats and shirts for the upcoming All-Star game scheduled for Cincinnati in July. To the chagrin of many Reds fans, other American League games were already in process despite the protest of Cincinnati's city council. The members had blasted the schedule makers again and voted to have the clock in the Reds clubhouse set back two hours, as if that would matter.

Proving that even death takes a holiday when it comes to Opening Day, Marilyn Holt of the Gump-Holt Funeral Home was asked by a reporter if the funeral home was busy. "We haven't had any deaths at all. I'd let you talk to my husband, but he's down at the stadium." But before the game, the teams recognized two former Reds greats who had died recently, Ted Kluszewski and Ed Roush. Everyone was asked to bow their heads during a moment of silence for these beloved former players.

In the news outside of Opening Day, there were two signs of things to come. The Associated Press reported on a baseball card show in Louisville, Kentucky, that had taken place several days before when the Reds played an exhibition game there. Pete Rose, aided by promoter Paul Janzen, sold each autograph for $8. Rose noted that he never charged fans for an autograph when he saw them out in public, but it was different at official events when recipients were likely to resell the autographs. As Rose said, "Why should I let

It's Opening Day: Let's play ball!

somebody use me to make money and not make money myself?" He got to keep $7 from each autograph. Ironically, Rose needed the money later to pay legal fees, as he would go on to be convicted of tax evasion.

Meanwhile, in Washington, the United States Supreme Court upheld a $3 million libel award won by a tobacco company against CBS and a television anchorman in Chicago. The anchorman had claimed that a Viceroy cigarette advertising strategy was designed to attract young people to smoking by relating cigarettes "to pot, wine, beer, and sex." Years later, the tables would turn. The tobacco companies were found to have lied to their customers for decades about the addictive qualities of nicotine.

1989: Say It Ain't So, Pete

Pete Rose was once again the center of attention on April 3 but for all the wrong reasons. Rose was being investigated by Major League Baseball. The allegation was that Rose had violated a long-standing rule against team players or officials betting on baseball. The rule emanated from the 1919 Black Sox World Series gambling scandal in which the Reds were supposedly the beneficiaries of White Sox players throwing games in the Reds' favor. (The players were banned for life even though they were found not guilty in court.) When reports surfaced of Rose's possible infraction, there was a nationwide media frenzy. Rose had been the poster child for all that was good about the game. His work ethic and hustle were undeniable. He was said to be less talented than other players, but he had overcome any athletic weaknesses with middle-class grit. During the exhibition season, Reds games became a media circus. That circus joined the Cincinnati carnival on Opening Day. For his part, Rose

denied any wrongdoing. "I haven't done anything wrong. I keep reading the articles in the papers looking for something … I have never done anything but try to give them my best and give them a winner. That's all."

Fans always eagerly anticipated an opener with the rival Los Angeles Dodgers. The 1989 game was sold out within 24 hours when tickets went on sale December 1. Even 79-year-old Olivia Lemker of Fort Mitchell, Kentucky, could not get tickets for her fifty-fifth consecutive opener. She used a wheelchair, and the stadium's wheelchair section was sold out. Fan frenzy was whipped up all the more when Reds fans learned that seven Dodgers had dined on the eve of the game at Montgomery Inn's Boathouse Restaurant as guests of the owner. They left afterward without tipping the servers, making fans even more motivated to root against their rivals.

Supermarkets and businesses had painted their windows with baseball scenes. "We're Reds Hot!" and "Turn Dem Dodgers Blue!" "Red Flu" swept the region. Adults and children lined the parade route, where they saw major-ettes, huge hot dogs riding in classic convert-ibles, a beaver masquerading as a balloon, jalopies, and marching bands. A 10-year-old girl proclaimed "Baseball is for girls and boys. We go every year."

At the park, banners in favor of Rose adorned the façades: "Free Pete." Fans interviewed by the press supported their hero and believed the team would have more incentive than ever to win. While other dignitaries were being introduced, Rose made his first appearance in front of the crowd since the investigation had begun. He was introduced and given an award for his contributions to youth baseball in the city. He received a standing ovation. Fifteen minutes later, he received a second, minute-long standing ovation when he was intro-duced with the starting lineups. He later noted that each tribute gave him goosebumps. He reported that he had received extraordinary stacks of fan mail.

As country music star Lee Greenwood sang "God Bless the USA," several boxes of pigeons were released. The flock circled the stadium twice before taking flight over the left field wall. Greenwood then sang the national anthem, and hundreds of helium-filled red balloons were released from behind the center field fence. Recent Hall of Fame inductee Johnny Bench then received an ovation before he threw out the ceremonial first pitch. The game was on and, in what would be the last Opening Day for Peter Edward Rose, the Reds

scored early and hung on for a 6–4 win.

Baseball fans, like most Americans, are forgiving people. Rose should have read the paper that day and taken a lesson from the officials of Exxon. The Exxon Valdez had crashed a week earlier and spilled 10.1 million gallons of North Slope crude in Prince William Sound, Alaska. Exxon had taken out newspaper ads costing $1.8 million to apolo-gize for causing the nation's biggest oil spill. The company also promised to clean up every beach in Prince William Sound. Exxon Chairman Lawrence Rawl stated, "I want to tell you how sorry I am that this accident took place." He did not blame the ship's captain, Joseph Hazelwood, who at that moment was on the run. Rose, on the other hand, refused to acknowledge any wrongdoing until 2004, when he finally admitted he had bet on the Reds and other teams while he was still a player-man-ager. His lack of contrition when first charged was instrumental in MLB banning him from baseball four months after the allegations first surfaced. Local judge Norbert Nadel ruled that the initial investigation was a sham, but it did not matter. The only Hall of Fame that Rose would enter was the Cincinnati Reds Hall of Fame, which admitted him a quarter-century later. If only he had apologized.

1990: Lockout and Delay

For only the fifth time in their storied history, the Reds were forced to play their opener on the road in Houston. Season opening rainouts in 1877, 1885 and 1966, and the only sched-uled opener on the road in 1888 had resulted in little fanfare when the Reds returned home. Those teams, however, were not owned by Marge Schott. She refused to allow anything to interfere with the holiday in Cincinnati.

The season had been scheduled to start on April 2, but that date was scrapped after an owners' lockout of the players delayed spring training. The season start date was pushed back a week, and teams were to begin playing what would have been their second week's

Red-hot Reds welcomed back
City, team give first home game fanfare of Opening Day

schedule. The games from the first week on the schedule would be made up later in the season. That meant the Reds were on the road during the first week that play occurred. The parade organizers canceled the parade as a result. President George H.W. Bush had been scheduled to be the first president to throw out a pitch at a Reds opener, but with the schedule modification, Bush attended a political fundraiser instead. A home opener in Cincinnati would not occur until April 17. Still, Schott wanted her parade. "How many days do you need to [organize] a parade?" she asked parade chairman Jeff Gibbs. He replied, "21." You've got 20," Schott retorted. "Done," Gibbs answered.

Hamilton County, which includes Cincinnati, has traditionally been known as a bastion of conservatism. (That reputation is changing.) While Gibbs scrambled and the fans waited two weeks for the home season to start, the media was consumed with the criminal indictment on obscenity charges of the Contemporary Arts Center and its director, Dennis Barrie. It was the first time criminal charges had been levied against a museum in the United States. The controversy surrounded "The Perfect Moment," a retrospective collection of 175 Robert Mapplethorpe photographs that had just opened in Cincinnati. It included classical nudes, sensual flowers, two portraits of nude children, and five explicit images of gay culture. Cincinnati's city council believed that the museum should not be charged, but the city solicitor was bound to follow the dictates of the county. In an unusual Sunday court session on April 8, District Court Judge Carl Rubin ordered city and county authorities not to interfere with the continuation of the exhibit even though the museum and its

director had been indicted. Another silver lining for the museum was that its membership increased nearly 50 percent in the first two weeks of April. Months later, an eight-person jury found the defendants not guilty on all counts.

Gibbs vowed to plan "the biggest [parade] we've ever had." The market area was in the midst of a transformation, as the area's revitalization program using federal community development funds was picking up steam. Indeed, the lockout-delayed edition of the

parade became the largest in history. Up to 50 groups entered the parade to replace some rooters who could not reschedule. A Reds fan who had attended 70 consecutive openers, Marie Determan of Kenwood, Ohio, was honored to be the grand marshal. She was joined in her car by a six-year-old T-ball enthusiast attending his first opener. The two would later throw out the first pitches as relief pitchers for the president. The festivities included 22-month-old Christopher Reardon of Amelia, Ohio, named America's Most

Beautiful Baby, a Wienermobile sponsored by Oscar Meyer, ten mini–Grand Prix cars, and a restored trolley car from the Cincinnati Historical Society. Schott walked the entire parade route, receiving well wishes from thousands of fans.

When game time arrived, the fans had reason to celebrate the string of games that preceded the Cincinnati opener. The Reds had been perfect on the road trip, winning six straight games against Houston and Atlanta. Red, white, and blue bunting along the stadium railings gave the stadium a World Series look. The ushers and grounds crew were dressed in tuxedos and tails. The pregame hoopla lived up to previous standards, including an appearance by the US Army Reserves 100th Division Band, another special release of pigeons, and tricks performed by Princess Schottzie, an elephant. Gibbs's organizational skills over the coming years would put the parade over the top.

Two members of the self-proclaimed "Nasty Boys," Norm Charlton and Randy Myers, pitched three scoreless innings in relief, and

the Reds extended their streak to seven games in a 2–1 nail biter. (Rob Dibble was the third Nasty Boy.) When the Reds' new manager Lou Piniella, a rookie when it came to Opening Day in Cincinnati, saw 100 reporters waiting in the press room after the game, he asked, "Is this the postseason or what?" Only 38,354 fans bought tickets for the delayed opener, but Piniella was impressed with the hoopla. The fans, in turn, would have occasion to be impressed with the club's performance during the season, as the Reds shocked the baseball world by going "wire to wire," meaning they were in first place in the National League for

Opening Day fever grips Queen City

every single day of the season. They went on to win their division and later sweep the heavily favored Oakland Athletics in the World Series. Not a bad run for a new skipper!

1991: Rings!

Five weeks after President Bush ordered a cease-fire to end the Persian Gulf War, Cincinnatians were in the mood to celebrate the world champions. Marge Schott had battled a life-threatening infection for two weeks, but she recovered enough to take part in the festivities. Opening Day fever gripped the Queen City.

Four preview shows on local TV stations covered every aspect of the day, including live coverage of the Findlay Market parade. On those stations, it was "all Reds, all the time." Local radio personality Jim Scott perched himself on a billboard above a local bar, Caddy's, to describe the festivities happening on the city streets. Renowned editorial cartoonist Jim Borgman drew a sketch of a plane flying over the ballpark with a banner saying, "Go Marge! Love, Reds." CBS late-night comedian David Letterman told Reds manager Piniella that he wanted to pitch for the Reds. Piniella responded by telling Letterman he needed to give up hope for a long-term, no-cut contract. Said Piniella, Letterman could pitch batting practice "as long as it's on his own expense, [with] no meal money, no guaranteed contract and he takes the manager and coaching staff out to dinner." In a nationwide poll, many baseball fans across the country picked the Reds to return to the World Series against the Oakland A's, though they predicted Oakland would win.

Downtown streets became fashionably red on the morning of April 8. The outfits included the expected baseball hats, satin bomber jackets, and cotton T-shirts emblazoned with the World Series championship logo. There were also blue denim jackets plastered with Reds buttons; goofy-looking, wide rain hats; and big baggy shorts that resembled candy canes. Girls wore red-trimmed, white cotton dresses with Cincinnati Reds Fan Club on the front. There were even plastic brooms with red bristles, a reminder of the Reds' World Series sweep of the A's. Reds logos were splattered everywhere.

The 1991 rendition of the Opening Day parade was easily the loudest ever. The record number of entries (165) included 14 bands! There was a first-ever float contest with a requirement that all entries be decorated in red and white. (The "Free Pete" entry did not win.) There were two elephants from the Cincinnati Zoo, antique fire engines, and the now traditional Clydesdales. Elderly "Captain Bingo," who ignored the requirement to wear red and white, strolled along looking like a World War I flying ace in a blue cape. There was a tribute to Peanut Jim. Did the organizers forget anything? Parade chairman Jeff Gibbs's only worry before the spectacle was that the parade would last too long.

Arriving at the ballpark, the fans again encountered picket signs carried by umpires. They were in yet another contract dispute that was resolved just a few hours before the game. Since negotiations were still underway close to game time, the replacement crew that had been called in went ahead and worked the game. Umpire Randy Marsh of northern Kentucky explained, "We don't want people to think we're a bunch of jerks. We want people to enjoy Opening Day, but we also want our presence felt."

On the field, Schott repeated a strange ritual that she had initiated in 1990: she pulled a

manners and grace. Eric Davis was the most expressive player in the ring ceremony. He dashed eagerly from the dugout to accept his ring, faked a move toward the owner's microphone as if to make his own acceptance speech, and then bounced back to the dugout, smiling broadly as he waved his prize.

> "Cincinnati stops for Opening Day. To Cincinnati it's the best thing that happens."
>
> José Rijo, Reds pitcher

fistful of hair from Schottzie and applied it to the chest of Piniella for good luck. The routine had seemingly brought good luck to the Reds in 1990, so Schott was determined to repeat it. As *Enquirer* columnist Tim Sullivan aptly wrote, the "bizarre ritual … surely constitutes cruelty to managers if not to animals."

After the parade entered the ballpark, the focus turned to the ring presentation. With a light rain falling, the owner began the ceremony. She barely realized that Ohio's governor, George Voinovich, had become her personal assistant by holding an umbrella over her head, as she was determined not to let the weather spoil the special occasion. Schott presented rings to anyone who had any claim at all to a ring, including Ron Robinson, who was traded during spring training well before the championship run. Schottzie also received a ring, and it was the only time the crowd booed. The fans loved that the team was generous in giving rings to all the club's officials and to players remotely associated with the championship, but giving one to the Saint Bernard was too much even for the Reds faithful. Schott clumsily presented the rings, giving the appearance that she didn't even know the players' first names. When calling two of her top pitchers forward, she said "Our player Charlton" for Norm Charlton and "Another little cutie named Dibble" for Rob Dibble. Throughout her tenure with the Reds, Schott was not known for having smooth

After the Reds defeated the Houston Astros 6–2, fans left the ballpark shouting, "Wire-to-wire, take 2!" That dream would end with a thud when the Reds went 74–88 on the season and ended in fifth place.

On the morning of the opener, two local firefighters were honored in Firehouse magazine for saving lives after a massive explosion the previous summer. The inferno at a BASF plant in a Cincinnati neighborhood resulted in the death of two workers, injuries for 90 others, and $50 million in damage to homes and buildings in the surrounding communities. Meanwhile, in California, controversy raged on as the embattled police chief of Los Angeles, Daryl Gates, was allowed to return to work. Riots had erupted in the aftermath of the videotaped beating of an African American motorist, Rodney King, by white policemen. (The police response was said to be a contributing factor in O.J. Simpson's "not guilty" verdict in 1995.) And in the space race, two astronauts aboard the shuttle Atlantis deployed an astronomy satellite to enable NASA to observe galaxies and black holes in space.

1992: Nuxhall Survives

The Reds boasted about their radio network being one of the largest in professional sports. Cincinnati's WLW radio was and is the flagship station, but there are about 80 affiliate stations in seven different states. The team has had its share of legendary announcers, from Red Barber and Waite Hoyt to, more recently, Marty Brennaman. However, reverence for these three pales in comparison to the city's love for "the old left-hander," Joe Nuxhall. For 38 seasons, Nuxhall was a true partner in the booth. When he signed off the air after his "Star of the Game" show after each game, Nuxy (as he was commonly known) would tell listeners that he was "the old left-hander, rounding third and heading for home. Goodnight everyone." (His tag line would later adorn the outside façade of Great American Ball

> '*Our act wouldn't fly everywhere. But I think what we do — by talking about my tomatoes, or his golf game, or my golf game now — is humanize ourselves.*'
> — **Marty Brennaman**

Park, the Reds' home stadium since 2003.) He developed the signature phrase two weeks into the 1967 season when a Reds coach, Whitey Wietelmann, told him he needed a sign-off phrase. The coach gave him the famous line, but Nuxhall thought it was corny so he gave up on it after a few weeks. Then, fans sent him letters saying they missed it, so he decided to "round third and head for home" each night. His wife wondered why it took him so long to actually make it home, but he often detoured to the Montgomery Inn ribs restaurant.

As plans were being made for another opener, fans learned that Nuxhall was scheduled for prostate cancer surgery on February 18. It became a major news story, and the reaction was both swift and heartfelt. Nuxhall recalled that get well wishes came from everywhere, and soon his hospital room was filled with a dozen floral arrangements. The city was holding its collective breath until the folksy announcer was released to work the final days of spring training—just in time.

The game was a sellout. Chip Goff of Verona, Kentucky, did not have a ticket for the first time since the early 1970s. He awoke early on April 6 and was first in line at the ticket office at 4:30 a.m. The sun was not even up, and Goff admitted it was "pretty lonely" before a second fan arrived 90 minutes later. The line would grow from the ticket office over the bridge that connected the stadium with downtown. The lucky ones would later become part of the 55,356 fans who jammed the stadium to the rafters that afternoon.

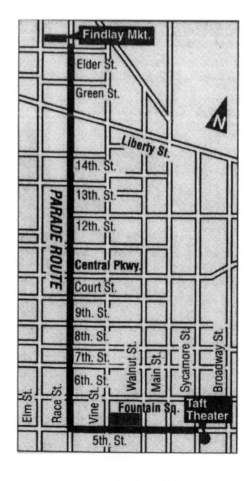

Throngs of spectators gathered downtown as well in the damp, early morning chill. They jockeyed for the best spot to watch the parade. Fans in the ballpark who had box-level seats were greeted by ushers in tuxedos. Everyone was later introduced to two elephants, Princess Schottzie and Mai Thai, and one of them lumbered out to the pitcher's mound with Nuxhall. The center of attention, though, was Nuxhall. He received a thunderous standing ovation when he bounced the first pitch to home plate. No one seemed to notice or care that the American League had once again started before the Reds. For the first time in ten years, the Reds lost on Opening Day.

In national news, President Bush was running for reelection. The administration had admitted over the weekend that it had been off target in its claims during the Persian Gulf War that Iraq's

nuclear sites had been eliminated. A column by Charles Madigan of the Chicago Tribune that appeared in the *Enquirer* on Opening Day opined that the Democrats were "stuck" with a front-runner who had the "stability of a sailor on shore leave" and "an amazingly changeable challenger whose campaign runs on resentment." He believed the Democrats were missing an opportunity to regain the White House. The front-runner? Arkansas governor Bill Clinton. The challenger was California governor Jerry Brown. Clinton would go on to become the next president in an electoral college landslide seven months later.

238

Marge Schott loved elephants, and this one delivers the ball to be used for the first pitch.

TROUBLE IN PARADISE

It's spring; it's rebirth;
it's a great festival.
It's great having a non-religious reason
to celebrate spring.

Greg Rhodes, author and baseball historian

As if Reds fans had not endured enough with the banishment of Rose, the next four seasons would really test their love for the Reds and Opening Day. The club's owner would be suspended, and a legend would be impetuously fired. The dictates of television and a strike by players would result in chaotic Opening Days in 1994 and 1995. Worse yet, there would be a tragedy during the opener in 1996. It would be the strangest four-year period in Opening Day history. It's a wonder the traditions surrounding Opening Day survived.

1993: "The Big Dog"

After the Reds finished in second place in 1992, popular manager Piniella resigned to become manager of the Seattle Mariners. Reds fans were stunned. New general manager Jim Bowden discovered the perfect panacea:

he hired Tony Perez, aka "The Big Dog." Aside from Rose, Perez was likely the most popular member of the Big Red Machine. The fans were placated. The opener was sold out in December. Dismay came next, as MLB suspended Marge Schott and banned her from day-to-day operation of the team while remaining as owner. Schott was accused of making racial and ethnic slurs. At age 32, Jim Bowden took complete control of the club, and he made a flurry of trades and acquisitions.

On the morning of April 5, even though Schott had been suspended, she was still an ardent supporter of Opening Day traditions. She arrived in Over-the-Rhine near the start of the parade, signing autographs and acknowledging well-wishers. The parade, then in its seventy-third year, wound its way from Findlay Market past Fountain Square. There were 155 entries with the customary

position behind home plate. Mrs. Perez then threw a perfect strike, keeping the ball low. The crowd erupted in laughter and applause.

> "All this is possible, of course. On Opening Day, all things are possible."
>
> Tim Sullivan,
> Enquirer sports columnist

When the Reds were introduced, the spectators noticed a new look. The players' white uniforms featured sleeveless, button-front vests with red pinstripes. The Reds had last worn sleeveless jerseys, including pinstripes, in 1966. Their new caps were white with red pinstripes, a red bill, and a red wishbone "C" similar to the caps last worn in 1966 as well. When the game started, Montréal's Felipe Alou and Perez became the first Latin American–born managers to face each other in a major league game. (Respectively, they were the fourth and fifth Latin American–born managers in history.) Having them at the helm of two clubs simply acknowledged the fact that there were so many more Latin players in the big leagues than in the past.

floats, bands, and animals. The organizers of the parade displayed a huge "We Love Marge" sign on their float near the front of the parade. Thousands lined the streets. Many wore Marge Schott face masks that had been sold along the parade route. Talk show host Jerry Springer, who was a former mayor and news anchor in the city, served as the grand marshal.

During the broadcast of the parade, Channel 5 introduced the new play-by-play announcer for Reds games. He was George Grande, who was best known as one of the co-anchors on ESPN SportsCenter when the cable channel began its service on September 7, 1979. Grande's inaugural duty on Opening Day was to describe the pregame ceremonies that were highlighted by Pituka Perez. As the wife of the Reds' new manager, Mrs. Perez was accorded the honor of throwing the first pitch. When she took the mound, her husband moved into position as catcher. Mrs. Perez peered toward home plate like a wily veteran. She playfully shook off the signal her husband gave her. That prompted catcher Perez to trot out to the mound for his first discussion with a pitcher as the team's manager. After a brief chat, the catcher gave the pitcher a kiss before returning to his

On this chilly and cloudy day, Perez got the better of Alou, and the Reds won, 2–1. Perez celebrated his first win as a manager by opening champagne in the clubhouse. Forty-three games later, he was out of a job. The new general manager, Bowden, became impatient after a 20–24 start to the season, so he fired the Reds legend—by telephone, no less. At the time, it was the earliest firing of a manager in MLB's previous 65 years. The decision and the method of communication outraged frustrated fans. Bowden would need around-the-clock police protection as a result of death threats to him and his family. Under new manager Davey Johnson, the Reds then compiled a record of 53-65. Bowden was more patient with Johnson, who returned for the following season.

1994: ESPN Be Damned

Reds fans were tired. Tony Perez had not been given a chance, and now the city was debating whether Riverfront Stadium was still good enough. The team had played with considerable success in a concrete bowl that was envied as a modern ballpark when it opened 24 years earlier. The stadium had Astroturf, but now some fans and baseball purists wanted grass. It was roomier than Crosley Field, but was it too roomy? Sharing the stadium with a football team meant there was no place to commemorate the team's legends or to celebrate its accomplishments. There were no statues of famous players. There was nothing to tell the history of the longest professional team in baseball. Sportswriter and author John Erardi explained, "It's a shame when you walk into Riverfront Stadium and don't see anything to say what has happened there. It's like baseball was never played here before 1970." The issue would be debated for years, with some politicians even advocating a move to northern Kentucky.

Fans across the country had become accustomed to television and cable networks deciding the dates and times for various sports events. TV executives naturally wanted to schedule games for dates and times that would maximize viewership and advertising revenue. That was one thing, but Cincinnati fans were left wondering: Why would you mess with Opening Day? MLB had inked a new television deal with ESPN that called for the opening of the baseball season to be on the first Sunday night in April. ESPN invited the Reds to host the occasion so viewers around the country could witness the traditions that accompanied Reds openers. The Reds had long asserted that the American League should not start games earlier than the traditional opener in the National League. Opening on Sunday evening with the only major league game being in Cincinnati solved that problem. It would be good for the city, and the Reds initially agreed. So what was wrong?

The wrench in the works was that suspended Reds owner Marge Schott belatedly realized April 2 was Easter Sunday. The Findlay Market organizers wanted nothing to do with a parade on Easter. When Schott tried to back out of the deal, the schedule had already been finalized. Schott claimed ESPN should have told her it was Easter. She was rebuffed and was told the official National League opener would be on Easter Sunday night. Schott reacted by saying that the Reds would consider the second game of the season to be Opening Day. There would be no bunting on display for the national TV audience at the opener, and there would be nothing more than a ceremonial first pitch by the National League president. On Easter Monday afternoon, the city would celebrate Opening Day.

> *"The parade was Monday; the ushers in tuxedo were Monday; the big crowd was Monday. That's what Opening Day is, honey! Monday afternoon!"*
>
> Marge Schott

Mark Purdy of the *Enquirer* acknowledged that fans were confused about how and when to celebrate Opening Day. He suggested fans wear two pairs of red pants, two red shirts, and two baseball caps to be ready to support the Reds on both days. On Easter Sunday, the *Enquirer's* Geoff Hobson asked rhetorically, "Is today Opening Day? Is it Opening Night? Is it Opening Daze?" The fans could not decide which day to celebrate, but one thing was certain: this was not normal. The ESPN telecast was a bust, short on festivities and missing the enthusiasm that typically accompanied the opener. It seemed the only fans treating Opening Day #1 as a holiday were four young men who wore white, full-length bunny suits. Each wore one letter of "ESPN" to attract the cameras. The game had all the excitement of a rain delay as the men pranced

through empty seats in the upper deck. The Reds ended up laying an egg in every respect, losing 6–4 in front of 32,803 spectators in 39-degree weather.

The fans decided to follow the lead of the owner the next morning and afternoon by embracing Opening Day #2. Just before 11:00 a.m., Schott boarded a big red Cincinnati fire truck, pounded on the engine's horn for several earsplitting blasts, and kicked off the parade. The procession of 175 units was witnessed by spectators standing four to five deep. The Clydesdales were back, Schottzie the elephant lumbered along, and there were even greyhounds from a dog-rescue organization. The crowd waved at the "Rosie Reds" and the "Hooters Girls" marching team, two groups of supporters with no overlapping membership. It looked and felt like Opening Day. Everyone seemed to forget that it was the second game of the season.

Inside the park, the traditional bunting was visible during pregame ceremonies. Fans were dressed in red from head to toe and, mercifully, there was sunshine. The players were introduced, wearing emblems commemorating the 1869 Red Stockings. The crowd reacted as if it was the first day of spring. Then, Gordy Coleman, former Reds first baseman who had died recently at age 59, was honored with a moment of silence. The 55,093 fans who bought tickets apparently knew the difference between a cable television production and a baseball season opener.

The Reds won on a dramatic home run by Kevin Mitchell in the bottom of the tenth inning, and afterward the town celebrated as if the team had not lost the night before. Not that the team's record mattered, as a strike in August—with the Reds in first place—resulted in the World Series being canceled. Both the Reds and the television networks would end up coming out on the short end of the stick given that unwelcome development.

1995: Not Again!

More turmoil returned in 1995. The players' strike continued into spring training. The umpires were locked out. Would there be a season at all? The owners had hired replacement players to start the season on April 3.

On the eve of the opener, the owners accepted the union's offer to play without a labor agreement, and they canceled their plan to use replacement players. There had been little or no fan interest for attending replacement games in Cincinnati or elsewhere around the country anyway. Instead of starting on April 3, there would be an abbreviated spring training before starting a 144-game (instead of 162-game) season, with the Reds opening on April 26 in Los Angeles. If that happened, it would be the only time the Reds would be scheduled to start their season on the road since 1888.

The Reds immediately petitioned the league to change the schedule and allow the Reds to open at home. A few days later, the league agreed, and Opening Day was on! Well, sort of. The parade organizers had planned the annual procession to coincide with the replacement players' game on April 3, and it was just too late to ask participants to wait 23 days. There would be a parade on April 3, but it would stop at Fountain Square and not proceed into the stadium.

> "Opening Day is not modern. It may not be everything that it was in the time of our parents and grandparents, when the world seem simpler and baseball had no rival for the fan's attention, but, in form and substance, it has not changed all that much. It is still a holiday in Cincinnati; a once a year happening that is unique to this town in all of baseball."
>
> Howard Wilkinson, Enquirer columnist

With the ongoing strike and the prospect of replacement players diminishing fans' enthusiasm, the number of entries in the parade was already down to about 125. The streets were less crowded with spectators than usual, and many of the units decided to mock the players and owners instead of celebrating them as was customary. Members of the Findlay Market Association led the ridicule with shirts that read "Replacement Parade Marshal." A 10-year-old girl, Stephanie Patton, pulled her ordinary red wagon with a three-foot sign backed by a wooden frame and decorated with balloons and a Findlay Market pennant. The sign revealed the wisdom or sarcasm of youth. It read "REPLACEMENT FLOAT." The float was described as one of the best for producing smiles along the route. A pickup truck sponsored by FM station WARM 98 featured a sign that said "Replacement Fans." There was no indication that these efforts were coordinated, but the message was clear: you can pound sand, players and owners. You can't rain on Cincinnati's parade.

Despite the gloomy mood of many fans, the sun was shining. The parade's biggest cheerleader, Marge Schott, once again started the parade by sounding the fire engine horn. Schott handed out team decals during the procession, which lasted more than two hours. The parade featured the usual cadre of politicians, zoo animals, beauty queens, food merchants, and marching bands. Students from Fairview Bilingual German School were dressed in traditional German garb. Along the way, fans groused about the players and the owners. Bob Layton of Lawrenceburg, Indiana, came to the parade to watch his daughter march in a band, but he promised he would never go down to the ballpark again. Police officer Dan Mitchell, who had led 20 consecutive Opening Day parades on his motorcycle, called it "the strangest parade because there's no ball game."

Missing from the day were the parties that usually accompany Opening Day. Local catering companies had seen a dramatic decline in engagements when there was a prospect of replacement games. Hotel occupancy rates were down, too, and even season suite holders at the stadium showed little or no interest in putting on their usual parties. By the time the opener on April 26 rolled around, there still was no significant uptick in enthusiasm. Many fans had simply lost interest. The effects of the cancellation of the 1994 World Series and the delay of the 1995 season would be remembered for years.

It took until game time on April 26 for all 51,033 tickets to be sold, but despite the sellout, there were 15,000 no-shows. The Reds apparently could not locate a fan willing to throw out the first pitch, so they turned to an elephant that was actually trained to throw a ball. It proved a fitting symbol. Elephants are famous for their memory, and fans do not easily forget. The player introductions received tepid applause. The fans booed lustily after public-address announcer Joe Zerhusen called the players "Your 1995 Cincinnati Reds." Flint Cornett, a 35-year-old Knothole baseball coach from Florence, Kentucky, summed up the feelings of even the most loyal followers of the game: "I'm disgruntled but I am here. This is such a love-hate relationship. I love the game; I hate what the professionals have done to it." Without a doubt, the biggest cheer of the day came for local vocalist Larry Kinley when he sang the national anthem.

To show the extent of the fans' ire, while the first inning was in progress, a small plane appeared above the stadium. A banner trailed behind it with large red letters: OWNERS & PLAYERS: TO HELL WITH ALL OF YOU! All in all, the day was certainly a spectacle, just not the kind that the owners, players, or fans wanted. The Reds lost 7–1 to the Cubs in a lackluster performance. So many spectators had left by the sixth inning that radio

announcer Marty Brennaman wondered if the fans had forgotten how long a baseball game lasts.

In a show of remembrance that the world did not revolve around baseball, the crowd observed a respectful moment of silence for the victims of the Oklahoma City bombing that had occurred a week earlier. Timothy McVeigh and Terry Nichols, domestic terrorists, had loaded a truck with fertilizer-based bombs. They killed 167 people, including 19 children, and injured more than 600 others. The blast destroyed one-third of the federal courthouse. McVeigh was later executed, and Nichols was sentenced to life in prison.

On the day of the opener, the sensational trial of football legend O.J. Simpson was continuing. Simpson's lawyers attacked the credibility of a Los Angeles police department evidence collector, sarcastically suggesting that she fabricated testimony to cover up her sloppy work. They claimed she was part of a police conspiracy to frame Simpson. The trial was a media circus and was covered live by cable news outlets. Simpson was found not guilty several months later.

And, since violence appeared to be the topic of the week, the United States Supreme Court joined in the discussion. In a 5–4 decision, the Court struck down a federal law banning gun possession within 1,000 feet of schools. Little did the public realize that shooting sprees at schools would seem almost commonplace two decades later.

The Reds went on to have a successful season despite a rocky start. After being denied the chance to be in the playoffs in 1994 because of the strike and the cancellation of the World Series, Davey Johnson guided the Reds to the playoffs in 1995. They swept the Dodgers in the division series before being swept by the Braves in the league championship series. The biggest story coming out of that series was that the Reds failed to sell out the first two games before the teams headed to Atlanta. Pundits blamed the fans' lingering resentment about the disruption of the 1994 season.

Ray Knight, a popular former Reds player, became the team's new manager. Even though Johnson had led the team to success, the club had inexplicably announced before the season that he would not manage beyond 1995. Instead, he would become a consultant, and Knight would become the skipper. The Reds would not return to the playoffs for 15 years.

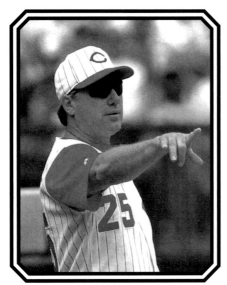

Ray Knight

1996: Tragedy Strikes

MLB clubs witnessed a 20 percent decline in attendance in 1995. The 1996 season began with the two leagues sounding like convicts who were seeking parole. Their plea was simple: "Forgive us and come back." The empty seats in Cincinnati during the 1995 playoffs had become a symbol of fans' anger and loss of interest. Over the winter, the sports talk shows were not buzzing about the excitement of a new season or the hope for another return to the playoffs. Instead, the topic of discussion was whether the fans would bother to return to the game.

Early indications were not positive. For the first time in years, the April 1 opener was not sold out in advance. Worse, Cincinnati was hit with an April Fools' Day joke in the form of several inches of snow on the ground. Meteorologists had been caught by surprise. Parade coordinator Jeff Gibbs decided the snow would not stop the annual traditions surrounding the parade. Fortunately, a warming sun appeared, making for more favorable parade conditions; unfortunately, clumps of melting snow fell from the market's roof onto the heads of high school musicians practicing "Louie Louie" in the street below.

As the snow dissipated, Marge Schott was sure the day had been saved. As was customary, she arrived early with her 160-pound Saint Bernard. She was greeted by the grand marshal, the ever-popular former manager Sparky Anderson. Schott sounded the siren that started the festivities. Mayor Roxanne Qualls presented Anderson with a framed proclamation and thanked him for returning to the city. "This is a very special day because we have Sparky back in town. You turned many Opening Days into victory celebrations."

Kevin Luken and Jim Scott

It seemed that one local radio station was in an April Fool's mood. When the parade began rolling at 11:00 a.m., listeners who tuned to WEBN-FM instead of the pregame show on WLW were treated to a rival, though fictional, parade. The station was conducting its twentieth anniversary "Fool's Day Parade." Since it was to be the station's last parade, the DJs filled the airwaves with flashbacks from previous April 1 "parades." There were edgy commercials for Billy Graham Crackers, Quaker's Mate condoms, the Lard Rock Café, and Martin Luther King Kwiks (a takeoff on the local convenience grocery, King Kwik).

Sparky Anderson Throwing First Pitch

In the real parade, Anderson led the usual array of floats and marching bands. This year, though, camels and llamas became part of the procession, too. The snow likely discouraged some spectators from attending, but the diehards returned to line the streets. Schott was dressed in a red pinstriped jacket with MARGE on the back and a red rose pinned to the front. She waved and carried on as if it were a 70-degree day. Anderson waved as if it were a 1970s victory celebration.

The game had not sold out until the morning of the game—a notable departure from the days of sellouts four or five months before Opening Day. When the capacity crowd of 51,033 arrived at the stadium, they were entertained by the high-stepping Clydesdales. Schottzie pranced on the field as a marching band played "God Bless America." Anderson threw the first pitch, after which the band played the Canadian national anthem. (The Montreal Expos were in town from north of the border.) The umpires soon emerged from their dressing room, but popular home plate umpire John McSherry was called back because "The Star-Spangled Banner" had not yet been performed. McSherry retreated, joking that former Expo manager Gene Mauch claimed, "Montreal led the world in anthems." Ten-year-old Kara Halbersleben then belted out the anthem, and the Reds took the field as the crowd roared. McSherry, who had an imposing presence at 6'2" and 328 pounds, engaged in friendly banter with Reds catcher Eddie Taubansee. McSherry downplayed his role as the game's arbiter, suggesting to Taubansee, "You call balls and strikes the first two innings and we'll be all right."

But things were not all right. Two batters and seven pitches into the opener, 51-year-old McSherry stepped away from his position behind Taubansee, saying, "Hold on a second." Taubansee turned and asked, "John, are you all right?" but the umpire did not reply. McSherry seemed to motion for assistance before walking toward the backstop from which he had emerged ten minutes earlier. McSherry then collapsed. Paramedics raced to his side, pounded his chest, pumped an IV into his body, and used electric paddles to shock his heart. The rescue attempts lasted for several minutes on the field behind home plate. The crowd, along with the Reds and the Montréal Expos, stood in silence. McSherry was taken off the field and rushed to a local hospital, but he could not be saved. He was pronounced dead 54 minutes after his collapse. McSherry suffered "sudden cardiac death" according to the coroner. Sadly, he was scheduled to see a doctor the next day for an irregular heartbeat, and his fellow umpires had asked him to take the day off.

After McSherry was taken to the hospital, the other umpires vowed to continue play, but the Reds and Expos players refused, some with tears in their eyes. The game was postponed until the next day. Some boos greeted the decision, but that may be because no one had disclosed McSherry's death to the crowd. Ninety minutes after McSherry collapsed, the flag in center field made a slow, graceful descent to half-staff. The scoreboard simply read, "Due to the unfortunate circumstance during today's Reds–Expos Opening Day game, the game has been canceled." It was rescheduled for the following day. Regrettably, Marge Schott, who was informed of the decision to cancel before the fans were, made insensitive remarks, including, "Why are they calling it? Whose decision is it? Why can't they play with two umpires?" and "I feel cheated. This isn't supposed to happen to us, not Cincinnati. This is our day. This is our history, our tradition, our team." She repeatedly referred to the umpire as "the man" or "the umpire" rather than by his name. Her actions and comments provoked a new wave of criticism of the already embattled owner. She was Jekyll and Hyde. At one moment, she was a gracious and generous ambassador for her hometown; the next moment, she was an insensitive, self-absorbed embarrassment for the city. She was simultaneously loved and despised. Later in the year, Schott agreed to give up day-to-day control of the team through the 1998 season because of still more controversial comments. One of the club's executives, John Allen, was put in charge.

It was the most shocking Opening Day game in history. (The only other time in baseball history that a death had occurred on the playing field was during a game 76 years earlier. Cleveland shortstop Ray Chapman died from a pitch by New York Yankee pitcher Carl Mays that struck his head.) When the 1996 rescheduled opener occurred the next day, few people were in the mood for baseball. The stadium was half full, even though 53,136 tickets had been sold (including those from the previous day). The umpires received a standing ovation when they walked onto the field. There was no hoopla. A chaplain said a prayer for McSherry and his family, and the crowd sat hushed during a moment of silence for the fallen umpire. The Reds won, 4–1, but the entire day was somber.

John McSherry, Opening Day 1996

Ken Griffey, Jr.

GOODBYE, RIVERFRONT; HELLO, JUNIOR!

Many things have gone modern, but Opening Day in Cincinnati will not change.

Cincinnati Reds 1952 Yearbook

1997: Looking Forward

After three consecutive openers were marred by controversy and tragedy, Reds fans were ready to turn a new page in 1997. There was excitement surrounding the planned construction of a new ballpark that would be less utilitarian and would be designed strictly for baseball. Riverfront Stadium was a lame duck. Despite its days being numbered, it had been renamed "Cinergy Field" in 1996 in a sponsorship deal with the local energy company. The only controversy about building a new ballpark involved its location. Urban development proponents urged that the park be constructed on the northeast edge of downtown, known as "Broadway Commons," where there was a view of historic Mount Adams. The Reds preferred a location on the riverfront and were trying to outmaneuver the

NFL's Cincinnati Bengals for what was viewed as the prime piece of real estate.

John Allen, who by 1997 was the club's "interim managing director," worked hard to hasten the renewal of fans' attention after a lot of upheaval in recent years. He brought back "Mr. Red," a popular mascot from the Big Red Machine era. Flags were painted on top of the Reds dugout to commemorate pennant-winning seasons. Two jerseys were displayed on the left field wall to honor manager Fred Hutchinson, from the Crosley Field era, and Hall of Fame catcher Johnny Bench. Bench returned as a consultant and dressed in uniform for the pregame activities. A new, spongier artificial surface replaced the Astroturf that was worn and rigid. Allen wanted Cinergy Field to look like a ballpark that housed a franchise with a proud and distinct history.

251

> *"If your response to 'Opening Day' is "for what?" … We cannot be friends."*
>
> Becky Freking, Reds Fan

Allen's moves paid off. In contrast to the 1996 opener, April 1 did not involve death, postponement, or bad weather. Instead, fans

John Allen

eagerly embraced Opening Day and the first sign of spring. The game was sold out, including all standing-room-only tickets. Rooters came out in force for the parade, which had more than 200 entries. Fans lined the streets five to ten deep, with thousands arriving early to claim prime locations with their lawn chairs. One fan, Jeff Wise, smartly noted, "The emphasis is back where it belongs, on the game, not on Marge Schott. This year, baseball belongs to the people again. Look how they've responded." Mr. Red was greeted like he was a long-lost friend. Cincinnati public schools were on spring break, and young students were particularly evident in the crowd. Many saw the Clydesdale horses, Cincinnati Zoo camels, and marching bands for the first time. The water in the Tyler

Davidson Fountain in Fountain Square even had a bubble-gum pink tint to it. The crowd wore red of every shade. Fan Matt Naglor carried on his own eight-year tradition by painting his face white with red stitches.

Proponents of locating the new stadium in Broadway Commons dominated the parade route. Men, women, and children showed their support for the urban location of the new ballpark by waving yard signs, lifting posters, and holding balloons. Lucy May of the *Enquirer* declared that Broadway Commons would be the winner "hands down" if Opening Day hype decided the future location of the new ballpark. Urban restaurateur Jim Tarbell, dressed in his traditional garb honoring Peanut Jim Shelton, walked the parade route and urged supporters to put their signs high in the air.

While the parade was underway, the Reds held a noon memorial honoring John McSherry. A plaque was unveiled as the team renamed the

umpires' dressing room in his honor. It was a fitting tribute that was well received by the public as another example of the first-class approach taken by John Allen. The club also put out slick yearbooks and media guides, and the Reds website made its debut. The Reds became the first major league team to create its own a CD-ROM (a compact disc that stored data). Reds season ticket holders were out in force along the parade route and in the ballpark, proudly wearing sweatshirts that were presented as gifts from the team.

A jazz band blared as the parade entered the field. Dignitaries included two local heroes, Olympic gold medal gymnasts Amanda Borden and Jaycie Phelps. Marge Schott said a few words that violated a strict reading of her MLB agreement prohibiting her from speaking for the club. The breach was ignored, as Schott was still appreciated for her role as a cheerleader for Opening Day festivities. Ohio governor George Voinovich delivered the first pitch to US senator Mitch McConnell of neighboring Kentucky. When the players were introduced, outfielder Reggie Sanders wore his pants bunched at the knees in honor of the Negro Leagues and his favorite player, Cool Papa Bell. Seven-year-old Cincinnati native Kali Armstrong's voice was strong enough to shake the cheap seats when she sang the national anthem. The crowd roared. A moment of silence quieted the crowd in memory of McSherry. Allen, a soft-spoken leader, stayed out of the limelight.

The play on the field put an exclamation point on the day. NFL defensive back Deion Sanders, newly acquired by the Reds, was Joe Nuxhall's "Star of the Game" as he garnered two hits and stole two bases. (Sanders played for five different NFL teams during his career, as well as five MLB teams.) The Reds thrashed the Colorado Rockies with four runs in the bottom of the first inning en route to an 11–4 victory. The run total equaled the franchise record for most runs scored on Opening Day. The party was complete. Opening Day was back!

1998: The Trade That Rocked the Opener

The airwaves of Cincinnati sports talk radio were filled with debates during the early months of 1998. There was the issue of Marge Schott's unresolved status, continuing debate about the location of the new ballpark, and budget cuts that yielded a $22 million, no-name roster. Then, after all this off-the-field chaos, the Reds shocked their fans on the eve of Opening Day. The club traded its best pitcher, Dave Burba, who was slated to start the season as the Opening Day hurler on March 31. In return, the Reds received 23-year-old first baseman Sean Casey. Casey was a minor-league star for the Cleveland Indians, but he was an unknown commodity in Cincinnati. This swap rocked already pessimistic Reds fans.

Sean Casey

Reds general manager Jim Bowden tried to allay the fans' skepticism. Bowden admitted that the Reds were rebuilding and promised, "Five years from now, fans will look back on this like the Joe Morgan trade in the '70s. This kid is that type of player." Cincinnatians were well aware that "rebuilding" is equivalent to saying that the team would not be very good that season, but Bowden's promise was largely fulfilled. Although Casey did not become the star that Joe Morgan became, he was later embraced by the fans as he lived up to his nickname, "The Mayor." The personable first baseman played the next eight seasons and became a fan favorite.

Preceding the opener, which was the earliest in the team's history, the busiest person in town seemed to be Linda Vester. A native of Milford, Ohio—a 30-minute drive from the ballpark—Vester was the anchor of *NBC News at Sunrise*. She was chosen to throw out the first pitch of the season, and Findlay Market organizers selected her as the parade's grand marshal. On the weekend before the opener, Vester narrated—ironically enough given the recent trade—"Casey at the Bat" for the Cincinnati Pops Orchestra concerts. On the eve of the opener, Johnny Bench invited her to the ballpark to receive throwing instructions before she took center stage the next day. Afterward, a Linda Vester "roast" and dinner featuring *Today* show weatherman Al Roker occurred at the Gregory Centre, just a few blocks east of the pitching mound at Cinergy Field. Mayor Roxanne Qualls declared Opening Day as "Linda Vester Day in Cincinnati, U.S.A." The Cincinnati Zoo named its rare Asiatic golden cat "Sunrise" in homage to her anchor role on the early morning news. Vester was the toast of the town.

Linda Vester

As Opening Day dawned, hundreds of people scrambled to be on camera on Fountain Square, where Roker appeared live on the *Today* show to give his forecast. The crowd cheered as Roker predicted 80-degree temperatures at game time. The spectators booed when he declined to sample chili, a Cincinnati delicacy. A few hours later, Vester assumed her duties as grand marshal. After Marge Schott sounded the siren, Vester led the marchers, clowns, and zoo animals. A special guest in the parade was Kathleen "Katy" Conway, a Cincinnati police officer who had been shot four times by a gunman two months earlier. Riding in a black Camaro convertible between the color guard and the marching bands, Conway waved to her supporters and received a hero's welcome. Fellow officers, on duty to monitor the tens of thousands of spectators lining the route, saluted her as she passed. Children held up signs and posters with her name on them. The politicians, basketball all-time great Oscar Robertson, Sparky Anderson, and astronaut/US senator John Glenn followed behind the marching bands. They, in turn, were followed by Miss Chiquita Banana, the Budweiser Clydesdales pulling a beer wagon, and a vintage 140-year-old H. J. Heinz Company tallyho wagon pulled by another eight-horse team.

Slightly off the parade route on Fifth Street, Main Auction Galleries on Fourth Street continued its tradition of decorating its windows with pieces from its extensive collection of Reds memorabilia. The assemblage contained items that spanned a century of baseball in Cincinnati, and the galleries were always a popular destination for window shoppers before and after the extravaganza. The owner of the auction house, Phyllis Karp, had been going to Opening Day games since the 1930s. Karp reminded observers, "[Opening Day] should be bigger here than anywhere else; this is the home of baseball."

On the other side of the river, controversial sports talk hosts Andy Furman and Tracy Jones were criticizing the Reds' off-season moves. The traditional Opening Day broadcast of *Sports Talk Extra* emanated that morning from Yeatman's Cove, a renovated riverfront bar on the Kentucky shore of the Ohio River. The pair questioned the Casey trade while extolling the virtues of baseball. Former NFL great Cris Collinsworth was stationed in the Reds dugout and took over the radio show during pregame ceremonies.

John Allen, meanwhile, was still sprucing up the ballpark. Fans entering the ballpark noticed that each of the five world championship teams was honored with a placard above the right field wall. Montgomery Inn, a popular barbecue restaurant, launched a rib stand behind the box-seat level. And for children, there was a new addition called "Kids Zone." Kids could go there to enjoy Sony PlayStation and Pop-a-Shot basketball.

When the parade finally arrived at the field, the sold-out crowd of 54,578 gave Officer Conway a standing ovation. After the usual festivities, left-handed Linda Vester took her windup and delivered a strike to her battery mate, Al Roker. The season was on, and the hometown girl received a roar of approval. The parade and pregame celebrations would be the highlight of the day as the San Diego Padres beat the Reds 10–2. Pokey Reese, subbing at shortstop for Cincinnati native Barry Larkin, went down in infamy by tying the modern record in baseball for most errors (four) in an opener. The headline the next morning was, "How many E's in Pokey Reese? Well, 4."

For many fans, Opening Day provided a welcome escape from the unseemly stories coming from the nation's capital. In Washington, there was an ongoing scandal that almost brought down the presidency of Bill Clinton. His escapades with intern Monica Lewinsky had first been revealed earlier in the year, and the national media outlets were consumed by them. Clinton famously asked an opposition lawyer for his definition of "sex" when he denied having extramarital sexual relations in the White House. On the local front, Hamilton County was continuing its campaign against obscenity. On the eve of the opener, employees of Larry Flynt's Hustler store were subpoenaed to appear before a grand jury later that week. Flynt had previously been convicted by the county prosecutor in 1977 on obscenity charges but that verdict was overturned. Hustler had not been sold in the county for 20 years until Flynt opened a new store in October 1997.

> *"It was a day everyone looked forward to all winter long."*
>
> Harry Heskamp, 1998, before his 68th Opening Day and his wife, Betty's, 57th Opening Day

The pageantry of Opening Day had been firmly reestablished in the minds of the citizenry. Eight months later, the voters were asked to decide the location of the new ballpark that would be the scene of future Opening Days. Siding with business interests close to the riverfront, the idea of moving to Broadway Commons was soundly rejected by the voters. The new ballpark would be close to Cinergy Field.

1999: A Parade of Runs

Anticipation for the April 5 opener returned to levels that preceded the mid-decade players' strike and the infamous ESPN opening-night fiasco. The Reds sold out Opening Day more quickly than in any year since 1993. The early ticket sales may be partly attributed to the fact that the Reds became the only team in baseball to televise their games exclusively on a cable network. Since 35 percent of homes in the area did not have cable, this financially driven decision meant many could not watch games at home. The move angered many in the community.

The Reds stuck with their cable contract, but they did do something to win the support of fans: they agreed to end the club's 30-year ban on facial hair. (The last Cincinnati players to sport beards or mustaches had been Jake

Beckley and Tom Daly—in 1903!) The change in policy came after the acquisition of goateed Greg Vaughn prompted an onslaught of letters from fans who believed the policy was outdated. Right fielder Dmitri Young took advantage of the change by growing a goatee and dying it and his hair yellow-orange.

The logistics for getting around on Opening Day had become problematic for fans. Development along the riverfront had elimi-

> *"In Cincinnati, Reds Opening Day means last season is forgiven and forgotten, April is the month of fresh starts, fans are back in the seats, God is in his heaven and all is right with the world. For one gloriously innocent day, hope hits its high for the season."*
>
> Enquirer editorial

nated 1,200 parking spaces, mostly due to construction of the Bengals' new stadium. That stadium would open two years before the Reds' new ballpark. Fans knew they needed to arrive even earlier than usual just to be sure they could navigate around the construction.

Nonetheless, parade attendance was estimated to be the largest in years.

One major development in 1999 is that it was Schott's last hurrah as majority owner. She sold her controlling ownership to a group headed by financier Carl Lindner that would take effect on October 1. (She retained a small minority share that would allow her to appear on the field but in a less conspicuous role.) For her final act, Schott showed up early as usual. "It's sad, real sad," she confessed to reporters, but she added that she had had a good run over 15 years and was proud of the growth of the Opening Day spectacle. After she started the parade, she chose to retreat to the sidelines. An array of motorcycle police from Cincinnati and Dayton led the eightieth annual procession. They were followed by fire trucks, soldiers carrying flags, and a handful of military bands playing martial music. Rumors in Washington were circulating that the United States might be forced to send ground troops to deal with a mushrooming humanitarian disaster unfolding on the ground in Kosovo. Public support was growing for that intervention, and the parade reflected that sentiment.

The parade featured co–grand marshals: Joe Nuxhall and country music legend Kenny Rogers. They were accompanied by the usual array of marching bands, politicians, radio personalities, red cars, and fire trucks. An added treat for the younger spectators were the oversized figures from the popular TV show, "Rugrats." In total, there were 140 entries, but the highlight for devoted Reds fans was Nuxhall. He rode in the back of a red GTO convertible, and fans left their curbside seats to shake his hand as the procession lumbered along the 18-block route. Two camels separated Nuxhall from Kenny Rogers, who could be seen sitting atop a 1957 canary yellow Chevy convertible. One walker was dressed in a dog suit with a seeing-eye person as an attendant, and Jim Tarbell pushed a vendor's cart in honor of the late Peanut Jim Shelton. After Nuxhall, the biggest ovation was for the Budweiser Clydesdales. Many fans couldn't resist yelling, "Hey, Pete" at James Patrick White, who marched with a huge Pete Rose head on top of his broad shoulders.

Ticket holders who chose to skip the parade warmly welcomed the Clydesdales as they entered Cinergy Field. Close behind the horses was another country music star, Loretta Lynn. Lynn received a hug from the soon-to-be ex-owner and then capped off the pregame ceremony by throwing the first pitch and singing the national anthem. When she neared the end of "The Star-Spangled Banner" and sang "and the land of the free," Rita Flege of suburban Sharonville took her cue. Flege and her assistants opened the doors on a series of pigeon coops, and 400 pairs of flapping wings emerged from spots along the warning track in center field. The grey and white birds became the stars of the pregame festivities as they took flight and circled the playing field. Three pure white birds with dangling streamers were released near home plate and likewise circled the field. According to Flege, they would find their way home to Sharonville within 20 minutes. As she explained, "They

don't have to stop for lights like we do." When one of the three white pigeons landed on the scoreboard, Flege's daughter predicted the bird would stick around to watch the game. After all, she said, "He has a bird's eye view."

Although the Reds had a young team, fans were optimistic. Jack McKeon was entering his second full season as the Reds skipper. Sure enough, under bright sunshine and 70-degree temperatures, the crowd of 55,112 witnessed a parade of runs by the San Francisco Giants and the Reds. The Giants prevailed, 11–8. While fans weren't happy about the loss, the new uniforms that the team introduced were an immediate hit. The addition of black to the traditional red and white uniforms was well received, and fans began to incorporate black into their game attire as the season went on.

> *"In Cincinnati, the activity that best brings us together is baseball- the sport that began as a village game and drew the whole community in as spectators."*
>
> Howard Wilkinson,
> Enquirer columnist

Opening Day received rave reviews the next morning. "Baseball is back in the Queen City," a reporter noted, adding that fans did not show the same irritation with club executives and players that they had in the previous four openers.

The opener was followed two days later by a plea of guilty to four counts of fraud from Cincinnatian Charles Keating Jr. Keating had been a champion swimmer at the University of Cincinnati in the 1940s. He was an anti-pornography activist best known for his role in the savings and loan scandal of the late 1980s. In that decade, Keating ran American Continental Corporation and the Lincoln Savings and Loan Association. Investors lost $200 million and taxpayers lost $3.4 billion after the companies took advantage of relaxed restrictions on banking investments. While he was being prosecuted, Keating made financial contributions to, and made requests for intervention from, five sitting members of the United States Senate. Those lawmakers were later dubbed the "Keating Five" for their support of the man who would eventually plead guilty to fraud.

On a lighter note, young adults were wild about J. K. Rowling's new book, Harry Potter and the Sorcerer's Stone. By the day of the opener, the magical first novel by Rowling had landed on the adult best-seller lists in the United States and Great Britain. Rowling went on to write six more Harry Potter bestsellers, and eight hugely popular films were made about the series.

The youthful Reds tried in vain to cast a spell on the New York Mets in a one-game "wild card" playoff at the end of the 1999 season in Cincinnati. After 54,621 tickets were sold out in seven-and-a-half hours for the unexpected showdown, Al Leiter delivered a magical two-hitter as the Mets advanced, 5–0.

2000: Ken Griffey Jr. Comes Home

Named to MLB's "All-Century Team" after playing only 11 years as a center fielder for the Seattle Mariners, Ken Griffey Jr. was a superstar by all accounts. Raised in Cincinnati from the age of six, Griffey came to be known as "Junior" to distinguish him from his dad, Ken Griffey Sr. "Senior" starred for the Reds in the 1970s. Junior was everything general manager Jim Bowden and new owner Carl Lindner wanted for Christmas in 1999. Negotiations that began in early December culminated 45 days after Christmas, but Bowden and Lindner got their prized gift. They traded four players for Junior, and he signed a $116.5 million contract for nine years. No acquisition had ever been this big in the history of the storied Cincinnati franchise.

Every Cincinnati TV station carried the live press conference announcing the trade. Local

Ken Griffey Jr.

baseball fans were ecstatic. Even before the Griffey announcement, Opening Day had sold out in record time of three and a half hours. When the Griffey trade was announced, the phone lines to the Reds ticket office were so overloaded that ten additional phone lines had to be installed just to handle fans' orders. The addition of Griffey resulted in the Reds selling a half-million additional tickets during the season even though the team's record proved to be a disappointment. The excitement about seeing Junior play was not limited to Cincinnati. The Reds would play before three million fans on the road in 2000. No club had ever reached that milestone.

Before the April 3 opener, the talk was only about Junior. Nothing else seemed to matter. Junior had been a high school baseball star at local Moeller High School, and he was considered a hometown legend. How could the Reds not be destined to win world championships? After all, the team had surprised pundits in 1999, and there was already a strong nucleus that could play a supporting role for the game's best player. Sports talk radio compared the trade to the coming of Babe Ruth. Reds player Pokey Reese echoed the fans' excitement: "The place is going to go crazy."

With so much enthusiasm for Opening Day, there were more than 200 parade entrants. As a result, the parade had to start an hour earlier than usual, at 10:00 a.m. The weather did not match the fans' sunny outlook about the season, as there was a downpour on and off throughout the spectacle. Schott kicked off the procession, as usual, before retreating to

> *"I love our Reds. Any extra tickets?"*
> Alex Lay, age 5, Reds Fan

the background. Draft horses led the march. The co–grand marshals were not as famous as previous grand marshals, but they were a big hit with the crowd. Six-year-old Whitney Ramos and 12-year-old Robbie Schlensker were chosen by the Make-A-Wish Foundation. The foundation gives severely ill children experiences they might not otherwise have, and this was no exception. Whitney was battling acute lymphocytic leukemia, and Robbie had osteosarcoma. Thousands of onlookers cheered the

two youngsters. The crowd stood 20 deep on Fountain Square, and thousands of others jammed the sidewalks. Scalpers were hawking tickets that had a face value of $21 for up to $100. Streets were awash with fans of all ages wearing replicas of Griffey's number 30 jersey. Men dressed as horses pulled the Barrelhouse Brewing Company's keg float. The rain seemed to have no effect on the fans' good mood.

Griffey's parents attended the game, and Junior made sure that his six-year-old son, Trey, followed in his footsteps and skipped school on Opening Day. Griffey explained, "It's a tradition. Cincinnati expects a lot of kids aren't going to be there [in class]." Unfortunately for Schottzie, tradition did not work in his favor when it came to being at the game. The new owners outlawed pets on the field except for service dogs. Schottzie's free run of the ballpark had come to an inglorious end.

As game time approached, the rain continued, but a Mardi Gras–style party was in progress on the plaza outside the stadium. A local rock band, Big in Iowa, played before die-hard fans outfitted in rain slickers. The party had moved to the plaza from the heart of downtown. Inside the ballpark, representatives from 176 media outlets were scrambling for seats in the press box. Credentials had been issued to 63 newspapers, four magazines, 55 photographers, 36 television stations, and 18 radio stations.

The governor of Ohio, Bob Taft, took the day off to throw the first pitch in his hometown. The hit group 98 Degrees played the national anthem. Five planes buzzed with advertising banners over the stadium. When Junior was introduced during the pregame ceremonies, the standing ovation lasted for 31 seconds. All 55,596 fans made sure they were there on time to witness the electric moment. (Unfortunately, Junior's mom was stuck waiting for an elevator to a private box and missed seeing—but not hearing—the ovation.)

The only glitch in the festivities was one that many fans would have been unaware of. For 81 seasons, the Findlay Market shopkeepers had ended their parade at home plate and presented the Reds with a fruit basket and two flags. One flag—a new red, white, and blue model—was designed to be flown over the stadium for the entire season. The other flag carried a host of signatures and the market insignia. That flag was traditionally raised only on Opening Day and was then put away until the next opener. When the April 3 opener was getting underway, it became apparent that someone had forgotten to deliver the flags to the stadium's upper deck, where they were supposed to be hoisted over the left field foul line.

When the game started, Junior received a 34-second standing ovation before his first at bat. The Reds got off to a quick 3–0 lead. Junior made the best catch of the day to end the first inning, snatching a 402-foot fly ball in front of the wall in dead center field. The stadium was practically shaking with glee. Four innings later, after the Milwaukee Brewers tied the game, the game went on a rain delay. After three hours, the umpires waved a white flag and canceled the game. Although the game officially ended in a tie, the Reds voluntarily elected to honor all Opening Day tickets for the next evening's game, too. Reds player Dmitri Young explained how Mother Nature tried to ruin Griffey's day: "I am woman, hear me roar." The media circus left town. It was the first time since 1966 that a Reds opener was rained out.

The next day, in addition to featuring a lot of news about Junior's homecoming, the Associated Press reported that the State Department had issued visas for another reunion. Six-year-old Elian Gonzalez, a Cuban, had been at the center of a custody dispute after he had been rescued off the Florida coastline when his boat capsized, killing his mother and ten others, on November 25. The government's action cleared the way for Juan Miguel Gonzalez, Elian's father, to visit the United States in an attempt to bring his son back to Cuba. Elian's relatives in Miami sought to keep him in the United States, leading US attorney general Janet Reno to order armed federal agents to seize Elian and return him to his father. In business news, America Online, Inc., became the first Internet company to break into the Fortune 500.

The Brewers won the second game of the season the next night. There were no pregame festivities, but one tradition stayed alive after all: both Findlay Market flags were hoisted in their rightful places before the game.

2001: "New" Cinergy

The Reds' inaugural season in the "Griffey Era" did not live up to expectations. The team was in first place when a June swoon sent them under .500. Shortstop Barry Larkin had an injury-plagued season, and the club could not overcome the deficit. The team eventually finished in second place behind the Cardinals. Popular manager Jack McKeon was fired.

The excitement for the April 2 opener was as much about the renovation of the concrete bowl formerly known as Riverfront Stadium as it was about the team. Construction of Great American Ball Park had begun just east of the stadium. The new ballpark was so close to Cinergy Field that 14,000 seats in left field had to be removed to make way for the new ballpark. The bite out of the stadium resulted in unprecedented views of Mount Adams, the river, and the twin towers of Procter & Gamble headquarters. The new look provided relief to any fan who had previously felt claustrophobic in the bowl-like confines of Riverfront Stadium. With about 30 percent of the seats eliminated, access to tickets was a simple matter of supply and demand. All Opening Day tickets that had not been spoken for were sold within a few hours of going on sale, including 1,500 standing-room-only tickets. "Only" 41,901 patrons could squeeze their way into the scaled-down version of Cinergy Field.

> *"Everyone celebrates the start of the new season. Spring's here. Summer's coming. The scent of hope is in the air and it's wafting from Findlay Market."*
>
> Cliff Radel, Enquirer columnist

Unlike the soggy conditions in 2000, the weather was sunny and slightly cool in 2001. A record number of people came out to enjoy the spectacle of another parade. The 18-block route was packed to capacity. The usual array of zoo animals, marching bands and floats, Clydesdales, and vehicles of every make and model had been assembled by the Findlay Market merchants. For the eighty-second annual parade, members of Historic Southwest Ohio dressed in uniforms of the 1869 Cincinnati Red Stockings, the first professional baseball team that was romanticized by Reds fans everywhere. A mere 132 years earlier, that first team had paraded to Union Grounds in the West End in a caravan

Carew Tower

of fancy, ribbon-adorned carriages, followed by hundreds of so-called "merry cranks" for the first-ever Opening Day. On this day, the members of the historical society marched in a similar fashion, but this time there were 100,000 fans watching as they paraded by in their white flannel uniforms and blazing scarlet hosiery. Harry Wright's boys would have been proud.

High above the crowd were Reds season ticket holders Matt Ridener and Joyce Brown. They had ascended to the top of a landmark building, the Carew Tower, that bordered the southern edge of the parade route on Fifth Street. Built in 1930, the tower had an observation deck 49 stories above the crowded streets. Ridener, a retired police officer, and Brown, a retired sheriff's deputy, were dressed in gray suits, with Ridener sporting a red pinstriped shirt accented with red roses. They had decided to tie the knot in a 15-minute ceremony that featured the sounds of the parade in the background. Carew Tower officials declared that the wedding was a one-time occurrence. No other weddings would be permitted on the observation deck in the future.

After the parade, fans lucky enough to have secured a ticket proceeded to a type of ballpark

1869 CINCINNATI RED STOCKINGS
presented by
Historic Southwest Ohio
Playing at Heritage Village in Sharon Woods Park

they had not seen since Crosley Field hosted games in 1970. Reds second baseman Pokey Reese said it best: "Sweet. Now, it looks like a baseball field." Instead of artificial turf, there was grass. The retro makeover had required home plate to be moved 10 feet closer to the stands, giving the park a more intimate feel. In center field, there was no longer an eight-foot fence but rather a new "Black Monster" that was 40 feet high. Batters that previously hit long home runs over the center field wall would now see them carom back into play, and they could only hope for a double or perhaps a rare triple.

Speaking of old ballparks, Harry and Betty Heskamp, both 83 years old, reminisced about the first of their 61 openers together at Crosley Field in 1940. (Harry had also attended ten previous openers before he knew Betty.) They must have had a good time at the 1940 opener, as they married later that year. Back then, a slice of apple pie at the ballpark was 10 cents, and the Reds became world champions. Could history repeat—if not in the price of pie, then at least the world championship part?

United States senator Mike DeWine, a longtime Reds season ticket holder, threw out the ceremonial first pitch. His toss was low and in the dirt. Martina McBride, a country music star, prepared to perform her rendition of the national anthem. As the crowd faced the American flag, they noticed four big birds ten miles away. But these were not the traditional pigeons released on openers, and they were coming in at 350 miles per hour! Slowing down to a mere 300 miles per hour, the four F-16 fighter jets from the 181st Fighter Wing of the Indiana National Guard roared over Cinergy Field seconds after McBride's voice rang out with the last note of "The Star-Spangled Banner." The formation of the planes was perfect. Colonel J. Stewart Goodwin later told a reporter that the flyover was no wasteful joyride. The pilots had recently returned from a month-long tour of duty over Iraq's "no-fly zone." On this day, the jets had just finished a practice bombing run in neighboring Indiana.

When the starting lineups were announced, Ken Griffey Jr. was not one of the players named. He had suffered a strained left hamstring at the end of spring training and was sidelined. The injury would portend a series of health issues for the superstar that would cloud his nine years of playing for the Reds. The Atlanta Braves spoiled the party even further by scoring six runs in the last three innings, winning 10–4. Fans, however, got to see something they had not seen since the days of Crosley Field. Braves shortstop Rafael Furcal launched a home run over the left field fence in the seventh inning that traveled outside the stadium. A construction worker picked up the ball and returned it to the ballplayers by heaving it over the 8-foot wall.

Seven days later, Over-the-Rhine would experience four days of riots over racial justice issues. The disturbance, called by some the largest instance of civil unrest since the Los Angeles riots of 1992, marred the city's reputation for several years.

2002: Buy Me Some Peanuts and ... Vegetable Lasagna?

The core of downtown Cincinnati drowned in bad news after the April 2001 riots. Protesters boycotted downtown businesses such as restaurants, and they taunted diners with signs such as: "Eat, Drink, and Be Racist." The Reverend Damon Lynch III declared that no day should include "wine and dance and fun" until justice came to town. The parade started in its usual spot—the very neighborhood that had been at the heart of the riots—and it would conclude near the federal courthouse just past Fountain Square. A hearing to settle a lawsuit alleging racial profiling that had been a flashpoint for the riots was scheduled to begin that after-

noon, just after the Reds took the field in the first inning. The April 1 Opening Day parade was nearly 12 months after the riots proved to unify the city in a much-needed way. Parade organizer Jeff Gibbs boasted, "Look around us. There's every color, every race. Everyone's having fun."

> "This is Cincinnati's best day of the year. On Opening Day, everyone—young and old, black and white, rich and poor—stands next to each other, rubs elbows and talks and gets along. We need to have that Opening Day spirit all year long."
>
> Tawanda Johnson, Reds Fan

Ken Griffey Sr. was honored as the grand marshal. Wearing the requisite red, he had his own response to Reverend Lynch's austere declaration: "I look at it this way: I'm enjoying myself. That's what I've got to do." Senior explained his duties: "I'm to sit in the car, wave and smile." That he did. But first, there were some preliminaries. A Charolais cow with a new name of "Cinci Freedom" had become famous nationwide. She had avoided certain death when she escaped from Ken Meyer Meats in Camp Washington, just a few miles from downtown. The 1,000-pound animal had been on the run for ten days following her liberation. She eluded police, as well as the Society for Prevention of Cruelty to Animals (SPCA), until she was spotted in Mount Storm Park just a mile or so east of where she had escaped. Cinci Freedom was given to Peter Max, a pop artist who planned to take the cow to the Farm Sanctuary in upstate New York. He decided to donate $100,000 of his artwork to the SPCA.

The planners invited Cinci Freedom to join the other animals in the parade, and she was to be given a key to the city. Moments before the start of the procession, Max decided to keep her in her pen. "The drums, the noise, the people—it was all too much for the sweet girl," he later explained. Undeterred, Mayor

Charlie Luken presided over a brief ceremony during which Cinci Freedom received her key. Her former owner, Ken Meyer, bid her adieu and said he was glad her life was spared. "She earned her freedom." Mayor Luken, Meyer, and Max then posed for pictures while Marge Schott quietly slipped over to the cow's pen. She softly petted her and said, "Goodbye, honey." (Schott called everyone "Honey," including beloved animals.)

Tens of thousands of spectators from the tristate region surrounding Cincinnati were decked out in red hats, shirts, and jackets. It was a Midwestern Mardi Gras. When the marching bands, floats, unicycles, fire engines, police vehicles, and pickup trucks carrying politicians completed their pilgrimage, Taft declared that the parade was a success. "Opening Day is something that unites everyone. It brings everyone together." There were few tears shed for, and little mention of, the fact that this would be the last opener for the 32-year-old stadium that was once a crown jewel. The time had come for a new ballpark that was slated to be ready in time for the next season.

Speaking of ethical treatment, Cinergy Field was named the fifth most vegetarian-friendly major league stadiums in the country by the People for the Ethical Treatment of Animals (PETA). While the park certainly sold large quantities of burgers and hot dogs washed down with beer, patrons could now buy veggie hot dogs or tossed green salads. The item that particularly impressed PETA was the park's offering of veggie lasagna. PETA's sports campaign coordinator, Dan Shannon, called the menu item a home run.

Barry Larkin

With Great American Ball Park scheduled to open in 2003, the Reds presented fans entering the park with a lapel pin that replicated patches on the players' uniforms. The pin featured a picture of Cinergy Field and the skyline of the city. During pregame ceremonies, Governor Robert Taft threw out the ceremonial first pitch. He was tired from having marched through downtown, and his toss was a slow lob. President George W. Bush's taped message to the crowd played on the video scoreboard. He greeted fans and then declared, "God bless you all; God bless America and, now, play ball!" The fans applauded for 10 seconds.

The Reds responded with a proper send-off to the ballpark. Barry Larkin sprinted home from third base in the bottom of the ninth inning to secure a 5–4 win over Chicago. The team had performed well at Riverfront/ Cinergy on Opening Days, winning 20 of 32 openers, with one tie. The Cubs were dejected, but Cinci Freedom held her head high.

GREAT AMERICAN BALLPARK

People want to get in on it because Opening Day is a big party, a celebration. It's an event that carries with it all of the romance of a first date.

George Vredeveld, University of Cincinnati professor

When Ken Griffey Jr. joined the Reds in 2000, Reds fans anticipated a decade of championships or at least ten years during which the club would compete annually for a right to participate in the World Series. After a somewhat competitive first season with Griffey on board, the team would see Junior saddled with injuries that tarnished his reputation as the most exciting power hitter in the game. The Reds' win total of 85 in his first season would never be exceeded during his tenure. None of the injuries was career ending, so fans waited, often impatiently, for his return to greatness. He had achieved so much success while in Seattle that even his above-average performance with the Reds enabled him to reach significant career milestones during his time in Cincinnati. Those occasions would prompt celebrations of his personal accomplishments, but the fans wanted something more for the team. Each year they anticipated that Junior would become Junior again. The tie score in his first game as a Red epitomized his tenure. No fan likes a tie, but it's better than a loss. Fans wanted a "win" with Griffey, but his frequent trips to the disabled list diminished his playing ability.

Fortunately for the Reds, a new ballpark would still lure most of the faithful until the later years. Griffey would then be traded to the Chicago White Sox in July 2008. His years in Cincinnati were appreciated but were never fulfilling for dedicated Reds fans.

> *"I wouldn't have missed this opener for the world."*
> Jeff Betts, Reds Fan

2003: Unveiling
Great American Ball Park

March 31 was an opener anticipated not just since the conclusion of the 2002 season, but rather for several years as the city, county, and team made plans for a new retro ballpark. The venue would have features reminiscent of the parks that preceded Riverfront Stadium and others of its era. Great American Ball Park would be more intimate than Riverfront Stadium (later Cinergy Field), having 10,000 fewer seats, and it would have lush, green grass instead of artificial turf. Fans eagerly anticipated seeing the notch in the upper deck that would reveal the city skyline and allow views of the Ohio River and the hills of Kentucky. They were also eager to see the bleachers in right field that were modeled after the sun and moon decks of Crosley Field.

The Iraq War was just 11 days old, so the Reds adjusted the hour-long pregame ceremonies to resemble the ceremonies preceding openers during World War I and World War II. During the weekend preceding the Monday opener, US warplanes bombed Baghdad, Iraq's capital. The air attack was a prelude to a ground assault by American troops. Iraqis responded with suicide attacks against American forces and threats to kill Americans on US soil. Pope John Paul II warned of a "religious catastrophe" stirring hatred between Christians and Muslims, while President Bush declared, "We are now fighting the most desperate units of the dictator's army." On the morning of the opener, a headline read, "Noose tightens on Baghdad." Cincinnatians were grateful to read good news about a local soldier, 21-year-old Jeff Klein of Independence, Kentucky. He was reported to be alive in a southern Iraqi desert after having been stranded there with another soldier for a week. After Klein was located, he was able to have a two-minute conversation with his family back home.

Opening Day was going to be a long day. Game time was not until 4:10 p.m., so the parade was scheduled to start at noon. But that didn't mean the party could not start as early as it always did. Local bars began to fill even before 9:00 a.m. A rousing "Reds Rally" took place on Fountain Square. The rally was broadcast live on local television for those waiting for the temperatures to warm, but 30,000 others chose to clutch blankets and parkas to combat the chilly weather. The day had started off cold and cloudy, but eventually the thermometer read 50 degrees once the parade began to roll. Former Reds pitching star Tom Browning served as grand marshal. Browning had earned the nickname "Mr. Perfect" because in 1987 he had become the first and only Reds pitcher—and only the twelfth in major league history—to throw a perfect game. Shortly after the parade started, Browning halted the march as he took time to embrace his old boss, Marge Schott, who appeared to be in frail condition.

Tom Browning Embraces Marge Schott

Special additions to this year's parade were several floats that were part of the "Bats Incredible!" public art project of Cincinnati ArtWorks, an art-oriented employment and job training program for youth in the Cincinnati area. The floats drew attention to the fifty or so signature Louisville Slugger bat displays that had been stationed along the route, at Fountain Square, and in building lobbies. Each display was created by local artists who transformed the bats into works

of art. Paid sponsorships supported the artists' work, with the number of bats in each piece reflecting the level of sponsorship. A $10,000 "Grand Slam" sponsorship allowed the artist to use up to one hundred 34-inch bats and to earn a $2,500 honorarium. A total of 200 displays were scheduled to be in place for the official kickoff of the project in June.

The Clydesdales were part of the parade as always. Two of the horses had done extra duty by visiting patients at Cincinnati Children's Hospital Medical Center on Sunday afternoon. "The Bucket Boys and Buckettes" featured two dozen teenage boys and girls dressed in blue jumpsuits. They seemed to be making more noise than the marching bands that were in front of them. In a show of love for the banished hometown star, the Contemporary Arts Center chose 50 men named Pete to march in red jackets that read PETE in big white letters. One lucky man—not named Pete—was Mark Hobbs. He was the winner of Findlay Market's Pete Rose look-alike contest. He got to sit in the back of a red Corvette dressed in a Reds cap and jacket. The square-jawed man was besieged by dozens of fans who wanted autographs and photos. They were taken with his striking resemblance to "Charlie Hustle." Tom Browning received a rose to clench in his teeth as he waved to the crowd. Business people taking a lunch break found themselves craning their necks to spot celebrities or friends participating in the annual rite of spring.

As the parade ended, the festivities at the ballpark began. At 2:00 p.m., the Reds celebrated the opening of Great American Ball Park by unveiling a statue of Ted Kluszewski in "Crosley Terrace," which served as the new park's front entrance. Kluszewski's widow, Eleanor (aka "Little Klu"), pulled a red tarp off the larger-than-life statue depicting the Reds first baseman standing in the on-deck circle holding a pair of bats on his left shoulder. The statue had been sculpted by Tom Tsuchiya, who would be commissioned to create other statues honoring Reds greats over the next 14 years. As fans entered the park, they received a commemorative baseball and a lanyard to protect their valuable souvenir: their ticket to the game. Once inside, the patriotic feel began to take hold. Every fan was given a miniature American flag, and the Pete Wagner Band played patriotic tunes.

After a number of introductions of dignitaries and speeches, the players were introduced along the baselines. After the Reds starting lineup was introduced, members of the Ohio Historical Society emerged from the outfield tunnel through a cloud of smoke. They were dressed in their 1869 Cincinnati Red Stockings uniforms. The crowd roared its approval. Singer Lee Greenwood sang his trademark song, "God Bless the USA," before the introduction of two special dignitaries. They were New York City's "Singing Policeman" Danny Rodriguez and former president George H. W. Bush. Rodriguez had gained national attention for his performances after the 9/11 attacks. He sang the

national anthem while Great American Ball Park construction workers unfurled a giant American flag that covered much of the outfield. Two C-130 military transport planes from the Ohio Air National Guard's 179th Airlift Wing rumbled low over the ballpark. Red, white, and blue streamers were released from the top deck as fireworks flew from the smokestacks in center field. The former president threw a high, arching ceremonial first pitch to Reds shortstop Barry Larkin. Bush received a huge ovation after telling the crowd of 42,343, "It's an honor to be here today, off the bench, substituting for another guy you know, President George W. Bush … I'm the proudest daddy in the world." Fans waved their American flags in appreciation.

The game was broadcast to the Middle East and Africa on the American Forces Network. Griffey recorded the first hit in the new ballpark, a double down the right field line in the bottom of the first inning. That was the last of the celebrations, as the Pirates rolled to a 10–1 victory.

The game result was not what the Reds fans had dreamed about, but everything else surrounding the debut of the long-awaited park was perfect. Even Tom Browning was proud.

2004: A Tribute to Schott

Marge Schott, the most visible and controversial owner in Reds history and a strong supporter of Opening Day traditions, passed away at age 75 just 34 days before the April 5 opener. The Findlay Market organization paid tribute to its biggest fan by retiring her Reds jacket and displaying it along the parade route. Larry Porter of Newport, Kentucky, summed up the feelings of many in the tens of thousands that came out to view the parade: "She had her faults, but she did a lot for the Reds and the city. I'm glad they're doing a tribute to her today." Because she was a strong supporter of the Cincinnati Zoo and helped pay for a new elephant house in 2000, an elephant sporting a Reds hat and a red cape was chosen to sound the siren (using his trunk) that kicked off the parade. Schott's sisters took her place in the procession, accompanied by 21 Saint Bernard dogs.

Spectators arrived as early as 8:00 a.m. to stake out a location at the prime viewing spot, Fountain Square, just short of where the parade traditionally ended. Former Pittsburgh Pirate and Cincinnati Reds great Dave Parker was the grand marshal. Parker had been invited well before Schott's passing, but having him head the parade turned out to be an ironic choice. In 1992, Schott had infamously and shamefully called Parker and outfielder Eric Davis her two "million dollar n-----s". Parker had long forgiven her after he got to know her better. After her death, he said, "The sad thing would be if she is remembered for what she said, rather than what she did. I think she was a product of her upbringing. But the lady did a lot of good. She did a whole lot of good for the Reds and Cincinnati." Parker waved, smiled, and laughed along the route, leading 182 entries past the throng of well-wishers. He was a popular native Cincinnatian.

Dave Parker

The parade included the customary cast of celebrities and politicians riding in their convertibles, 20 marching bands and drill teams, and the Belgian horses leading a replica tallyho wagon. Popular radio personality Jim Scott walked in the parade in front of the 21-dog salute to Schott. He was accom-

panied by Steve Stewart—"the new Reds guy," according to Scott. Stewart was the heir to Joe Nuxhall's spot in the radio booth that Nuxhall shared with Marty Brennaman. Stewart was scheduled to be in the booth in 2004 to learn the ropes during Nuxhall's final full-time season.

> *"In Cincinnati, this is New Year's!"*
> Jim Borgman, Enquirer cartoonist

The march snaked its way to Over-the-Rhine and past Fountain Square, ending just beyond the point at which two white-haired women had planted their chairs in front of Taft Theatre earlier in the morning. The sisters and had been coming to the parade and game for more than 50 years. Nancy and Marge Roetker, ages 79 and 77 respectively, had waited for members of the Rosie Reds to pass by and nod to them. They were charter members of the philanthropic organization that had formed in 1964 to prevent the Reds from leaving town. "[Opening Day is] like a holiday," Marge explained. Nancy added, "Winter is over and you've got baseball to go back to. It just makes it very exciting." They were among the most ardent of Reds supporters, either attending games or listening to them on radios stationed in every room of their modest Mount Washington home in eastern Cincinnati. Neither woman ever wanted to miss seeing or hearing a pitch. No doubt they enjoyed the 1950s-style flannel uniform worn by Jeff Wehmeier in the parade. The uniform had been donned by his father, Herm, a Reds pitcher for eight seasons. Wehmeier strode beside Jim Tarbell, who did his traditional impersonation of Peanut Jim Shelton.

American troops were still in Iraq, so fans were presented with small flags as they entered the ballpark. It was a day to remember the troops and to honor the memory of Schott. Reds management played a video tribute to the former owner during pregame ceremonies that reminded fans of her best qualities. The presentation showed Schott waving to the crowds at the parade, planting kisses on the cheeks of players, and leading her big, friendly Saint Bernard around the stadium turf. The message included a quote from the former first lady of the Reds: "Opening Day is history, honey, and you've got to keep history going."

A second tribute was dedicated to Dernell Stenson, a young Reds outfielder murdered in Chandler, Arizona, on November 5. Video highlights of Stenson's life and baseball career played on the ballpark's big screen. Then country singer Sara Evans belted out "God

Vice President Dick Cheney

Bless America," followed by Nick Lachey singing the national anthem in a Johnny Bench jersey. Cincinnati native Lachey had performed the anthem with the group 98 Degrees in 2000, but this solo performance had teenage girls gathered behind home plate squealing when the pop star took center stage.

The spotlight then turned to Vice President Dick Cheney. A vocal proponent of the war, Cheney was applauded as he walked to the pitcher's mound and delivered the first pitch. After that, Reds fans would again be disappointed in the result, losing to the Cubs 7–4.

In local news, there was continuing controversy over a case that made headlines for months. Families had sued Hamilton County after the bodies of deceased relatives were found to have been photographed at the county morgue by photographer Thomas Condon. The photos showed the bodies posing with seashells, dollhouse furniture, and sheet music. The county denied that Condon had authority to take the pictures and said he had only been permitted to do research for a training video. On the day of the opener, it was revealed that the families were seeking a $12 million settlement. The local prosecutor, Mike Allen, complained that the families' lawyer, Stan Chesley, was also representing the county in a case against the Cincinnati Bengals over their stadium deal with the county. Chesley was known as the father of the modern class-action lawsuit and was nicknamed the "master of disaster."

2005: The Hoopla Factor

Reds fans were hoping for a return to the victory column on April 5. After two successive defeats on Opening Day, they realized that no Reds team had ever won the World Series without winning the first game of the season. Hopes were high, as center fielder Ken Griffey Jr. was expected to be healthy coming off a season-ending injury in late 2004. (In 2005, he would end up playing 128 games, the most since 2000, but he still missed 34 games due to injury.) Demand for Opening Day tickets was at an all-time high. Individual tickets sold out in 12 minutes—a record—on February 19. Scalpers were asking and receiving $125 for standing-room-only tickets with a $15 face value. The city fire marshal allowed the Reds to add to the number of standing-room-only tickets, so 451 more people could attend the opener than had been permitted just two years earlier. George Vredeveld, director of the

University of Cincinnati's Economic Center for Education & Research, explained that the demand was so high because of "the hoopla factor" caused by "the pageantry of the event."

> *"Opening day is to baseball what stargazing is to astronomy. It's a day for poets and dreamers, and for that first warm wind that moves the curtains behind the open window in the living room. In Cincinnati, it's the one day every year were guaranteed to feel good about ourselves."*
>
> Paul Daugherty,
> Enquirer sports columnist

It was a perfect day for baseball. Bobbie Unnewehr, Marge Schott's sister, assumed the duty of signaling the beginning of the annual parade. She blew the horn of a fire engine, sending six loud and long blasts into the air. She then hopped into a car provided by one of her sister's former car dealership competitors. Six men wearing monks' robes called themselves "The Brothers Inebriate," and they were hitched to a giant wooden goat made out of beer barrels. The goat pretended to nibble an extra-large baseball cap of the day's opponent, the Mets. The grand marshal was a football player, Rudy Johnson of the NFL Bengals. He received applause as he led the parade, but his reception paled to the one accorded to the Reds' legendary radio voice, Joe Nuxhall, who was semi-retired from the broadcast booth. Fans leaped from the sidewalks to shake Nuxy's hand and ask for his autograph. He willingly obliged. (After the game, the spectators could go home and watch the first episode of a four-part series that would debut that evening on public television, "Joe Nuxhall, My Life: Baseball and Beyond.") Jason Edwards, age 30, and his family marched with the Rosie Reds. Jason had thrown out the first pitch to Johnny Bench on Opening Day 25 years earlier. Jason was born with spina bifida, and his parents fondly recalled the honor bestowed upon him in 1980.

Joe Nuxhall (seated in rear)

Inside the ballpark, 100 soldiers, sailors, airmen, and Marines carried a giant American flag to the outfield. The flag bearers included 67 members of the Ohio National Guard's 216th Engineer Battalion, a Hamilton, Ohio-based unit that had returned earlier in the year from a tour in Iraq. Three members of the battalion had been killed in action. Staff Sergeant Greg Arthur's mind returned to Iraq as the flag was slowly unfurled. "I think of all the little things we take for granted here that we didn't have there," he told a reporter. The national anthem was then performed by Air Force Staff Sergeant Felita Rowe before a jet-black B-2 Stealth Bomber soared over center field. US Congressman Rob Portman then signaled the start of the season with the first pitch. Newly acquired third baseman Joe Randa would hit the last pitch of the day over the left field wall to give the Reds a 7–6, come-from-behind win in walk-off fashion. Hopes were still alive for a world championship.

Cincinnati has long been known as a city with a rich Catholic heritage. It is understandable, then, that the passing of Pope John Paul II two days before the April 4 opener dominated the news and the minds of the Reds faithful. Cincinnati and Northern Kentucky Catholics mourned the pope's death following his years of struggling with Parkinson's disease and other health challenges. The Sunday *Enquirer* on the eve of the opener contained a bold headline proclaiming, "Millions mourn His Holiness," devoting six pages that day to the pope's life and legacy. The paper also noted how local congregations were marking his death. Meanwhile, in Rome, the pope, clothed in a red robe, laid in state at the Vatican's frescoed Apostolic Palace. His hands clutched a rosary, and his pastoral staff was under one arm. People from around the world came to the Vatican to pay their respects. Residents of Rome lit candles in their windows. The pope's funeral was scheduled for the following Friday afternoon.

CASTELLINI COMES CALLING

Today is a day when Cincinnatians—baseball fans or not—can kick off the winter drabs, throw open the doors and windows, and take a deep breath of renewal. It's about more than baseball. It's about nostalgia and hope, tradition and youth. It brings us together—people of all ages, ethnicities and backgrounds. For one day everyone's a kid again, peeking through the slats in the outfield fence. Or at the real-time update tucked behind the spreadsheet on your computer screen.

Enquirer editorial

Despite fans' thrill at welcoming Ken Griffey Jr. back to Cincinnati in 2000, the only winning season the team enjoyed during Griffey's tenure came during his inaugural season. During the next five years, the team endured a string of losing campaigns, the club's longest such streak in 50 years. Robert Castellini, Reds fan and part owner of the St. Louis Cardinals in conjunction with Cincinnatian Bill DeWitt, decided to take control of his hometown team in an effort to return the Reds to championships.

Castellini was the owner of Castellini Company, a fruit and vegetable wholesaler based in Cincinnati. Castellini was a self-made man, much like his predecessor, Carl Lindner. He had been involved in baseball for the previous 30 years by having minority interests in the Texas Rangers, the Baltimore Orioles, and the Cardinals. Castellini led a group of investors that purchased majority control of the Reds from Lindner in January 2006. According to *Enquirer* columnist Paul Daugherty, Castellini was partly motivated to buy the team after

Bob Castellini

Daugherty wrote a column headlined "RIP Baseball Town" about the disillusionment of Reds fans in 2005. Castellini wanted the club to be a source of pride for Cincinnati residents. He commented, "At my core, I am a fan."

Castellini was 65 at the time, but retirement was not in his plans. He said, "I would not be the lead person in ownership outside of Cincinnati. I just would not have had that passion to do that." His heart was in Cincinnati. He did not waste any time telling Reds fans that he was intent on returning the Reds first to competitive play and ultimately to the World Series. A month after purchasing the team, Castellini replaced general manager Dan O'Brien with Wayne Krivsky. Under Castellini's and Krivsky's leadership, the Reds built a young team through a strong farm system that produced one of the future great hitters in the game, Joey Votto. Reds fans put their faith in Castellini and were eager to support a winning team again.

2006: A New Start

Ninety years before Castellini bought the team, the Reds were urging fans to vote for an upcoming rapid transit bond issue for a subway and an above-ground commuter rail system that would provide easy transportation for fans. In 2006, the club was busy promoting a local initiative to develop "The Banks," a section of the riverfront slated for commercial development. The Banks was envisioned as a dining, drinking, and entertainment district between Great American Ball Park on the east and the Cincinnati Bengals' Paul Brown Stadium on the west. The transportation system that the team had promoted nearly a century earlier had run out of money and public support when World War I took hold, and it was never completed. Reds fans were optimistic that The Banks would not suffer the same fate.

> "Opening Day is to Cincinnati as Mardi Gras is to New Orleans. The start of another Cincinnati Reds season gives the city the license - just for a day - to trade its tight-fisted, tight-lipped Teutonic tendencies for a light-hearted, laissez-faire lifestyle. Carefree, the town throws a day long party. Everyone's invited. Come on down."
>
> Enquirer editorial

As April 3 approached, the opener had the look of an official state holiday. Castellini had arranged for something that had never occurred in the 137-year history of the Reds: a sitting president (George W. Bush) would throw out the first pitch. (President Reagan had been slated to cast the ceremonial pitch in 1981 until an assassination attempt precluded his appearance.) Bush would become only the third sitting president to attend a professional baseball game in Cincinnati. William Howard Taft had visited the ballpark in 1912, and Richard Nixon appeared at the 1970 All-Star Game, but neither had thrown the first pitch at an opener. Castellini had orchestrated Bush's appearance to drum up excitement for Opening Day, and he succeeded. Castellini also made other off-the-field moves that were popular with fans. Throughout the season, the ballpark would open 30 minutes earlier than in the past to allow fans to watch batting practice, and a bar in the stadium would be kept open two hours after the games. The Reds had also invited former stars to spring training and coaxed beloved announcer Joe Nuxhall to return to the radio booth to provide color for more games during his semi-retirement.

Johnny Bench, George Brande, and Bob Castellini

Fittingly, Reds Hall of Fame pitcher Mario Soto, who had started five openers from 1982 to 1986, was chosen as the grand marshal. Soto traveled slowly in a silver Corvette convertible, hanging over the side to sign autographs as the spectators applauded. He was followed by former Reds pitcher Jim O'Toole, who rode in a vintage Oldsmobile convertible. The club's first African American player, Chuck Harmon, came next in a vintage black Corvette convertible. Mayor Mark Mallory joined other politicians on the route, but unlike the others who paraded on foot, Mallory was seated on the back seat of a red Mustang convertible accompanied by ten mounted police officers. The most unusual entry in the parade was a group of white and orange Bobcats (the earth-moving variety) that snaked through the downtown streets. The Bobcats stopped occasionally to perform spins, twists, and circles to entertain the spectators.

When the parade ended, fans hurried to the stadium. Metal detectors had been installed, and Secret Service agents were stationed outside the park to search bags. Anti-war protesters marched as fans stood in line for an hour. The picket signs had baseball themes, such as "Go Reds, Stop the War in Iraq!" and "Reds Steal Bases, Bush Steals Your Kids." Most of the impatient patrons were not happy with the picketers because they were there to enjoy Opening Day, not debate politics. Arriving in their seats, patrons received free mini–American flags in their cupholders so they could wave them during pregame ceremonies. While the fans were waiting in line, President Bush practiced for his big moment by tossing about 20 balls to catcher Jason LaRue inside the underground batting cage.

After the usual pageantry that preceded the game, President Bush took center stage. He was accompanied by two wounded war veterans, Paul Brondhaver of Union Township, Ohio, and Michael McNaughton of Louisiana. Brondhaver was a National Guard sergeant severely wounded in Iraq, and he walked with a cane. McNaughton lost a leg in Afghanistan and had bonded with President Bush during Bush's visit to an Army hospital there. Bush was also joined by John Prazynski, the father of Marine Lance Corporal Taylor Prazynski, who had perished in action in Afghanistan. Bush waved to the cheering, standing-room-only crowd that was eager to watch his

President George W. Bush

delivery. Bush later said, "[It was] my best pitch, which was kind of a slow ball." He then joined Castellini, MLB commissioner Bud Selig, and two Republican senators (Mike DeWine of Ohio and Jim Bunning of Kentucky, a former pitching great) in the owners' box to enjoy the game.

Unfortunately, the first game of the Castellini era did not go as planned. The Cubs won easily, jumping to a 5–1 lead in the first inning and scoring the most runs (16) by a visitor on Opening Day since May 14, 1877. Meanwhile, Congress was debating a comprehensive immigration bill. Bush supported the bill that would provide undocumented workers a temporary legal status so they could stay in the United States. The country was divided on the issue, as was the Republican Party. While Bush was in Cincinnati, Senate Majority Leader Bill Frist of Tennessee called for a vote on the bill that was seen as a compromise. The bill never passed, and the issue still plagues political discourse in the country.

Castellini's first year would bring marked improvement after a bumpy start on Opening Day. The Reds rebounded from the embarrassment on April 3 to finish in third place in their division with 80 wins. It was the highest win total since 2000. During the season, Marty Brennaman's son, Thom, joined him on radio broadcasts on a part-time basis; they became part of a small fraternity of family acts in baseball commentating, as there had been only three others in the history of the game. Both continue to do broadcasts—Marty on radio and Thom on TV.

2007: A Fresh Start for Josh Hamilton

As April 2 approached, Reds Country was reinvigorated by the team's improvement during the previous season. At Castellini's urging, fans were being patient; most simply wanted to see more progress. Finishing above .500 was a goal for many fans. The Reds and Cubs were meeting for the fourth time in six openers, and it was the thirty-sixth time (more times than with any other opponent) that they would face each other on Opening Day. The club continued to enhance the ballpark, this year adding a two-story riverboat in center field for group outings.

The biggest off-season move intrigued fans. The Reds acquired Josh Hamilton via what is called a "Rule 5" draft trade. Rule 5 requires the team acquiring the player to keep him on the major-league roster for the entire season or risk losing him. Signing Hamilton was a feel-good story. The Miami Marlins' vice

Josh Hamilton

president of player personnel opined that Hamilton had been the best amateur player he had ever scouted other than Alex Rodriguez (A-Rod), one of the game's greats. Hamilton was left unprotected in the Rule 5 draft after drug addiction and multiple suspensions cost him nearly four seasons in baseball. When he was finally reinstated in June 2006, he played only 15 games with a team in the lowest level of the minor leagues. General Manager Krivsky convinced Castellini it was worth taking a risk on Hamilton. During spring training, Hamilton had exceeded expectations and was welcomed on the Opening Day roster. Reds fans prayed that, despite his addiction, he would be a spark for the club and would stay free of drugs for his own sake.

Eric Davis

The day began under partly sunny skies with warm temperatures. It was a perfect day for a parade. Findlay Market organizers reported that the march would include 6,600 humans and 288 vehicles, including bicycles, unicycles, cars, trucks, motorcycles, and horse-drawn carriages. Fans of every age filled the sidewalks and Fountain Square. Many had tickets to the game, but most came downtown simply to be part of the festivities. The 2.5-hour spectacle featured a star player from the 1990 world championship team, Eric Davis, as the grand marshal. Davis, decked out in a black suit with small red checks, rode on a fire truck and was warmly received, mostly because he was one of the former greats but also because Castellini had invited him to spring training as a special assistant. Although Davis had played with other teams, he identified as a Red.

Applause for Davis took a back seat to cheering for the parents of Matt Maupin. Maupin was a local soldier who had been missing in action in Iraq for three years. His parents received a deafening welcome. Coco, the singing parrot from the Cincinnati Zoo, could be heard perfectly despite being slightly ahead of the Anderson High School marching band. Members of the Oak Hills High School dance team showed off their moves while wearing

their signature red lipstick. Forty men from Wapakoneta, Ohio, entered the parade as the "Precision Power Mower Team," with their roaring lawn mowers cutting through any weeds that happened to be on the city streets. Mr. Red strolled along with the Reds cheerleaders, who wore replica jerseys. The cheerleaders would later entertain the crowd during the game, an innovation that lasted for a few years but seemed out of place at baseball games.

Not to be outdone, the crowd got into the act as well. Scott Pohlkamp from Cleveland arrived in his Elvis Presley–style red jumpsuit. Dan Thomas of Florence, Kentucky, was dressed in a replica uniform of the 1869 Red Stockings. He was a member of a vintage baseball team that played at a local park during the summer. Thomas was accompanied by his wife wearing an outfit from the mid-1800s.

> *It's a blessing to get the whole family together. Every opening day is an occasion for hope, for the team and for life in general."*
>
> Jimmy O'Toole,
> son of Reds pitcher Jim O'Toole

At the ballpark, Doug and Adam Fickert arrived four hours before game time. The father and son tossed a baseball while waiting to be the first ones to enter the gates. Meanwhile, Castellini was continuing his efforts to run the team the right way. As preparations for the day's events were being made, Castellini greeted each employee by name. The employees reciprocated, most simply calling him "Bob" and thanking him for their new red uniforms that replaced staid yellow uniforms from previous seasons. Castellini had built momentum among the employees and fans but conceded, "It's all about winning."

The pregame ceremonies included the revival of the old mustachioed mascot of the Reds from the Crosley Field era: Mr. Redlegs. As the market organizers came on the field for the customary presentations to the Reds, great pomp and circumstance was reserved for Mr. Redlegs. He entered the ballpark, circling the field while swinging a baseball bat atop a sport-utility vehicle. The next noteworthy feature of the pregame was a moment that will live in Opening Day infamy. Mayor Mallory had practiced for his ceremonial pitch, isolating himself in the batting cages under the stands next to the Reds dugout in order to warm up. When the big moment came, the mayor walked to the mound and then turned and joked with the crowd. He assumed his pitching stance but playfully walked to the bottom of the mound before going back to the pitching rubber. With the ball in his right hand and his black glove in his left hand, he pretended he was holding a runner on base. When he finally threw the ball, it was undoubtedly the worst toss in first-

Johnny Bench and Mayor Mallory

pitch history on Opening Day. It was well short, and way left, of catcher Eric Davis. The home plate umpire, Randy Marsh, jokingly threw the mayor out of the game. Mallory did not laugh, and the crowd booed the pitch. The cringeworthy 15 seconds would become a sensation on YouTube as one of the worst first pitches anywhere. The mayor's office released a humorous list of the top ten reasons for the blooper. One of them was that Eric Davis had missed a sign, so the mayor thought he was supposed to do a pitchout as if he were intentionally walking a batter.

The fans were then treated to one of the best-played Reds openers. The club thumped the Cubs 5–1, starting with Adam Dunn launching a home run in the first inning. The highlight, though, was reserved for Hamilton. When he was announced as a pinch hitter in the eighth inning, the crowd gave him a 22-second standing ovation. The cheers nearly brought him to his knees. He then hit a line drive that was caught, but the crowd gave him another ovation as he trotted back to the dugout. Hamilton dominated media coverage of the game because he was on the road to recovery. Fans hoped the Reds were, too.

Fans were ecstatic leaving the ballpark, but the season would be a major disappointment. By midseason, Castellini had grown frustrated, so he fired manager Jerry Narron. Narron was replaced by Pete Mackanin, and the Reds would finish the season with only 72 wins. It was a far cry from a .500 season. Hamilton had a good year and was a fan favorite, but he became valuable trade bait during the winter. The Reds sent him packing to Texas.

> *She said "Tell me the three things every woman wants to hear."*
> *And I said "It's baseball season."*
>
> Bob Freking, Reds Fan

After the disappointing 2007 season, about the only excitement for March 31 related to local construction. Later that week, Governor George Voinovich was scheduled to break ground at The Banks—the same riverfront site that was once called "the Bottoms." It was where the first settlers of Cincinnati landed in December 1788, and city and county officials hoped it would turn into a vibrant destination for people to live, work, and play. Fans looked forward to visiting "The Banks" before, during, and after Reds games in the coming seasons. Another positive development was that the reinvigorated Reds Radio Network added dozens of stations, enabling fans throughout the region to tune into games.

Pete Rose lookalike

There were two sad events affecting fans' spirits on a rainy Opening Day. First, fan favorite Joe Nuxhall had lost his battle with cancer on November 15. The 2008 season would be dedicated to him. Then, on the eve of the March 31 opener, Keith and Carolyn Maupin learned that their son Matt's body had been found nearly four years to the day that his fuel convoy had been ambushed west of Baghdad. That evening, President Bush called the family. The Maupins had planned to continue the family tradition by attending the opener, and they were scheduled to appear in the parade as they had in 2007. Matt's parents decided to continue with their plans despite receiving the heartbreaking news. They would join with the community that had supported them through the hard years of Matt being missing in action.

Former Reds center fielder Cesar Geronimo, a member of the Big Red Machine, was the grand marshal. The cloudy, wet weather matched the fans' mood: sad and reserved. The parade was dominated by tributes to Nuxhall and the fallen soldier. A WLW float with a chair and microphone symbolizing Nuxhall's career as a legendary announcer was followed by Nuxhall's 1989 Lincoln Continental. Riding in the car was Nuxhall's son Kim and Kim's wife. Fans applauded throughout their journey. When spectators saw the Maupins' car, they applauded, saluted, placed their caps over their hearts, and cried in the rain. Just past Fountain Square, fan Ken Gannon sprinted from the sidewalk and presented Carolyn Maupin with a single white rose. At the end of the route, in response to a spectator saying he was sorry for their loss, Keith Maupin stated simply, "Matt's coming home." The rest of the parade played second fiddle to the Nuxhall and Maupin families.

The rain continued at the ballpark. Pregame ceremonies were delayed, but F-18 jets from Marine Fighter Attack Squadron 224 arrived during the downpour as scheduled. The families of Nuxhall and Maupin were introduced on the field, and there was a moment of silence for Matt Maupin and his family. As one fan noted, Nuxhall was "everybody's grandpa," and Maupin was "everybody's little brother." When the Reds were introduced, each player darted from the dugout to the first baseline. A murmur became a roar as the crowd realized that each player had the same word and number on his back: Nuxhall 41. Aaron Harang, the starting pitcher, received permission from MLB to wear the commemorative jersey during the game; the other players removed theirs after introductions and donned their regular jerseys. Each jersey had a black patch on the sleeve with "NUXY" in white, a tribute that would remain throughout the season. The Banks' chief proponent, County Commissioner Todd Portune, threw out the first pitch. Luckily for him, it was a strike, so he would not become the brunt of jokes on late-night television as did Mayor Mallory the year before. Harang took the mound to start the game but not before he drew a "41" in the dirt on the mound. The sad atmosphere of the game was compounded by the Reds losing 4–2.

Local, national, and international news swirled around Opening Day. Gas prices were at record highs, so club officials wondered whether far-flung fans from the tristate area would make the two- or three-hour drive during the season to catch a game or two. Local parishioners at Holy Family Church were protesting the potential hiring of a longtime Catholic priest who had faced sexual misconduct charges years ago. In politics, the junior senator from Illinois, Barack Obama, had caught Hillary Clinton in the delegate fight for the Democratic nomination for president. The Israelis and Palestinians reached an agreement on the eve of the opener that was aimed at paving the way for a peace deal between the perennial enemies. In Baghdad, Shiite cleric Muqtada al-Sadr announced a cease-fire between warring Shiite factions.

Meanwhile, US officials were preparing to brief a skeptical Congress the following week about the prospects for bringing troops home and leaving Iraq.

Dusty Baker joined the Reds' managerial carousel in 2008. During the season, Griffey and power hitter Adam Dunn were traded. Castellini continued to hope for a turnaround, but the Reds won only 74 games. The fans were disgruntled.

2009: Fickle Mother Nature

Despite the disappointment of the previous two seasons, Reds fans continued to believe in Bob Castellini and his plan. The team had young hitters that seemed to form a productive nucleus: Brandon Phillips, Joey Votto, and Jay Bruce. There were also young pitchers, such as Johnny Cueto and Edinson Volquez. If the ball bounced the right way, maybe the Reds would repeat the surprise success of the 1961 Reds. As baseball historian Greg Rhodes explained in the Sunday *Enquirer*, the Reds had gone into 1961 with only one winning season in 15 years. They were not expected to contend, but they shocked both pundits and fans. That team won the National League championship and went on to have the best record in the league over the next 40 years. Fans hoped Rhodes's analogy was spot-on. This season could be the start of another magical run if everything went right.

> *"To me, opening day means the kind of hope that only a new season of baseball in Cincinnati can bring. Every new season says winter is over and that not only is summer coming, it just might be a very special summer. Only baseball has the potential to unite us in a way that supersedes reality and actually lets us all taste hope."*
>
> George Corneliussen, Reds Fan

Everyone was geared up for April 6. The opener was a little later than it had been in recent years, and fans figured there was a better chance of nice weather. The game was another early sellout. There were plenty of opportunities to begin the daylong party early in the morning and continue it well into the evening. Streets were closed as early as

7:30 a.m. and an all-day party was planned on Fountain Square beginning at 9:00 a.m. There was to be live music and televising of the game on the giant screen above Macy's that faced the square. Game Day Sports Café, which was offering "kegs and eggs," opened at 5:00 a.m. WLW radio was scheduled to broadcast from the location all day. There were no less than 14 other venues within blocks of the parade and ballpark that opened early in the morning with food and drink specials. Parade organizers expected another huge crowd, as Hall of Famer Frank Robinson was the grand marshal, and two of the young Reds, Volquez and Cueto, were going to ride in the parade. The day preceding the opener was a beautiful Sunday with 70-degree temperatures.

Suddenly, Mother Nature decided to switch things up. Temperatures dipped into the low 30s, and along with the plummeting temperatures came a chance of snow. At best, Opening Day was certain to see rain. Fans planning to take in all the festivities suddenly decided to stay indoors. The crowd lining the parade was the smallest in years, as evidenced by spectators being only one or two deep along the sidewalks. Even Canadian Joey Votto objected to the cold conditions, observing, "I never headed outside when it was anything like this," he said. "You play hockey in this weather, not baseball." Only in Cincinnati would people call this the first day of spring.

Despite the inclement weather, Robinson was a big hit with the crowd. The brave souls along the route waved to him enthusiastically from under their blankets and ponchos. Robinson, dressed in his pinstriped Reds jersey with number 20 on the back, rode in the back of a white Mustang convertible with a red interior. It was a throwback to the white Thunderbird with red interior that he had driven when he played for the Reds in the late '50s and early '60—that is, before he was traded in one of the most controversial trades in Reds history.

Rock & Roll Hall of Famer Bootsy Collins, a native Cincinnatian, traveled the route sporting red, star-shaped glasses. He was part of the Yellow Ribbon Support Center contingent. His SUV followed a vehicle with a sign saying "Remember my face" that also displayed photos of the late soldier, Matt Maupin. Maupin's father was scheduled to ride with Collins, but ironically he had to attend a funeral instead.

Fans shivered on their way to the ballpark. Once inside, they marveled at the new 39-foot by 138-foot scoreboard that was showing high-definition highlights of previous championship teams. Digital "ribbon boards" graced the fascia of the second deck of the bleachers and ran along the first and third baselines. Longtime official scorer of the Reds, Glenn Sample, was remembered with a moment of silence in pregame ceremonies for his 29 seasons of service. He had passed away five months earlier. The Reds also honored armed forces members wounded in battle in Iraq and Afghanistan, and a parade of colors featured honor guard units from each military branch. Four F-16s from the 178th Fighter Wing of the Ohio Air National Guard roared over the park. Nick Lachey was brought back again, this time to throw out the ceremonial first pitch. Brian Kelly, the coach of the University of Cincinnati Big East championship football team, then delivered the game ball to Aaron Harang, starting his fourth consecutive opener.

Despite the closely contested game that was very much up for grabs, the cold was too much even for hard-core fans, many of whom decided to leave the park early. The Reds eventually lost 2–1. The next morning, well-liked *Enquirer* columnist Paul Daugherty committed heresy. He advocated that the Reds give up the annual tradition of opening at home. Daugherty argued that the weather was simply too uncertain and that openers should be played in more hospitable climates. His theory gained little traction with Reds supporters, much less with Reds management. The team improved slightly over the previous year but still won only 78 games. By the time the season ended, Dusty Baker's job appeared to be in jeopardy.

Opening Day had begun with news of other losses besides those acknowledged at the game. Cincinnati was the only city in Ohio with its own retirement plan, and the 2008 financial crisis had taken its toll on the plan's fiscal well-being. The Cincinnati Retirement System's assets had been depleted nearly 40 percent, so city employees were naturally anxious about the long-term solvency of the fund. On Xavier University's campus, just a few miles west of where the University of Cincinnati was celebrating its football championship, students and fans were worried about something in the short-term. Xavier's basketball coach, Sean Miller, had guided the team to another NCAA Sweet 16 appearance, but he was being courted by other top-tier college basketball programs. The day after the Reds lost the opener, fans' fears became reality as Miller signed on to coach at the University of Arizona.

2010: Could This Be the Year?

An out-of-town businessman arrived in Cincinnati on April 4, complaining to himself about the higher-than-normal hotel rates that went hand in hand with Opening Day. He then picked up the Sunday *Enquirer*. Even though he was a baseball fan, he had to chuckle. "Are these people nuts?" The local team had not had a winning season since 2000 and they were having a parade? Yes, and the paper had a special insert section called "Defining the Decade" claiming, "The Reds have good reason be optimistic about the next decade." What were these folks thinking? Well, Reds general manager Walt Jocketty had created headlines during the off-season by rekindling Cincinnatians' memories of the Griffey splash of 2000. This year, Jocketty had signed pitcher Aroldis Chapman, a Cuban defector, to a six-year, $30 million contract. Chapman was lauded as an ace pitcher who threw the ball over 100 miles per hour. A week before the opener, Jocketty proclaimed the team "was much better" than it had been. Fans believed Chapman would eventually become the cornerstone of a young pitching staff that would change the trajectory of the Reds.

> *"But for some of us, the best thing we see on Opening Day is each other. The ebullience of the day is as much about saying what Cincinnati can be as what the Reds can be. It is a day when the sketches of development projects come to life—when the streets really are filled with people, when there's electric vibe in the air and life not only seems good here, but vital and fun."*
>
> Enquirer editorial

The Reds needed to do something to keep the faithful interested. With a recession that continued to pound family and corporate budgets, the Reds' 2009 attendance was down 400,000 from the previous two seasons. The local level of interest compared unfavorably with all-time attendance records throughout MLB and with increased TV viewership for baseball overall. Castellini spruced up the ballpark again by adding the likes of sushi in the concession stands and a new restaurant on the suite level for season ticket holders, but he knew the best way to bring back fans was for the team to start winning consistently. The club hoped to capitalize on the "Aroldis Chapman Factor" and the addition of four veteran players who could mentor their younger teammates. The make-up of the team seemed to portend a brighter future, but the *Enquirer* would only go so far: it predicted the Reds would finish in third place.

As the visiting businessman walked out of the Westin Hotel across from Fountain Square early in the morning, he saw hundreds of people sitting in lawn chairs on the sidewalks. He was still scratching his head when he counted no fewer than 18 bars and restaurants that were already open for business within blocks of the ballpark. The day of partying had begun early. Neil Luken had already been at work since sunrise, as he was again the organizer of the ninety-first version of the annual procession. He expected the number of spectators to easily double the size of the 2009 parade when cold and rain kept the crowd at a low level. Up to 100,000 fans were expected to come and see the grand marshal, legendary catcher Johnny Bench. Bench was joined by current Reds pitcher Bronson Arroyo, Reds Hall of Famers Ken Griffey Sr. and George Foster, broadcaster George Grande, and Miss Ohio USA 2010, Amanda Tempel, who had graduated from local Roger Bacon High School in 2008. Two hundred parade units lined up behind Bench. Luken's prediction about the crowd was correct, as spectators flooded the streets on a mild day.

The parade was eclectic in its usual entertaining fashion. The Cincinnati Rollergirls roller derby team interacted with the crowd while skating along. The Crosby Elementary Pop Cycles demonstrated their skills on unicycles while trailing several floats featuring a nineteenth-century theme. Marching bands were heard throughout the 18-block carnival, with the Cincinnati Hawks marching band featuring a clown called "Poppie." There were vehicles of every size and model. Even though the team had been unsuccessful for many years, the unofficial city holiday was still going strong. Grand marshal Bench said he was stunned to be chosen for the role. He recalled his days as a player when the team had no idea what was going on outside the ballpark. Said Bench, "We'd stay down at the ballpark, get warmed up and then have to wait two hours for the festivities to get over with on the field. We'd say 'Let's get this over with.' Now, I know what goes on. This is like Cincinnati's Mardi Gras. This is like Augusta and the Masters tournament, only better."

When the march finally subsided, the fifth-largest crowd (42,493) in the park's young history witnessed the show that occurred outside and inside the stadium. The Goshorn Brothers and Pete Wagner's Dixieland band performed pregame concerts. The time-honored traditions of Reds Opening Days played out once again with the Rosie Reds and Findlay Market officials presenting gifts to the team. Four F-16s did the now traditional flyover. Former Bengal Ben Utecht displayed his softer side by singing the national anthem. TV announcer George Grande, wearing a jersey autographed by each Reds player, tossed the ceremonial first pitch to none other than Bench. Bench squatted behind home plate for the first time since his retirement in 1983. The beauty queen, Amanda Tempel, delivered the official game ball to Aaron Harang. Harang was honored with his fifth consecutive Opening Day start, tying a Reds record.

Katie and Nancy Freking

Reds fans witnessed a close game until the ninth inning when the St. Louis Cardinals scored five runs en route to an 11–4 win. The Reds made good on the preseason optimism when Jay Bruce hit a walk-off home run on September 28 to clinch the first division championship since 1995. Although the club was swept in the playoffs by the Phillies, Reds fans hoped the season marked the start of a successful decade.

Jay Bruce

Johnny Bench's reference to the Masters golf tournament was timely in that the tournament was about to begin later in the week in Augusta, Georgia. As Opening Day was underway in Cincinnati, disgraced golfer Tiger Woods was holding a press conference in Augusta. Woods was returning to golf after 45 days at a rehab facility that stemmed from his infamous Thanksgiving night car crash. The crash followed a domestic dispute with his wife, Elin. Over the winter, a dozen women claimed to have had an affair with Woods. Woods stated that he planned to compete as hard as ever, saying, "Nothing's changed. I'm still going to go out there and try to win this thing." His next several years in golf would be marred by injuries and a reputation that had been forever sullied.

2011: Health Concerns

Coming off a division-championship season, Reds fans looked forward to a successful opener and season. Health concerns soon consumed them during spring training. The Reds believed they were deep in pitching talent, but suddenly two starters landed on the disabled list (Johnny Cueto and Homer Bailey). A third, reliever Jared Burton, would not pitch for at least two weeks, and a fourth, starter Bronson Arroyo, was dealing with mononucleosis. These concerns detracted from Cincinnatians' excitement about how The Banks was taking shape next to the ballpark. Plans called for 1,800 apartments and condos, up to five hotels, an office tower, and at least 200,000 square feet of shops, restaurants, bars, and entertainment venues. The Holy Grail Bar would be the first business to welcome fans by Opening Day. The rest of downtown was also in the midst of a renaissance, including a renovation of Washington Park in Over-the-Rhine and completion of the 41-story Great American Tower that capped off the skyline with its distinctive tiara. After more than 15 years of decline, the downtown area and Over-the-Rhine (rebranded as simply

"OTR") became a destination for residents and tourists alike. Suddenly, at least 38 bars and restaurants were ready to celebrate the opener within walking distance of the park. One, Arnold's Bar and Grill, was ten blocks away. It had opened eight years before the Red Stockings took the field in 1869 and celebrated its 150-year anniversary in 2011! It remains the city's oldest eatery.

Arnold's Bar and Grill

With all this activity swirling around the ballpark, Opening Day fever reached a high point. Michael and David Schuster, local architects, circulated petitions along the parade route and outside the ballpark to make the annual rite of spring an official city holiday. Joe Morgan, a member of the Big Red Machine and arguably the greatest second baseman of all time, became a huge draw for the parade when he was named grand marshal. Some business owners worried that attendance might decline because the opener was on a Thursday instead of the customary Monday. Those fears were misplaced, as more people poured onto the downtown sidewalks than had in 2010. Following Morgan in the procession were Reds pitchers Travis Wood and Mike Leake.

Among the horde of fans entering the ballpark were Bev and Lou Dollin. Married 57 years, they were attending their sixty-fifth consecutive opener. The Dollins had attended Opening Day separately with their families before they got married in 1954. Another special patron

was Mildred Tuttle. She was 100 years old and lived in Seymour, Indiana. She explained, "It's like a family reunion." She had attended 33 previous openers and at least one game a season for the previous 50 years.

In the pregame ceremony, Reds first baseman Joey Votto was presented with his 2010 Most Valuable Player trophy. A highlight of the program was a video tribute to former Reds manager, Sparky Anderson. He had passed away on November 4. Public-address announcer Joe Zerhusen reminded the crowd that Anderson was not only the first manager to win the World Series with teams from both leagues, but that he was also "one of the greatest humanitarians the game has ever known." When the tribute ended, the Reds unveiled a sign that read "Sparky 1934–2010" that would hang during the season above the Reds bullpen. The location was chosen to commemorate a manager known as "Captain Hook" because of his penchant for using relief pitchers. The Reds wore a patch on the left sleeves of their uniforms in honor of Sparky. Retired Cincinnati police chief Tom Streicher then threw out the ceremonial first pitch, which sailed over the head of his catcher, Joe Morgan.

The game was a thriller. Ramon Hernandez hit a three-run homer in the bottom of the ninth inning for another walk-off victory in an opener. The Reds topped the Brewers, 7–6. Reds fans celebrated, as many knew that no Reds team had ever won the World Series without winning the opener. At least on this day, it appeared Reds pitchers were healthy enough to go the distance. Unfortunately, Bailey and Cueto would each miss 15 starts each during the rest the season, and the Reds failed to repeat as division champions. They finished in third place, winning only 79 games. Castellini vowed not to run short of pitchers in 2012, making four significant acquisitions during the winter.

2012: Votto Goes to The Bank(s)

> *"Opening Day is our local first day of spring. As winter ends, it is time for pasty Midwesterners to emerge from our sheltered confines. Time to embrace the sunshine, the green grass, and the hope that this could be the Reds year … We relish the protracted digestion of a pastime which lacks the frenetic pace or the intense chaos of our other games, yet is no less complex."*
>
> Ben Shooner, Reds Fan

Reds fans believed 2011 was an aberration due to bad luck with the pitching staff, and they hoped the Reds' off-season moves would bring dividends. The city council voted unanimously for Opening Day to be recognized as a ceremonial holiday (whatever that meant, but it certainly was not a paid holiday for city workers). All of a sudden, there was an abundance of events competing for fans' pregame attention. Of course, there was the annual two-hour parade that would draw tens of thousands. Then there was the party on Fountain Square that included live music followed by the game being shown on the big screen. On the riverfront, a seven-hour festival with food, drinks, and music was to take place on the Schmidlapp Event Lawn in the new Smale Riverfront Park. The park perked up the previously drab shoreline of the Ohio River. In The Banks entertainment area, even more bars and restaurants had opened in time for the 2012 opener. Most significantly, a new tradition was born on the streets outside the park: a block party that would draw thousands between the end of the parade and the first pitch. It benefited the Reds Community Fund, a nonprofit that seeks to improve the lives of young people through baseball. The mob outside the ballpark filled several blocks as fans listened to music by Frankly Speaking and enjoyed ice-cold beer. Without question, 2012 was the largest party on any single day

in Cincinnati history. On the Internet, game tickets were being hawked at prices ranging from $140 to $600.

Joey Votto, a reserved, introverted star known for his intellectual approach to hitting, became the face of the franchise. He was the league's MVP in 2010, and in 2011 he became the first Reds first baseman to win a Gold Glove. Two days before the Thursday, April 4, opener, dressed in a dark, three-piece suit, the star promoted a new breakfast cereal: VottO's. The product was a honey-nut toasted oat cereal in a limited-edition collector's box featuring a drawing of Votto in action. Rumors had been circulating that the Reds and Votto had reached a long-term deal that would keep him as a Red beyond 2013 when his current

Joey Votto

contract expired. On the eve of the opener, the Reds held a press conference at which Castellini announced his next gamble: he was "all in" with Votto and signed him to a ten-year deal worth $225 million. Votto said afterward that larger-market teams may have offered him more after 2013 season, but he added, "Bottom line is I like it here … I enjoy coming to the ballpark and playing in front of the Cincinnati fans. I like the momentum we're building with the fans. That's a big deal for me." He joked that his girlfriend probably hoped he was willing to make another long-term commitment. (He was not.)

The huge contract for a player in a small market was the talk of fans throughout the day. "How can anyone be worth that much?" one asked. A Catholic nun hoped Votto could buy the sisters a new grotto. Pete Rose, buying two blankets in the store inside the ballpark, said, "I'd give him a lot money, but not that much." (Rose had been the first "singles hitter" to earn $100,000 in a season.) Mark Herr, a truck driver from Dillsboro, Indiana, put the contract in perspective. Dressed in a vintage Red Stockings uniform, he talked about George Wright, the 1869 captain who made $1,500 for the season. "Baseball players have always been overpaid. [$1,500 was] not $225 million, but $1,500 was a lot of money back then." Herr was correct; Wright's salary was exponentially larger than the average worker of his day, but still, there was reason to wonder whether the Reds had paid too much. History will be the judge of the price tag.

The parade route was jammed with optimistic fans. ESPN baseball announcer Aaron Boone was the grand marshal. He had played with

The Neff Family

the team for seven seasons. In his first two seasons in 1997 and 1998, he played alongside his brother Bret. In his last three seasons, his father, Bob, was the manager. The Boones were still popular. Behind Boone were more than 200 parade entries. There was the "Made It Official Float" carrying Mike Schuster and Councilman Wendell Young, who had spearheaded the effort to make Opening Day a holiday. Four US Army soldiers in camouflage units chauffeured soldiers from the Wounded Warrior Project. Three generations of the Gray family waved from a float honoring their

Party at the Banks

mother, Kathryn, of Hamilton, Ohio. She was described as "the world's greatest Reds fan." Her family commented that when her casket was lowered into the ground at the cemetery, her children all sang, "Take Me Out to the Ball Game" in her honor.

While the block party continued in The Banks, the pregame ceremonies featured Miss Ohio 2012, Audrey Bolte of Batavia, Ohio. She delivered the ceremonial first pitch to the retiring sheriff of Hamilton County, Simon Leis Jr. Leis had been sheriff for 25 years after previously serving the county as a prosecutor and judge. He became nationally famous for prosecuting Larry Flynt and Hustler magazine in the late 1970s and was featured in the movie The People vs. Larry Flynt. Much like his prosecution of Flynt, Leis' toss was slightly off target. Senator Rob Portman was honorary captain of the Reds for the day, and he accompanied manager Dusty Baker to home plate to exchange lineup cards with the Miami Marlins and review ground rules for the game.

Everyone was having a good time at the game except for the Miami Marlins. Votto collected a hit and a walk, Jay Bruce hit a home run, and Johnny Cueto pitched seven scoreless innings. The Reds cruised to a 4–0 shutout win. The crowd of 42,959 set a record for attendance. The team would go on to replicate the success of the 1970s Big Red Machine, winning 97 games. They traveled to San Francisco to open the playoffs and breezed to two easy wins. Disaster struck at home when the Giants eliminated the Reds with a three-game sweep.

In national news, it was reported that Mitt Romney had achieved an insurmountable lead over Rick Santorum in the Republican race to oppose President Obama in November. The former Massachusetts governor had picked up 86 more delegates in Maryland, Wisconsin, and the District of Columbia. During the three days prior to the opener, USA Today and the Gallup organization conducted a survey of national attitudes regarding the controversial shooting of Trayvon Martin in Sanford, Florida, in February. The results showed a racial divide as to whether people believed George Zimmerman, a neighborhood watch captain, should be charged with murder.

Reds fans spent the winter with a severe case of indigestion. Castellini may have been "all in" on the Reds, but they were declared "all out" of the chase for the pennant.

2013: Unfinished Business

The prevailing mood in Cincinnati as April 1 approached was that the Reds needed to finish their drive to a championship. Fans' biggest worries centered on how Joey Votto was healing from two knee surgeries and whether the pitching staff would stay healthy. In 2012, the Reds' five starters had remarkably started every game of the 162-game season except one. (A doubleheader caused them to miss the one start because it would have cost one of the five regular starters a normal day of rest had he pitched.) Reds management had done their part, increasing the club's payroll to over $100 million for the first time. It was the thirteenth-highest payout in MLB but was dwarfed by the $151 million tab of the Opening Day opponent, the Los Angeles Angels. Every baseball fan realizes that money is important in baseball, but it does not necessarily guarantee success. Teams, not individual stars, win championships.

> "Opening Day is celebrated, revered and altogether cherished here. It's part of what makes us, us. It's also the weirdest day of the baseball season, and one most players are glad to get behind them. After six weeks of regimentation, in the warm cocoon of spring training, they're thrown into this one-day ball-apalooza … "
>
> Paul Daugherty,
> Enquirer sports columnist

Some fans in Cincinnati have long celebrated the day before Opening Day as if it were New Year's Eve. Clubs, organizations, and families have traditionally held luncheons and other parties on the day preceding the new season of baseball. This year, a local law firm hosted the first annual "New Year's Eve" party at The Phoenix, the historic event center near OTR. The evening featured live music from Chuck Brisbin and the Tuna Project. Goings-on included dancing, prizes, and appearances by local sports celebrities and Reds mascots.

Party at the Phoenix

Popular WLW radio talk show host Bill "The Great American" Cunningham (the self-proclaimed "voice of the common man") promised the 200 attendees a World Series championship. The night concluded with a balloon drop as the band played "Auld Lang Syne." The party benefited the Reds Community Fund and has become an annual tradition.

Even more than treating Opening Day eve as New Year's Eve, many fans prefer to compare Opening Day to Christmas morning. In 2013, it was an apt comparison, as stray morning snowflakes put people in the holiday spirit. The official festivities started at 11:00 a.m. with the second annual Reds Community Fund Charity Block Party on Joe Nuxhall Way and Freedom Way in The Banks. Beer drinkers could also enjoy the newly opened Moerlein Lager House that allowed patrons to procure their beer alfresco straight from the on-site brewery. Findlay Market organizers expected 100,000 people to line the streets to watch 189 entries, including 13 marching bands, march in the parade starting at noon. At least 250,000 more were expected to watch the parade on TV in Greater Cincinnati and Dayton. The parade lineup was led by Reds Hall of Famer

Phil Castellini Taking Selfie

George Foster. Foster was a member of the Big Red Machine but was often lost in the shadows of Pete Rose, Johnny Bench, Tony Perez, and Joe Morgan. He was the National League's Most Valuable Player in 1977, played 11 of his 18 seasons with the Reds, and remained a popular figure who was active in the community and the Reds organization.

Foster was involved with Impact A Hero, an organization supporting wounded war veterans and their families. Two dignitaries, Chief Warrant Officer S. Alan Hartley of Fairfield, Ohio, and the father of Lance Corporal Taylor Prazynski joined Foster. Hartley lost the use of his legs while serving in Afghanistan and Prazynski had been killed in Iraq eight years earlier. The crowd gave Hartley and Prazynski's father a rousing ovation. Another crowd pleaser was Teddy Kremer. Kremer, 30, from White Oak, Ohio, has Down Syndrome. He was a guest batboy during a game in the previous season, and he bonded with Reds players and became a crowd favorite. Kremer waved from his perch in a

Pregame Managers' Awards, 2013

convertible. There was also a restored tallyho wagon that had carried players to Crosley Field on Opening Day in 1920. A team of eight world-renowned Budweiser Clydesdales returned once again, hitched to a beer wagon. The Clydesdales had been a Budweiser symbol since 1933. Some jump ropers from Anderson Township entertained the crowd with their ropes and pogo sticks. Many of the parade spectators wandered through the new exhibit at the Reds Hall of Fame & Museum on their way into the game. It was called Signature Reds: A Century of Reds Autographs, and it displayed signatures from virtually every player since 1920.

Wounded heroes were the first honorees in pregame ceremonies. They were recognized by Senators Rob Portman and Sherrod Brown. Members of the nation's oldest professional fire department, Cincinnati's own, unfurled a giant American flag as the Angels and Reds

> *"This is our special day, a day for a dad to be with his son. Opening Day lets us bond. We talk about everything. Opening Day is much bigger than a game."*
>
> Gary McMasters and Brady McMasters, Reds Fans

were introduced. The festivities turned somber as a moment of silence was observed for the 26 innocent victims of the December 14 shooting spree at Sandy Hook Elementary School in Newtown, Connecticut. Cincinnati firefighter John Winfrey then stirred the crowd with a beautiful rendition of the national anthem capped off by a flyover by two T-28 Trojans and one B-25 Mitchell. The planes came from the nearby Tri-State Warbird Museum in Batavia, Ohio. Former New York Yankee manager Joe Torre, the manager of Team USA in the recently concluded World Baseball Classic, tossed the ceremonial first pitch.

During the game, fans could visit the new Bowtie Bar in right field. Reds TV announcer Chris Welsh liked the concept so much that he began a tradition of wearing a bow tie during each Tuesday-evening home game. A local quartet, the Mistics, performed "God Bless America" during the seventh-inning stretch. The teams were tied 1–1 after nine innings, and the Angels eventually prevailed in 13 innings. Many in the record crowd of 43,168 had already left the nearly five-hour game as the temperatures plummeted to the low 40s.

The game ended just in time for interested fans to walk across the plaza on the east side of the ballpark to U.S. Bank Arena. There, a 90-minute program called "4,192—An Evening with Pete Rose Live" was on tap. Rose made fans howl as he told stories from his playing career. Opening Day was the fiftieth anniversary of Rose's Crosley Field debut. He remained immensely popular with Reds fans despite the troubles that came to light at the end of his career. Rose, then 71, recalled what it was like to play for his hometown team. Said Rose, "I was the happiest guy in the world, playing second base for the Cincinnati Reds on Opening Day." Rose reminisced about his first appearance on Opening Day. He recalled his thoughts after being photographed with his parents in the stands, saying, "That woke me up to what was going on. Geez, I'm the starting second baseman for the Cincinnati Reds! It was like someone slapped me in the jaw. Up to that time, having the kind of spring training I did, and making the team, was just all a fantasy."

Rose was not the only one feeling nostalgic on Opening Day. The opener was the last one for Reds clubhouse chief Bernie Stowe. The Delhi Township resident, then 78, had not missed an Opening Day since Harry Truman was president 67 years earlier. He started as a batboy for the Reds at age 11 and went on to become one of the most beloved employees in the history of the franchise. Stowe retired at the end of the 2013 season.

Bernie Stowe

Speaking of stories from a previous era, the Associated Press reported that morning about a single-page FBI memo that had become the most popular document in the bureau's electronic reading room. Dated March 22, 1950, the memo contained a report of three flying saucers allegedly found in New Mexico. An informant whose name was redacted had advised the FBI of several bizarre details. Inside each saucer were "three bodies of human shape but only 3 feet tall, dressed in metallic cloth with a very fine texture. Each body was bandaged in a manner similar to blackout suits used by speed flyers and test pilots." The report said that the government's high-powered radar in the area could have interfered with the controlling mechanism of the unidentified flying objects and forced them to land. The FBI filed the one-page memo away in its headquarters and "no further evaluation was attempted."

The Reds would return to the playoffs in 2013 but this time as a wild card participant in a one-game playoff against the Pittsburgh Pirates preceding the division series. The Pirates won, and it would be the last playoff game for the Reds in the first 150 years of their history. Dusty Baker was fired (or was he scapegoated?) for the team's lack of success in the playoffs. It was a disappointing season, and regrettably the team's unfinished business was left unfinished.

OPENING DAY EVE EXTRAVAGANZA

C.

THE C DOT SHOW

MOTR PUB · 1345 MAIN ST.
SUN 3·30 / 5PM

SPECIAL GUEST REDS BEAT REPORTER JOHN FAY AND CARDINALS BEAT REPORTER DERRICK GOOLD

CO HOSTS C. TRENT ROSECRANS AND JOSH SNEED

2014: Aberration?

The citizens of Cincinnati were continuing to debate the merits of the streetcar project that had been a matter of controversy for years. In December, after a scaled-down version of the transit system had been approved, there was a 20-day delay while the city council again debated whether to move forward. That delay cost the city $1 million, according to a report on the morning after the March 31 opener. When completed, the streetcar would connect OTR on the northern edge of downtown with the ballpark and the riverfront on the southern end. One mile of the 3.6-mile track was already installed in time for the opener, but the ongoing streetcar project and other building projects guaranteed traffic congestion.

> *"The game will start shortly after four, and right then, we'll get back that eternal feeling that, no matter what else happens, the Reds will be on the radio, and we can retreat to the backyard or the front porch and suspend reality for a few hours."*
>
> Paul Daugherty,
> Enquirer sports columnist

Aside from people wondering how they would get where they wanted to go, Reds fans were debating whether the club could top the 90-win mark for the fourth time in five years. There were questions in abundance, not the least of which was whether the team was better off with a rookie manager in Bryan Price or the veteran, Dusty Baker, whom the club had discarded impetuously (or so it seemed) after a pretty good season. True, the Reds had lost 4–2 in their 2013 wild card game, but can a manager really be blamed when his playoff pitcher (Johnny Cueto) seemed nervous, and the rest of the team did not hit well against a good pitcher on the road? Most fans realized that in baseball, perhaps more than in any other sport, a single game hardly ever tells you which team is better. The wild card round is

strictly a made-for-TV event and an attempt to pull in more viewers. So instead of hanging their hopes on winning one game, the Reds were eager to be one of the better teams over the long haul so they could not be bounced out by just one loss. They wanted to play at least a best-of-five series where they could settle in and play winning baseball.

The Reds made another move over the winter that left fans scratching their heads. Homer Bailey, a former first-round pick who had few noteworthy accomplishments during his career other than two no-hitters, was offered a six-year contract worth $105 million. WLW radio's Ken Broo (on Sunday mornings) and Lance McAlister (on weeknights) needed no other topics to be guaranteed callers and listeners for their three-hour Sportstalk radio shows. Fans sort of understood the 2012 Votto deal for $225 million, as Votto had won both the MVP and Gold Glove awards, but the Bailey contract baffled even the most ardent supporters. The oversized salary made the move a real gamble, as the Reds were also betting that three other players being asked to take over new roles—Billy Hamilton, Devin Mesoraco, and Tony Cingrani—would help them return to the playoffs. The weather was not helping to calm fans either. There had been a seemingly endless run of frequent snowfalls causing school delays and closings.

Parties and Reds-related events took over the town during the weekend before the opener. On Friday, a four-week display of artwork debuted in Covington, Kentucky, touching on the themes of baseball, Cincinnati, and Opening Day. Named "199C," the exhibit featured artwork inside the building and various activities outside the building, including street wiffleball, live music, vintage video game competitions, a live art installation, and food trucks. On Saturday night, there was a Baseball Art and Memorabilia party at Christian Moerlein Brewery and the Opening Day eve benefit party once again at The Phoenix. On Sunday, local sportswriter

305 C. Trent Rosecrans hosted an "Opening Day Eve Extravaganza" at MOTR Pub called "The C Dot Show." On Monday, other parties in various locations from OTR to Mount Adams to northern Kentucky to The Banks started earlier in the day and were better attended than ever before. Opening Day was becoming exponentially more than just the parade and the game. Parties and early-morning tavern openings had always been part of the holiday, but this seemed like an explosion of interest. The Reds topped it all off by unveiling the Brewery District Bar inside the park. The popular attraction was an 85-foot bar with 60 taps serving 22 craft and domestic beers.

With the sun out and thermometers reading 66 degrees on the morning of Opening Day, there were no excuses for staying home from the parade. Renovations of Music Hall and Washington Park had resulted in easier parking access and wider sidewalks so fans could sit or stand along the popular viewing area in OTR. Big Red Machine shortstop

Davey Concepción, grand marshal, left, and Teddy Kremer, honorary grand marshal, second from left

Davey Concepción was the grand marshal, and he was joined by Teddy Kremer, honorary grand marshal. Along the route, Kremer received a welcome that nearly equaled that for Concepción. Kremer apparently enjoyed the perks of being a star in the parade, saying, "I get to hug some pretty babes with some others folks."

The Flyover.

Spectators were relieved to see the smile on the face of Reds pitcher Aroldis Chapman, who rode along with his daughter Ashanti. Chapman had sustained fractures above his left eye and nose when Kansas City catcher Salvador Perez drilled him with a line drive during spring training. During surgery, a titanium plate and screws were inserted in his face to stabilize the bones above his eye. The scary incident jarred Chapman, his teammates, and fans, but he was expected to be able to pitch for the team soon.

Mr. Red strolled along sporting his patented smile, and Jim Tarbell was back impersonating Peanut Jim Shelton. Once again, the lawn mower specialists of the Wapakoneta Optimist Precision Lawnmower Drill Team reprised their fancy footwork. The marching bands returned in force, and accordion player John Keene performed on a float. Said Keene, "Our first tune will be 'Beer Barrel Polka' in line with what so many people along this parade route have already been drinking." The most creative float seemed particularly appropriate as the Reds' nemesis, the St. Louis Cardinals, were this year's opponent. A group from Goshen, Ohio, crafted a "Goshen Horse Thief Detectives" float. The crowd sparred with the six jailbirds in the cage, who were dressed in Cardinal uniforms! (If they really were St. Louis players, the Goshen jailers probably would have received a key to the city.)

As fans arrived at the stadium, many of the faithful waited in line to enter the Reds Hall of Fame & Museum. Two new exhibits were on display: Kings of the Queen City showcasing the first 145 years of Reds history; and Hometown Reds, honoring more than 100 native Cincinnatians who had played for the team.

The pregame festivities were highlighted by two great shortstops. Barry Larkin grew up in Cincinnati watching the grand marshal, Concepción, play shortstop for the Big Red Machine. Larkin had gone on to an 18-year career with the Reds that landed him in the Reds Hall of Fame in 2008 and in Cooperstown in 2012. (Concepción was inducted into the Reds Hall of Fame in 2000 but did not receive the nod from Cooperstown during his fifteen years of initial eligibility.) Larkin was Concepción's successor as the Reds' shortstop. On this day, the Reds selected the two great infielders to throw out the first pitch simultaneously. The crowd went wild, as both players were beloved. Concepción was a great player who was often in the shadow of the more famous members of the 1970s Reds, and Larkin was a hometown boy.

Speaking of which, another hometown boy had the honor of handing the lineup card to the umpires at home plate. He was Mayor John Cranley. Cranley had grown up in Price Hill and had never attended Opening Day as a kid. "I remember growing up in Price Hill and in grade school at St. William a kid went to the game and came back and showed us his ticket. I always thought that was the greatest possession on Earth."

Billy Hamilton, hailed as a player who would wreak havoc on the base paths with his blazing speed, received one of the loudest ovations when the players were introduced. Unfortunately, he had no opportunity to show off his speed, as he struck out four consecutive times and never reached base. The Reds lost 1–0 in an excruciatingly frustrating loss. They had their chances to score, but they left men on base and could not deliver in the clutch. The loss broke the streak of 60 Opening Day games in which the Reds scored at least one run. A disappointing loss aside, it was a perfect day for an opener. *Enquirer* columnist John Faherty summed it all up eloquently:

> The noon parade through the streets of Cincinnati was a celebration of spring. It was a day so ideal, after a winter so withering, that it almost felt pretend. The team will play 162 of these games this season, and it is likely that few fans will recall the particulars, the frustrations, of Monday's 1–0 loss. But the day they will remember. The warm breeze and bright sun, that will stay with them.

The loss foreshadowed a maddening season, as the Reds fell below .500 and finished in fourth place. They were never in contention. The offseason would be dominated by questions about the strategic direction of the club: Should they rebuild, or was 2014 an aberration?

Meanwhile, the city was helping spruce up downtown in anticipation of the 2015 MLB All-Star Game. Cincinnati and the Reds would be the hosts. Days prior to the 2014 opener, the city council voted unanimously to issue $8 million in bonds to help Smale Riverfront Park reach its milestones by July 2015 in time for the game. That money would be combined with a $4.5-million grant from the US Army Corps of Engineers and $41 million in corporate, foundation, and other private gifts. Over the next year, the money would be well spent, making the park a crown jewel. Citizens still debate the merits of the streetcar, but Smale Park draws no criticism.

2015: Time to Rebuild?

Reds manager Bryan Price took 2014 in stride. Votto had been on the disabled list with a nagging thigh injury for 100 games.

> "So as a new season begins, the game reminds us of the continuity of history. It reminds us to control our worst instincts and celebrate our virtues. The politics of divisiveness will pass. People want a return to tradition. They want institutions that work and earn our admiration and praise. Just like our national pastime, hope springs eternal. Happy Opening Day."
>
> Ryan McGoren, Reds Fan

Price declared, "Internally, we feel very good about our ability to win within our division and throughout the league." Votto agreed, calling 2014 "an aberration." Reds management concluded there was no need to rebuild, so the Reds tweaked the roster and believed they were already good enough. Veteran *Enquirer* sports reporter John Fay, a keen judge of the team's talent, predicted the Reds would exceed expectations. He did not climb far out on the limb, though, as most national experts were forecasting another subpar year. The fans were not as optimistic as Fay, so the Reds ticket office put on a full-court press to maximize ticket sales. Opening Day sells itself, so there was no need to solicit buyers for those

seats. The bonus dangled before the fans was that new season ticket holders would get not only tickets for the opener but tickets for the highly sought-after All-Star Game as well. In addition, the Reds invested $5 million in improvements to the ballpark in anticipation of the midsummer classic. Reds management said the improvements were planned anyway, but it was like getting ready to host a party at your house and having home-improvement projects become a high priority. The city and team definitely wanted to show off the ballpark and share the city's love for all things baseball.

Ohio attorney general Mike DeWine issued advice for fans who didn't have a ticket for the April 6 opener. DeWine reminded people that Ohioans had lost large sums of money on phony tickets due to various ticket scams. He warned that if a seller asked them to pay using a prepaid card or a wire transfer, it was likely a scam. Tickets were not the only thing in high demand. Applications to participate in the annual parade hit an all-time high of 300, and parade organizers had to turn away 100 potential entries. The result was the most engaging procession in history with more floats and, most importantly, many professionally made floats.

The day's agenda, though, did not start with the parade. There were the usual early-morning tavern openings, and Arnold's Bar and Grill was always a traditional headquarters for Opening Day Reds aficionados. The city's oldest eatery opened its doors at 9:00 a.m., offering nine hard-to-find beers on tap and hosting its annual trivia contest. An hour later, the Reds Hall of Fame & Museum opened to accommodate families and other sober patrons as they came out to enjoy the festivities. At 11:00 a.m., Fountain Square became the site for live music and a pep rally called Rally on the Square. The Phoenix welcomed back customers who wanted to watch the parade from ringside seats along Race Street. The Opening Day Block Party benefiting the Reds Community Fund opened its taps and offered live music and

entertainment for the next five hours. Funky G and the Groove Machine got the crowd dancing early to the Commodores' "Brick House." Up in OTR, the band Glory Days kicked off the celebration in Washington Park, a premier spot for viewing the parade. Across the river in Newport, the German-themed Hofbrauhaus had its house-brewed Hopfen Spezial beer on tap. There were various contests and drawings all day, not to mention wursts and schnitzel. The party was on, and spectators and fans had plenty of options.

Up at Findlay Market, the marching bands were lining up. Various bands started bumping into each other and, in the spirit of the day, the members formed instrument groups with musicians from other bands. An observer noted that it looked like a symphonic dating ritual. The day's grand marshals were a famous trio in Reds history: the relief corps of Rob Dibble, Randy Myers, and Norm Charlton known as the Nasty Boys. The trio was unhit-

table during the 1990 wire-to-wire championship season and World Series. Police on motorcycles had normally been first in line to lead the parade, but the organizers decided to add some additional firepower. Rozzi Famous Fireworks, the company responsible for the rockets at the ballpark that celebrated home runs and victories, sparked the procession with a ground-level fireworks display along the route that was a block ahead of the police. The Nasty Boys followed, and they were met with screams of "wire-to-wire!" Further back, wooden carousel characters entertained the old and young at heart. They were part of Carol Ann's Carousel at Smale Riverfront Park that would open in May. At that time, patrons would be able to ride them in their permanent spots on the merry-go-round.

Ray Wegman and his family had entered their Belgian draft horses in the parade since the days of Crosley Field. Two of the horses pulled a "Free Pete" wagon filled with party-goers blowing horns and shooting streamers as if it were New Year's Eve. On one side of the wagon, a banner proclaimed "Free Pete!" and on the other "Happy New Year!" This

year, Wegman, 82, had also secured a tallyho carriage that he had coveted for more than 50 years. The carriage once belonged to James Gamble, son of the founder of Cincinnati-based Procter &Gamble and the inventor of Ivory Soap. Wegman had spent the winter restoring the carriage. The refurbished carriage was paired with another tallyho wagon that the Wegman family had entered in the procession for decades. The Wegmans also paraded a horse-drawn Wiedemann Brewery wagon that had been used to deliver beer around Cincinnati. In the midst of the horses and their handlers, the 2015 Bockfest Sausage Queen, Pam Kravetz, smiled and waved at her admirers along the route.

The local semi-professional soccer team rode in Melvin Larson's 1941 Ford truck that once carried explosives for the Kings Powder Company. Not far away, the Hamilton County Sheriff's Office marching band wore their traditional kilts, described as "man skirts" by one mother to her son. The Red Stockings in vintage uniforms were well represented once again, the lawnmower guys did their choreographed routine, and Kathryn Gray's family was back on their float to honor their deceased mother. A poodle named Stuart strutted his stuff with his hair dyed a magnificent red. All in all, it was an all-star spectacle worthy of an All-Star year.

At the ballpark, thirsty fans headed to Bootleggers, one of the improvements Phil Castellini made to the ballpark's concourse. (Phil Castellini is the son of the owner who has made his mark by mark by enhancing the fan experience at the ballpark.) Bootleggers' façade and wood bar were modeled after Wielert's Café, an OTR saloon that was home to Cincinnati's political puppeteer, George "Boss" Cox, in the early twentieth century. He was an associate of President William Howard Taft. Cox's Italianate home, built in 1894, remains a historic residence located near the Cincinnati Zoo.

Pregame ceremonies featured US Navy Reserve members unfurling a giant American flag during the national anthem, which was sung by Marlana VanHoose. The Navy Reserves were celebrating their one hundredth anniversary. VanHoose hailed from Denver, Kentucky, and she was blind. Once the ovation died down after VanHoose's stirring rendition, another erupted as the Nasty Boys took the mound once again (their first time doing so as a group!) and threw three ceremonial first pitches. Later in the game during the seventh-inning stretch, Cincinnati firefighter John Winfrey reprised "God Bless America." Winfrey, no relation to Oprah, dedicated the song to the first-ever Cincinnati firefighter to die in the line of duty. Daryl Gordon had perished 11 days earlier while fighting a blaze.

Even before the first batter had stepped to the plate, everything about this opener was off the charts! What could make the day any better? Well, Reds third baseman Todd Frazier launched a mammoth, upper-deck, three-run home run in the eighth inning, leading the Reds to a 5–2 win over the Pirates. Another record crowd of 43,363 fans danced out of the ballpark. The feat presaged a remark-

able first half of the season by Frazier. He was selected to appear in the Home Run Derby conducted by MLB on the Monday evening preceding the Tuesday All-Star Game. The hometown hero electrified a standing-room-only crowd with a stunning power display to win the Derby. The noise emanating from the ballpark was said to be heard a mile away at Mount Adams's historic rooftop bars. Frazier's power surge would be the highlight of the 2016 season for Reds fans. The team suffered through its worst season in 33 years with only 64 victories. Price and his inner circle went back to the drawing board.

Todd Frazier

For Cincinnatians who didn't follow baseball, there was plenty of local news swirling around to capture their attention. Retired court of appeals judge Mark Painter resigned from the Cincinnati Bar Association. His resignation served as a protest about the censorship of his legal-writing column that appeared in the group's monthly publication. The association had declined to publish his April submission because his examples of poor writing identified local judges. Painter was offered the opportunity to include examples from outside the area, but he refused and called the censors thin-skinned. Another judge, Tracy Hunter,

was indicted on a charge involving the alleged misuse of a credit card. She had been convicted on a different charge the previous fall. Hunter pleaded not guilty, and her supporters threatened to disrupt the festivities surrounding the All-Star Game.

Meanwhile, local hero Pete Rose was appealing to another judge. He had long ago applied for reinstatement to MLB, but Commissioner Rob Manfred had never ruled on his appeal. Three pages of the Sunday *Enquirer* were filled with opinion pieces on the subject, with the *Enquirer* advocating for his reinstatement. The editors, even while admitting they were not his biggest fan, argued, "Rose has served his time" after 26 years of banishment. The controversy continued through the midsummer classic. Manfred did not heed Cincinnatians' advice, however, and Rose remained banned. The only concession made by Manfred was to allow the club to induct the "Hit King" into the Reds Hall of Fame in 2017.

2016: Campaign Promises

Opening Day on April 4 received the traditional media pregame and postgame coverage, but in some ways, the coverage was lighter than usual. That was because the presidential primary season was in full swing. Local and national media were consumed with Republican candidate Donald Trump and his long-shot bid to win the nomination. Ohio governor John Kasich spoke at a press conference four days before the opener and told Trump supporters that Trump was not prepared to be president. A poll claimed Ohio was increasingly uninterested in Trump, by then the Republican frontrunner. Trump's presidential campaign was accusing Tennessee Republican Party officials of attempting to steal his delegates to the national convention. On the Democratic side, the bickering between Hillary Clinton and Bernie Sanders was reaching a peak, as some began to believe that Sanders had a chance to knock off the presumptive nominee, Clinton.

In Reds Country, the fans were looking for on-the-field candidates who could give them hope for a brighter future. After boom times earlier in the decade, the Reds were in the midst of a recession. Reds officials had a choice to make: continue to believe that their core of players could compete or else accept the advice of local and national pundits and commit to a rebuilding process. In their campaign to win back fans, the team's president of baseball operations, Walt Jocketty, and general manager Dick Williams made the hard decision to publicly commit to rebuild. Without admitting that there was already a rebuilding effort underway, the team had traded veteran pitchers before and during the 2015 season, including ace Johnny Cueto. Now they were ready to say it out loud even though the confession would send a message to fans that the Reds would not compete in 2016. Barring a miracle, they would not even be competitive for a few years beyond 2016 as well. It was tough medicine that second guessers said should have been administered in 2014 or 2015. The Reds traded star players Todd Frazier and Aroldis Chapman as part of their strategic plan to unload players who had enough value to acquire high prospects in return. Management's plan for rebuilding was published on the eve of the April 4 opener.

> *"My dad always made sure I missed school and spend time with him on Opening Day, which was something very special. We wouldn't buy our tickets ahead of time. We would come down here and see what happened. We'd see the parade. It was a special day to miss school and be part of something very special in Cincinnati."*
>
> Alex Keller, Reds Fan

Fans were nonetheless in good spirits, and the previous year's raft of parties came back in force. Washington Park, The Banks, and Fountain Square were full, as were several other venues. Of note, Arnold's featured an appearance by Jeremy Dubin and Justin McCombs of the Cincinnati Shakespeare Company. They performed "Casey at the Bat" and "Who's on First." Jim Tarbell, aka Peanut Jim Shelton,

played the mouth harp while more than 100 prizes were given away, including autographed baseball cards and memorabilia that had been used in games. "Kegs and eggs" were on the menu at Rhinegeist Brewery. WLW continued its tradition of broadcasting live from the Holy Grail across from the ballpark entrance. Parties continued throughout the day, with some patrons sneaking off to the parade and others waiting for the game to start at 4:00 p.m.

> *"We started at 12 o'clock last night. It took about four and half hours to dye my hair. We actually bleached it, then dyed it red … We actually decided this like three nights ago. I'm like, 'let's do a mohawk, dye it red, and go from there.' My girlfriend, she's like, 'I've never done it but I'll try it.' She watched a couple videos on YouTube and it went from there. I love the Reds. I got 'em tattooed right here above my heart."*
>
> Timmy Teuger, Reds Fan

The number of applicants for the parade was down from the record number in 2015, but there was another impressive array of floats, vehicles, and performers. The grand marshal was the manager of the 1990 world champions, Lou Piniella, who wore his signature broad grin. Piniella had managed the Reds from 1990 to 1992, and he now served as a consultant to the club. Pitchers Brandon Finnigan and Alfredo Simon represented the current Reds players, while former pitcher Ron Oester stood in for players of old. Oester played his entire 13-year career in the big leagues with the Reds, winning MLB's prestigious Hutch Award in 1988. He also scored the winning run in the pennant-clinching game over the Pirates in Game Six of the 1990 NL championship series.

Another sports dignitary was Anthony Munoz. Munoz was the most decorated former Cincinnati Bengal and remained a popular resident. He is the only Bengal to be

enshrined in the NFL's Hall of Fame. He was also honored as a member of the NFL's seventy-fifth anniversary team in 1994.

Also marching along and waving, mostly to the children, were the various Reds mascots: Rosie Red, Gapper, Mr. Red, and Mr. Redlegs. The Red Hot Dancing Queens, a diverse adult dance crew, strutted their stuff. "We are red-hot and love to dress up, have fun, and dance in the streets!" said one of its members. The streets were again lined with spectators five to ten people deep, with even more packing Washington Park and Fountain Square. While it was a rebuilding year for the team, at least the parade was going strong.

Inside Great American Ball Park, there were the traditional pregame ceremonies, complete with Lou Piniella throwing a perfect strike.

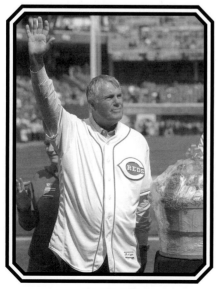

Lou Piniella

The strangest thing occurred when the Reds were introduced before the flyover by the US Navy. As the Reds' starting lineup was introduced, public-address announcer Joe Zerhusen announced "Joe---y Votto" as the third hitter, but no one came out of the dugout. Then, during the national anthem, Votto was still nowhere in sight. His teammates, who claimed not to know what was going on, were left to wonder if something had happened to Votto. The fans wondered, too. After lineup cards were exchanged at home plate and the Reds took the field, Votto finally assumed his rightful position at first base. Where had he been? Votto later explained that he decided to do "the LeBron" and "the Ronaldo." "I figured Opening Day, I'd do the no-show." Apparently, Votto was inspired by the theatrics of NBA star LeBron James and soccer phenom Cristiano Ronaldo, but he refused to give any further explanation. The first baseman also appeared to be missing in action in his first three plate appearances of the day, going hitless, but he came through when it mattered most. His RBI single in the eighth inning gave the Reds a two-run lead en route to a second consecutive win in the opener. It was another comeback, this time 6–2 over the Phillies. The momentum did not carry into the regular season, however, as the youthful team improved by only four wins. The team occupied the cellar at season's end. Right fielder Jay Bruce was traded mid-season as part of the effort to shed payroll and acquire younger players whom the team could control for several years.

On the day before the opener, FC Cincinnati of the United Soccer League played its first-ever game. They won 2–1, and Cincinnati had hopes that what it would be awarded a Major League Soccer franchise when the league announced future expansion. The local soccer team proved to be incredibly successful in terms of attendance its first season, perhaps benefiting from Reds fans turning out in lesser numbers during 2016.

The media had decided before election night that Hillary Clinton would become the next president, but they and most pollsters were wrong. Donald Trump became the forty-fifth president of the United States with a decisive electoral college victory, aided in large part by voters in Ohio. *Enquirer* writer Jeremy Fugleberg was wrong about the eventual national results and wrong about Ohio's role in shaping them. Wrote Fugleberg on April 3, "Ohio, get ready to give Hillary Clinton the keys to the Oval Office. If Donald Trump is her general election opponent, that is." Trump, who snatched Ohio's 18 electoral votes, won 52.1 percent of Ohio's popular vote compared to 43.5 percent for Clinton. As had happened in 29 of the past 31 presidential elections, the candidate who won Ohio won the presidency.

2017: The Rebuild Continues

The best that Reds fans could hope for in 2017 was a more competitive team. The town was discouraged by two consecutive last-place finishes. A seemingly inconsequential acquisition of second baseman Scooter Gennett two weeks before the opener did not change the outlook. Gennett was a Cincinnati native who had been cast aside by the Milwaukee Brewers. The Reds had traded popular second baseman Brandon Phillips to make room for José Peraza. Peraza had been part of the earlier Todd Frazier trade, and he was destined for second base. Gennett was slotted for a utility role. Hope springs eternal on Opening Day, but fans did not have much faith after the departures of Bruce and Phillips. Only Votto remained from the playoff teams of 2010 to 2013.

> *"I think I was, like, six or seven. That was obviously a good experience with all the streets shut down and stuff like that. It was pretty unique. I only remember Schottzie, Schott's dog and the naked cowboy guy with the tighty whities playing the guitar."*
>
> Scooter Gennett

Local news of a much more serious nature pushed the Reds off the front page as Opening Day approached. Eight days before the April 3 opener, on a Sunday evening, the worst mass shooting in Cincinnati history occurred. It

The Banks

happened inside the crowded Cameo nightclub on the city's east side near the shore of the Ohio River. The shootout occurred when two men allegedly decided to engage in a gun battle. Seventeen people were shot, one of them fatally. O'Bryan Spikes, 27, died at the scene. A 911 caller reported that there was blood everywhere. The victims who survived ranged in age from 24 to 33. It was not yet known how the men bypassed security with loaded guns. The coverage naturally dominated the news. Four days later, two men were charged with murder. Arraigned with his bail set at $1.7 million, one of the alleged shooters denied firing any shots or even having a gun that night.

In light of a pessimistic Reds fan base, the Findlay Market organizers smartly chose one of the most popular Reds players in a generation to serve as grand marshal: Sean Casey, aka "The Mayor." Casey played with the Reds for eight seasons, leading the team in hitting six times while being selected as an All-Star in three of those seasons. Casey was honored for his intensity and enthusiasm by winning the Hutch Award in 1999, the season the Reds lost a one-game playoff with the New York Mets. He was named the team's MVP in 2004. After retiring, Casey was inducted into the Reds Hall of Fame in 2012. Following recent tradition, the Reds had two current players participate in the parade as well: pitcher Rookie Davis, who had been acquired in the trade with the New York Yankees for Aroldis Chapman, and fellow pitcher Robert Stephenson. Stephenson was the Reds' first-round draft pick in 2011 and had worked his way up through the farm system, but he had not yet fulfilled the promise associated with his high draft selection. The two young pitchers were being counted on as the rebuilding continued. Former pitcher Tom Browning was the guest of the Federation of Lutheran Churches of Cincinnati. He pitched the only perfect game in Reds history and was the author of a book entitled Tom Browning's Tales from the Reds Dugout. He once famously escaped to a rooftop venue outside of Chicago's

Wrigley Field during a game, earning a fine of $1,000 from manager Davey Johnson, who was not impressed with the stunt.

The parade was a hit as always, as were the other parties around town. Pregame ceremonies were highlighted by Marlana VanHoose's return to sing the national anthem, another F-16 flyover, and Casey's introduction as the honorary Reds captain. During the game, Phil Castellini introduced his favorite fan attraction, Redzilla. Redzilla is an ATV that

Redzilla

contains the first-ever triple-barrel souvenir launcher for shooting souvenir items high into the stands as it circles the field during one of the half-inning breaks and after each win. Said Castellini, "We designed Redzilla to be a spectacle that adds to the fun by launching t-shirts and balls unprecedented distances into the upper decks." Fans quickly came to love Castellini's favorite toy.

As for the game itself, the utility player signed just the previous week, Scooter Gennett, came off the bench. His two-run home run in the ninth inning highlighted another comeback attempt by the Reds, but the Reds still came up short. Milwaukee won 4–3. The rest of the season ended in disappointment again, as there was no improvement in the win column. The results of the rebuilding effort were not yet visible.

2018: Rebuilding Fatigue

After four consecutive seasons during which the Reds averaged fewer than 70 wins per season and never finished higher than fourth in their five-team division, Reds fans were becoming disenchanted with the rebuilding efforts. To make matters worse, MLB decided the season would start on Holy Thursday, just three days before Easter and the earliest date ever. No opener had ever been scheduled in the days leading up to the Christian holiday. Why would MLB do that? Like most scheduling issues that seem odd, such as early-morning college football games or late-night NFL games, you only have to "follow the money." MLB wanted to eke out as much television and ballpark revenue from the season as it could,

so it wanted to squeeze in some games before Easter. And, since the proprietors of Findlay Market establishments couldn't operate their businesses while the parade was going on, and because they typically saw a bump in revenues during Holy Week, the merchants didn't want to give up a day of sales to conduct the parade on Holy Thursday. (There was also the issue of Holy Thursday being a sacred Christian holiday that many fans would choose to observe rather than turn out for a parade.) Because Monday, with a few recent exceptions, had traditionally been the day of the week when Opening Day was held, the market parade organizers decided their parade would be on the Monday following the first game. MLB was not going to dictate the schedule of the parade to Findlay Market!

Cincinnatians were confused. Is the holiday Thursday, March 29, or is it Monday, April 2? The answer? Both days! Businesses planned all-day events Thursday and Monday, and there was even a five-day party hosted by Taft's Ale House, Washington Park, and Cincinnati Center City Development Corporation (aka 3CDC). On March 29, there would be a family-

friendly celebration on Fountain Square with live music and food trucks beginning at 11:00 a.m. and lasting at least until the final out of the 4:10 game with the Washington Nationals. For their part, the Reds reprised their annual charity block party with live entertainment headlined by the Naked Karate Girls. As in previous years, many bars and eateries hosted parties.

Plans would change, however, when the bleak weather forecast for Thursday forced the Reds to postpone the game until Good Friday. That change created another stir, because many Christians observe Good Friday as an even holier day than Holy Thursday. The Reds reluctantly announced the delay on Wednesday so fans could make necessary plans. Reds chief operating officer Phil Castellini apologized to anyone affected in a negative way, announcing that concession stands would sell fish sandwiches to accommodate Lenten traditions. He also said ticket holders could attend another game of their choice if they preferred. It was the first postponement of Opening Day since the death of umpire John McSherry resulted in a one-day delay in 1996. Prior to that, the most recent postponement was when the entire three-game series was washed out in 1966.

All the events planned for Thursday were shifted to Friday, and the crowds came out in force for the block party and the events around town. There were pregame parties at Rhinegeist Brewery, Fountain Square, and on the street in Covington, Kentucky. "Mr. Perfect," former Reds pitcher Tom Browning, opened his new tavern, Browning's on York, that morning. There were cloudy skies, but the rain held off. The pregame festivities went off without a hitch. The Clydesdales arrived at the ballpark on time for their usual prance around the park. There was a moment of silence for departed members of the Reds family of staff and players, and singer/songwriter Nicki Bluhm belted out the national anthem. Two F-16 Fighter Falcons soared over the ballpark as area firefighters displayed the giant flag on the field. Indiana native and Olympic gold medalist in men's slopestyle, Nick

Goepper, tossed out the ceremonial first pitch to Reds catcher Devin Mesoraco. The game? The Nationals beat the Reds 2–0 before another record crowd of 43,787.

The team stumbled out of the gate and was swept in the weekend series. Many speculated whether interest in the parade would wane because of the club's shaky start, but those concerns were erased as tens of thousands celebrated a second holiday before the Monday afternoon game against the Cubs. Grand marshals Danny Graves and Sam LeCure, both former Reds pitchers, received warm welcomes from the throngs lining the streets. Behind them were 187 parade units of every variety. One of the many prized entries was the Hamilton County chapter of the Ohio Horseman's Council. That organization brought dressed-up miniature horses, and the crowd loved them. The block party outside the park was packed just as it had been on Friday. The Monday afternoon game commenced with no pregame pomp and circumstance, and unfortunately, the Reds dropped their fourth consecutive game. The good news? Two Opening Days worked out just fine and had hefty crowds on both occasions. The fans enjoyed four days of parties in a most unusual opening weekend.

Die-hard fans saw glimmers of hope for the future during the season. Joey Votto continued to make good on his long-term contract. There were promising young pitchers and a cadre of young hitters that could blossom in 2019. As was their custom, Cincinnatians looked forward to another Opening Day in 2019. Findlay Market would celebrate its one-hundredth parade. The Reds would celebrate the 150th anniversary of the storied franchise that had its roots in a band of ten players—baseball's first professional team, the famous Red Stockings. From the motley procession of fans heading to Union Grounds on May 4, 1869, stemmed traditions that would enliven and unify a city for one and a half centuries. It all started with a parade!

Opening Day Joke, April 1, 2013

Epilogue

After attending Opening Day in 2013, at the urging of my friends Doug and Joan Raftery, I began thinking about writing this book. I considered writing about my years celebrating the opener but put the idea on the shelf for a while, uncertain as to how to proceed. I then looked at how the Reds' success compares with that of other franchises. With so many cities hoping for the same result—a world championship—our small city has had its fair share of success, less than some but more than most. But that topic has been well documented.

Instead, the urge to conduct research about the event that is so unique to Cincinnati kept tugging at me. I began to read a few books on the subject (see bibliography), but researching 150 years of Opening Day happenings seemed particularly daunting. Plenty of other books have been written about the Reds, mostly about specific seasons, specific teams, or specific years, and there is even a noteworthy book that chronicles the games on Opening Day. I called Sue Bradley, my editor, and warned her that I had a big project.

My curiosity was piqued by thinking about how Opening Day traditions have evolved and yet have remained so constant, at least from what I recall and had read about over so many years. Baseball is a unique sport in that if players from the very earliest years of baseball could come back to life, they would see a game that is strikingly similar to the one they had played years before. Sure, there have been tweaks to the rules here and there—there's a designated hitter in the American League, for example—but the essential nature of the sport has remained constant. One unique point of consistency is that there is no clock to artificially change the flow of the sport (only recent efforts to speed up play between innings and during pitching changes). It is precisely because baseball has no artificial constraints on how long a game lasts that many people are drawn to the leisurely sport. When does a baseball game end? It's over when it's over. In the meantime, the leisurely pace of the game allows fans to enjoy each other's company and take in the whole ballpark experience. In addition, over the course of an MLB season, no single game during the regular season means all that much. Lose one day? Oh well, there's another game tomorrow. Lose a three-game series? Ah, there are more games this week. And so it goes in the unique sport that is baseball.

Since there are already books and articles that describe Opening Day, I decided that I wanted to research how baseball intersected with local, national, and world history. The game had remained so constant while the country and world had changed so much. Unlike ballplayers who could come back to life and not notice much difference in the sport they loved, nineteenth-century citizens as a whole would not recognize our current culture or understand the complexities of modern life. Everything, except for baseball, would be different. My goal has been to summarize the evolution of Opening Day traditions in the context of events that were happening in Cincinnati, the nation, and the world. It was delightful to find out that Opening Day has been surprisingly impervious to the kind of cultural transformation that has affected so many of our societal institutions. Cincinnatians have worked hard to protect the unique and treasured spectacle represented by Opening Day.

What has surprised me the most in immersing myself in Opening Day history is how I now look at Opening Day. As a lifelong fan of baseball and particularly of the Reds, I have always tended to focus my attention on the results of each game. Up one day, down the next. As I researched the years in which I had attended openers, I was surprised by how often I could not remember who won or lost, who had been the star, or if anyone had been a goat. Sure, there are some Opening Days that will always remain in my memory bank. Among these are my first in 1967; the night in 1994 when ESPN and MLB tried to dictate that Cincinnati not have an Opening Day; and the day in 1996 when John McSherry died on the field. Other than the most recent years, I have long since forgotten the game results. As a fan who hangs on every pitch, I was amazed at what I was reading about the games. Why didn't I remember anything about most of the games?

> *"In the retelling and the remembering of that special day, time will sharpen the focus. Those Opening Day memories will come down to what truly matters. They become a celebration of not who you saw play, but who you are with."*
>
> Cliff Radel, Enquirer columnist

As I was researching, I read a brief 2013 article by Cliff Radel in the Enquirer. He pointed out the obvious. The holiday in Cincinnati draws people not because of the game, but rather because of the people. It hit me like a lightning bolt. What do I remember? I remember who I was with much more than the games themselves. I remember going with my brothers Ted, Robert, Mark, and Jay in 1967, with my parents or Uncle Harold and Aunt Jeanne in the late 1960s, and then again with my parents and siblings while I was in high school. I treasure the memory of sitting next to my parents in 1974 on the day Hank Aaron tied Babe Ruth. While I was in college, I remember the friends who went with me to the openers. Since I've been married, my wife and I have always enjoyed the game together surrounded by family members. My brother, Jay, and his wife, Debbie, were regulars with us before his untimely passing in 1996. When children arrived, we carted them to the openers at very young ages. Eventually, extended family members such as nieces and nephews and my sister-in-law, Nancy, would accompany us. As our children grew, they often were excused from school in keeping with

the Cincinnati tradition. In more recent years, my sister, Sue, and her husband, Glenn, along with their daughters, Emily and Lydia, and their husbands, Clarence and Will, have become fans of the Opening Day tradition.

Where do we meet downtown before going to the parade? We meet at the very place my dad took us in 1967: The Red Fox Grill. Emma Watson, the server, knows to reserve a couple tables for us, or even more if we have a large group. In some recent years, we have been fortunate enough to ride together on a float in the parade. What a thrill!

In my research, I found that the stories about other families always seemed to mirror our story. I read about entire families that came to the game together in the late 1800s. The Enquirer archives are full of tales about families and friends who regularly celebrated the opener with each other. Throughout the 1900s and now in the early 2000s, that storyline has not changed. Indeed, most of the coverage around Opening Day is about the people, not the game. While many game-day conversations are focused on the Reds and how they might do during the opener or the season, the real enjoyment comes from catching up with family members and friends whom we may only see on those other holidays that are recognized by the rest of the country. That is why Opening Day is so often compared to Christmas in Cincinnati. During our busy lives, Opening Day is special not because of the game itself but because we can share it with people we love.

Cincinnatians have been fortunate. Through all the turmoil of world wars, economic disruptions, terrorism and the like, we have enjoyed an extra holiday thanks to Harry Wright and the original Red Stockings, along with those "merry cranks" who supported them. I, for one, am forever in their debt for the joy they have brought to my life and the lives of countless others.

Bibliography

Newspapers and Periodicals

Special thanks to The *Cincinnati Enquirer* for much of the research material for this book, as the only local source of authoritative information throughout the entire 150 year history of the Cincinnati Red Stockings, Redlegs, and Reds. The paper has been published daily for all but one day since 1841. Quotes in chapters throughout this book come from the *Enquirer's* coverage of Opening Day, unless otherwise indicated.

Cincinnati Commercial Gazette

Cincinnati Commercial Tribune

Cincinnati Daily Star

Cincinnati Magazine

Cincinnati Post

Cincinnati Times-Star

Dayton Daily News

Humanities

Spitball

The New York Times

The Nippon Times

The Sporting News

The Telegraph

Time

Books

Allen, Lee. *The Cincinnati Reds*, 1948

Conner, Floyd and Snyder, John, 1983

Erardi, John and Rhodes, Greg. *Opening Day*, 2004

Guschov, Stephen D. *The Red Stockings of Cincinnati*, 1965

Kaplan, Ron. *501 Baseball Books Fans Must Read Before They Die*, 2013

Lee, William F. *American Big Bands*, 2006

Lewis, Dottie. *Baseball in Cincinnati: From Wooden Fences to Astroturf*, 1988

Rhodes, Greg and Snyder, John. *Redleg Journal*, 2000

Seymour, Harold and Mills, Dorothy Seymour. *Baseball: The Early Years*, 1960

Shannon, Mike. *Riverfront Stadium: Home of The Big Red Machine*, 2003

Shannon, Mike. *The Good, the Bad, & the Ugly*, 2008

Smith, Curt. *Voices of the Game*, 1987

Tilton, Liz. *Cincinnati's Historic Findlay Market*, 2009

Wheeler, Lonnie and Baskin, John. *The Cincinnati Game*, 1988

News Reporting Services

The Associated Press

United Press

United Press International

Websites

answers.com

baseball-almanac.com

baseball-reference.com

blogredmachine.com

cincinnati.com

city-data.com

cnn.com

dates andevents.org

jfklibrary.org

mlb.com/dodgers/history/timeline-1950s

newspapers.com

ronkaplansbaseballbookshelf.com

reds.com

space.com

thisgreatgame.com

thoughtco.com

wikipedia

who2.com

Photo Credits

Most of the photos, drawings, and cartoons before 1923 (Chapters 2-7) are reprinted from The *Cincinnati Enquirer*; a few are reprints in the public domain from various sources.

Post 1923 photos are courtesy of, and with permission from the Findlay Market Association, the Cincinnati Reds, the Cincinnati Reds Community Fund, or are otherwise in the public domain. Color photos are all courtesy of the Findlay Market Association, the Cincinnati Reds, the Cincinnati Reds Community Fund, and family collections referenced below.

Family photos are courtesy of, and with permission from, Clarence and Emily Miracle, Sue and Glenn Showers, Debbie Freking, Katie Freking, Mark Freking, and Bob Freking.

The photo of Al Schottelkotte is courtesy of, and with permission from, WCPO (Cincinnati).

The photo of Marian Spelman is courtesy of, and with permission from, WLWT-TV (Cincinnati), Hearst Television.

The photo of Pete Rose and Tom Linz in Chapter 11 is courtesy of, and with permission from, the Tom Linz family collection.

The front cover photo (bottom) is courtesy of, and with permission from, CincinnatiUSA.com.

Randy with his Pete Rose wig

Biography

· ·

Randy Freking is a lifelong baseball fan. He lives in Cincinnati with his wife, Sue, and they are proud parents of four children, Becky, Bob, Laura, and Jen.

A lawyer by occupation, Randy is the author of "*The Real Employee Handbook*" (CreateSpace Independent Publishing Platform, 2012) and the "*ABA Consumer Guide to Employee Rights*" (American Bar Association, 2015). He is listed in every edition of "*Best Lawyers In America*" since 1994.

Randy attended his first Opening Day game in 1967 at the age of 10. He vows to keep the streak alive.

Index